Social History of Africa

WOMEN OF PHOKENG

Social History of Africa

Series Editors:
Allen Isaacman and Luise White

WOMEN OF PHOKENG

Consciousness, Life Strategy,
and Migrancy in
South Africa, 1900—1983

Belinda Bozzoli

with the assistance of
MMANTHO NKOTSOE

HEINEMANN
Portsmouth, NH

JAMES CURREY
London

DT
1058
B34
B69
1991

Heinemann Educational Books, Inc.
361 Hanover Street
Portsmouth, NH 03801-3959

James Currey Ltd
54b Thornhill Square,
Islington
London N1 1BE

ISBN 0-435-08054-7 (Heinemann cloth)
ISBN 0-435-08056-3 (Heinemann paper)
ISBN 0-85255-653-5 (James Currey cloth)
ISBN 0-85255-603-9 (James Currey paper)

First published 1991.

Credits for reprinted material are on p. xi.

Library of Congress Cataloging-in-Publication Data
Bozzoli, Belinda.
    Women of Phokeng: consciousness, life strategy, and migrancy in South Africa,
    1900-1983/Belinda Bozzoli, with the assistance of Mmantho Nkotsoe.
        p.   cm. — (Social history of Africa)
    Includes index.
    ISBN 0-435-08054-7. — ISBN 0-435-08056-3 (pbk.)
    1. Women, Bafokeng (African people) — South Africa — Phokeng — Interviews. 2.
    Women, Bafokeng (African people) — South Africa — Phokeng — Social conditions.
    3. Group identity — South Africa — Phokeng. 4. Social structure — South Africa — Phokeng.
    5. Phokeng (South Africa) — Social conditions. 6. Phokeng (South Africa) — History — 20th
    century. I. Nkotsoe, Mmantho. II. Title. III. Series: Social history of Africa series.
    DT1058.B34B69 1991
    305.4'0968.2'94 — dc20   91-9326
                                                                        CIP
British Library Cataloguing in Publication Data
Bozzoli, Belinda
    Women of Phokeng: consciousness, life strategy and migrancy in South Africa
    1900-1983. — (Social history of Africa).
    1. South Africa. Social life
    I. Title   II. Mmantho, Nkotsoe   III. Series
    968.063

    ISBN 0-85255-653-5
    ISBN 0-85255-603-9 pbk

Cover design executed by Jenny Jensen Greenleaf.
Text design by G&H Soho Ltd.
Printed in the United States of America.
91 92 93 94 95 9 8 7 6 5 4 3 2 1

CONTENTS

ILLUSTRATIONS

ACKNOWLEDGEMENTS

For so modest a study, this book has taken an inordinately long time to produce. It is based upon interview material originally collected in the early 1980s, with the generous support of the Human Sciences Research Council, Pretoria, under the auspices of the University of the Witwatersrand's African Studies Institute. The Ford Foundation, the University of the Witwatersrand's Senate and Council Research Committees, and the Department of Sociology Research Incentive Scheme have also provided funds for the translation and indexing of interviews, the production of the manuscript, payment of my salary during periods of leave, and a variety of other expenses.

The initial research for and drafting of the book itself took place within the intellectually rich and personally supportive milieu provided by members of a variety of departments and disciplines at the same university. Friends and colleagues such as Luli Callinicos, Stephen Clingman, Isabel Hofmeyr, Jon Hyslop, Paul la Hausse, Duncan Innes, Debra James, Tom Lodge, Bruce Murray, Patrick Pearson, and Ian Phimister made intellectual life possible, and even sometimes enjoyable, in the fraught and tragic circumstances of South Africa during the 1980s, many of which impinged upon universities in painful ways. Betsy Coville, Denise Moys, Helene Perold, Diana Wall and Ilse Wilson also provided moral support and friendship in difficult times. The Department of Sociology provided me with time off, and space to teach in the fields of women's studies and cultural studies, both of which have drawn me into reading material that has enriched the interpretation put forward here. I have been particularly privileged to have benefited from the collegiality and insights of Phil Bonner, Tim Couzens, and Peter Delius, three friends whose understanding of African societies far surpasses my own. Their contributions to the making of this book may have been mainly indirect, because of my tardiness in presenting its findings to formal seminars, but they were invaluable, and deeply appreciated, nevertheless.

The book has been completed in the comparatively peaceful milieu of Cambridge University, where the African Studies Centre has generously provided me with a base, and where I have benefited from closeness to the vigorous community of Africanists in England. Here, both Shula Marks and Stanley Trapido have set intellectual standards to which one can only aspire. Their friendship, together with that of Barbara Trapido, whose literary creativity puts to shame any academic pretensions to innovation, and of Rosa de Lauro, Stanley Greenberg, Karin Shapiro, and Marcia Wright in the United States, has often been a lifeline to sanity. Josh Brown, Kate Pfordresher, and Steve Brier of the American Social History Project in New York helped me both expand and focus my ideas about the "view from below" during projects we undertook together, in their inimitably imaginative way.

Mmantho Nkotsoe's sensitive contribution to the collection of material for this book — as the text makes clear — influenced its very shape and form, although like everyone else thanked here, she bears no responsibility for any errors and distortions in the interpretation that has been put on it. Nita Leyleveld, Denis Mashabela, Carol Traill, Nesta Madlala, Mapula Molefe, Celeste Emmanuel, Arlene Harris, and Margot Ford, all at one time members of the African Studies Institute, contributed in various ways to the compiling, typing, indexing, and management of the tapes and documents emerging from the interviews. Robert A. Hill, in his capacity as director of the Marcus Garvey Papers in Los Angeles, generously assisted with research into the life of Kenneth Spooner; Graeme Simpson kindly shared with me his findings on the history of the Bafokeng; Mrs. Shole helped me with Setswana words and phrases; and Santu Mofokeng helped provide, and advise on, photographs. In the final stages of revision of the manuscript, the encouragement of Luise White and Allen Isaacman have been invaluable. I hope that the women of Phokeng and their families, all of whom gave of their time and themselves, will find their thanks in that the book tells their stories in the proper way.

I am deeply grateful for the help of my parents and the rest of my extended family, who have always been unstinting in giving both their time and their friendship to the overworked academic in their midst. But my greatest thanks are due to my husband, Charles van Onselen. His companionship has always been an inspiration; his dedication to the hard slog of writing has provided an unwavering example to follow; and he has borne the brunt of the pressures on time, emotions, and family relations that a project such as this seems inevitably to entail, without losing his sense of humour. The book is dedicated to our children, Gareth, Jessica, and Matthew, who have been curious and often perceptive about it, but who have never allowed purely intellectual preoccupations to cloud their rich visions of life, the universe, and everything.

CREDITS

The author and publisher wish to thank the following for permission to reprint material appearing in this book:

Passages from Naboth Mokgatle, *Autobiography of an Unknown South African*, copyright © 1971 Naboth Mokgatle, are reprinted by permission of The University of California Press and C. Hurst & Co.

"Sketches in the Life of K. E. M. Spooner, Missionary, South Africa," collected and arranged by Mrs. K. E. M. Spooner, A. E. Robinson, and Dr. P. E. Beacham, and *Sketches of Native Life in South Africa* by Kenneth E. M. Spooner are part of The Marcus Garvey Papers. Passages are reprinted by permission of The Marcus Garvey Project at the University of California, Los Angeles.

The map on page 56 is based on information in P.-L. Breutz, *The Tribes of Rustenburg and Pilansberg Districts* (Pretoria: Government Printer, 1953) and in *Ordinance Survey, 1970*.

The cartographer for the maps in this book was Wendy Job.

The photographs of the women are courtesy of the African Studies Institute Oral Documentation Project.

The photographs of Phokeng today were taken by Santu Mofokeng and are used with his kind permission.

Introduction:
Oral History,
Consciousness,
and Gender

This is a study of the lives of a small group of black South African women. It has three modest aims: to examine the broad processes and events that have shaped their experiences as black South Africans; to explore the specific ways in which their gender has affected their lives; and, most importantly, to study the forms of consciousness they express in their own interpretations of their histories.

Unlike those who dominate society, oppressed peoples are not often able to choose and shape the institutions within which they live. In the endless debates that pose "structure" against "agency," and that ask how much of our lives is determined for us and how much by us, we are apt to forget that the balance between the two differs depending on where we stand in relation to social power.[1] In South Africa, the ruling classes have possessed considerable political and economic power, enabling them to design social structures, to create and manipulate classes, borders, and communities, to destroy and reconstruct families, and even to enter most brutally into the private domain of sexuality. Intoxicated with their visions of perfect, conflict-free systems of accumulation, of pure ethnic or racial communities, or of man realising himself through a privileged relationship with God, they have often found it unnecessary even to disguise their social engineering. Liberal mystifications of bourgeois rule are a rarity in this stark order. Men here have indeed made their own history in ways quite remarkably of their own choosing.

By contrast, the objects of these hegemonic designs — black and white working people — have experienced history largely as a series of defeats and enactments, through which their choices have become ever narrower. Land removals, proletarianisation, geographical and other forms of segregation, and the powerful impact of racist ideology, have been only some of the forces and structures with which the poor have had to contend — and indeed which will affect their lives for generations to come, whatever the outcome of current political affairs in that country. The physical geography of segregation alone, the permanency of the hundreds of thousands of homes and homesteads locked within urban and rural areas defined as "black," has ensured that the lines of struggle have been defined thus for at least a further century — and this is only one feature of the social order which has emerged since the 1860s.

What happens to consciousness when the forces of structure and agency are so unevenly balanced? In the case of the South African ruling classes, we find that self-consciously designed and promulgated ideologies are common. Intellectuals and strategists have created world views which coherently and often successfully express ruling class interests, and with which, less successfully, they have attempted to seduce the hearts and minds of the oppressed. Powerful media carry and publicise these ideas, while a large buffer stratum of journalists, teachers, and culture brokers perfects and elaborates upon them.[2]

The consciousness of the powerless contrasts vividly with this.[3] It has rarely attained a similarly deliberate character. Not only has the very power of their rulers made it difficult for the intellectuals of the poor, few as they are, to articulate successful and refined national ideologies — the millennial, spontaneous and riotous behaviour of township youth is not easily harnessed by social movements with definite goals[4] — but the facts of alienation and oppression have meant that the ordinary person has infrequently been drawn into a vision of herself as capable of exerting power beyond a certain limited sphere. Consciousness here has been formed within and against structures, rather than above and around them.

As a result, the ideologies of the poor in South Africa — like those elsewhere — have often been an incoherent mass of ideas and attitudes, whose logic is to be discovered by exploring patterns of experience.[5] They have at times been pulled together and rationalised into the powerful and internally more consistent social visions of such social movements as the Industrial and Commercial Workers' Union (ICU), the African National Congress (ANC), or the Black Consciousness Movement. But the moments at which consciousness becomes transformed into ideology need to be explained rather than taken for granted, a task that cannot be undertaken without an examination of the grassroots forms taken by both the experience and the associated consciousness with which this book is primarily concerned. We should not assume that subjectivity only exists, or is important, when it is manifested in organisations. The raw material of "common sense" comes to be shaped and moulded only at particular times into the finished product of social ideology. We need to ask: what have the forces been that have shaped experience, how have they been expressed as consciousness, and at what points has that consciousness coalesced into ideology?

While we may postulate that ruling and subordinate classes have differing capacities to shape their own destinies, this does not mean that either group exists in a fixed relationship to the social order. Hegemony is, after all, a process, a "moving equilibrium," in which spaces are created, fought for, and won by those at the bottom from those at the top.[6] But those at the bottom are often more capable of influencing than overturning the forms whereby domination is expressed. This study sees black South African women asserting their dignity, class capacity, cultural patterns, and gender identity; it sees some of them evolving coherent ideologies of opposition. But these assertions occur within a framework of inequality and structured brutality. To ignore this by romanticising the popular cultures of the oppressed is to bypass the crucial question of power. What this study seeks to do, rather, is to examine the "moving equilibrium," which is hegemony from the perspective of its objects, in order to assess both its effects upon them, and their assertive impact within and upon it. To suggest that popular consciousness and social resilience are important, that they influence the form taken by hegemony, and that at times they may provide the basis for radical social movements is not, as some critics would claim, mere romanticism or populism. It entails a hard-headed understanding of the cultural and ideological bases of social power, and the ways in which these are modified or even overthrown when social and cultural assertiveness "from below" is felt.

Because its aims are to expose the elusive, the invisible, and the intangible, this book is unconventional, both in form and in content. Things look different from below. Particular methodological weapons have been brought to bear on its subject matter — the analysis of consciousness.[7] Conventional sociological methods — the structured attitude survey, the questionnaire, or the rigid interview — are poor tools for understanding this elusive force.[8] Informants responding to these will fail to speak honestly, and researchers find their own preconceived notions of consciousness being flung back at them by the results of their "scientific" survey. Nor are historians, conventional tools always suited to analysing the consciousness of oppressed, illiterate, poorer people, particularly women, who might be excluded from access to the kinds of public forms of expression recorded in most archival and documentary sources. While historians have overcome this problem to an extent by inferring the consciousness of the mass from its public expression in various cultural arenas (such as religion) or in times of social upheaval and organised protest,[9] even they acknowledge that what may be called the "inherent" (as opposed to the "derived") ideologies of ordinary people[10] are less easy to grasp, let alone in an underdocumented African context.[11] This study uses life stories, based upon lengthy recorded interviews, as its major source — and more will be said about this below.[12]

The handling of this material is also unconventional. The reader will not always find here the neat weaving together of the words of informants and social context characteristic of most studies that use interviews as a source, where the experiences of the poor are validated by their accordance with other sources of information and interpretation.[13] These approaches to the words of interviewees, whether of the left or of the right, tend to be imbued with a positivistic flavour, born perhaps of the "halo of second-rate reality" usually attached to notions of people's subjective views.[14] This is not a study of broad patterns of political and social power, where experience is merely illustrative of wider points; of how interviews can help us understand "what really happened"; or of the opinions of people about certain predefined issues. Rather it is an exploration of one of the more intimate private domains within which power is fought over, and consciousness born — those of personal life, family, community, and experience. It examines the evolving subjectivity of informants, usually the domain of phenomenologists. This matter does not lend itself to interpretation through existing, structured concepts and notions of reality. Indeed, as one commentator has observed, oral history's very promise lies in "the discrepancy between oral sources and most of the interpretive categories so far elaborated by the social sciences."[15]

Yet this is also not a purely phenomenological book, in which a decontextualised compilation of "experience" is explored, although such an approach would imply more sensitivity to the human mind and psyche than would the positivist one. Instead, located within the Gramscian concerns of the relationships between social power and social consciousness outlined above, this book seeks to follow the birth and vicissitudes of that consciousness over time and space, drawing it into a consideration of context willy-nilly.

The context is not portrayed as the "base" upon which the "superstructure" of consciousness is constructed. Such notions have long been abandoned (in theory, although less so in practice) by students of culture and subjectivity.[16] Instead, the trajectories of the lives of the informants are explored, with varying references to the contexts in which particular forms of consciousness and ideology appear at particular stages. As such the study sets out to be deeply historical, without reducing history to the mechanics of simple causation and determination. The "life worlds,"[17] "life cycles,"[18] and "life strategies"[19] of the women of Phokeng are at the centre of the study. How have these been approached, and what are the methodological principles that have been used?

* * *

My name is Nkotsoe. I am a girl from Mabeskraal, the nearby village. I think you know that village.

Yes I do. My name is Ernestina Mekgwe. I was born here in Phokeng and brought up here also.[20]

The twenty-two women whose interviews are analysed here were all residents of Phokeng, an old and typically Tswana settlement, now in the officially designated and legally "independent" homeland of Bophuthatswana. Their stories exemplify some of the complexities involved in the formation of modern South Africa. Born at the turn of the century, they grew up in a rural economy that was both viable and resilient, but one that had already had to make significant adaptations to survive the newly emerging order of the times. Many of them became migrants to the city, however, in their early twenties, as migrancy became both an economic necessity and an institutionalised expectation. For many, what were planned as temporary sojourns in the city lasted for up to forty years, during which they lived a life defined by family, work, and community, a life that was only partially proletarian in character. In the end, they returned to their village to live as pensioners and grandmothers in the "homeland" of Bophuthatswana.

The women were interviewed, up to four times each, by Mmantho Nkotsoe— also a black South African woman—who, as she says, was born in a "nearby village." The conversations between Mmantho and the women were recorded as part of a larger oral history project (the Oral Documentation Project, or ODP) initiated at the University of the Witwatersrand in 1979. Some one thousand oral histories of black and some white South Africans, mainly from the countryside of the Transvaal, have been collected since the project began.

The ODP has focussed on the life experiences of rural black South Africans in the Transvaal, and has a variety of analytical and geographical focal points. Methodologically, it adopted a pragmatic and eclectic approach.[21] No fixed procedure for obtaining life stories was decided upon in advance; researchers and interviewers worked together to construct a viable set of ground rules as the material was being collected and problems emerged. Fundamental to the ODP was the initial decision that interviews with rural people, often barely literate and certainly unfamiliar with the English language, needed to be undertaken in the vernacular, preferably without the presence of a translator or other intervening party. Setswana- or Sesotho-speakers were the obvious candidates for the role of interviewer in the case of the Transvaal, and the ODP has over the years employed a succession of interviewers fluent in either or both of these languages, who would undertake interviews in collaboration with a researcher or team of researchers, and then transcribe the tapes and translate them into English. The ODP archives have been used by a variety of authors and interpreted in a range of different ways. Some have used them as a source of information not obtainable elsewhere;[22] others have used selected interviews as the basis for essays on individual life experiences;[23] and a major biography of the ODP's most loquacious informant is under way.[24] This study has chosen a different means of interpreting the material, which was generated as a result of specific choices over time about the direction the interviewing should take.

Mmantho Nkotsoe, a university graduate, was trained by the ODP, and she and our initial research team — Tim Couzens, Charles van Onselen, and I — worked cooperatively on the project during 1981–1983. Her mandate was to find interesting elderly women who lived in the countryside and to record the stories of their lives. At first, the intention of the study was simply to record the stories of those whose lives are hidden from history; Mmantho was asked to travel around the Transvaal from village to village, and enquire whether any of the elderly women of the village would be willing to talk to her. She was working together with the other similarly trained oral historians in the ODP, but she alone had been asked to interview only women (the others interviewed men or women). Mmantho was given guidance as to the kinds of sociological questions which the study of the lives of African women in South Africa might involve. She was introduced to modern feminist literature, to the comparative literature on African women, and to the history of women in South Africa. She was trained to record life stories in roughly chronological sequence, and to prompt her informants with indirect questions about issues that she and we considered to be particularly interesting or informative. She was not, however, asked to administer anything like a structured interview schedule in the early stages of the project; when appropriate, she was to allow her informant to guide the interview.

In the early part of the project, Mmantho interviewed women from Potchefstroom, Kuruman, Vryburg and Phokeng.[25] But she developed a particularly striking rapport with the Phokeng women. Using her native Setswana to speak to Setswana-speaking informants, she elicited from the first few women from this particular place life stories and statements of world views that rang with intimacy. One obvious reason for this was Mmantho's own background in the neighbouring village. Now, of course, she was a University-trained historian and sociologist. But to the women she was interviewing, as will become evident in the body of this study, she was almost a kinswoman, a young girl, a child to some, who wanted to know the stories of the past. Thus, what to positivists might seem to be Mmantho's weakness (her subjective involvement in the lives of the informants, and their perception of her as having a particular meaning in their lives) proved to be her greatest strength. It was in the light of this that Mmantho was then asked to continue her interviewing only with women from Phokeng, and to focus her questions more directly on their specific experiences. In the subsequent months, the full twenty-two life stories of women living in Phokeng, in their late seventies and early eighties, were collected. These provide the basis for this study, a remarkably coherent collection of stories with a similarity of context that enabled this "cohort" of women to be examined using sociological more than biographical tools.

This collection of stories has been both reported and interpreted somewhat unconventionally. The life stories have been treated as texts, imperfectly reflecting lives, and more accurately revealing "cultural and psychological myth,"[26] rather than as sources of "gobbets" of useful answers to key questions, as the positivist approach might have it. While the "texts" have not been given full priority over the "context," in poststructuralist fashion, literary methods of analysis have certainly been brought to bear upon them.[27] The seventy or so bare transcripts that make up the twenty-two life histories have been subjected to a variety of different readings; they have been treated variously as documents, narratives, stories, histories, incoherent ramblings, interlinked fragments of consciousness, conversations, and/or recitals of fact.[28] Each of these ways of looking at them has revealed a different set of meanings.

The first, and most conventional, use to which they have been put has been as reflections of the history of the places and times experienced by the women interviewed — they have indeed provided us with "more history." This aspect of their usefulness is particularly evident in the first three chapters of the book, where the history of Phokeng — a relatively unknown village, in an underre-searched part of South Africa — is undoubtedly illuminated by the recollections of the women who have lived there.[29] The conversations throw light on the way of life in early peasant and sharecropping households, the standard of living attained, the sexual division of labour that prevailed, the history of schooling, family relations, ethnic divisions, and particular Bafokeng struggles, for example. As the women migrate, they are drawn into relationships that are far better documented by other researchers. But we may still see their stories as sources of information about the conditions of labour in domestic service, wages, networks of support, and social relations, as well as about the nature of life in freehold townships such as Sophiatown and Alexandra during the interwar years in particular. Of course the interviewees tend to romanticise their childhood, to get dates wrong, to abandon all chronology, and simply to forget. The reading of these transcripts has involved the craft of sifting the valid piece of information from the invalid, the weak informant from the strong one. But what source of sociological and historical information does not involve these processes? Can we assume that the witnesses to government commissions of enquiry, or the government officials and public figures who write official letters to one another — sources that have all the grave respectability required of historians' footnotes—are freer of the sins of bias and distortion than the women of Phokeng? Thus, as with any source of information, there are crucial times and places where the informants interviewed here can and do provide valid, important, and useful insights, which might emerge as much in spite of their intentions as because of them. Of course these testimonies need to be read with a critical eye and with enough knowledge of the context to make it possible to sift the gold of true evidence from the bulk of ideology, poor memory, and wilful misleading that occurs. But it would be a poor researcher who did not perform this sifting process with every source available to her.

This book will have failed, however, if it is read as yet another contribution to the detailed understanding of "what happened"—whether in Phokeng, Parkview, or Pimville. It is not designed to add, in incremental fashion, to our store of information about sharecroppers or peasants, servants or beerbrewers, although it does reveal a lot of interesting detail about these things. But more importantly, these texts have revealed themselves to be unsurpassed sources for revealing otherwise hidden forms of consciousness. In the case of interviews such as these, which take the form of a dynamic conversation, expressions of consciousness and social identity are evident which do not normally find their way into the kinds of sources and methods conventionally used—where black South Africans are in any case thinly represented, and women hardly at all.[30] How has this aspect of interpretation of the texts occurred?

The very intimacy and interactiveness of the interviews has lent them a special character, and the study has not pretended that these life stories were obtained through the sterile means of removing the interviewer as far as possible from any involvement in the interaction, and turning her into the "absent" listener. Instead, the interaction itself is analysed here,[31] and the book acknowledges the transcripts of these interviews for being precisely what they are—records of conversations between black South Africans of differing backgrounds and levels of education, but with sufficient similarities between them to lend authenticity, richness, and depth to what is being said. As such, the interviews reveal things about the women and their mentalities that would otherwise remain opaque. Mmantho's questions as well as the women's answers are usually included, as are fairly lengthy extracts in which the full flow of their interaction is revealed. We see how even the most canny of informants tells Mmantho, the educated young girl from the nearby village, a little about her childbearing and marital experiences. Mmantho allays the suspicions of most of her informants about her political credentials in a culture riddled with suspicion and fear. It is Mmantho who draws out of her subjects stories of home and work that many white, or male, or "outsider" researchers might struggle to obtain, even using the most "scientific" of methods. Let us examine more carefully the various components of this process of interaction, in order to help us understand what precisely it is that these interviews are capable of yielding.

The interviews are not treated as having a clearly defined beginning and end, as perhaps a pseudoscientific interpretation of them might suggest.[32] Of course they have boundaries—between the "formal" period of actual interviewing, where questions are asked and answers recorded, and the "informal" preliminaries, interludes, and lengthy farewells which surround and cushion what some think of as the "actual" interview. But both the informal and the formal parts of the interaction have their functions, and are interpreted as part of the text—again providing us with insight into the kinds of people being interviewed. In the former, for example, Mmantho establishes the crucial rapport discussed above; in the latter, she requires the interviewee to respond to her questioning initiatives, to submit to a certain degree to the authority she claims to possess. In these conversations it becomes clear that what is formally recorded is informed and indeed inspired by what is not. Many of the insights these interviews give us are not derived from any clear-cut and formalised set of interview questions; nor are they insights that any interviewer, administering the same set of questions, could have gained. Rather, they are a product of the unique formal and informal exchanges between this particular interviewer and her interviewees.

Mmantho herself brings particular characteristics to bear upon the situation. The fact that she is "a girl from Mabeskraal, the nearby village" is perhaps the most important of these[33]—the focus on Phokeng was selected at an early stage in the study precisely because of Mmantho's ability to call upon common understandings between herself and her interviewees from this particular place. As the "local girl," Mmantho can appeal to common conceptions of space, community, boundary, property, history, hierarchy and culture, both on the broad level (she is a Tswana too) and on a local level (she knows Mrs. X who lives down the road; her sister went to Y school, which Mrs. J's daughter went to, or of which Mrs. M has heard). These are areas where her knowledge of the society is more experiential and intuitive than learnt. On the level of class, too, Mmantho is not an outsider—for she shows great sensitivity to and empathy for those whom she interviews, in spite of her better education. Mmantho "knows what is going on" in Phokeng. The interviews display a sense of conversation and intimacy between interviewer and interviewee, which is obviously aided by Mmantho's fluent use of rural Setswana. The interviews are replete with references to Tswana words, some with a local meaning, to surnames, clan names, and regional realities.[34] Her local origins allow a particular type of interview to emerge, one rich in local detail, and one which allows us to "overhear" interactions. This means that what is taken for granted between Mmantho and her interviewee is often of as much significance as what is regarded as of unusual and extraordinary value by both of them. The structure that both parties almost unconsciously attribute to Bafokeng society and the world around it is one that contains categories which are of great interest to the sociologist. Often, as suggested earlier, social scientific categories of analysis prove inappropriate for, or have to be adapted to fit, reality as it is perceived locally. This is not to say there are not hidden, invisible structures that common consciousness does not perceive. Of course there are—and part of Mmantho's quest was to discover them. But often these hidden forces are better understood by starting with the common consciousness of existing forces, than by assuming that categories derived from other contexts are appropriate by virtue of their theoretical pedigree. In the interviews, the women assume that Mmantho is aware of such matters as the boundaries of the community, its inner workings, and the roles it attributes to its members, as well as a whole range of other matters they feel she "knows," assumptions that give us a lot to work with. Sometimes this rapport fails, and the interviewee gets irritated with Mmantho because she hasn't indicated the common ground the subject thought they both possessed; or Mmantho finds her question gets the "wrong" answer, because she has assumed common ground that does not exist.

Mmantho is also black, and to the white outsider, the interviews sometimes read like private conversations.[35] Interviewees will sometimes express a hostility towards whites that they feel Mmantho will understand. At other times they confide in her, with a sense of amazement, about the extraordinary behaviour displayed by whites. Elsewhere, they show simple interest, treating her as a source of potentially important and useful information about whites — what can you tell me about these people? The impression given is that whites are mysterious, they come in a variety of different "types,"[36] and their behaviour requires constant explication. There are, it is assumed, nice whites and not-so-nice ones.[37] Whites are the outside category in these interviews, blacks the inside one. "We blacks" is a commonly used phrase, for example. Mmantho herself does not indulge in exchanging information about "good" and "bad" whites. But her interviewees assume she is a ready listener to such information because of the assumption of a common universe.

Thirdly, Mmantho is also a woman. Common womanhood is appealed to less frequently than Tswana-ness or blackness as a basis for mutual understanding. But Mmantho was trained to ask questions about the female experience, and about relations between men and women. Although the sociological categories she brings to bear on the interviews do not always "work,"[38] there are few examples of places in the interviews where such questions are brushed off or ignored. Rather, interviewees participate eagerly in discussions of such matters as how "women get rich through farming,"[39] how "men do not worry about women who dislike arranged marriages,"[40] or how women took out their breasts and showed them to the police, shouting "you were fed from this breast."[41] Perhaps the fact that Mmantho is a good fifty to sixty years younger than her informants made them less than forthcoming about the details of childbirth, or about the role of prostitution in township life — and the study is unable to pursue the issue of sexuality beyond a limited sphere. Still, childbirth rituals, fears of rape, and the difficulties of arranged marriage are issues raised by several of the women.

Mmantho's youth often causes her to be subjected to the older women's homilies about the evils of the younger generation, the virtues of the good old days, and the decline of moral and ethical standards. They like Mmantho because she shows respect towards them, and because she does not objectify them as "old people." Reminiscences are often treated by the women as opportunities for them to educate the younger girl about the culture, history, and achievements of her own people, and to draw her into an acknowledgement of the failures of the present. Her high level of education, while often treated as something to be valued, is assumed by some of the women to render Mmantho ignorant of local history and culture. She combines, therefore, the roles of a learned authority, whose questions must be answered, and an ignorant junior, who must be told about reality. At the same time, some of the women prefer to present themselves to Mmantho in terms they know will be understood by a younger, modern person.

The very interviewing technique used by Mmantho — the pursuing, in as near chronological order as possible, of the trajectory of the life of each woman through her experiences as a young girl, a married woman, a peasant and an urban worker, a mother and a churchgoer — also contributed to the special character of the interviews. Mmantho was sensitive, for example, to the fact that most "ordinary people," especially less educated ones, do not think of their lives as an elaborate curriculum vitae, arranged in chronological order and divided up into neat compartments such as work, home, and leisure.[42] Her interviewing technique adapted itself to the rambling style of many interviewees, to the fact that personal histories are a jumble and that they contain inconsistencies; or to occasions when the interviewee herself would wish to lead the discussion at certain crucial points rather than allow herself to be led — all of which would be anathema to the positivist. The consciousness of the interviewees is most often revealed, here, where they are not necessarily being "led" by Mmantho, but when they make unsolicited or seemingly irrelevant statements, in the "wrong" chronological order, about matters they consider to be important. Often it is what is spontaneous about the interviews that is most revealing.[43]

Some of these special characteristics of Mmantho as an interviewer were very clearly highlighted when, after the first thirty or so interviews were completed, we decided to "advance" to a more "scientific" stage in the research, by devising and administering a more formal questionnaire, based on the findings of the first interviews. The questionnaire was designed to overcome the problems of inconsistency between the interviewees — all would now be asked the same set of questions in the same order — and of major gaps that existed in the testimonies. The resulting more tightly structured interviews were factually informative, and probably, in case it appears that this book lacks any commitment to structure whatsoever, essential in giving us a bank of information common to all members of this "cohort" of women. But they lacked qualitative insights. They told us about the ages and dates of birth of each member of the informants' families, for example, but informants failed to take the opportunity to make their own statements, answer their own questions, lead the interview, or give their own opinions. The interviews became less interactive, more one-sided. Subjectivity vanished. The terms of reference were dictated by myself; Mmantho became simply the channel of my structured views, and the resulting words of the informants were often static and shallow, although Mmantho managed to make more imaginative use of the questionnaire than seemed possible.

This problem became even more obvious when Mmantho left the project, and the final round of questionnaires was administered by a second interviewer who, although black and with every intention of sympathy, was male, from an entirely different region and social class from the Phokeng women, and not a native Setswana speaker. The women failed to respond to the questions with more than yes or no answers in some cases; and some expressed feelings of resentment and anxiety about being interviewed. The rapport was lacking, the women became reticent, and they presented themselves to him in less open a manner.

Thus when we look at each interview as the text of a conversation between Mmantho and another woman, we are able to ask questions about the self perception of older Tswana women vis-à-vis the younger generation, or about the boundaries of common identity established between interviewer and interviewee, which suggest something about the meaning of being a "Tswana," a woman, a black, or a Mofokeng. We can probe how the relating of historical tales and details is seen as an important and socially underestimated activity, or how complex is the matter of the value given the high level of education of a woman like Mmantho.

Besides the process of interaction that produced the texts, the interviewees themselves have brought certain personal and individual qualities to the interviews, which add to their value. It should be said that the interviewees here were all informed that their stories were to be recorded, translated, and made fully available to scholars. The women who agreed to participate did so for a variety of reasons, each of which leaves its mark on the kind of interview they give. Some agreed because they believed they had an interesting and important story or series of stories to tell. They show a sense of their place in history, and their significance as historical actors. Naomi Setshedi, for example, stops Mmantho and changes the direction of the interview completely at times, with the sense that she knows important things that Mmantho is not particularly good at getting at. Others believe that by participating in the interview some aspect of their lives will perhaps be bettered. One woman refused to be reinterviewed, claiming that "nothing had come" of her previous interviews, so why, she asked, should she be interviewed again. Some treat the interview as an occasion to tell Mmantho all the things they have been longing to convey to the younger generation — either about the lost past, their own lost dignity, or about the lost struggles that achieved things which the younger generation now take for granted. The women regard themselves as "stores of information and history." They talk about times long ago, and about old practices, sometimes patronising Mmantho with a cultural heritage she "should" know about, but at other times simply telling her that there are things she has not heard of.

The women are almost all keen to be interviewed. They wish their village and their people to be known. They place a value on history, on recording the deeds of people, and on genealogy. They display a feeling that the past contains truths and inspirations that the present has crushed. As "ordinary" women, few interviewees give Mmantho the sense that they might think they are not worthy of being interviewed,[44] although it might be Mmantho's special status as an interviewer that brings their self-confidence and assertiveness to the fore.

Each interviewee constructs her life story in a different way. The different personalities of the interviewees of course affect their responses. But there are also ideological and cultural perceptions that have a social determination, varying from person to person. While the least successful interviewees treat the interview as something rather official, answering questions in a static, monosyllabic way, and giving even Mmantho the status of an outsider, denied access to the interviewee's inner feelings, the best become story tellers, creating a series of well-told anecdotes.[45] In telling stories, the informants construct the past in ways that place them at the centre of important events, and convey to us what they think is important about their lives — the pleasure or horror of living in Sophiatown, their courage, or their trauma, in difficult circumstances; and what type of person they wish to present themselves as being. Certain character "types" emerge, whether by the artful design of the interviewee or as a reflection of different social patterns of identity. The "Mayibuye" woman, who saw Christianity and education as a means to other ends, who took part in social protest, rebelled against arranged marriage, and has a coherent sense of her reasons for her various dissatisfactions, may be distinguished from the more conservative church-going woman, who tends to accept authority, to be overwhelmed by defeat, and to show a suspicion of social movements, for example. The study does not often try to label each individual woman as such. It is difficult to do so without obscuring the way in which the women's stories are also repositories of different fragmented components of consciousness and identity; the same woman who presents herself as having a rather clear sense of herself as a "Mayibuye" woman, also reveals aspects of her identity as a tribeswoman, churchgoer, wife, mother, daughter, township dweller, and so on. What the study attempts to reveal are the patterns of interplay between the inconsistent and fragmented aspects of identity, the myriad building blocks out of which a particular individual is constructed, and the larger patterns she might try to present. We ask when and why it is that at certain times, identity appears to cohere. Does it have to do with the presence of an "organic intellectual" (in Gramsci's terms) who seeks to and is able to organise consciousness?[46] The study does not seek to suggest that the presence of a variety of aspects of identity confirms the currently fashionable view that all subjectivity is "decentred," but suggests that there is an interplay between the self and its multiple components, an interplay that may be historically examined, and which involves processes of social interaction and ideological creativity.

A shortcoming in the book lies in its use of translated versions of the interviews, and their interpretation by myself, a non-Setswana speaker. No self-respecting literary analyst would allow this to occur in his or her field, and there is no doubt that this whole study would have benefited had it been written by a native Setswana speaker. The book has been limited by the fact that only broad generalisations can be made about the meaning of particular statements made by the women, and it has been impossible to draw conclusions about the more intricate, subtle, idiomatic, and nuanced expressions of their views. If I have done injustice to the Setswana, which no doubt I have, let us hope this is compensated for by the fact that here the interviewees are speaking to us in fully translated versions of their own language, rather than in the halting English they themselves speak (although Mmantho's translations do at times reflect her own late twentieth-century idiomatic English). At least this is the English version of a Setswana original. But students of South African society await the day when a new generation of fluent Bantu-speaking sociologists emerges, able to convey to the English-speaking world what insights they gain from the analysis of the words of ordinary speakers of their own tongue.

It may seem insensitive to impose upon qualitative and subjective material such as this the heavy artillery of the sociological armoury, weighing down modest life stories with a massive interpretive framework. It is to be hoped that a good deal of the material in this book will be interpreted by the reader, much as would a work of literature. But, Studs Terkel aside, "raw" oral histories are often opaque or merely anecdotal to those who lack a detailed historical understanding of the contexts that have generated them. This is not a work of phenomenology, as is made clear above. Some interpretive structure has been imposed or generated, although every effort has been made to reduce its intrusiveness.

This book addresses a wide audience, but a good deal of it is directed to sociologists of Africa in general, and of South Africa in particular. Sociology is, along with psychology perhaps, a discipline that has singularly failed to confront the challenges of interpretation that have been presented to Southern Africanists by historians and social anthropologists over the past two decades. Perhaps because its disciplinary heritage lies in Western capitalist societies, where it was born and where its greatest theoretical and substantive contributions have been located, the sociology of Africa is strangely rootless. Originally created as an offshoot of either philosophy or social work, South African sociology has perhaps too readily accepted its own separation from social anthropology — a separation justifiable (barely) in the West, for whom "primitive" societies have been geographically distant. This has led to a blindness to the special features of African societies, and an almost unqualified acceptance of the broad conceptual models provided by Western sociology — be these Marxist, Weberian, or Durkheimian — with perhaps some concessions to the essentially Eurocentric "underdevelopment" theories of the 1970s. While an eclectic internationalism is commendable, and should not be replaced by a chauvinistic introversion, their flirtation with the grander jargons of large theories has excused sociologists from having to confront societies such as African, and even Afrikaner, ones, which have distinctive and often non-Western characteristics such as chiefship, paternalism, patronage systems, powerful kinship structures, particular cultural formations, and particular configurations of age and gender. And while sociologists might well argue that such matters have been treated in a static and normative way by social anthropologists in the past, they have also not taken full cognisance of the substantial and successful attempts made in the field of African history to redirect the arcane concerns of social anthropology by seeking new sources, new theoretical and conceptual inspirations, and new subject matter.

While it is impossible to summarise here the whole reorientation of South African studies over the past twenty years,[47] it would seem essential to suggest briefly how much the conceptualisation of this study owes to the work of Southern African Marxists and Africanists, so that the significance of its conclusions may be assessed, and its distinctiveness as a work of sociology made explicit. The first intellectual heritage on which it draws is that of the writers of the early 1970s, whose major contribution was to recast the history of South Africa over at least the past one hundred years in materialist terms. The apparently determining force of long-entrenched racism in shaping modern South African institutions was reexamined, and shown to have been itself an ideology that was both cynically used and complexly reconstructed by various interests created by an increasingly successful capitalist revolution after 1867. The major policies of the twentieth century were about land, labour, and wages, each constructed in different ways around the races, and not simply about the gratuitous domination of white over black. The influence of this school of thought can be seen in the way in which this book is constructed. At the very broadest level, a system based primarily on the process of capital accumulation looms at every point in the story, which shows how it has been used and shaped by ethnic, racial, and gender forms and ideologies in Phokeng and outside it, and suggests that it has been overseen by a powerful state. The very rise and decline of the Bafokeng peasantry, part of a process originally identified for the broader region in the early 1970s, may be attributed to the African response to, incorporation within, and subsequent rejection by this system. The creation of black ghetto-like living areas in the cities was also part of a strategy designed to reduce the costs of labour as well as to control it, a strategy epitomised by the infamous pass laws themselves.

But a second influence on the book — the work of Africanists who have examined the impact of this revolution upon indigenous societies — has bred a caution about an unmodified "political economy" that would explain everything in terms of large-scale processes such as these. Of course here, as elsewhere, the broader pattern taken by events has engendered large, historically changing, and encircling material limits within which smaller struggles occur. But the need for caution is made especially pertinent in the light of the fact that the capitalist revolution in South Africa, powerful as it may have been, had always had to take account of, adapt to, and attempt to incorporate and control surviving and relatively resilient noncapitalist African societies and economies. These societies were not simply overwhelmed and destroyed (as in the United States, Australia, and New Zealand); nor did they contain class cleavages and ideologies that were transferable to capitalism (as feudalism or slavery did, for example). Powerful residual ideologies remained for many decades in South Africa, even when, in later years, precapitalist economic relationships became unviable. As we will be seeing in the case of the women of Phokeng, these ideologies contained notions of gender, age, royalty, property, and patterns of deference and assertion that differed fundamentally from those which a more purely "class" system might breed. And their presence has had a substantial impact upon the structural position, experience, and consciousness of the women as a result. Over time their behaviour as well as their ideas (which in turn influenced their behaviour) came to embody the complex interplay between the larger forces encircling and often squeezing them, and the cultural and structural attributes they brought into the situation. A combination of a materialist and an Africanist understanding is surely necessary for this process to be adequately captured.

Thus this study shows that not only has popular consciousness been forged out of the complex and mobile interplay between class, race, and gender ideologies, but it has also been forged in the context of surviving preindustrial world views. And because our concerns are with women, this draws us into an even further, important refinement: our conception of "hegemony" should in fact be modified to cope with the fact that the women of Phokeng are and were not simply the objects of the policies of white government and industrialising power-brokers — but they were affected by the policies of their own black chiefs and elders as well, so that their oppositional visions contained within them contradictory forces. Opposition to one's parents' choice of a marriage partner might well entail an embracing of the individualism offered by the new society, while resisting the imposition of passes upon women may be cast in terms of a preindustrial ideal vision of the family. The complexities involved in understanding the terms "resistance" or "opposition" are considerable when one perceives people as being so intricately enmeshed in different types of domination that opposition to one type may involve collaboration with another. The notion of "domestic struggles" developed in the body of the book represents one way of handling these multiple and mutually intersecting contradictions.

The social and historical complexities surrounding the lives of African men and women are thus only minimally explicable by reference to "political economy." These facts explain why a South African sociology without African history and without anthropology is forced to abandon what should legitimately be a substantial proportion of its own terrain. This study does not of course claim to solve all the problems and weaknesses of South African sociology through the oral and historical techniques used here. For one thing, not every question can be answered

by the use of oral history. But it does claim to reveal the existence of a world —
already fairly substantially documented by other disciplines — that should be the
domain of the African sociologist but that is, generally speaking, neglected. The
realities of African culture, childhood, family, gender, class, race, and resistance —
all staples of the sociological menu — are at least brought into focus through this
study, by the interplay of disciplines and concepts, the local and the universal,
and the worlds of culture, society, and political economy. Perhaps other sociologists will take them further, and open up new possibilities for us to explore.

Perhaps in conclusion it should be said that, whatever the theoretical pretensions
of this introduction, the reader should approach the book more as a source of
insights about people than about theories. Theory, after all, is mainly a means
to other ends, and not an end in itself. This book will have achieved its aim if, at
the end of it, the reader feels he or she has a better understanding of the kinds of
people the women of Phokeng are, and of why they think, feel, and act as they
do. If a work of sociology can achieve that, it will have made a small contribution
towards creating that most elusive of all things — a humane and democratic
society, in which all are respected for who and what they are, and in which
"liberation" refers to the freeing of subjectivity as much as to the altering of
structure.

Prelude:
Lives in Portrait

There follow brief biographies of seventeen of the twenty-two women whose stories provide the basis for this study. All references to places, people, and events have been left unembellished, in the hope that they will acquire significance and meaning in the body of the book.[1]

DIKELEDI MAKGALE was born on a white-owned farm in the Rustenburg area in approximately 1900, where she, her Bafokeng parents and sister, and her grandfather worked as labour tenants, cutting tobacco and tending their own and the farmer's sheep and cattle. She had very little schooling, and remembers her parents moving from farm to farm in search of better contractual conditions. She married a farmworker and they moved to Rustenburg, where she worked in a tobacco factory for twenty years, until "I retired because my feet were no longer strong enough to stand for a long time and so I was afraid I would become crippled," while he worked in a dairy. She bore twelve children, of whom seven died during this time. She did not plough the small amount of land she managed to retain in Phokeng, where she lived with two of her children in her old age, and spent a large amount of her time and pension on burial societies, saying that she would still be prepared to "go back and stay at the farms and still continue working if I feel strong. I know that the Boers will give 'boermeel'" [boermeel is coarsely ground cornmeal].

MAHUBE MAKGALE was born in Phokeng in 1901, and remembers driving the oxen behind her father's plough as a child. She attended the Reverend Penzhorn's Lutheran school, and remained loyal to his memory. After confirmation, at the end of Standard 2, she left school and worked seasonally on a well-known Rustenburg citrus estate, making marmalade. She then went to work as a domestic in Pretoria, and remembers the dangerous life of Marabastad, the township she visited on week-

16

ends. In 1921 she went to Johannesburg, where wages were higher. She stayed there, moving from job to job, until 1940, when she was recalled to care for her elderly parents. She was sceptical about whites, saying they "are only interested in your hands, when you get sick and you can't work, they forget about you and get somebody else." She never married or had children, and remained in Phokeng for the rest of her life, working "with my own hands for survival," her family having retained a number of cattle and good access to land. On her parents' death, however, her "brothers and sisters were there to take their shares, but in Setswana, cattle are for men." Her brothers sold the cattle, and she lived on a meagre pension in her old age.

MMADIATE CAROLINE MAKGALE was born in Chaneng, near Phokeng, in 1903. Her father once worked on the Kimberley mines, and her parents were wealthy peasant farmers, who told her stories of how the Bafokeng had been brutally dispossessed by Paul Kruger, and who employed others to help them weed, harvest, and herd. "We were healthy and shining," she recalled, with many cattle, abundant crops, and plenty to eat. She went to the local Lutheran school, where she did well; she finished school and was confirmed at the end of Standard 2. She went to work as a domestic to "manage to buy things that I would need in my matrimony," in Rustenburg and then Johannesburg, where she worked for "good Boers." Her parents arranged her marriage to Gideon Makgale, a much older Mofokeng who was related to her, and who was a horsecart driver for a liquor store in Braamfontein, Johannesburg (and who was later put out of a job when the firm began to use motor vehicles in the 1960s). They had three children, the first of whom was born in 1923 (before their marriage of 1929) and was born retarded, because, she said, she suffered a severe beating by police when she was pregnant with him. Both he and her youngest child died young. During her time in town, she would visit "Fietas" (Vrededorp), where, after 1932, she lived as a married woman, in a rented house, sewing, brewing beer, and experiencing arrest and harassment. She hated the city, and built herself a house back in Phokeng during the 1940s, injuring herself badly in a fall while doing so. There, her family's fields had been expropriated by the chief for mines and roads, but she lived an energetic life caring for grandchildren, participating in a variety of societies, sewing to earn extra money, and taking part in community affairs.

MARIA MATHULOE was born in the Rustenburg area in 1911 of wealthy peasant parents who lived in Sefanyeskraal, a small area where black landowners clustered and which they called "Mensekraal" (people's kraal), "because we owned it and had no king." Her father produced "hundreds" of bags of maize, grew tobacco and graded it with the help of "a certain Whiteman," and sold both in town. His cattle were "many in such a way that he had to be on horseback when looking after them." She went to the local Lutheran school up to Standard 4, when she was confirmed. She, like all her siblings, went to work in town after finishing school. After a year as a domestic in Rustenburg, she went to Johannesburg, where she worked as a domestic again, until she married a Mofokeng who worked in a Johannesburg dairy and was fairly well-off; they rented rooms in Alexandra township, and ran a small cafe there, while he also bought a stand in Alexandra and rented out "cottages" on it. In the meantime, (presumably in the late 1940s) her father's land was expropriated as a "black spot" and the people removed to "another place." This appears to have destroyed his wealth, and she recalled that he had no children to care for his remaining cattle in his old age, and that he sold them all eventually. Maria and her husband continued to run their cafe in Alexandra through the 1950s, and did well enough to send their daughter right through high school and on to become a teacher, but they were vulnerable to gangster raids and protection rackets during this turbulent decade. Maria came to dislike the city and never involved herself in the political and economic campaigns of the time. In 1962 the couple moved back to Phokeng, where she built a house. She lived there in her old age, caring for her great grandchildren.

 ERNESTINA MEKGWE was born in Phokeng in 1906 of moderately well-off peasant parents and remembers her childhood as a golden age, in which "farming was number one," traditional values were strong, their fields were large and fertile, and the family produced "hundreds" of bags of sorghum for sale to "the Boers in Rustenburg town" — although they were far from being the richest in Phokeng. She was educated by the Lutherans at first, but soon joined the alternative and more Western-oriented school run by the West Indian Pentecostal missionary, the Reverend Kenneth Spooner, who taught her English. She was confirmed at seventeen and went to Johannesburg as a domestic in 1925; her wages supported her family after her mother had died in 1919. She was called home in 1931 to an arranged marriage to Thomas Mokua, a Mofokeng, which she futilely resisted. "It was painful," she said, but she moved with Thomas to Benoni, where he worked in a grocer's and they had three children. They lived in "Twa-Twa" — the Benoni township — which she found "decadent" and "immoral," until he died in 1937. She went home for a time, but was forced by economic circumstance to return to domestic work. She worked for liberal employers in Johannesburg, who did not object when she lent her impassioned support to the bus boycotters and pass campaigners of the postwar era, although she did not join them. In the meantime, in 1950 she married Josiah Mekgwe, a wealthy farmer and widower with five children, from neighbouring Luka, who had a tractor, ample fields, and cattle. She carried on working as a domestic until 1960, after which she retired to Phokeng where she and Josiah lived in the house she had built. He died in 1970. She lived on her pension in Phokeng in her old age, and looked after her grandchildren. Farming was out of the question because of the dangers introduced by the presence of mineworkers in Phokeng. One of her children became a teacher, but died in 1952, one became a "witchdoctor," and the third a worker in a soft-drink firm in Rustenburg.

MMAMATLAKALA MOJE was born in Phokeng in 1904. Her mother was widowed a year later, and her only sister died in the great flu epidemic of 1918. She helped

her mother—who could also afford to hire labour—to plant, weed, and harvest her fields of sorghum, and tend her pigs. The crop was sold in Rustenburg. Her mother wanted her to go to initiation school, but she rebelled and went to the Lutheran school instead, at the age of ten, where she completed Standard 3 and was confirmed. She then went to work as a domestic in Pretoria, where she stayed, moving from one job to the other, until 1930. For the subsequent twenty years she lived with Ephraim Moje, a deliveryman at a Johannesburg butchery, who had been "chosen for her" in her childhood. They lived in Alexandra township and sometimes Sophiatown, in a whole series of rented rooms. They had eight children, born before and after their marriage in 1940, of whom two died. Mmamatlakala was a *fah-fee* runner,[2] and also brewed "plenty" of beer at home in the townships, and was arrested a number of times; her husband was, moreover, brutally assaulted by an Alexandra gang in 1941. In the late 1950s, they moved back to Phokeng, after her mother-in-law's death left her husband's family home empty. They resumed farming for a while, but in her widowed old age Mmamatlakala could not continue with this activity and lived, with three of her children, on her small pension. She belonged to several burial societies, saying "All my hope lies in Societies." None of her children remained in Johannesburg—they became domestic or factory workers in the Rustenburg area or at Sun City, or remained unemployed in Phokeng.

NTHANA EMILY MOKALE, Naomi Setshedi's niece, was born in Phokeng in 1908 and had a strict upbringing as the daughter of well-off peasant/migrant parents. Although her father was rich enough to hire people to work his land while he worked in town, she remembers her childhood as a personal "struggle." She had no brothers, and would undertake "boys' work," such as herding her father's cattle, milking cows, and helping with ploughing. She completed Standard 5 at the Lutheran school in Phokeng, but, anxious to leave her difficult home, chose to go to work as a domestic in Johannesburg in 1927 instead of going on to Standard 6 as her parents and teachers wished her to. She worked in various "live in" jobs and had three children during these years, but only married her policeman husband, Hazael Mokale, in 1938. She had a further three children, but two died at birth, while her husband died in 1946. In 1947, after a year of mourning, she returned to domestic work, but in 1952 moved to Sophiatown and became a factory worker after her mother could no longer care for her children. Long hours of work in a jam factory could earn her enough money to keep the family going, but she was jailed after joining a union-led strike for higher wages. She remembers her years in Sophiatown as having been relatively content, and she joined the antiremovals campaign when "the white man pierced our hearts with a spear," and Sophiatown was destroyed in the mid-1950s. Nthana was left bitter and cynical by the defeat of the latter campaign, saying that "there isn't a single black who can defeat a white man." She retired to a house she had built in Phokeng in 1973, keeping her house in Emdeni in Soweto, and still retaining some liking for city life. She spent her old age living on a pension. Three of her children ended up in upper-working-class or white-collar jobs, and were married and settled in towns, one of them in the Emdeni house.

 MMADIPHOKO CAROLINE MOKGATLE was born in Siega, not far from Phokeng, in 1899. Siega's poor soil drove her peasant parents, along with the rest of the village, into sharecropping upon white-owned land near Koster and, later, Ventersdorp. The village community would migrate by ox-wagon to the lands seasonally, and live in shacks constructed there. Her father would also sell timber during dry seasons. Her mother, the daughter of a wagon-builder from Luka, was an accomplished potter and basket weaver, who sold her wares as well, skills which Mmadiphoko was reluctant to learn, believing that they were more trouble than they were worth. Instead, she was taught by the local missionary to sew and crochet, skills which stood her in good stead later. Her father carved wooden figures, and was also a scout in the Anglo-Boer War. She helped her parents in the fields, and attended the local Lutheran school until she was confirmed in Standard 2 (Standard 3),[3] after which she travelled by ox-wagon to work in Johannesburg as a domestic. There, during the 1920s, she married a cousin, Edward Mokgatle, who came from Phokeng and who worked in Johannesburg. She left Gauteng (Johannesburg, the Golden City) for the birth of her first child and never returned, believing strongly that migrant workers and city dwellers made poor mothers, and disliking the urban treadmill. At first they stayed in Siega, but later her husband persuaded her to move to Phokeng, where they built themselves a house, and farmed on several fields, practising crop rotation; she also did freelance washing for a Rustenburg boarding house while her husband took a job with a tobacco company there. They had a further five children, all of whom survived. Their three daughters became professionals in either teaching or nursing. The coming of the mines to Phokeng inhibited the couple from ploughing the four fields they still had in their old age, and after her husband died in 1978, she lived with two of her children and survived on very little.

SETSWAMMUNG ERNESTINAH MOKGATLE (photo unavailable) was born in Phokeng in about 1885 — a full generation earlier than most of the other women — and was both born into and married within the royal clan. Her maternal grandfather was a man of high status, who had three wives and worked in the great Chief Mokgatle's office as secretary, "and wrote everything about what the chief was doing." Her father had many cattle, and also worked on the Kimberley diamond fields for a spell, while her mother did "the usual duties of a woman" — tilling the fields, building, potting, and caring for her three children. She also recalls that her mother was amongst those sometimes sent by Chief Mokgatle to work on Paul Kruger's farm nearby, and that after her father died, she "produced enough to feed us." Although her father was not a Christian, her parents succumbed to her refusal to go to initiation school, and she attended the Lutheran mission school, and was baptised in 1897. Her parents arranged her marriage — presided over by the Lutheran missionary Ernest Penzhorn — to her cousin Chere Mokgatle soon afterwards. Chere was an educated man and clerk in the chief's court, who subsequently went as leader of a Bafokeng age regiment dispatched to fight in the First World War (elsewhere she says it was the Anglo-Boer War, but this seems unlikely). But Setswammung remembered seeing "a great cloud of dust when some Boers on horseback were being chased by English soldiers" one day while she was collecting wood — this was surely the latter war. Although her brother Thomas migrated, neither Setswammung nor her mother ever worked in town. As women, she said, "we were not allowed." She and Chere had six daughters, most of whom were taught by the Lutherans, and many of whose own children became teachers or nurses. (In fact, when the Reverend Spooner came to Phokeng, she refused to send her own children to his school, remaining loyal to the Lutherans and finding his Baptist practices embarrassing.) She vividly recalled the "Bafokeng wars," in which she and her husband were reluctant defenders of the royal house against the "rebels," but was vague about her later life, mentioning only her children, and her membership, in her old age, of the church *manyano* (women's league) — which provided a great deal of support to her, as did the dignity and respect she was accorded as the oldest royal woman in Phokeng.

JOSEPHINE MMAMAE MOKOTEDI was born in Chaneng near Phokeng in 1905. Her father was born in Botswana (then Bechuanaland) and had moved to Phokeng in his childhood. Both her parents were Lutherans. Her father had worked on the Kimberley mines, and the whole family worked on their fields, which were only moderately productive, particularly after her father died in 1921. Although hers was one of the poorer families in the area, whose members sometimes worked for others to earn a little, Josephine remembered a happy childhood. She went to school for five years, between 1917 and 1922, and was proud of the good English she learnt there. She was then confirmed, and went to Pretoria to work as a domestic in 1923. She bought furniture and helped support her family with her wages. She remembered visiting the township of Marabastad in her free time. In 1929 she married Martins Mokotedi, a military policeman who worked in Pretoria, but who was from Phokeng, whom she had chosen for herself as husband, and after their first child was born went to live with him in the military camp. There she did washing, and they had ten children, of whom four died. Some time during the 1940s, she moved to Phokeng and ploughed their limited fields using donkeys and with the help of her children. Her husband continued to work in Pretoria, and died in 1975, after which she stayed on in their house on a small pension. She belonged to ten burial societies. Most of her children married and settled in and around Phokeng, or were in working-class jobs in town.

IDA MOLEFE was born of a Mofokeng mother and a Zulu father (a mineworker at one stage) in West Roodepoort in 1910, and was taken to Phokeng where she was brought up by an aunt after she was orphaned at the age of nine or ten. She went to both Penzhorn's and Spooner's schools, where she was a bright pupil; because of family poverty, she left school in 1926 (or 1923), having completed Standard 5 and having been confirmed by Penzhorn, to work in Rustenburg and then Johannesburg as a domestic. Later, she returned to the countryside and worked on a "Boer's" farm. In 1939 (date uncertain) she married Phillip Kwele, already the father of one of her children and also a Mofokeng, and moved to Randfontein location with him. Together they had an unnamed number of children, of whom six survived, while she did washing, ran "fah-fee," brewed beer, and did other "piece jobs." She joined the antipass campaign in Randfontein in the 1950s, and in the 1960s she returned to Phokeng, where she was a stalwart of the International Assembly of God Church in her old age. Three of her children were in white-collar jobs in Randfontein or Sun City, in their adulthood.

 BOTO FRANCES NAMENG was born in Luka near Phokeng in 1903, and grew up on a highly productive farm, which harvested "large quantities" of sorghum and maize. "We ate and drank, our life was smooth, everything OK," she said. Her father was Abednigo Mneia, a teacher and evangelist, who had been to school at Tigerkloof and converted to the African Methodist Episcopal (AME) church in his adulthood, and who, she said, "decided to call some Americans" to Luka; the Reverend A. A. Morrison, Luka's charismatic AME missionary, came at Abednigo's request in 1916. At the age of nine Frances went to school in nearby Phokeng, where the schools were "better," and she went up to Standard 4 there. Perhaps as a result of the American connection, she then spent two years as a boarder at Wilberforce College in Vereeniging, where she trained as a teacher, and returned to become an assistant teacher in Luka. Because her qualifications were so low, however, she left after two years and some time in the 1920s, went to work in Johannesburg as a domestic. In 1932 she met her future husband, who was from Searone and worked at Lever Brothers in Johannesburg, and who had been chosen for her by an agreement between their parents, and moved to join him in Sophiatown where he had a rented room. They lived there together during the 1930s and early 1940s, a time which she says was peaceful and pleasant, and had four children, marrying only in 1939. She earned a living by brewing beer and sewing clothes for sale. Later in the 1940s she moved to Phokeng while her husband moved to the company hostel, because her "money was going down the drain" because of high rents. She stayed there, apparently living off her husband's income, until the need for her children's school fees drove her back to work as a domestic again in the 1950s, during which time she was saddened by what she saw as the decay of Sophiatown, and by its ultimate removal. She built a large house, with three bedrooms, a kitchen, dining room, and pantry, in Phokeng during this time, and retired there some time in the 1960s. Their children all had a relatively good education and were settled in houses in Meadowlands, while Frances spent her old age and widowhood deeply involved in burial societies and church affairs.

NKWAPA RAMORWESI was born in Phokeng in 1914 — a decade later than most of the women — and grew up with her grandparents while her mother worked as a domestic in Pretoria. She helped them plough, weed, and harvest their fields, cooked, ground grain, and kept the homestead "clean and well decorated" — a sign that "in that particular home there lived a hardworking girl." Those were times, she said, when good traditional values were still intact. She attended the

Lutheran school from the age of fifteen, and completed Standard 3 and was confirmed in 1931. One of the Reverend Penzhorn's most loyal followers, she also went to Kroondal, the Lutheran mission station, a "university of domestic work," which "prepared" her for her subsequent years as a domestic. She had several children during her first years in Johannesburg, while working for a succession of different families, but never married their father, a man from nearby Kanana, who "could not even afford to pay *bogadi* [brideprice] for me." In the early 1940s, soon after the violent murder of her youngest brother in Johannesburg, she went with her current English employers to live in Cape Town, leaving her children in the care of her mother in Phokeng. She stayed in the Cape for thirty years, living in, learning to speak Xhosa, and subsequently obtaining a house in Nyanga township with her son, who married a "coloured" girl from Cape Town. She visited Phokeng annually to see her children. She found the Cape pleasant and peaceful until the 1960s and '70s, when she took an interest in the turbulent black politics of Cape Town, but was restrained by her employers from becoming too involved. She declined to join her employers on their return to England. Her children's father died of tuberculosis while she was away, and after her son died in the mid-1970s, her children in Phokeng "ordered" her to go home, and she and her daughter-in-law and grandchildren moved back to Phokeng, where she lived in her old age on a pension, in her son's house — opposite the one in which she grew up. Her relationship with her daughter-in-law, who had left her people and now cared for her devotedly, she said, was like that between the biblical Naomi and Ruth: "'This girl,' she lost her well-built gentleman but she left her people, Coloureds of Cape Town, and said 'I want to follow *die Kaffirmeid*, she is my mother because I agreed to get married to her son.'"

MOKETE PHALATSE was born in Heidelberg in 1905 (1904). Her father was from Phokeng, and a Wesleyan preacher, and her mother from Dewildstad, but they were labour tenants on a white farm in Heidelberg between about 1900 and 1917. She remembered having had a happy, well-fed childhood there. She particularly remembered herding the cattle. After her mother died in 1917, the family returned to Phokeng driving her father's fifty-two cows and a span of oxen, few of which survived the less prosperous times of Phokeng in the 1920s. There Mokete attended the Lutheran school until her confirmation in Standard 2, after which she went in about 1923 to work as a domestic, first in Rustenburg and then in Johannesburg. She worked there until 1936, returning home for harvesting each year, until her father's blindness and subsequent death forced her to return to Phokeng to tend the farm. In the meantime, she had met her husband, Okker Phalatse, who had come from Botswana in the early 1920s, and had various jobs as a farm worker or shop assistant in the Phokeng area, and together they had nine children, three of whom survived. They only married officially in 1948, in Botswana itself. Mokete preferred not to live in Botswana, and eventually they built their own house in Phokeng where they stayed as farmers — with her husband, it seems, retaining a fairly good labour tenancy in Rustenburg — until Okker died in 1975. After that,

Mokete, by then paralysed by an unknown illness, and shocked by the sudden and inexplicable death of most of her remaining cattle, lived on a small pension and on money sent to her by her children; she had six grandchildren in her care.

SOPHIE SEROKANE was born in Potchefstroom district, where her parents were Bapedi labour tenants on a series of white farms, in 1907. Her father would move from farm to farm seeking better conditions. She used to help in the farmer's house, cook and clean at home, and also help during weeding and harvesting seasons in her father's fields. She attended school for a short time, until Standard 1, and was brought up as an Anglican. After school, she went to work as a domestic on the Rand, where "all of my friends" were already working. Her first job was in Florida, but later she moved to live in Julia Location in West Roodepoort and then, when in 1967 (1957) Julia Location was demolished, she obtained a four-room house in Dobsonville. In the townships she lived by washing and liquor-brewing, and was never politically involved, saying that she had no option but to accept a pass when it was forced upon her. She had met her husband, Ramokgopana Koriah (Oriah) Serokane, in 1941; he was a deeply religious man who worked in a dairy in Randfontein, and a Mofokeng. He subsequently went to work in Johannesburg while she stayed in their Dobsonville house. Although they visited Phokeng from time to time, they did not settle there until 1976, when their old age and the expense of life in town became too much for them. They had three children, but two died; their surviving daughter worked as a domestic and had a house in Dobsonville. They lived on pensions, grew a little maize, and had money sent to them by their family for caring for several of their grandchildren and nieces and nephews in Phokeng, where schooling, said Sophie, was good. She felt herself to be a stranger in Phokeng in many ways, but took an active part in Anglican church affairs in spite of a crippled leg.

NAOMI SETSHEDI was born in Phokeng in 1904, of comfortably-off peasant parents. She remembered cooking, housebuilding, sewing, washing, and cleaning in the home, and later her widowed mother hired workers to do the ploughing and harvesting for her. She went to the Lutheran school and reached Standard 2 in 1922, and then went to Johannesburg to work—not, she insisted, for economic reasons, although she sent money to help her mother, but because it was what all the young girls of the time were doing. She worked as a domestic in the suburbs, where she had a number of friends from Phokeng, including Joseph Setshedi, her future husband, who had been at school with her, but who was not her parents' choice for her and who at the time worked on the Kimberley mines. Some time in the early 1930s she moved with Joseph to Alexandra Township, while he took a job as a shop assistant in Johannesburg, and they stayed there for the subsequent thirty years, marrying in 1935, and having five children, of whom four survived. Naomi gave up full-time domestic work and became the archetypal informal sector worker, brewing beer, hawking apples, sewing, and taking in washing to boost the family income, although she never fulfilled her ambition of buying a stand in town. She enjoyed life in Alexandra in the earlier years, but gangsterism and later political and economic circumstances drove her to evolve a fairly militant political consciousness. She joined bus boycotts, the potato boycott, and the women's antipass campaign, and in spite of experiences of jail and repression, remained loyal to the spirit of these causes in her later life. Finally, however, the threat of removals, particularly of militants, from Alexandra to Soweto led the family to build a house back in Phokeng. Her husband died in 1962, before the house was completed, and soon afterward her son was murdered in Alexandra. Naomi moved back to Phokeng alone. She began by cultivating their fields but gave up, out of a combination of fear of attacks by mineworkers from the nearby Bafokeng mines, a desire to care for her grandchildren, and the difficulties of farming in her old age. She lived on her pension and remained involved in Christian affairs.

Rosinah Setsome (photo unavailable) was born in Krugersdorp in 1901. Her parents were not Bafokeng, but of the Bangwato of Botswana (then Bechuanaland), and she had only lived in Phokeng since 1969. Her grandfather was an Anglican preacher, and her father, who owned a cafe in Krugersdorp, was killed in the Anglo-Boer war, in which he had acted as a scout for the English. Her widowed mother ran the cafe and sewed for a living, but then remarried (this time to a Mopedi from Phalane), sold the cafe, and moved to Olifantsbrug (Ntseedimane) in the Magaliesberg, where they were sharecroppers on a profitable farm, producing sorghum and rearing cattle. She went to school there and passed Standard 6, after which she worked for two years as a domestic servant in Johannesburg, and then married a local man, Zachariah Setsome, who had been chosen for her by her parents, some time in the early 1920s. For the first few years of their marriage she lived with her parents-in-law, bore two children (both of whom eventually died), and found the strictly regulated life of a hard-working junior wife very difficult. After that, in the late 1920s, she joined her husband, a horsecart deliveryman for a grocer in Johannesburg, in Alexandra Township, where they lived rent-free in a back room in his sister's house. They had a further two children, one of whom died, and Rosinah brewed liquor and experienced frequent arrests. In the 1930s, they moved to Boons, where they became labour tenants on a white farm where they grew wheat and tobacco, and worked with sophisticated farm machinery. They had a further five children, three of whom survived. "Oupanyana" (Rosinah's husband) had a good and profitable relationship with Steenkamp, the white farmer, and administered his farm while he went away during World War II. Rosinah did some domestic work for the farmer, who eventually sold his farm, forcing them to move into another tenancy relationship. There Rosinah took up brewing again, under the protection of the white farmer, Charles Pieters (Piet Smith), but was nevertheless jailed for it at least once. After the latter farmer died in about 1969, and his children "were a bit fussy, they could not look after the tenants well," the family moved to Phokeng, where Rosinah had an aunt. They were strangers, and Rosinah worried a lot about whether she had burial rights in the village. Her husband died in 1973, and she lived alone in her old age, on a pension and money sent to her by her surviving children, one of whom became a traffic inspector in Johannesburg, and another a self-employed manager of a brick-making firm in Rustenburg.

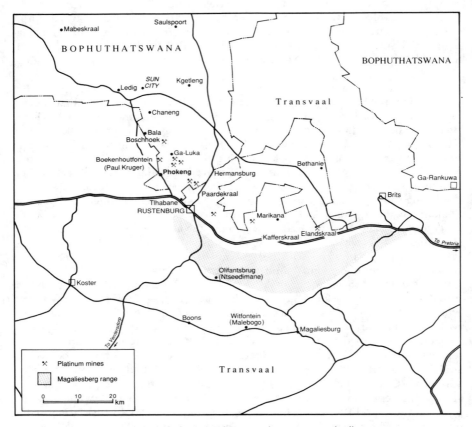

Rustenburg, Phokeng, and surrounding towns and villages

1

The Bafokeng: Myths and Realities of the Past

White South Africans do not know the small town of Phokeng, which is situated outside Rustenburg in the Western Transvaal. The most they may know is that they will pass it as they make their frantic trips between Johannesburg and the decadent pleasure resort of Sun City, for it is just over one of the many "borders" between South Africa and Bophuthatswana. The region in which it is situated is subtropical in climate, and the Rustenburg district is characteristically fertile, with many citrus estates and colourful vegetation. Road signs do not direct one to Phokeng—somehow black towns do not warrant that status—which is reached after passing through the mainly "white," historic town of Rustenburg, with its associated township Tlhabane—the name given to Rustenburg itself by many Africans. Those who are not blinded to the subtleties of variation within and between the places where black people live, might note that Phokeng itself looks relatively prosperous in comparison with other "homeland" centres of its kind. Hundreds of low, concrete-block or older brick houses cover the spread-out town and the low hills surrounding it, each with a corrugated iron roof and a tiny yard of its own. Some have maize and other crops growing there. Less sturdy tin shacks are visible on the periphery of the town, where squatters and refugees from other parts of the region have attempted to make a home. There are several prominent churches, small scruffy and busy country shops, a substantial civic centre, and a number of schools. There are some well-tended surrounding fields, each with evidence of large numbers of tractors. But most striking are the looming great platinum mines that surround Phokeng, lending it an industrialised tone, which indicate a place of greater wealth than whites are accustomed to seeing in the so-called self-governing homelands. Indeed, some may wonder why the border is situated before rather than after you reach Phokeng and the mines— surely such wealth is normally carefully embraced within South Africa's peculiarly constructed geography?

To black South Africans, particularly those from the Transvaal, Phokeng is better known and understood. It is a place which elicits a tone of respect and even envy. It has relatively high standards of education, for example.[1] Doctors, lawyers, writers and teachers lay proud claim to coming from this area.[2] The standard of housing is regarded as good,[3] while the town itself, as some of the informants in this study reveal, is seen as a desirable place for settlement by those who wish to escape the massive cities of the Reef, to own a home of their own, and to remain within easy reach of the urban areas where many of their kin may live. Chief Edward Lebone Molotlegi, who held office there from 1964 until his ousting in 1990,[4] articulated, in his public statements, a desire to work for the social, educational, and cultural upliftment of the people of the town, using the wealth of those of the mines owned by the Bafokeng themselves (but leased to mining companies) as a means to higher ends. "We are going to use every cent we get to fight illiteracy," he said early in his period of office.

Accompanying the acquisition of wealth on the part of the Bafokeng has been an increasing "ethnic"[5] and political assertiveness. In 1987, the Bafokeng were implicated in an abortive coup against President Mangope of Bophuthatswana, and Chief Edward Molotlegi and his wife Semane were detained for a few days after the coup attempt. Later Mrs. Molotlegi obtained a court order to forbid the Bophuthatswana government from harassing and interfering with the women's club she ran, claiming that she and her family, along with the club, had been "victimised and harassed" since the attempted coup, while reports were received by the South African Council of Churches that "hundreds and hundreds of ordinary Batswana in the so-called Bafokeng region have been hunted and detained by the Bophuthatswana Defence Force...." Rumours have also claimed that Phokeng threatened to secede from Bophuthatswana during the late 1980s. Further evidence of the Bafokeng's increased confidence and assertiveness came in 1988, when Chief Edward (unsuccessfully) appealed to the Bophuthatswana Supreme Court for the right to challenge Impala Platinum, the company to which platinum mining rights had been leased since 1977, for the right to mine on their land. Other examples of "ethnic" consciousness are referred to by the women themselves, as we shall see towards the end of this study, where they describe how during the 1970s it had become increasingly difficult for non-Bafokeng to settle in the town, and suggest that "outsiders" were being denied burial and other rights. This type of reinvention of ethnicity, and ethnic closure, is typical of black homelands, particularly where access to land is limited, and chiefs seek means of rationalising and focussing their patronage.

But the relative wealth and the "ethnic" assertiveness of the Bafokeng are not simply a result of the discovery, in the 1940s, of platinum and chrome in the surrounding hills and plains. While this study does not pretend to give a history of the Bafokeng, to the student of consciousness it appears, even from the meagre available secondary sources, that their group pride has its origins in times which precede those covered by the interviews in this book. Both in fact and in communal myth the Bafokeng appear to have an earlier history of resilience and self-assertion that plays an important part, as we shall see, in the evolution of consciousness in the twentieth century. This chapter is the only one in this study that explores a version of reality not mainly derived from the women's stories. It examines published missionary, autobiographical, explorer, and ethnographic materials, side by side with academic works; and sketches out, in a rudimentary fashion, some of the basic elements of Bafokeng history. It should be said,

The mines and town of Phokeng, 1990

however, that even this history takes on a form that is unusually contoured — for many of the published sources are in fact simply distillations of oral traditions taken from the Bafokeng themselves. Thus it is not certain whether the stories, particularly of the period before the nineteenth century, constitute "actual" history, or some sort of myth of historical origin.[6] I have deliberately left the chapter ambiguous on this point, taking the liberty of drawing readers in to the ways in which it is likely that the women perceive their own past, in order to prepare them for the emergence of the women's own version of reality in later chapters. Throughout the account we pursue three themes. We ask whether the myths of historical origin give us any indication of the extent and nature of the patriarchy that the society is bound to have possessed.[7] We explore the "senior status" of the Bafokeng in relation to other groups, particular other Tswana groups nearby. And we examine the particular economic and cultural patterns taken by their interaction with colonialism — in particular, their relative economic resilience, their rapid embracing of Christianity, and their migrant labour tradition.

Accounts of the origins of the Bafokeng place emphasis on their longevity. There is no doubt that the women think of the Bafokeng as a group with a long history and deep roots in the region. Commentators suggest that the present-day inhabitants of Phokeng originate from an ancient and fairly independent group. According to one ethnologist, the Bafokeng are "a very ancient tribe,"[8] while another commentator writes of their having "at least a thousand years of history" behind them.[9] Their arrival in the Transvaal is said to have been circuitous: some say they came from Egypt or Ethiopia originally, and crossed the Zambesi into Southern Africa, probably moving into Lesotho, in the 12th century.[10] Bafokeng oral histories of the subsequent centuries suggest that while many remained in what was to become Lesotho, at least some of their ancestors left that area "many generations ago" and settled first in what was to become Botswana, and then in the Transvaal.[11]

While their self-identification,[12] and their identification by ethnographers, always notes the affiliation of the Bafokeng to the "Bakwena" (crocodile) totemic social grouping (i.e., a grouping wider than that of "tribe" or "clan"), this is often qualified. Commentators sometimes note that to be Bafokeng denotes an affiliation to something at once smaller and more elevated than the "Bakwena." One author suggests that this is because the Bafokeng as an independent group actually long preceded the Bakwena, and that it was only their "peacable ... nature that led them into affiliations of this sort." Their pottery and huts show distinctive and long-standing cultural patterns,[13] while some have referred to the phenomenon of Bafokeng intermarriage with San people, which led to their possessing particular physical characteristics.[14] They were perceived locally, according to one source, as the "senior tribe," with a tendency to attach themselves to other groups while retaining a sense of their own position. In one commentator's words, "they have continued, even up to the present day, to retain their individual seniority and influence. They were regarded as clever and able by the other tribes, whose chiefs frequently chose Bafokeng wives."[15]

In his autobiography, a well-known figure from Phokeng, Naboth Mokgatle,[16] recounts the oral traditions passed on to him by his uncle, a repository of information and myth about the past of his people. These too reflect the presence of a myth of common origin, which, whatever its basis in fact, serves to reinforce notions of Bafokeng uniqueness.[17] He suggests that after massive migrations in the sixteenth century a branch of the Bafokeng established their first independent village at Mogoase (relatively far to the north-east of what was to become Phokeng) under the chieftainship of Tsukudu (spelt Tshukudu elsewhere). They settled there, between the Pilanesberg mountains (thaba tsa Bakgatla), the Elands River, and the Crocodile River. While Mokgatle is not as blind as are some chroniclers of African communal pasts to the realities of preindustrial cleavage, conflict, and contradiction, his evocation of the Mogoase period is of something of a golden age of traditionalism, hierarchy, and ordered tranquillity: "They were a large group who constituted families, with possessions, owning cattle, sheep and goats ... the land was open, roamed by wild animals and birds of all kinds, big and small," he writes, in the nostalgic tones echoed in some of the interviews in this study. The people flourished at Mogoase, according to Mokgatle. They became agriculturalists, and "they had the whole field open to them, their animals grazed anywhere they chose, and they hunted everywhere at will." The tribe grew, "cherishing the crocodile symbol which lent them the totemic name 'Bakwena.'" In these times, "women tilled the land and grew food, and men took care of the animals, the building of houses, and the maintenance of law and order." While work was collective, he suggests, this sexual division of labour extended throughout. Men helped each other build homes, women to kill weeds, reap and build the storage containers for grain (difala) that kept it fresh and free from insects. The fields were planted with sorghum, naoa (African butter beans), ditlhodi (African peas), sugar cane, and marotse (African pumpkins). What Mokgatle perceives as the golden age of the Mogoase period was presided over by a series of chiefs of the Tshukudu house, but the Bafokeng eventually split as a result of vicious succession disputes, common to Tswana communities, into three sections, each founded by one of the three wives (with her son) of one of the dominant Tshukudu chiefs. The Bamanape, the Bamaramokoka, and the Bamogopa each moved to a new place. One account even refers to numerous subdivisions of the Bafokeng during this period, into "little clans, spread all over the country and forming close relationships with various tribes as each little party came into contact with them,"[18] leaving the rump of the tribe in the Magaliesberg region from the sixteenth century till the coming of the Matabele invader and conqueror, Mzilikazi. Ellenberger attests to the ancient nature of the occupation of this region by Bafokeng by suggesting that "all the other tribes except the Maphetla on their arrival in these regions found Bafokeng already there."[19]

Mokgatle suggests that each of these groups based on one of the sons formed a separate settlement. The first made their home at Phalane, the second at Thaba-ea-Nape, and the third at Koamogopa, where the town of Brits now stands. He suggests that the sense of kinship between these three groups remains strong, and also that the Bamanape (to become the Bafokeng of modern times) were the strongest of the three. This sense of strength and relative power is conveyed in Ellenberger's account as well, where it is suggested that the Bafokeng are seen in some senses as the primary grouping among a variety of lesser ones. "They were much respected by reason of the antiquity of their race and their intellectual qualities" he writes, and even when they were conquered or absorbed by other groups, or in cases where they scattered, "their dialect was adopted as well as their manners and dress by the tribes whose subjects they became."[20] Mokgatle also exhibits a kind of ethnic pride and sense perhaps of the Bafokeng as some sort of aristocracy in the region when he describes how "our population has always outnumbered theirs (the other split-offs from Tshukudu), we occupied more land than they did, and were richer than they were. It seems to me also that they looked to us for guidance in some things; for instance, we adopted Christianity first and they followed."[21]

Of the Bamanape, writes Mokgatle, "the legend is that at that time they were rich, had large herds of cattle, sheep and goats, large quantities of corn, and other things." The ancient claim of the Bafokeng to a place in the Transvaal is reasserted by Mokgatle, for he says that while they kept their land at Thaba-ea-Nape,[22] "they settled at a place they called Tlhabane, the place where Rustenburg, the European town, now stands. My tribe even today still calls Rustenburg Tlhabane." On the way to Tlhabane, "those who did not want to go to the new site established villages, but remained loyal to the chief who led the emigration to Tlhabane. The villages they established became branches of the main tribe.[23] The land they passed through to the new place became the property of the whole people."[24] Two famous chiefs, Sekete and Makgongoana, ruled in these times. It was the latter who, before the arrival of Europeans, moved his people to settle along a hill named Direpotsane. This place was subsequently named Phokeng.

The first chief who ruled at Phokeng was Mokgatle, popularly called Mokgatle-oa-Makgongoana-oa-Sekete. He was clearly a descendent of the Sekete line. His grandson Naboth estimates that this settlement began towards the end of the eighteenth century — at least we know that he was an established ruler of the Bafokeng by the 1830s and that his rule continued until the 1890s, covering almost the entire period of early European contact, and spanning the decline of the first perceived "golden age," and the rise of perhaps a second — that of the peasantisation of the community. Mokgatle Mokgatle, Naboth's grandfather and the first paramount chief to rule at Phokeng itself, was (according to his own family's perceptions at least) a wealthy, just, and revered chief who "treated all the people in the same way, and intensely disliked injustice being done to some people because those who provoked them thought they were of the lower class in the tribal society." A patriarch and polygynist (he is said by Naboth to have had up to four wives, the "top three" of whom were the most important), he appears to have ruled with a feudal sense of justice towards commoners and "old people in my tribe still swear in his name when they testify to the truth, while they cannot imagine anyone making a false statement in his name." Mokgatle himself "stored large amounts of *mabele*-corn[25] at his home, and when some people in the tribe were unfortunate and had had a poor harvest, and their stock of food could not carry them through to the next harvesting time, they could go and tell him that they were facing starvation, and he would not hesitate to give them *mabele*-corn."[26]

Naboth Mokgatle refers to the role of women in these early times. Polygynists, practitioners of traditional Basotho female circumcision and marriage customs, the Bafokeng were "male dominated":[27] "Men were masters, made laws mostly in their own favour, and to suit their needs, and made it appear that this was right." He also describes the sexual division of labour in some detail. Women were the key craft producers of the society: "Before the introduction of European containers, steel tins and cooking pots," he writes, "there were very artistic women in the tribes ... there were women experts in pottery who made pots from dark, soft clay called *letsopa*. The pots that they made were of two different colours and some were artistically decorated with animals, birds, flowers or other objects." He also writes about how "before the arrival of Europeans, when all young women of marriageable age spent more time in the tribe with their mothers, they were taught the art of brewing. A woman found good at brewing beer is regarded as a copy of her mother, and the unfortunate one who cannot is also taken for granted as a copy of her upbringing." We shall see in later chapters how some women, wishing to keep their "respectability" intact, tried to play down the traditional roots of the art of beer-brewing.[28]

But more important, women were the gatherers and farmers; they provided grain and edible wild food for the family's survival. This vital productive role did not lend them an equal or superior status to that of men, because "Men maintained relatively exclusive control over their products, which allowed for their accumulating property and acquiring social standing over time," while women "were cast into largely communal forms of ownership, which locked them into a situation of dependence and lifelong subordination."[29] Women's subservience was reinforced by the punishing work schedules imposed by subsistence production, their vulnerability to deprivation and violence, and the "work ethic" prevalent in Tswana society.[30]

The sense of the order prevailing in pre-European times, called, interestingly, *pele-a-lekoallo*, or "before literature," that is conveyed in Mokgatle's testimony is one that is indeed reminiscent of feudalism — society was hierarchical, patriarchal, and divided into royals and commoners. Bafokeng society resembled most African preindustrial societies of the period, although it seems to have benefited from the rule of a particularly paternalistic chief.

Oral tradition suggests that from the 1820s onward, a series of wars in the region devastated the previously prosperous settlements. A Bafokeng chief named Sebetwane waged widespread war in the region of the Kwena and elsewhere in the mid-1820s, until his defeat by the Ngwaketse in 1826. At the same time, the region was subject, during the upheavals of the Difaqane, to the conquest and invasions of the hated Matabele expansionist, Mzilikazi (Moselekatse in Setswana). The population was cruelly defeated and Tswana society was devastated over a period of sixteen years.[31] The collective memory of this period of conquest and humiliation is still powerful in the women's testimonies, and the Matabele (Ndebele) are still considered to be "the Tswana's worst enemies," according to one account. So central was Phokeng to the workings of his empire that Mzilikazi established his headquarters for the region there.[32] In the turmoil many Bafokeng fled back to Lesotho, and today there are numerous connections between the groups who remained there and the Bafokeng of the Transvaal.[33] Mzilikazi ruled and exacted tribute from local tribes until his defeat by "Boers"[34] in 1839 — and Chief Mokgatle himself, displaying the pragmatism which appears to have been the key to Bafokeng survival in this period, ultimately gave recognition to Mzilikazi.

Visiting the region during Mzilikazi's reign, in 1829, the missionary and traveller Robert Moffat, in his *Matabele Journals*, observed the devastated remains of what Naboth Mokgatle's grandfather had so clearly portrayed to his grandson, perhaps providing support for what might have appeared an overromanticised depiction. He saw the ruins of the towns and villages that had clearly held together an agricultural and pastoral society of considerable stability and prosperity:

> the country ... became more plain, beautifully studded with small chains of mountains and conical hills, along the bases of which lay the ruins of innumerable towns, some of amazing extent. The plains and valleys, of the richest soil to a great depth, had once waved with native millet and been covered with pumpkins, water melons, kidney beans, and sweet reed.... The ruined towns exhibited signs of immense labour and perseverance, every fence being composed of stones, averaging five or six feet high, raised apparently without mortar, lime or hammer.[35]

It was during this time of the decline of the early Kwena culture that the first European travellers came to the area. Given the devastation that had occurred, it is not surprising that by 1836, it was the wildlife of the region, rather than the prosperity of its indigenous inhabitants, that attracted attention. Moffat commented on how, with the destruction of Kwena society, the area "had become the habitation of wild beasts and venomous reptiles, where lions roam at large as if conscious that there is none to oppose," and according to one vivid early description:

> Three hundred gigantic elephants, browsing in majestic tranquillity amidst the wild magnificence of an African landscape, and a wide stretching plain, darkened, far as the eye can reach, with a moving phalanx of gnoos and quaggas, whose numbers literally baffle computation, are sights but rarely to be witnessed.

Moffat described how people of the area constructed houses in trees, in order to remain safe from wild animals.

The conquest of Mzilikazi by Dutch-speaking Voortrekkers in 1839 permitted the Bafokeng to regroup. Indeed, oblivious of what to later generations would be seen as the ironic freeing of a black community by a white one, Chief Mokgatle rapidly switched his support from Mzilikazi to Hendrik Potgieter, the Voortrekker leader who settled near Phokeng in late 1839[36] at a farm called Doornkop, and made contact with the local chief.[37] From there he attempted (largely unsuccessfully, it seems) to control the area across the Vaal and several other districts. In the same year the Trekker settlers founded the village of Magaliesberg, which later, in 1850, became Rustenburg. By 1852, some 20,000 "Boers" had settled in the Transvaal area, and had established widespread townships and farms. As the clans scattered by Mzilikazi's conquest and rule began to "creep back from the desert,"[38] Mokgatle "reassembled the tribe."[39] But the Bafokeng encountered new attempts to subjugate them: the settler Boers set out to claim local blacks as their subjects and to exact forced labour from them.[40] For the subsequent twenty years, massive changes were wrought in local economic relations. Chiefs and Boers engaged in struggles over the supply of farm labour, and several communities moved across the border into what was then the Bechuanaland Protectorate to escape these.

By the mid-1860s, white Rustenburg itself had become better established,[41] and it continued to grow during that decade. Oral traditions about this time convey a sense of loss and deprivation. Boer labour exactions were experienced as harsh;[42] the fields that used to be tilled by the local inhabitants were no longer theirs to cultivate. Chiefs collaborated in the supply of labour; we shall see how one of the earliest memories in the interviews in this book is that of the oldest informant, who recalls her ancestors' having to work on white farms, under instructions from the chief.

Between the 1860s and the 1880s, the Trekkers attempted to extend their influence over the local Tswana groupings. Responses were ambiguous, indeed contradictory. The Bafokeng themselves were on the one hand driven to take up arms against the Boers,[43] in an unsuccessful attempt to persuade the British to extend their protection to Bakwena land. This at least might have made it difficult for the Trekkers to lay claim to control of all the land of the region, and made more viable the second Bafokeng response, which was to compromise and indeed collaborate. Thus Bafokeng and other Bakwena communities supplied regiments to aid Trekkers in the suppression of another, less compliant, Transvaal community, the Bapedi,[44] during the Sekhukhuni war of 1876−77; and to aid Paul Kruger, by then president of what had become the South African Republic, under Boer rule, during the 1880−81 war against the British.[45] According to one source, "Mokgatle did what the Boers wanted, and was respected by them."[46] Paul Kruger visited the tribe in 1883, and established his Transvaal residence at Boekenhoutfontein, very near to Phokeng. The way this episode was related eighty years later by the contemporary chief of the Bafokeng was as follows: "It all started during the days when Paul Kruger decided to settle in Rustenburg. He got on so well with the Bafokeng that he forced them to buy the land they occupied. He issued the tribe with the deeds which they still have. So, as you see, we are entitled to the land and its mineral rights."[47]

But in fact, Trekker-Bafokeng relationships were much more complex than this folk account would acknowledge. They were shaped by a complex interplay between the gender, class, and age hierarchies within each social group. This is well illustrated by Naboth Mokgatle's story of the marriage between Chief Mokgatle and Matlhodi Kekana, Naboth's own grandmother. She was an *inboekseling*, or indentured slave,[48] who had been captured by the Boers at Potgietersrus during a battle with the Ndebele, at the age of two to three, and taken away by a Dutch family to the Rustenburg area. The man who kept her as a slave, nicknamed "Mangoele" (knees) by the Bafokeng, became friendly with Chief Mokgatle. They "paid each other visits and gave one another presents.... It is said that each time Mangoele arrived at Phokeng he brought presents to his friend, and through these presents their friendship deepened. According to legend, there was no feeling of a white man meeting a black man, one thinking that the other was not his equal, but man meeting another man and accepting him into his household."[49] During one of his visits, where Chief Mokgatle was enjoying the European food cooked by the *inboekseling* Paulina, Mokgatle "asked his friend to allow him to marry Paulina, so that she could cook him European food at his headquarters, Phokeng." Mangoele agreed, but suggested that "his marriage to Paulina must be performed according to his [Mokgatle's] law and customs, so that Paulina could acquire social standing in his tribe." In an amazing collaboration between two systems — one of slavery and one of patriarchy — "grandfather paid Mangoele dowry [*bogadi*] which would make her grandfather's legal wife."[50] A series of complexities followed, since "her status was never defined to her or her children"; a fact that led Naboth himself to resent greatly the degree to which other, legally more secure, members of the Mokgatle royal line attempted to "relegate [my father], my mother, my sisters and myself to the last position in our tribal society." Later, through an extraordinary set of coincidences, Paulina's Ndebele family found her in Phokeng, and demanded the payment of a second dowry, and the celebration of a second marriage.

Two further events — the coming of missionaries and the discovery of diamonds in Kimberley — were also treated as opportunities for the assertion of the chief's vision of Bafokeng interests. Like many other chiefs in the region, Mokgatle sought to enter the land market, making use of what resources the Bafokeng possessed — mainly mission protectiveness and cash income from migrancy, as well as the patronage of Kruger — to acquire more land. It was after 1853 that the first missionaries came to the region, when Setshele, a Kwena chief, invited the Trekker leader Pretorius to send them in.[51] Later, the South African Republic government invited the Hermannsburg Lutheran Missionary society to come into the region.[52] However, the Christianisation of the Bafokeng was slow at first. According to Naboth Mokgatle, "one day, I was told, a man arrived in our village and introduced himself as a missionary for the Dutch Reformed church." Chief Mokgatle invited him to meet with his people and councillors, which he did. After a long explanation of the teaching of Christianity, he was asked "to give them time to consider alone what he had told them." When he returned, Chief Mokgatle responded in this manner:

> We thank you very much for the trouble you have taken to come here to introduce to us your religion and the church. We are sorry ... we cannot accept your religion and the God you urge us to accept and believe in. We have our own way of worshipping God and the way we think we can reach him. We think that our dead ancestors are the way we can

speak to God. Through them we firmly believe he can speak to us, by accepting our humble requests to him or rejecting them. We, therefore, think that it would serve no useful purpose for you or ourselves, to join together and worship the God you have spoken to us about. The best thing we think is that you pass on to try elsewhere.[53]

However, says Naboth, "the missionary left our tribe like a man who planted a seed in a dry soil, knowing well that one day rain would come to water the soil and the seed would grow and bear results."[54] Some had "silently accepted" his message, and two or three years later, when the Hermannsburg missionaries were heard to be in Durban, these "silent accepters" actually went by ox-wagon to attach themselves to them. "In Durban, among the Lutheran Missionaries, men from my tribe, like teenage boys amongst teenage girls looking for sweethearts to marry made their choice. They picked one for themselves and asked him to consent to become their teacher of the Christian doctrine and priest. His name was Penzhorn."[55] And indeed, in 1867, the Hermannsburg Mission Station was established at Saron in Phokeng,[56] with Ernst (also called Ernest) Penzhorn at its head.

The first conversions to Christianity were, significantly, amongst royal rather than common people — yet another example of royal initiative. The first man to be baptised, according to Naboth Mokgatle, was the son of the chief's third wife, Sekete, renamed on his baptism as Johannes, followed soon thereafter by his brother Petrus.[57] As a result "the ordinary people of the tribe felt free to join the Lutheran Church of Hermannsburg mission, or to stay out of it."[58] Naboth Mokgatle quotes a Bafokeng proverb, which asks "Worm, how did you manage to enter the large body of an ox and cause it to rot?" and the worm answers, "Through a tiny piece of flesh." "And that," writes Mokgatle, "was how the Christian Church entered my tribe, not to cause it to rot but to cause it to become Christian. It would appear that the word went round like wild fire that the Bakoena-ba-Phokeng had become Christians."[59]

Naboth's maternal grandfather was an early convert, a fact that led to a great, but perhaps typical, conflict between the demands of polygyny and those of Christianity. Mokgatle relates with great poignancy the story of Thomas Mororo, who was not a Mofokeng, but a Mokgatle of the Bagkatla tribe, a wealthy man with many cattle, sheep, and goats, and much corn, who emigrated from Kgatleng with his two wives, to Phokeng especially to become a Christian, his own tribe having "expressed opposition to it at all costs." He paid the cattle required of him to become a citizen of Phokeng, and approached the church. "He was shocked at being told that he could only be accepted with one of his wives, not the two of them." His first wife "being disappointed" suggested they should return home to Kgatleng. "It is said she was uncompromising in her attitude and refused to accept that one of them should go into the church with Grandfather while the other remained outside." She was unhappy in Phokeng as well and could not be persuaded to stay even if she were to become the only wife.

While grandfather's word was officially law, he could not force his wife into the church. "As a last stand," grandfather "left it entirely to her to decide what she desired to do." She chose to return home to her people and her children. The second wife went with Mororo into the church and the children of his second wife "were all born into the Christian section of our tribe" (implying that quite a large section remained un-Christianised at this time). Mokgatle relates that quite a few polygynous men faced the same problem, "but because their wives were women of Phokeng they did not have to see them go to live far from them. Others did not bother to join the church, but left the decisions to their grownup children to join if they wished."[60]

The Lutheran missionaries established themselves in the community over the subsequent decades. The Penzhorn family in particular became deeply rooted there, a fact that was to affect the women profoundly. The elder Penzhorn's first child was Ernest, who had been born shortly before the family moved to Phokeng. "His other children were born in Phokeng and therefore were Bafokeng. They grew up playing with Bafokeng children in the village and acquired the language of the Bafokeng, Sesotho,[61] in the same way as the children of the tribe."[62]

The elder Penzhorn taught the Bafokeng how to read the Bible; indeed he "transformed their lives entirely," also introducing the building of square brick houses in straight rows, for example. He introduced skills such as carpentry and brickmaking into the community. Mokgatle recalls a little more of the tales told to him by his parents and uncle of the early years of the missionaries, writing of how in the early years "nearly every family ... found itself divided in the middle, into Christians and non-Christians," and saying that the latter did "not find it easy to throw over their old beliefs and habits and adopt the Christian way of life."[63] The early Christians were, he says, strict with ritual and holy days.

Christianisation accompanied, and indeed assisted, the transformation of the Bafokeng into a progressive peasantry in subsequent years. Whereas in many other areas in the Transvaal the Trekkers laid claim to all the land after having routed the Ndebele, here in Phokeng Mokgatle's special relationship to Potgieter and Kruger led to his being given permission to retain land, as we have already seen.[64] The "gift" of land was, however, augmented by a strategy of land buying. Mokgatle's chiefly authority over junior men, in an act typical of chiefdoms of the time, allowed him to "send" about five hundred young men to the diamond mines soon after diamonds were discovered at Kimberley in 1867, to earn five pounds each, a portion of which would be levied by the chief, so that the Bafokeng could buy farms.[65] Although Africans were not allowed to purchase land, the Lutherans — themselves substantial landholders in the region (Kroondal, the mission station, provided the young Naboth Mokgatle with a place to escape to, from an oppressive uncle; missionaries themselves farmed there, and youth and runaways were taught crafts and agricultural arts there) — did for the Bafokeng what missionaries in many parts of the region were doing. They allowed them to purchase land in the mission's name, providing Chief Mokgatle, along with many other chiefs of his time, with a clear material motivation for continuing Christianisation. It is probably the case, and certainly the women's interviews later in this book give weight to this suggestion, that Mokgatle's strategy of "communal" purchase of land was in fact a means to some degree of individualisation of land holdings in the emerging peasant society, although elements of communalism did and do remain.[66]

When in 1881 the Native Locations Commission established reserve areas of land for African occupation ("locations"), in which land could be transferred to African ownership if it was held in trust by an officer of the government, those African groups with substantial land holdings, such as the Bafokeng, found themselves the subjects of further attempts at dispossession. White farmers sought to extend a "squatters law" to such lands, limiting the number of families residing on each plot, and thus forcing the surplus into farm labour. As far as the Bafokeng were concerned, this led to negotiation over what was to be defined as a location and what was to be subjected to the squatters law. In the end, "of the eighteen farms belonging to the Fokeng, ten were considered to be in excess of the area required by the population and as such subject to the squatters law." But by 1908 negotiations were still going on, and the situation seems always to have remained ambiguous.[67] The Bafokeng once again appear to have avoided outright dispossession.

It was during the latter years of Chief Mokgatle's rule, between 1865 and 1895, thus, that Christianisation, strategic migrancy, and land acquisition wrought great transformations in Bafokeng society. Whereas in the early part of that period, the whole community owned only one plough and one wagon, by the end of it "every family" possessed a plough and enough oxen to plough their land. While they were not the wealthiest community in the generally resilient Western Transvaal region, the Bafokeng were indeed "progressive." "All Fokeng women wore European style clothing"; there were five stores doing good business on their land, the people were "thriving," and goods were acquired through increased production and the strategic use of migrant labour as a means to acquisition of goods and land, as well as to introducing a totally new way of life.[68] This reinforces Mokgatle's view that they were amongst the "moral leaders" of the region.

It would seem fair to conclude, even while taking account of the element of myth in some of the sources used here, that while the Bafokeng, like most other Tswanas of the region, were systematically brought under European influence and control by the late nineteenth century, they were not the victims of full subjugation. Relationships of negotiation were frequently entered into, and substantial holdings of land were retained in black hands[69] as trust land, native locations, or reserves.[70] The Bafokeng thus were to become part of the South African progressive peasantry of the late nineteenth and early twentieth centuries. At that time, in fact, Western Transvaal Africans were outproducing white farmers. Some did so as sharecroppers or labour tenants on white-owned farms. But in the case of the Bafokeng, this productivity took place mainly on what remained of their own land. Africans from this region placed themselves in a relatively strong position in relation to the emerging, labour-hungry capitalist economy after gold was discovered in 1886, their participation in migrant labour remaining discretionary and centred upon the needs of the rural economy (rural-centred), rather than involuntary and centred upon the labour needs of the urban economy (urban-centred) as late as the 1930s.[71]

Mokgatle used his authority — that peculiar mixture of royal, male, and age-based control that characterises power in African precapitalist formations — both to protect his domain and to make possible the accumulation of land and the Christianisation of his people. This stance was lent support by and indeed supported an ideology of Bafokeng longevity, individuality, strength, and uniqueness that accompanied the process of peasantisation. It was into the resulting context that the women who are the subjects of this study were born.

2

Peasant Daughters,
1900−1915

The majority of the women interviewed for this study were born between 1900 and 1910, and their childhood memories are of the days when the Bafokeng reaped the fruits of Mokgatle's strategy of land buying, Christianisation, and peasantisation. These were times of both prosperity and change. It is not as if they were the first generation to experience extensive contacts with white society, the cash economy, or Western and Christian values. But they were certainly one for whom such contacts had profound implications, both for their place as women in a patriarchal society, and for the nature of their community itself. This chapter explores the changing society into which the women were born, examining the implications these changes had for the position of girls, boys, men, and women in an economy affected first by the encroachments of mercantile capital, and later by its self-transformation into a peasant one. It shows the gender system as having been affected in numerous and complex ways by these changes. It also tries to give a more qualitative portrayal of the lives of subsistence farmers and then peasants than is usually found in the literature,[1] and presents to the reader the modes of remembering the women adopt when talking of their earliest days.

The generations preceding theirs had, indeed, already experienced a great deal of change. The oldest informant, Setswammung Mokgatle, of the royal house, was born in about 1886, and was herself, therefore, a member of the older generation. Her family was wealthy, and had many cattle: "we never ran short of meat," she says. She remembers that even her grandfather, Ramoralo Molefe, had been literate, having worked in the chief's office as a minute-taker, while her father, Montlafi Molefe, had, like many of his generation, worked at the diamond diggings in Kimberley, and seems to have served in the Anglo-Boer war. But these experiences were not sufficient to mark them, in Setswammung's eyes, as fully modern: "Education and Christianity were not as yet common," she recalls, and because her father was not Christian, on his death he was not buried at the church but at home, like all the "older people" who "had not been converted."[2]

In spite of, or perhaps because of, their royal connections, Setswammung's family became victims of Mokgatle's strategy of appeasing Kruger in those early times. She recalls:

> When we had to go to the towns for work, a certain white man who ruled over the people of Mokgatle at Moletsane called Piet [sic] Kruger[3] came to our village and asked Chief Mokgatle to provide him with women and children who could work on his farms at Boekenhoutfontein. Our mothers worked in those fields while we attended to our younger brothers and sisters who were too young to be left on their own at home.

Her mother had clearly not conveyed happy memories to her of this experience:

> *How much did Kruger pay the workers on his farms?*

> No, he did not pay them. The old man Mokgatle called the Bafokeng to the *kgoro* and told them that the following morning they should go and weed Kruger's farm.... He had farms on the other side of that big hill. Occasionally when Kruger held a party of some sort at his house, we would all go there to look at Boers dance. After they had eaten, the hardhearted Boers would throw us scraps of food for us to nibble.[4] When we were weeding on his farms, he would come on horseback with his big stomach heaving, shouting obscenities at our mothers and urging us to work faster.

> *When weeding, did they stand in single file?*

> Yes, they worked towards one end of the field and then turned weeding towards this end of the field.... He will swear and beat up the slower workers. At times the slow worker is your mother and you would be crying helplessly at the edge of the field when he beats up your mother.[5]

Mmadiate Makgale's testimony suggests that the figure of Kruger looms large in the mythology of ordinary Bafokeng, in spite of their chief's alliance with him. She was told as a child that:

> My great-grandmother's folks on my father's side were removed by the Boers. It is Paul Kruger when he came with the wars.[6]

Legend has it, she says,

> that he used to inspan people. My great-grandparents used to be inspanned in ox-wagons; they then physically pulled them. When the babies cried, Paul Kruger used to say "Let them keep quiet, they will suckle afterwards." I mean, that is what they narrated to us.... He used to persecute them, they drew those ox-wagons. They then escaped and crossed over down to Steinleter [sic].

Kruger did not buy Bafokeng land, "he annexed it through war," she insists. "When viewed objectively, the land still belongs to Phokeng people.... There is no part which belongs to whites really, I am telling you."[7]

The initiatives by the Bafokeng chief, in his self-protective alliance with the Boers, were more likely to have reinforced "traditionalism" than to have undermined it, as indeed Setswammung's memories of her mother's position in Bafokeng society as a whole suggests. She undertook "the usual duties of a woman, these being to till the fields, making walling enclosures and pots with clay and mud. Also to look after her children," while her own father took a harsh traditionalistic stance towards her widowhood:

[My mother] told me that after the death of our father she went to see her father Mokgatle and after spending most of the day sitting on the verandah she met her father and asked him to allow her back at home with her children since her husband had passed away and she could not look after us on her own. Mokgatle said to her "my child, those children are the responsibility of your husband's father, and he rightfully more than I should look after them." She told me she left her father's yard crying, and she came home to find us seated with our [paternal] aunts eating together.[8]

Setswammung remembers tales, correct perhaps more in spirit than in fact, but definitely echoing Naboth Mokgatle's version, told to her of the coming of the missionaries into Phokeng: Chief Mokgatle "said he wanted priests here in Phokeng, so he fetched them, driving an oxen cart from Germany," and recalls that her parents were far from anxious for her to embrace the new religion. Setswammung herself showed the kind of spirited ambition to go to school that most interviewees reveal:

When time went on the German missionaries came to Phokeng and began their church schools. When time came that I should go to initiation school, I refused to attend and asked my mother to allow me to attend school instead.

She describes her rebellion, a presage of the greater independence that the subsequent generation was able to obtain:

I was walking with my friends who were going to the school. I was crying, not wanting to go along with them, and then they grabbed me trying to pull me with them. I screamed and when they let go of me, I ran back home to my grandmother's house and I hid myself in her blankets and slept. When they completed their time at initiation and returned to the village they jeered and spat at me, calling me a coward.

She attended school and was baptised in 1897, and confirmed when she completed school.[9]

Like Naboth Mokgatle and several other informants, she was struck by the tensions produced by Christianisation:

When the Germans came here they said to Mokgatle that they would not allow anyone who had married more than one wife to join their church. The old man [Mokgatle] then left half of his women and remained with three whom he was allowed to register at the church.... He had a lot of wives in his court and its surrounding lands. I am sure there were more than six women who had borne him children. Mokgatle decided to remain with only three women.[10]

We have a clearer idea of what life was like for Setswammung's own generation (i.e. those born in the 1880s), because this was the age of most of the informants' own parents. Here we get a real sense of the growth of a secure peasantry: "Our main occupation during those years was farming and it was really profitable," said Ernestina Mekgwe of her childhood. "Farming was number one," says Naomi Setshedi. Mrs. Mekgwe gives the impression that to the Bafokeng, farming was the woman's sphere in more than just name: "No woman ever thought of going to work for a white man.... Women got rich only through farming."[11] Several of the women talk of "my mother's" fields, "my mother's" crops, and "my mother's" income from the sale of crops. Although he would, at times, sell eighty to one hundred bags "to the Boers," and had three fields, Mrs. Mekgwe's father was not as rich as some: "No, my father was not rich, he had just enough to support himself and his family." He had about thirty head of cattle, and about twelve donkeys.

> At home while growing up we made about fifteen bags [of sorghum] every season and these saw us through to the next season.... When we wanted sugar we sold some, when we needed paraffin we also sold some or exchanged it for paraffin and other various needs.[12]

By contrast, she says, "there were people who had more than two hundred head of cattle."[13] Nthana Mokale talked of how her father "was indeed a rich man," who "owned quite a herd of cattle" as well as "flocks of sheep and goats."[14] He hired people to look after them,[15] and produced "sometimes fifty, sometimes a couple of hundreds" of bags of sorghum per season, "more than enough to feed an army."[16] He was, she said, one of the richest men in Phokeng. Mmadiate Makgale, the daughter of an extremely rich family ("You know, wealthy people's children are rather spoilt," she says) talks of times when a good harvest was produced:

> After a good harvest we could get a hundred bags in one field, that is after the land has excreted....
>
> *Really? When you figuratively say that the field has been shitting, you imply a very good harvest?*
>
> Yes. There would be about five truck loads of maize from one field only. There were no harvest machines during those times. These bags would then be placed under a tree at home. We bothered little about cows eating the crop. We just went to bed, after shooing stray cattle away. Beer would be brewed. An old lady would be responsible for that.[17]

Producers of this sorghum would sell it — Mrs. Mokale's father sold it at 50¢ a bag to Raphalane, a buyer for the Boers.[18] Mmadiphoko Mokgatle talks of how her father "used to load the goods onto an ox-wagon including sorghum, these would be carried and sold to Boers in the North."[19] Her parents were well-to-do peasants, it seems:

> They had a big tract of land which they could till. We used to experience bad harvests during dry seasons. My father would, during such times, sell some of his crops from the previous harvest. It was normal practice in the community to sell even timber. The male folk usually went out to fell trees and would sell these as timber. This timber they used to sell through travelling outside our farming community. Our father would then bring home groceries.[20]

Mrs. Moje describes how her father produced many sacks of grain, and kept pigs. Even a female-headed household, such as that of Naomi Setshedi, whose mother was widowed young, was able to employ people to work in fields.

Status awareness linked to the old hierarchies persists — Mrs. Mokgatle, of the royal lineage, is proud of her connections. But commoners such as Mmadiate Makgale's father ("we were simple people") could become wealthy, and Mahubi Makgale ironically observes that her family was wealthy, but "not of the royal house." Other families appear to have become rather poorer, having to work for others in order to survive. Mmadiate Makgale describes what it was like belonging to a rich household that employed poorer families, or "gang labour,"[21] in the fields: "Other women would go to the fields to hoe the weeds so as to earn a twenty-five-gallon tin container full of maize. A woman would work for this tin as reimbursement for two days."[22] Josephine Mokotedi, a member of such a family, which produced only a few bags of corn or maize a year on fields given to them by the chief, and had "few cows," continues to interpret her family's situation in preindustrial terms, however, rather than as a result of the compulsion of economics: "we grew very little, so we helped others."[23]

In an indication of the value placed by her generation upon education, Mrs. Makgale makes a connection between the lower qualifications of her parents' generation, and the type of work they did when they migrated. Her father was less well educated than herself, and worked at the Kimberley diamond fields ("people went there on foot then")[24] and even her much older brother (born in the 1880s and thus of the older generation), Ishmael Mokua, for example, "belonged to a group that was not educated in this formal standardised type of setup. However, he did attend school, although he was unable to write, he knew how to do various tasks very well."[25] His work was old fashioned: "It was not the type that needed academic qualifications. It was not these types of special jobs. He worked this type of job which ... is the 'pick and shovel' type of work."[26] By contrast, Mrs. Mokale's father may have worked in town, but he did so as a peasant seeking cash to buy more modern farm equipment, and hired people to do ploughing for him while he was away.

A few became sharecroppers. But this, like migrant labour, was often a means to the end of becoming an independent peasant in the long run. Mrs. Phalatse's father sharecropped for a while, but moved back to Phokeng when he had earned enough cattle.

Thus the interviews suggest that the community showed signs of stratification, from the very beginning of its late nineteenth-century transformation, into a variety of different kinds of households, usually male headed. These included those of the rich peasant (by far the most common pattern in the case of the families of the interviewees), the migrant worker seeking to reinvest in the land, the sharecropper who left Phokeng to become resident on a white farm (but also kept his options open to reinvest in and return to Phokeng), and in one or two cases, the poorer families who began to work for others in order to survive. The seeds of such stratification may have been planted earlier, with differential access to literacy, chiefly patronage, or skill. But all that the interviews allow us to observe is the entering into this earlier generation of new modes of being, rather than their detailed sociological origins and consequences.

Although many of the interviewees have stronger memories of their mothers, relationships with fathers, the formal heads of the peasant households to which they belonged, were important. Control over children's labour seems to have been essential for the effective peasantisation of the economy. Such control was often vested in males, although mothers too were highly authoritarian at times. One obeyed one's parents unquestioningly:

> One would be given a milk pail to drink after milking time in the morning. One was supposed to finish the whole milk pail. Our elders would tell us that they want our stomachs to get used to milk during

such times of distress. One was obliged to do as commanded. Violation of such an order would result in one getting a good hiding, being naked except for a tiny bead skirt.[27]

Parental harshness appears in several accounts. Nthana Mokale talks of how both her parents whipped her, leading her eventually to escape to the town to get away from the family:

> I had to waste no time since my mother was a shrew ... [she] was very stubborn. At one stage I was of the impression that she was not my real mother. I think if ever we were living in this era at that time when she was ill-treating us, we could have deserted her.... She would sit down with a whip in her hand, ready to pounce on us when we made mistakes.[28]

Naboth Mokgatle himself had escaped to Kroondal from his oppressive uncle. Such situations may have been softened, as Mrs. Mokale suggests, in settings where the power of a single parental autocrat was lessened by the presence of other adults. She complains of having had "no other mothers" to help bring her up, and of thus being thrown onto her own "shrew" of a mother. Thus particular stress was thrown upon children when one parent died or was absent. Naomi Setshedi says that when her father died her mother ploughed her own fields, with the help of her children. (More often, however, she would hire people with cattle or donkeys to plough for them.) Ernestina Mekgwe was needed to help her father when he was widowed,[29] and indeed she worked to support him. But familial affection was not uncommon, even in situations where only one parent survived: "I was the only girl and daddy loved me," says Mokete Phalatse of her widowed father.

The sexual division of labour and responsibility was an important dimension of Tswana social organization.[30] Many of the women were asked who did the agricultural and pastoral work, in their parents' times, with this division in mind. Some portray a picture that could have come out of a social anthropology textbook. "All the hard jobs were done by women in those days," said Nthana Mokale, "It is only now that I see women relaxed and giving tougher jobs to men."[31] Ernestina Mekgwe says her mother's role on the farm was to decorate the house, and to do the agricultural labour. She sewed and farmed and "did not work for whites."[32] Mothers and daughters made the *seboana* (threshing floor) together, and went to the fields together,[33] sometimes for months. In the informants' memories, whilst mothers built houses, potted and wove,[34] made lamps, grew crops, guarded, weeded, and often reaped them, prepared and cooked food and cared for children, fathers aided with housebuilding, possessed or dealt in cattle, migrated to the city, or were key figures in setting up sharecropping relationships. Mmadiate Makgale's father was a thatcher:

> His house was built along the Boer homestead style. It had round side chambers. Even inside it was like that. When you entered a room, you could go out through the adjacent room. These rooms were not separated from each other.... It was my father who used to cut grass and thatch houses.[35]

Because this "Boer" house had brick walls, her father constructed them. If huts were built of mud, then her mother was expected to build the walls, and her father to do the roof. Her mother, like most, would then decorate the house.

Children's roles often reproduced this division:

I was never a herdgirl ... I was a mere courtyard girl, who used to imitate whenever my mother did some job in the courtyard. My first attempt was often a mess, but as time went on I went to the extent of decorating the courtyard more beautifully than my mother.[36]

Girls had to cook,[37] and "during those years a girl was regarded as her mother's assistant. A woman who happened to give birth to only boys was pitied," says Nkwapa Ramorwesi. Ernestina Mekgwe remembers that all children worked hard, and that girls and boys had some specific duties:

When we woke up the first thing we did was to draw water from the spring, others thrashed [sic] grain for cooking and another made fire. These duties we divided amongst ourselves. Before we left for school, we must cook something for our parents who will be all by themselves during the day. After school, we girls collected firewood and the boys go to the kraal to milk the cows. Doing something for your parents was each and every one's duty while growing up.

Each sex would play in ways which prepared them for their future contribution:

Who was responsible for plastering the walls and floors?

Our mother did those jobs, and when we were about twelve years old we played house games, and during these games we mixed mud to build houses, we also added small pieces of bottles to the mud that we used to cover the courtyard around our "houses." Later, when your mother sees what you have been playing at, she will be very happy and will compliment you on what you've been doing. Years later, when you are older, you go out and collect cow dung and you plaster the whole yard without waiting for your mother to tell you so.

Boys also played "with clay and made cows. You find your brother making a span of oxen 'ploughing.'"[38] We shall see below, in Chapter 6, how older daughters helped care for younger children.

But not every woman portrays a picture that conforms to normative expectations. It would appear that here, at least, the social anthropological conventional wisdoms — that girls and boys were deeply socialised into different roles, "constructed" into different "social identities" — are shown to be themselves as subject to change as any other historical variable. One woman, Josephine Mokotedi, points to the coming of cattle and oxen as the time when the men "took over" the old system, suggesting perhaps that the more rigid division of labour broke down with the advent of these animals, and certainly with the ploughs they drew.[39] But this was by no means a consistent theme in the women's memories. In families with no sons, for example, daughters did the "boys' work." Mrs. Makgale — a girl with no boys in the family — did the ploughing, while Nthana Mokale was a herdgirl as a child in a family with no boys, and actually did not help her mother in the fields at all, although she did do all the cooking, housework, and washing. In fact, her schooling was delayed by the need for herding. Evelyn Rakola, too, herded in the absence of brothers, and says "at that time there were a number of girls who used to herd cattle" — a fact that gave them protection against the normally aggressive young boys, who would torment a girl if she was the only one of her sex out in the veld.[40] But the absence of sons was not the only condition for breaking the norm: most of Mahube Makgale's brothers handled the sheep, while she and one brother handled the ploughing — supposedly considered "taboo" for women:

> I drove the oxen with a long whip while my brother came behind me sowing the seed and drawing the cattle ... [which is] to control and direct the cattle to a planted reed without having them moving into different directions, that is, they must face the distant reed and move towards it. This would enable the plough to go along a straight line. You move along praising and encouraging the drawing cattle, after that you go back and repeat again what you did, then you are finished with the whole ploughing procedure.[41]

Mokete Phalatse's brothers were all younger than she was, and she and her older sister had to care for them and her widowed father. She did all the herding, going out into the fields with the boys from the next farm, while her sister did the housework: "I rode a calf every morning and let them out to the veld, then in the evening I would see them in and go into the main house to look for something to eat." Mokete's father may have loved and treasured her, but this did not exempt her from strict discipline — the unpalatable side of being treated as a serious contributor to the household economy:

> That was a huge responsibility. If the cattle ate anybody's crops, I was to blame, and my father would punish me viciously for that.... Dare you walk slowly, you would find them in somebody's field, destroying months of effort within the wink of an eye, and the owners would want to know what you were doing when your cattle wandered into their fields and you had to stand it all, including some few licks on your bottom.[42]

Nthana Mokale's experiences were similar: if a cow went astray, "my father would not only beat me, but 'kill' me."[43] Mmadiate Makgale also helped with ploughing; Mrs. Moje's mother did all the ploughing herself, and Ida Molefe — from a poor family — ploughed "on weekends" when not at school. As Ernestina Mekgwe said:

> If a boy was not feeling well to herd the cattle or goats, a girl would volunteer to undertake such responsibility. Sometimes one would find a man grinding sorghum very excellently.... But even in farming a man would assist his wife with weeding if she did not have children to help her out. In this case a man would have to stay in the fields for as long as harvesting was uncompleted.[44]

Indeed, Nkwapa Ramorwesi, who suggested that a woman who happened to give birth to only daughters "was pitied," gives the strong impression that this normative system existed more in the breach than in the observance:

> Here in Phokeng, a woman who had girls and the one who had boys only received the same treatment from their children. Boys in Phokeng used to stamp and grind sorghum, go fetch firewood out in the veld, and they would go to the extent of smearing the floors of the courtyards with a mixture of cow dung [all "women's tasks," BB].... In other words children were treated alike during those years and they worked together irrespective of sex.[45]

We cannot assume that a uniform family structure and type of labour division existed in these times. Such things probably varied between sharecroppers, wealthier peasants, families where migration had set in, or poorer peasants. But since the mobilization of the labour of the entire family was vital to the system of peasant production, this may well have given rise to the undermining of previously stricter lines of cleavage by gender. This could be because the burden of authority may have shifted from the lineage as a whole, to the more "nuclear" household, upon which the emerging productive system came to rest. That Bafokeng women were less "role restricted" than the women of other communities is confirmed later in this study. It may possibly be attributed to their having come from relatively wealthy peasant backgrounds, as well as to their own particular toughness.

If fathers and mothers controlled their children in the interests of creating and maintaining peasant households, the authority of the chief himself controlled adult labour, in the interests of reproducing the community at large. It was the first Chief Mokgatle who had "sent" young male migrants to the Kimberley mines, and contracted Setswammung Mokgatle's mother to work on Kruger's farm. Both of these acts were designed to protect and expand the interests of the Bafokeng. It was the pattern of male-only migration, however, that persisted into later times. Very few women worked for cash outside the home. Setswammung Mokgatle herself may have gone to school, but she did not ever go out to work, suggesting that this was indeed forbidden: "At that time women were not allowed to go to the towns, only men went out to far places for work. Today women can work; we were not allowed, my child."[46]

Another older woman, Mmadiphoko Mokgatle, did go out to work, although she claims that in her earlier life "my mother did not allow me to go away from home so as to seek employment. She wanted me to help her during harvest time and with other home chores such as smearing the floors with cow dung, including decorating the walls with ochre."[47] Others describe their mothers as having occupied themselves with making clay pots and other clay items, and weaving grass mats, winnowing baskets, and various items.[48] Mmadiphoko Mokgatle is not inclined to romanticise these activities:

Do you mean you have no interest in handcraft?

I still repeat, I have no interest whatsoever, absolutely no interest. Even when I saw how my mother made a living out of that trade, I found it rather to be a nonsensical practice. One was supposed to cut cane from the river, collect grass for the winnowing of baskets. We had to keep this material wet and also to dry the finished articles.... They would spread the grass on the floor, they would then start to pierce and to weave. After weaving the grass, they would weave a round pattern.... Do you think this type of job one could manage it? I could not cope with this type of job.... Even a clay pot was rather a tiresome venture for me to undertake.[49]

While the children were away at cattleposts, their mothers often stayed at home:

They kept themselves busy by going to the fields or weaving baskets at home. We used to help her by grinding *mabele* [sorghum]. When she woke up in the morning, she would make herself porridge and carry it along to the fields when it was time for hoeing or harvesting.[50]

Cash relations seem to have given the women's mothers something of a source of income of their own.[51] In one unusual case an informant's mother worked as a domestic servant in Pretoria. "My mother was working for whites. . . . She was living a modern life even during that time," said Nkwapa Ramorwesi; "she was counted amongst people who were considered to be 'civilised.'"[52] But Nkwapa was the youngest of all the informants (she was born in 1914). Most informants' mothers earned cash rather through selling crafts or beer, or through such activities as dressmaking within Phokeng itself:

> My mother was very creative, though she was not educated. She was a dressmaker and was very good at wedding gowns. It was really surprising to see the beautiful gowns she used to design and sew. She used to buy cloth in Rustenburg, and used a hand-driven sewing machine.[53]

But the requirements of reproduction were paramount. Large families were common and expected, and female beauty was indeed defined accordingly:

> Yes, she was also fat.
>
> *Was she very fat?*
>
> She was not that obese, she was just fat in an acceptable way and her body suited her well.[54]

Rosinah Setsome was one of twelve children, Ernestina Megkwe's grandfather had eleven children; and her mother, a dressmaker and farmer with no education, had six. Naomi Setshedi's mother had five children, of whom the relatively high number of four survived, and was widowed young.

Very young children did not work hard in those times, Mmadiphoko Mokgatle suggests. "We were just preoccupied in playing games as children. It is nowadays that we find children being urged to seek employment so as to take care of their parents."[55] Of course her definition of the concept of "work" excludes the spells of hard agricultural labour that most children undertook at least between the ages of five and eighteen years. But what Mmadiphoko appears to be referring to is the sense that a rich children's subculture existed, which gave to the young a sense of place, importance, and fun. Mmadiate Makgale recalls her childhood on the farm of her grandparents, also, it seems wealthy peasants. It was a golden time:

> My grandfather used to look after his cattle. We also enjoyed spending our school holidays at the cattle post so that we could drink milk to our satisfaction. We used to take off our dresses and put on *makgabe* [a thin rope worn round the waist with threads hanging all over] when we arrived at the cattle post.[56]

The cattlepost was at Kgetleng: "Grandfather would give me a bucket full of fresh milk to drink. I used to enjoy that milk when it was warm and fresh from the cow."

Agricultural life for the peasantry was governed by Tswana landholding customs, which shaped childhood experiences substantially. The fields themselves were situated far from villages or towns, and families had to travel away from home for days, weeks, and sometimes even months at a time to work in the fields or herd. Mokete Phalatse describes it thus: "There are four places that are specifically meant for ploughing, and that's Belebokene, Mellwe, Tlhatlhe, and Rathipa."[57] Mmantho asked one woman what work children did in the fields and was told:

> We used to harvest the crops, weed the fields, and haul the harvest with an ox-wagon.... [At sunrise] our task was to weed or to fetch water early in the morning so that we could cook.... We used to camp there sometimes, as travelling to and fro was rather tedious....

She suggests that this rhythm was adjusted to cope with the requirements of schooling in the child's later years: "We as scholars were able to assist on Saturdays only as we would not be able to do that during the week owing to the fact that people sometimes slept there." The work was not easy:

> How could we relax? We usually bundled ourselves in blankets because after a hard day's work we would be too weary to even desire relaxation, we would then go to bed. We usually sat around the fire for a short time after our meals, then we slept.[58]

Ida Molefe talks of how the children and their mothers would go to their fields in Kgetleng, sometimes even by train, and would sleep in huts they or their menfolk had built there.[59] Similarly, Naomi Setshedi remembers going to Brits by train, donkey cart, or ox-wagon; staying at the fields at Kanana (also called Canaan) for several months, in small huts, and going home at weekends. Ernestina Mekgwe, whose father had cattle that were "to be admired, not to sell,"[60] remembers the isolation of the fields:

> On many occasions, we were forced to drink a lot of milk when we ran short of maize meal. It was dangerous to cross the Kgetleng River when in flood and go home to fetch maize meal. Therefore we preferred drinking a lot of fresh milk rather than taking a risk.

> *Did you enjoy it?*

> It was the only thing we could have. We got so used to drinking milk that it ultimately didn't act as a purgative. We gained a lot of weight through drinking fresh milk.

She doesn't remember those as hard times, in spite of the expectations placed on young girls:

> During the day we would play until late in the afternoon when we saw cows running to feed their calves, which they had left in the kraal. We would then know that herdboys were on their way home and we would make a fire and start cooking hastily, otherwise we would be beaten up if they found us not ready with food. Herdsmen expected to find porridge ready, so that we could eat it with fresh milk that they had milked immediately on their arrival from the veld.[61]

Josephine Mokotedi, too, recalls "We built thatched houses in which we slept while at the fields. We had a real happy time there, we weren't scared of anything, only scared of snakes."[62]

That the children had their own subculture was not surprising, given their frequent isolation. In one vivid anecdote, Mrs. Makgale gives a sense of the responsibilities and dangers involved:

> One day we ran short of maize meal and we decided to go home to fetch some because we had had enough of drinking milk. We crossed the Kgetleng River very safely but immediately when we looked back the river was in flood. We were terrified.... The herdboys from our cattlepost

came running to see whether we had crossed safely. They were also terrified. . . . They came running and saw us on the other side of the river bank. They were thinking of what could have happened if ever we happened to be caught up in the flood. One of the herdboys shouted, "Are you all safe?" They started counting us to make sure that all of us were safe. When we finally arrived home, our elder brothers and sisters started teasing us, saying that we had run away from drinking a lot of milk since there was no mielie meal at the cattlepost. We, the young ones, started telling them how we escaped narrowly from the Kgetleng River, which was in flood. . . . The following day when the flood had subsided, the herdboys crossed the river and they were so furious that on their arrival, they caused a lot of confusion. Those with whom we crossed the river the previous day, and who were a bit older than I was, were beaten. Our parents said: "They shouldn't be allowed to go to the cattlepost any more, otherwise they would get themselves drowned in that river. They have had enough of milk in any case."[63]

Boys and girls played together, says Ernestina: "We played 'rope,' skipping games, and *morabaraba*." While skipping, Mmadiate Makgale remembers singing:

Monna sule, monna sule
Ao, ao, ao, ao,
O rwele boloko (3)
Ao, ao, ao, ao,
Boloko ka tlhogo (2)
Ao, ao, ao, ao,
Ka tlhogo ya kgomo (2)
Ao, ao, ao, ao,
Nna ke nyetswe (2)
Ke radituku. (2)

[There is a man, there is a man. He is carrying cow dung on his head. His head looks like that of a beast. I am married, I am married to *radituku* (literally a man who puts on a headscarf, but referring specifically to the headbands worn by miners.][64]

Boys and girls played together. Often "we played naked," says Mrs. Megkwe (she means, it seems, wearing loincloths only) and "did not see a problem." But handball, she says, which was emphatically not a "white people's" game, but "our" game, was for girls only:

On a big open space, we erected makeshift goalposts like you have on a soccer field. It was a very painful game because we used a tin, beat up into a pulp as our ball. We made up teams of six or more and each player was provided with a wooden stick . . . with which she hit the "ball." The ball was hit all over the ground with these sticks and the aim was to hit it through the goalposts for a score to be recorded.[65]

Indeed, boys were "too rough," and "I would never accept food from a boy's mouth," says Ernestina.[66]

Although earlier generations were accustomed to the buying and selling of commodities or labour, the fuller encroachment of the cash economy into Bafokeng society took place during the time the informants were growing up. They were thus positioned to observe and participate in this most basic transformation of economic, social, and cultural relations. Setswammung Mokgatle, the oldest informant, describes the early economy as one based only marginally upon the purchase of goods:

Did your mother or yourself ever make clay pots?

We did. I used to make them myself with wet clay that was moulded into a conical shape and after that I put the pot in an enclosure and built a fire around it.[67]

Shops were there but not, at first, for buying: "We used to walk from here to town when Tlhabane was just a few houses with things to sell like mats and clay pots." The barter economy was powerful: "As time went on, Indian traders came to our village selling cloths and these we bought with grain. Still, we only covered ourselves from the waist downwards, we did not wear anything on our breasts." And still, in the majority of the informants' childhood years, according to Mrs. Makgale,

We used to survive through farming. We did not go to shops to buy maize meal. We did not become bothered about food when we went to sleep at the maize fields. We used to take maize on tick at the local shop only when we did not have the chance to grind corn in preparation for the task ahead at the fields.[68]

Even though anthropologists studying Transvaal culture suggest that iron-working was not common in these times, Mrs. Mekgwe mentions iron smelting in her parents' times. Certainly iron ore was to be found in the nearby Magaliesberg:

They made hoes from iron that was extracted from iron-bearing rocks by heating them. When hot, this molten iron would be fashioned into hoes and at times, spearheads would be made.[69]

Nthana Mokale says that even though her father was "rich," her parents "knew very little about furniture and its uses, they were quite comfortable to leave their utensils where they were placed and that was the floor."[70] Although they bought pots, razor blades, and knives:

We saw very little use for money, some people even went to the extent of hoarding it because it was practically of no use.... Even a farthing was enough to give a person who urgently needed an ox one.[71]

Purchased household and farm goods were also minimal: plants were extensively used, milk pails were made of cowhide, and floor mats, loincloths, baskets, and candles were often homemade, as was soap, made either in the style of "Boers," from pigfat, or obtained from "a certain plant that grew near rivers and when this plant was rubbed in water it produced a lather."[72] Setswammung Mokgatle describes firemaking:

My father had a log on which holes were made and in the evening when he made a fire, he took a stick and put a small part of the stick into one of the holes on the log. Using the palms of his hands he swirled the stick at a great speed inside the hole and after a while a lot of smoke evolves and then dry grasses were sprinkled on the log and these burst into fire.[73]

But things were changing, and the women appear to have little romantic nostalgia for the days when all was handmade. (That, perhaps, is the privilege of the twentieth-century urban intelligentsia.) Mrs. Mokale reports that "we bought calabashes from the bordering Bakgatla. Nobody was eager to make pots and calabashes any more. So we resorted to buying."[74] Mmantho asks one informant:

> *Now, things like candles, did you buy them at your home, as you were growing up? or what did you use then?*

> We used to light up with paraffin. We had some home-made can lamps. I can even show you one now.

> *Didn't you use spleen fat from the cow?*

> It is the older generation that used fat to light up. That is, my mother's generation. We, that is my generation, used tin lamps that are similar to that one over there. We used to pierce open a small can that had a lid on, we would then insert a small tube from a bicycle pump.... You would then screw it on to the tin lid, after piercing it, of course. You then insert a piece of rag through the tube, having poured paraffin into the can. Then you would light up.... We used these lamps at night when we went to the toilet. However we also used them in the house—that is, before we purchased lanterns.[75]

The informants contrast the time of their parents, who, like Setswammung, presumably went with very little clothing, with that of their own childhood, when at least at times more Westernised clothing was worn: "We girls were not into old-fashioned clothes (like those of our parents).... For us girls our parents sewed dresses."[76] When they weren't playing, young girls wore long *motweisi*[77] dresses, for which their mothers, clearly willing participants in these transformations in style, bought or bartered cloth from local Indian or Jewish traders. "We bought yards and yards of cloth and sewed beautiful dresses.... My mother was a good dressmaker; compared with today's standards, she would have been a professional dressmaker," says Nthana Mokale with pride. "The very *motweisi* [dresses] that you see here everyday, that's our own creation."[78] However, very few manufactured clothes or other commodities were bought during the girls' childhood, at least until the time of confirmation, when some wore shoes and new dresses for the first time in their lives. "Before that we just wore our usual tatters and during winter you took a scrap of blanket and threw it over your shoulders and went out to play, but we never became ill."[79] Everybody, even rich children, wore rags most of the time.

The Phokeng peasantry lived on a diet that was both adequate and, in the memories of the women, healthy. Nkwapa Ramorwesi says that sorghum had to be ground every day because "each meal ... consisted of sorghum"; but

> during those days people were strong enough to stand against diseases because they used to eat a lot of cucurbits [sic] and edible herbs. Those who had cattle would drink fresh milk and sour milk.[80]

We have already seen how important milk was to young children in the fields. Nthana Mokale remembers cooking for her younger brothers and sisters:

> It was enjoyable.... I cooked them vegetables, and fed them very well with so little, mainly with *kgodu* [porridge mixed with a pumpkin-like vegetable].[81]

Mmadiate Makgale remembers:

> We used to eat porridge made out of sorghum with *morogo* [a spinach-like vegetable]. At times mealie samp [coarsely ground maize] would be cooked and it would be mixed with Tswana beans.... At times only beans would be cooked. Sometimes only pumpkins would be cooked. We had plenty food at home, my dear.... We also had peach trees and pomegranate trees.[82]

She remembers her mother, along with other village women, taking grain by train to a nearby mill to be ground into wheat flour:

> They would then leave their tins of wheat at Boshout, at the mill. These would be milled for baking bread during Christmas time. They would then fetch their tins. Each and every tin had the owner's name labelled on it.

They would either buy fat, to make the flour into bread, or make their own butter:

> We used to pour milk into a clay pot. We would then use a wooden pestle to churn the milk.... The pestle had a spoon-like handle, and it was round at the base with a handle-like bud shape. We would then gently churn the milk.... The milk cream would then rise to the top.... You have to be careful not to carelessly dunk the pestle; you have to be gentle, lest you spill and splash the milk. You have to tie around the pot a clean cloth, so that when you blow the froth on top it should not spill down the clay pot. You would just hear a swish–swish–swish sound. You take some breaks when you feel tired. When you open the clay pot, you will find that it is full of butter. You then have to spoon this butter into a container, then continue again with the task at hand.... What remains is buttermilk.

Her elder sister was called "Mmamokaro," one who likes buttermilk. "Buttermilk was delicious": when served with "pap,"[83] it was so delicious that "you would then bite yourself before chewing this porridge. It was so delicious, one could bite off his lips before putting the meal into his mouth."[84]

Although meat was not a common part of their diet—Mrs. Mokale says that "cattle were not easily slaughtered, they were my father's pride but not our food. Their main part was for milk, both fresh and sour"[85]—Mokete Phalatse talks of her father making *biltong*,[86] and of eating *ronpens* ("until nothing can go in your stomach any more, a full round stomach").[87] To many of the women, people were healthier in those days:

> In today's life black people have discarded the values of their society and are imitating people whose values do not coincide with ours. The food that we eat today is not the same with [*sic*] what we ate in the past. We have changed to mielie meal instead of sorghum porridge, this mielie meal has no nutritional value and is not good for us. We ate sorghum porridge, soya beans, *thepe* [a spinach-like vegetable], all sorts of melons and lastly we drank milk in great quantities.[88]

She talks of maize as a "Boer crop," contrasting it with the indigenous and healthier sorghum.[89]

This captures the tone of nostalgia that pervades all of the women's recollections of the days of their childhood. Such nostalgia is common in oral histories, where childhood is almost always romanticised, and indeed where informants may regard interviews as places where nostalgic reminiscence is required. But here it attains the status of an ideology, rather than simply a form of remembering. The women talk with a sense of loss of a stable and wealthy past, which is often actively compared with the deprivations of the present. We shall see later that they perceive what they regard as the decline and decay of their own culture, at the hands of a variety of evil forces, ranging from Boers, through money, whites, mines, diet and climate, to modernity itself. A past has been ended; money, of which there is never sufficient, dominates; diets are poor; and people no longer have respect for each other or, particularly, for the elderly. As Mrs. Mekgwe put it, "We never went short of anything, we ploughed and our needs were met through selling our produce, not (like) today when our lives are controlled by a small coin." There weren't as many illnesses as there are today.

> Even babies were very healthy, because they suckled their mother's breast, not drink [sic] cow's milk from a bottle. Mother's milk is of vitamins that combat sickness and build his body. Sometimes when your sister or aunt who had a baby died while that child was still suckling, that baby would be given donkey's milk as a substitute and would grow very healthy.[90]

Money makes one poor:

> We were living comfortably, not like today where one has to pay thirty cents for a loaf of bread.
>
> *Were you not struggling with the life that you were leading?*
>
> Not at all, we were living a very comfortable and enjoyable type of life.... The world was very peaceful then.[91]

Mmadiate Makgale echoes this: "those were blissful days," she says, when "there was plenty rain," "we were healthy and shining."[92]

Nkwapa Ramorwesi also emphasises the association between changes in diet and in general well-being:

> Nowadays we eat all types of food, that is why we are prone to so many diseases. There are diseases like high blood pressure and sugar-diabetes, which were not there among people who lived some years ago.[93]

People respected one another in the old days: "the world was not yet corrupt like nowadays. One looked upon every elderly woman as one's mother, gave her all the respect":

> It happened that whenever an elderly woman came across children having a fight, she would intervene. As schoolchildren we used to quarrel and our fights were usually fought after school on our way home. Whenever an elderly person intervened, we used to respect her and gave her the same respect as we would to our parents.... Each and every man was respected as a father. This shows how obedient children used to be in those days.... The rules that governed our lives when we were young were good ones; nowadays we, who were able to taste what those rules contained for us, still cry for them. We still long for that strict discipline under which we were brought up.[94]

It is easy to see that this type of peasant vision would be compatible with an African nationalism that sought the return of the land and the revival of the peasantry. However, we should not be led to think that the women embrace a purely backward-looking nostalgia that finds "modernity" and all of its trappings unacceptable. This is only one aspect of their ideology, that concerned with the land and the family. As we shall see, they display quite different attitudes towards the past when such matters as education and Christianity are concerned. Indeed, we now turn to see the other side of the Janus-faced ideology that the women espouse — that which seeks to confront and control the modern world, and use it to their own advantage — a feature also compatible with nationalism, perhaps, but with its forward-looking side.

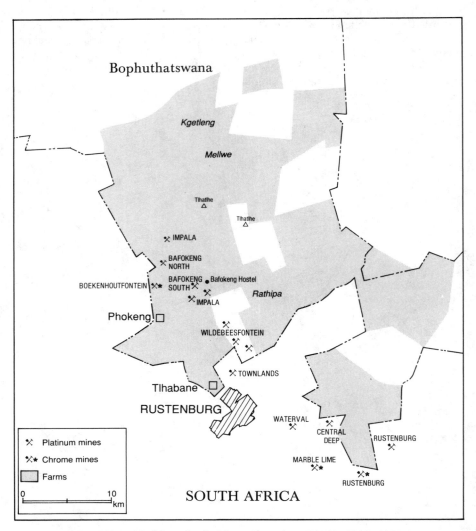

Bophuthatswana

Kgetleng

Mellwe

Tlhatlhe
△

Tlhatlhe
△

✗ IMPALA

✗ BAFOKENG
NORTH

BAFOKENG ● Bafokeng Hostel
✗★ SOUTH ✗
BOEKENHOUTFONTEIN ✗★   *Rathipa*
✗
✗ IMPALA

Phokeng ☐

✗
WILDEBEESFONTEIN
✗

✗ TOWNLANDS

Tlhabane ☐

RUSTENBURG

WATERVAL
✗   ✗
CENTRAL
DEEP   RUSTENBURG
✗
MARBLE LIME
✗★
RUSTENBURG

✗	Platinum mines
✗★	Chrome mines
▦	Farms

0   10
|____|____|____|____|____|
                    km

SOUTH AFRICA

Approximate Bafokeng landholdings, Rustenburg District, 1920−1970

3

Church, School, and Tribe, 1910–1925

The heyday of the Bafokeng peasantry was associated in the minds of ordinary people with the strategies and alliances of the "greatest" Bafokeng chief, Mokgatle Mokgatle,[1] who, as we have seen, sought to use every available resource — ranging from missionary protection to Boer patronage — to transform the economy of Phokeng. If at times this involved the exploitation and control of commoners by the chief, a sufficiently powerful ideology of "Bafokeng" communalism and interest appears to have existed to obscure these differences in the minds and memories of informants.[2] Royal enthusiasm for conversion to Christianity, as a consequence, gave this new ideology considerable legitimacy in the nineteenth century, and we have already suggested that the Bafokeng were early, rapidly, and relatively easily Christianised. As is well known, however, in no African society has Christianity written itself clearly upon the supposedly blank slates of African minds, however greatly those minds may be predisposed to its acceptance, and however anxious its proponents may be to colonise them.[3] In every case, Christianity has rather tended to provide a new discourse that interacts with old ones, and only partially replaces them. The precise degree of receptivity of particular communities to the new ideas varies, according to a whole range of factors. This chapter first explores the history of the introduction of Christianity in Phokeng and focusses more specifically on the meanings it came to possess for the women. It suggests that the new ideology came to be regarded in a contradictory manner. It was spiritually meaningful to the women, and indeed came to form a central pillar of their emerging consciousness but it never operated as a fully "hegemonic" ideology. They show, thus, a deep commitment to their (mainly Lutheran) religion, the "worm that had entered the body of the tribe ... to cause it to become Christian."[4] But they also demonstrate a "standing back," a distancing from the religion, a capacity to regard it as a resource to be taken or left, depending upon its usefulness. There is a sense in which, for this generation at least, there exists another set of values, outside of the religion, by and through which Christianity itself is judged.

The intentions to hegemony of the first Lutherans brought into the village, under Ernest Penzhorn, were distinctly Germanic. A cultural as well as spiritual vision prevailed, in which the Bafokeng were, it appears, to become skilled Christian farmers and craftsmen whilst retaining, and indeed building upon, elements of their own distinctive "Bafokeng" or "Tswana" culture, language, and tradition.[5] The first Penzhorn learnt Setswana, and conducted all of his religious and social relationships with the Bafokeng in that language, using a Setswana Bible and prayer book. Mmadiate Makgale believes him to have been a protector of the community during the times when Kruger was exploiting them:

> They lived like that through drudgery; they then fled. Kruger did not go after them. He then befriended our local white pastor.... He begged him to stop persecuting people. He preached to him about this matter....

> *Did Penzhorn pay Kruger regular visits?*

> Yes. He preached to Kruger. As he was a white person he managed to subdue Kruger.[6]

Penzhorn's son, also called Ernest, a tall, handsome man with a "loud, clear and frightening voice,"[7] had been brought up in Phokeng, a fact that impressed itself upon the memories of the women. "His [the older Penzhorn's] children grew up the same way as we did.... They ate porridge just like us and ground sorghum at their father's mill."[8] The younger Ernest was thus fluent in Setswana, called himself a Mofokeng and tribesman, and continued along the same lines as his father during the late nineteenth century and the first three decades of the twentieth.

> He hated it when someone referred to him as a German. He could speak Setswana very fluently, he used to tell us many Setswana praises and proverbs and also tell us that he used to herd cattle with our fathers. He only taught in Setswana and did not tolerate anyone mixing Afrikaans or English while speaking in class.[9]

According to Naboth Mokgatle, the younger Penzhorn taught people to read the Bible in their own language, formed a women's union, and changed the agricultural ways of the people so as to suit the Christian week and calendar. His intentions as a missionary were to reinforce the hierarchies and disciplines of Tswana culture, and at the same time to assist the transformation of the Bafokeng into a prosperous peasantry.

But as we have seen, in both Naboth and Setswammung Mokgatle's testimonies, reflections, perhaps, of popular perceptions of the coming of missionaries, the original Penzhorn had been invited into the community, and not imposed upon it. Indeed, Naboth's story places the responsibility for his arrival upon a group of ordinary Bafokeng who went to "fetch the German," rather than upon the chief, who only subsequently was said to have agreed to his coming. There is a sense, thus, that Christians are perceived as having been consciously brought "into" the community by a group seeking modernity and advantage. The duality of Penzhorn's influence — both as bringer of an imposing new hegemony, and as presenter of useful new ideas — is reflected in the women's accounts of the ways in which conversion to Christianity itself took place.

Most of the women were born into recently Christianised families. It was the previous generation that had experienced the transition from "traditionalism" to what the women perceive as "civilisation." Mrs. Mokale put it thus: "Penzhorn was the first preacher in Phokeng, his father brought the Bible, and consequently civilised all the people of Phokeng."[10] (In this case to be "civilised" was to be Christianised. Other meanings are attributed to this word, as we shall see.) Mrs. Mekgwe said that the Lutheran church was the church "we found our parents attending when we were born";[11] others suggest their parents were older when Christianised: "Some even asked to be baptised while very old, and this was done," said Nthana Mokale. Her father and grandmother were both adults when baptised: "My father was baptised late in his life and he knows not a thing about school."[12] The older generation liked church, but, she says, "it was not available in their youth. So much that when Christianity appeared on the scene, they were too old and their ways [polygyny, BB] not compatible with the teachings of the church, this they could not understand." Thus, "initially there were others who objected but had to submit in the end, because how were they to enter the kingdom of God without any Christianity?"[13] The second and subsequent wives of polygynists such as Naboth's uncle had, as we have seen, suffered considerably with the change to monogamy. But generally, Mrs. Mokale suggests that "those who already had more than one wife did not become Christians, only the ones with one wife or were unmarried enrolled.... They [the polygynists] did attend church services but could not be confirmed into Christians." Mrs. Mekgwe is slightly more cynical, however, displaying an awareness of a more instrumental attitude towards Christianity:

> Initially, I understand there were people who were against the church, but they later recanted and joined the church. When Penzhorn's father came to Phokeng, he found men here marrying more than one wife and he told them that if they wanted to be baptised they had to have only one wife. Now what the men did was, go to church for baptism with only one wife and left perhaps two others at home; after they were baptised they went back to their other wives and carried on with their normal lives.[14]

The women remember baptism for their parents as having meant the taking on of a new name: "The grandmother I am named after was initially called Maoto, but after baptism was referred to as Rebecca Maoto," says Nthana Mokale.[15] By the time they themselves were baptised, this was not perceived as anything special. Most of the women give Mmantho both their Christian and their Tswana names with little concern as to which she uses.

If the depth of religiosity in adulthood is any measure of the successful penetration of Christianity decades earlier, then both Penzhorns were indeed persuasive men. The younger Penzhorn himself acknowledged that in Phokeng, as elsewhere in polygynous, patriarchal Africa, conversion to the relatively more benign ideology of Christianity was more common amongst women than men.[16] Virtually all of the women perceive themselves as Christians, and many are very deeply religious:

> *So you all believed there was a kingdom of God?*

> We all believed it was true. None of my family members questioned the existence of heaven.[17]

As Mmadiate Makgale put it:

> Me, I trust in God. I do not put my trust on earthly beings, because an earthly person would promise to stand by you, but during times of crisis he leaves you in limbo.... He deserts you. But Jesus will never leave you. He never changes. He will stand by you until you arrive at his feet and announce yourself, saying "Here I am."[18]

Later she confirms that for her, at least, religious rituals provide an outlet that might otherwise not be available:

> During times of stress and crisis one is able to go to church. At times one finds that chapters that offer comfort are read. You then realise that you can put your problems at Jesus' hands. One can also be aware of the fact that had one stayed at home with his problems, one could have been having bottled-up, poisonous feelings, not knowing where to pour them. At church, such feelings are reduced, then you would feel relieved, and you would be like other normal beings.[19]

It was the Lutheran church that became the established — perhaps "establish-ment"[20] — spiritual home of the Bafokeng.

For several of the women, however, deeply felt Christianity is not incompatible with an ongoing and vibrant series of "traditional" beliefs and customs. To Nkwapa Ramorwesi, in fact, the coming of Christianity did not mean anything radically new was introduced into the community, as the people "already knew God":

> Here in Phokeng they arrived in 1866 when Phokeng was still backward. However, the people knew about God as it was common for every tribe to know something about God. Even a non-Christian whenever he is in difficulties would be heard saying, "I wish God would help me...." Even our great-grandmothers, who used to put on skins of animals since there were no clothes that we know of today, knew about the existence of God.

What the missionaries introduced to the Bafokeng, therefore, was not the knowl-edge of God: "The only thing which our great grandparents did not know, was how to worship him."[21] Thus it is not surprising that the women see no contra-diction between their holding traditional and Christian beliefs simultaneously. But this tendency is regarded with varying degrees of tolerance by the church. Nthana Mokale, for example, is a traditional healer as well as a Christian, who was trained at a Sowetan healing school, attends ancestral ceremonies on Sunday afternoons, at which a sheep is slaughtered, and runs a vigorous healing practice. When she stayed away from church in Phokeng because "I felt that my going to church would cause unnecessary friction with the priest," she was asked by the priest to return, and told that it was the use of herbs and drugs, rather than the healing practice itself, that was frowned upon. She suggests that her practice is now based almost exclusively upon the use of water to heal.[22] Mmadiate Makgale, by contrast, remembers a less tolerant Hermannsburg missionary, during the period after Penzhorn's death, objecting because the community, and the chief, engaged in "paganism":

> People had gone to pray for rain at that hill. It is only the malefolk who went there barefooted. The men went there and offered a cow for sacrifice.

This cow was killed with bare hands. It did not offer any resistance. In the evening, rain fell. That is when the minister started with his objections.... He said "These people had gone to worship a man-made god, that is sheer paganism." He continued with his criticism, having no room for the people's feelings.

Popular feeling appears to have run so high against the priest that "the chief then personally locked the church. He then declared he should, at no stage, hear church bells ringing again."[23] Penzhorn himself, as late as 1930, acknowledged that when it came to sustaining the family economy, neither men nor women were hesitant in abandoning Christian teaching:

[The natives] want large families; they want as many children as possible.... I know the average native, if he has a wife who has borne no children, he will take a second wife simply with the idea of obtaining children; that is what he wants. If he is a Christian, well, he doesn't worry about that; he takes a second wife whether it is right or wrong; he doesn't care.[24]

As we shall see, one of the chief Christian institutions affecting the interviewees — that of confirmation — came to possess a complex meaning, reflecting this retention of a commitment to traditionalism.

Side by side with the spiritual dimension ran the more material benefits that accrued to communities becoming Christianised under the aegis of paternalistic missionaries such as the Penzhorns. The mission farm, Kroondal, may have provided a refuge for runaways. But its main function was to assist in the acquisition of agricultural and other skills by those who went there, in an atmosphere of benign paternalism. Nkwapa Ramorwesi remembers going to work on Kroondal for money during her school holidays.

Girls of our age used to seek employment during summer vacation at Kroondal so that they could earn money for buying themselves Christmas clothes.... Kroondal was far away from Phokeng, we therefore had to stay there until we had finished our job. Germans were very friendly with us, they looked after us as though we were their children.... We even had our own rooms in which we stayed until hoeing was over.[25]

It was at Kroondal, too, that women acquired skills in domestic work:

Kroondal was where we used to gain experience of domestic work. Germans at Kroondal were very patient with us, they used to teach us domestic work. Kroondal was like a university of domestic work.[26]

Schools were set up, in which, as we shall see, basic skills of literacy and numeracy were taught, alongside Christian doctrine. The peasantisation of the Bafokeng must have been considerably aided by these developments. In addition, the missionaries' assistance in the buying of land enabled the Bafokeng to continue to protect themselves against the disintegration of their economy as the twentieth century began, as was common in the Western Transvaal.[27] But whereas spiritual conversion could mainly be seen as having provided the Bafokeng with a vast store of more or less useful, and more or less wholly absorbed, new ideas and symbols, the more mundane aspects of Christianisation and the accompanying peasantisation of the society had deeply contradictory results, which were to produce considerable tensions within it in the first decades of the new century.

The turn of the twentieth century had seen the beginning of a new era both culturally and economically. After the first Mokgatle died in 1889, he was succeeded (after a succession dispute that pointed to the beginnings of dissension in Bafokeng society)[28] by Chief Tumagole until 1896, when Mokgatle's own son, August Molotlegi, came to power and ruled until 1938. If his father's rule had coincided with the period of Boer ascendancy and Bafokeng defensiveness, then August presided over the less comfortable era during which full-blooded capitalism and segregationism placed almost unbearable pressures upon his community and his office. Three often mutually contradictory forces appear to have been at work.[29] In the first place, the Bafokeng clung to the land they had already acquired in the more flexible years of Boer domination. They were not, thus, to be dispossessed by the 1913 Land Act.[30] Indeed, land buying continued after the First World War, with the chief using the system of tribal levies upon migrants to continue to expand Bafokeng land. The progressive agricultural, educational, and land-buying strategies pursued by the community began to give rise to a stratum with distinctly modern ideas about "traditional" society. To this stratum, it appears that individual landholding was more appealing than the forms dictated by traditions of communalism. Secondly, the chieftaincy was deeply threatened by these developments, which had given rise to somewhat unintended consequences. It is not as if the chieftaincy was dedicated to pure communalism; after all, it had overseen the strategy of embracing modernity, of communal land buying, and of Christianisation. Indeed, the chief had become something of an individual accumulator himself over the years, much to the chagrin of some of his subjects. But he had ridden a tiger, for the survival of the chieftaincy as a legitimate institution depended upon his ability to retain access to some of the more traditional means to power, redistribution, and social reproduction. And thirdly, members of this stratum and of other less well off groups in the society found themselves drawn into an increasingly permanent relationship with the towns and cities, for which the peasant-based ideologies of Hermannsburg Christianity and schooling did not always equip them. The essential question for August Molotlegi (and others of his kind) was, how was he to survive in an institution that had been only just flexible enough to adapt to the nineteenth century, while overseeing the rapid move of his community into the much more volatile and indeed revolutionary, twentieth century?

The informants in this study reveal to us some of the ways in which these contradictions worked themselves out in the society. Presenting to us, as they do, the view from below, however, they see things in terms of their own, and the community's, access to key resources in the changing setting, rather than in terms of chiefly survival and decaying modes of production. It was they and their families who constituted one of the chief's constituencies, and we see them expressing opinions that were far from reflecting an uncomplicated allegiance to the established social order of late nineteenth-century Phokeng.

It was schooling that most clearly reflected the changing society, in the minds and memories of the women. In comparison with members of other Transvaal communities, and indeed with young girls in most newly colonised settings, Bafokeng daughters were extremely well educated both by Penzhorn and by other teachers in the community. "In our village we had many schools, even during those years," recalled Mrs. Mekgwe; "there was a row of schools on the southern part of the village."[31] Many of the women, it is true, say that schooling was not "taken as seriously" as it is today:

> We were ignorant about the worthiness of education then. Even then mistresses were not that plenty. We did not know that a young girl could teach. People during those times were unaware, I mean our parents.[32]

But for the times, the everyday culture of Phokeng was deeply influenced by schooling:

> *When did you go to school?*

> ... I was old enough to realise everything that was going on. Our sisters used to teach us how to write our names at home. One of our sisters would act as a teacher, with a whip in her hand, and we, the young ones, as pupils. This, in a way, gave us an idea of what to expect when we finally went to school.[33]

Parents encouraged girls to go to school. And in both cases where they did not, the girls themselves took the initiative.[34] Like Setswammung Mokgatle, Mrs. Moje resisted her mother's attempts to send her to initiation school at Mabeskraal, and instead secretly took herself off to Penzhorn's school for a day, after which her mother agreed to send her. "The main reason which pushed me to go to school was that all of my peers were attending school. I was tired of being an errand girl," she laughed.[35]

It does not appear that girls were less well schooled than young boys of similar backgrounds.[36] The relative wealth of the Bafokeng made it possible for many of them to leave their agricultural tasks for large portions of the day, the week, or the year, in order to attend school. Mmadiphoko Mokgatle describes how, although she worked hard in her parents' fields in her younger childhood, on holidays and when she left school, during the actual school week: "We as scholars were only able to assist on Saturdays as we would not be able to do that during the week owing to the fact that people sometimes slept there" [in the fields, BB].[37] Josephine Mokotedi's family fields at Chaneng were nearer the school, however: the mothers and children stayed in the thatched huts built there, and in the mornings the children went off to school:

> At times in the morning we waited there for the school bell to ring and would then go to a water stream nearby where we washed with soap; we also took along a comb and a little mirror to use afterwards.... I washed in the flowing water and then combed my hair. My dress would be alongside on the bank.

> *Weren't you worried that someone might see you while you were washing, naked?*

> No, you didn't care, because we often swam in that river naked.... I washed myself thoroughly and after wiping myself and combing my hair, I would take my satchel and rush to school.[38]

Nthana Mokale, however, like many others, says that her schooling was delayed until she was eleven—because she was needed to herd cattle at home.[39] Mmadiate Makgale, too, says that schooling was started late because of the demands of the household:

How old were you when you started to attend school?

I think I was over ten years of age. The problem was that we had to look after our younger brothers and sisters and this delayed us. During those years education was not regarded as important, otherwise we could have gone far with our studies.[40]

Still, she and most other girls like her were schooled for several years. She herself went to Standard 3, and appears to have attended school for a good seven years.[41] Mrs. Mokale went right up to Standard 5, the highest grade possible in Phokeng. For many of the women the bringing of schooling to the region was something which engendered deep loyalty to the Lutherans:

Are you aware that Penzhorn was the father of the whole of Phokeng community? He arrived here when Phokeng was still remote. Phokeng was just like *lentswe-tshipi* [chrome, indicating that the people were uncultured, BB]. When he came here, he started breaking apart that huge black rock into small pieces. In other words he found people of this village uncultured and he tried to make them improve their way of living.... Even if Penzhorn is no longer alive to date, I swear that he is the one who brought civilisation here.[42]

Here the word "civilisation" appears to mean "education."

What actually went on in the classroom is not entirely clear. The teacher with whip in hand was clearly an image with some basis in reality; certainly teachers were regarded with considerable respect, being considered "second only to the chief," in the words of one informant. Given Penzhorn's volkische ideas about schooling in the mother tongue, most of the children at his school seem to have concentrated on becoming basically literate in Setswana, through the "a, b, c." Mrs. Ramorwesi insists that what they obtained in those days was a good education, far better than that which children obtain today. "In other words, that education which we used to receive is superior to Bantu education.[43] Previously when one went to school, one was sure of being taught the same thing that was taught whites," she says:

To show that pupils during those days received good education, the following subjects were offered: Spelling, which was done in Tswana, was taught beginners.... *Thamagane*, which was a subject dealing with knowledge of deep Tswana, ... *Ditiragalo* [history], ... [and] the English language.[44]

The ways in which local world views incorporated and transformed outside religious ideas are revealed by the example of the rite of passage of confirmation, which was linked closely to Lutheran schooling. It is well known that initiation schools and ceremonies were an important part of a child's socialisation in Tswana society,[45] but these were abolished with the introduction of Christianity. However, it appears that to the women interviewed here, the ceremony of confirmation became transformed and adopted by the Bafokeng, with the support of Penzhorn, and perhaps the chief as well,[46] into a substitute for the initiation school. According to one source, "The problem of the missionaries was then how to draw the children from *lebollo* (initiation) schools to the church schools. The parents, though they attended church services in good numbers, were still for *lebollo*." As a strategy for undermining *lebollo*, missionaries denounced *lebollo* as "heathen and unchristian," and organised church confirmation classes in age groups "similar to that of *lebollo.*" "As was the case with the *bogwera* and *bojale* groups (boys' and girls' initiation groups, respectively), so the confirmants a day after the big confirmation formed themselves into a group to ask from the chief a name for their *mophato* (age-group)."[47] This strategy seems to have succeeded from the women's point of view. They remember that confirmation rites, like initiation schools, became rites of transition from girlhood to womanhood. Thus every child, no matter how far he or she had gone in school, was drawn from the school itself into "confirmation school" between the ages of about sixteen and eighteen. They attended this school for several months, after which they were discouraged from becoming educated further, and encouraged to work or undertake other adult responsibilities. Nkwapa Ramorwesi remembers:

> It was a common practice to leave school at a certain age and attend confirmation classes. Since we used to start going to school late in our lives, we couldn't go further with education because we had to leave school and go for confirmation classes. During those days, one simply took it for granted that once one had been confirmed in church, then school days were over. We thought that we were matured and old enough to go look for a job in the white area immediately after confirmation.[48]

Ernestina Mekgwe talks of how "We had to attend confirmation school for three or four months. After that period we were expected to know the rules of the church well."[49]

The actual ceremony is remembered by all the women as having been of considerable significance to them. "During the Confirmation Day we were then dressed up beautifully in German-style clothes."[50] Ernestina Mekgwe remembers that "my first pair of shoes I wore in 1924 for the confirmation ceremony at Penzhorn's church"; her parents bought "shoes, dresses, and this would be the first time in your life that you wore new clothes."[51] And Setswammung Mokgatle remembers that whereas the children wore any clothes to school, "It was only on the confirmation day that we were required to wear the same kind of clothes. We wore white dresses and shoes . . . we still wear those white clothes."[52] The details of what was taught in confirmation school are not known. Rangaka claims that "To the Bafokeng and their children . . . there was no difference; it was the same *Lebollo* clothed in religious garb."[53] But it is likely that its similarity to initiation school was one of broad function rather than of content—for, in initiation schools, the girls were taught explicitly about sex, and then "severely flogged, 'in order to inure them to suffering and to give them an idea of what pain they will undergo in giving birth to children.'"[54] Such practices were not to the liking of missionaries.

Penzhorn and the religion he represented are remembered with love and loyalty by many:

> He was . . . a good man, and above all, he was our Reverend. He always gave us good advice, and his words which I will never forget were, "If you leave school without completing you are already lost." He too always sought our advice.
>
> *Were there people who liked him and those who disliked him?*
>
> We all loved him, each and every one of us in his congregation.[55]

However, hints that all was not well with Lutheranism had developed as early as the 1890s, with the arrival in the region of a black American missionary, Mr. Morrison, of the African Methodist Episcopal (AME) church, who introduced an evangelistic, revivalist religion, which was blamed at the time for outbreaks of Ethiopian fervour and political radicalism in South Africa. According to Naboth Mokgatle, Morrison's arrival caused an initial split in the community — some favoured not allowing him in, as they "already had a church."[56] Probably as a result of this initial hostility, a reflection of the power and influence of the Penzhorns, the AME was never as strong in Phokeng as it was in nearby Luka, where the Hermannsburgers had little following and the AME was able to establish itself firmly.[57] But still, according to Naboth,

> Morrison's English day school attracted a great deal of attention among the people of my tribe. At that time, the people were aware that the white man's rule was spreading all over the country and therefore it was essential to get prepared and to learn his language. Those men of my tribe who had been to Kimberley to work for money in the claims had had contact with the English people there and were impressed by them and found them very clever. They found no comparison between them and the Dutch people they knew. Although the Anglo-Boer war had not broken out, they could sense that eventually the Englishman, with his cleverness, was bound to make an impact on the whole country.[58]

In making this direct link between migrancy and the desire to acquire English, Mokgatle demonstrates the degree to which missionaries were regarded as much as an "influence" upon the community as a "resource" to be used by it. In fact, so clear was the desire to learn English rather than to seek any religious message from Morrison that the English taught was not accompanied by religious conversion to his church. Many of those taught remained Lutherans. One informant was in fact brought up in Luka, and suggests that there too, the arrival of Morrison is remembered as something that resulted from community initiative rather than missionary imposition. Her story is that the local priest, Mr. West, was called a heathen by his colleague, because he chose to rescue a cow from a ditch rather than attend a service one morning. "His colleague called him a heathen because he placed earthly goods before the Lord God Almighty." This, says the informant, led her father, Abednigo Mneia, "to call some Americans to hold a service":

> He called one Reverend who was known as A.A. Morrison, whose grave is in Luka. He came as a missionary all the way from America and collected Reverend Mmutle at a conference. . . .

> *Where were they when your father called them?*

> They were overseas. . . . Rev. A. A. Morrison went straight to Luka on his arrival, and settled there.[59]

But a far more memorable challenge to Lutheranism was presented by the arrival in Phokeng in 1913 of the Reverend Kenneth Spooner, whose effect upon the lives of ordinary Bafokeng is vividly remembered by almost every informant. Spooner, a more charismatic and effective missionary of the Pentecostal Holiness Church,[60] was also perceived as a black American by the informants, but was in fact a West Indian, born in Barbados in 1884, and possibly even a Garveyite, though he was based in and sent from the United States. Like Morrison, Spooner was treated with considerable initial hostility in Phokeng. At first he and his wife seemed to be welcome. But then, Spooner discovered that the person who had brought them in had told the tribe that "he had imported us from America and that it cost him two hundred and fifty dollars to get us into the country and that they would have to refund him the money if they really wanted us to stay." They were treated more guardedly as a result.

A great breakthrough came when Spooner converted one of Penzhorn's protegés, Dan Rangaka, who was also Naboth Mokgatle's uncle and of the royal house. In Spooner's account:

> Brother Dan was given to us in answer to prayer.... I fell in love with him at first sight and really coveted him for the work of God. In a few days, God gave him to us. My dear wife saw him smoking and spoke to him about his pipe and how that in order for God to dwell in him he had to be clean. He threw his pipe away and shortly afterwards God sanctified him. It was not long after he was baptized in the holy spirit.[61]

The whole community came to watch Rangaka's baptism, but this did not necessarily indicate widespread support for the Pentecostal Holiness Church (PHC). Rather, Spooner was soon struck by what he interpreted as the instrumentalism of the community. At first, he wrote, "the people were somewhat disappointed in us. They thought we had come to give them an education and to preach politics," and recounts that he had a difficult time persuading them that the PHC was about religion. (From the point of view of the interviewees in this book, he never fully succeeded.) Although by then he had been given land by the chief, who was playing the role of enabler, he perceived some considerable hostility on the part of the people, and his inability to speak Setswana made it more difficult. In September 1916, there was a fight in the church. Dan Rangaka was attacked, as

> he was supposed to be the one who was putting me wise to all their secret moves against us. Of course that was what they thought but it really was not so. They said they were going to deal with Brother Dan, and that my dear wife and I would have to clear out and go back to America. No service could be held that day as they were guarding the door with sticks, ready to beat anybody who would enter the church."[62]

Penzhorn, to whom such great loyalty was being expressed, disliked Spooner, and attempted to have his mission removed from Phokeng, but he failed to obtain the backing of the chief, who decided to take the issue to the *lekgotla*, the tribal court. There, in an indication that perhaps support for Penzhorn was less powerful in the upper reaches of the society, the case was finally decided in favour of Spooner. Still,

> In those early days, things were made very warm for them and on more than one occasion our departed brother Spooner was brought before the native chief and at other times before the Magistrate of the district.[63]

Sections of the community harassed Spooner, even vandalising his church at one stage, with chunks of raw beef and blood.

There is no doubt, however, that what Spooner had to offer was wholly attractive to some people, and of partial significance to others. By giving him land for his church and school, the chief himself was acknowledging that Lutheranism alone was inadequate to the needs of the Bafokeng at the time. What was Spooner's attraction? He certainly brought a strange set of customs to the community. To Nkwapa Ramorwesi, he "belonged to the church denomination which was different from us. Theirs used to immerse a person in water at baptism, which was something we were not used to . . . but we never looked at it with scorn."[64] Mokgatle suggests that some people liked the institution of adult baptism, as they liked the idea that children could make their own decisions about baptism later in life. He also suggests that people liked the fact that prayer could be addressed directly to God, something echoed by one or two of the interviewees. People, he says, also liked having "somewhere to go" before they went to bed; and the Baptist prohibition upon beer brewing and drinking appealed to many:

> Men who were admitted to the church began to surprise their friends by telling them that they had stopped smoking and drinking beer. Some of them were men who could hardly allow two days to pass without enjoying a calabash of beer. Women who were noted for their skill in brewing good and strong beer before the Pentecostal Holiness Church arrived disappointed people who used to enjoy their brew by telling them that they had not known that they were engaged in an evil thing, beer making, until they joined the Pentecostal Holiness Church, which opened their eyes.[65]

But to Mrs. Ramorwesi, the great attraction lay in the healing mission of the church; "He claimed that he could pray for the sick to get cured. Therefore people flocked to him because they hoped to get cured of their diseases. There was a rumour that every sick person who joined Spooner's church got cured."[66] This revivalist spirit was present, if somewhat unevenly, throughout the region. Spooner and his chief Bafokeng converts travelled north to the land of the Bakgatle and carried out conversions there. Again, Bafokeng were taking the cultural lead within the region.[67] Successful conversions amongst several communities followed, and Spooner's own description suggests that there may well have been millenarian overtones to his popularity:

> After two years of the most strenuous labours, travelling and preaching night and day, fasting, praying and weeping, God began to move upon the hearts of the people. A revival broke out and the work began to spread from village to village like a mighty forest fire.

However here too, his opponents were vigorous: "along with this came much opposition," he writes, and at some places, he suggests, we were "not permitted to preach." Dan Rangaka was stoned on some occasions, while at others "we were simply given a hearing because they enjoyed hearing me, a black man, speak English and Dan interpret. This novelty proved an instrument in God's hand to bring many to the feet of Jesus."[68] In the subsequent years he established Phokeng as the headquarters of the PHC, holding its annual meeting there. According to Spooner himself, by the 1930s they had

> forty-two mission stations, thirty workers as preachers, eight teachers, fourteen buildings. Some of these structures have only mud walls and straw roofs and yet they last for quite a long time. The work spread over five districts, namely: Rustenburg, Middelburg, Waterberg, Potgietersrus, and Pretoria.

Later, he suggests, this revivalism spread to Natal.[69]

To all the informants, Spooner's greatest contribution lay in the field of education. Criticisms of the Lutheran approach clearly existed. Ernestina Mekgwe, admittedly a product of Spooner's school, is highly critical of the type of education given at that time under Penzhorn's aegis:

> He did not want Western Civilisation. He wanted us to remain ignorant.... All the Germans around here were missionaries. Now they seemed to be less interested in formal education. They did not want a black man to be enlightened.

In this use of the term, "civilisation" clearly referred to a body of knowledge and culture that was not contained in "traditional" Bafokeng society. Penzhorn's approach had, it seems, become outdated by the second decade of the century:

> The German guy was only interested in such talks as: "so and so is carrying a calabash to the river to draw some water, so and so broke her calabash." He gave no time at improving our level of education.[70]

But several women mention the fact that some of their most admired teachers had been Pedis who had mastered English, and had come from a far better educational system than their own (presumably these were men, as Pedi schooling for women appears to have been less adequate). And Spooner's most significant attribute for all the informants was the fact that he taught in English, encouraged literacy in that language, and promulgated an ideology of modernity and Westernisation.

Why was it that you preferred Spooner?

Spooner was a resilient teacher and taught mostly in English.

So, Penzhorn taught mainly in Setswana?

Yes, he was too much into Tswana, and those of us who preferred English left his school classes.[71]

Spooner, the "innocent man of God," who "came here from America without a slightest knowledge of our language,"[72] offered something that Penzhorn did not — secular training more suited to the rapidly industrialising economy into which more and more Bafokeng were being drawn. Naomi Setshedi indicates a somewhat pessimistic resignation to the emerging class structure:

> The Bafokeng tribe argued that they wanted to know English so that they would be able to communicate with their white employers. They used to have a very big problem of language with their employers. One white employer once said to her servant, "Make me a cup of tea please." The servant could not understand what the woman was trying to tell her, and she said "what is she talking about, she says please, please, I don't know what that means." The poor employer had to show her cups and a kettle, it was then that the servant could understand what she was trying to say. Now they wanted to know English so that they could have no problem with their employers.[73]

Another interviewee speaks of how "the person who introduced Western civilisation here was Reverend Kenneth Spooner.... He told the chief that he was sent by the Holy Spirit to Phokeng to teach the villagers the word of God." Thomas Rangaka, the son of the convert Dan, writes: "At the time there was already a stirring and hunger among the Bafokeng and others, for western kind of education and style of living. The people scanned the sky for a Messiah to lead them away from the church *lebollo* (initiation) to better and more meaningful education. That really meant from the grip of Lutheran Missionary influence."[74]

Was that missionary interested in the Word of God only?

No, his initial intentions were to preach the word of God, but he discovered that we were lacking in education. He then organised groups of pupils who came for lessons on several occasions.[75]

He started teaching and preaching under a tree, but then built a "big 'rondawel' with the stoep all around it,"[76] which acted as church and classroom. It was in direct competition with Penzhorn's school, and attracted a great number of pupils. Mrs. Mekgwe's brother was one of the first to attend his school. "People preferred Spooner because they saw us progressing under his school, and believed that Penzhorn wanted to make us stupid," she said.[77]

Reverend Spooner, that one was very intelligent. He was a real teacher.... Most of the people who were taught by Reverend Spooner know English very well. They are fluent in English, and they know the history of this village. Spooner was used to discussing everything with the chief, who was in favour of him. He supported the idea of using English as a medium of instruction.[78]

Spooner proved to have wide appeal to those who sought access, not just to the dubious privilege of speaking English to their domestic employers, but who, perhaps on the basis of greater wealth acquired through the peasant economy, had set their sights higher, aiming to become teachers, nurses, and other professionals. The trouble with Penzhorn had been that "because he was a German he did not want children to get a higher or better education than the one he gave."[79] Lutheran schooling ended when confirmation took place, and for most pupils, particularly those who had begun school late in life, this was only after five or six years of education. Also, as Nthana Mokale put it, "English was the language of the educated," and Penzhorn's failure to embrace it inhibited social mobility. Indeed, one informant suggests that Spooner was indeed favoured by the emerging elite, who saw his education as a means to power: "Many of those who went to Reverend Spooner's school are leaders, they are very active in the community, and seem to be interested in the welfare of the community."[80] Soon after his arrival several young men were sent to train as teachers at various training schools, and the trend continued.[81] Spooner also offered an Africanism and a radicalism to his pupils that may have appealed to this stratum — Naboth Mokgatle remembers being taught about the great continent of Africa, and its glorious past, while Naomi Setshedi suggests that not only do "most of the people around here who were taught by Rev. Spooner know English very well, they are fluent in English," but "they know the history of this village."[82] Rangaka says that his "favourite song when in meetings with the Africans was: 'Oh Africa, black Africa, God's love will make you free; we bring to you in Jesus' name, his love and liberty.'"[83]

Spooner's success was, according to the informants, deeply resented by the Lutherans. Penzhorn's own ideas about black education were far more gradualist than those of his rival. Some missionaries, he said in 1930, make them climb up that tree too quickly, and when they are sitting there at the top of that tree, they do not know where they are, and they fall down.... They want to climb quickly; they often do climb, and before they know where they are, they have tumbled right down—they have tumbled deeper than where they were at first.... Give him a chance as he climbs the tree of education and the tree of civilisation; give him a chance to look around a little, and to see for himself where he is before he climbs higher and higher.[84]

Penzhorn "hated Spooner and used to call him *Rabodiba*:

Spooner got this name from his method of baptising. *Rabodiba* means the one who owns a spring; this was where he baptised his followers. The name Spooner, Penzhorn used to translate it into Tswana as *Raleswana* (Man of *spoons*).... This is how he insulted Spooner. He didn't want his followers to visit "Raleswana's" church, but many people joined Rev. Spooner.[85]

Mrs. Mekgwe recalls:

The German guy used to hunt for us, to search for those who were going to Mr. Spooner's place. There were a number of thorn trees between our village and Reverend Spooner's place. One of us would shout, "A white man is coming," and we would hide behind those thorn trees in fear of the white man. Those who had some scraps of paper and pencils would wrap them and hide them in between their clothes.[86]

Penzhorn thought that Spooner should have gone to "areas which were still backward," and Nkwapa Ramorwesi, Penzhorn's staunchest defender, agrees:

We used to refer to those places as *Bokala* ... the area where the *Gaba* group lives.... It is those remote areas where circumcision is still being practised on a large scale and where education is not yet known. Spooner should, in fact, have proceeded to those places. He should have gone there to open the eyes of the people. Instead, he settled in our area, where he found people already cultured. He just came in like an intruder who has found one's kraal with beast and who wants to control that kraal which he never bothered himself to give a hand when it was built.[87]

According to one informant, what Penzhorn feared was that the Bafokeng would become "black English men and women." Penzhorn said that "when they ceased to read, speak and write their own language ... they would cease to know themselves and their backgrounds and cease to be a nation." The informant continued:

[Penzhorn] was not in favour of English used as a medium of instruction. He argued that if we could be taught English, we would try to follow English culture as well. The Reverend Penzhorn said that English culture is horrible. "They are going to show you horrible films at a cinema," said Reverend Penzhorn. He complained that our primitive way of life would be disturbed and we would experience rough life. "Hey, you are going to regret it because whites would be attracted to your place."[88]

Mokete Phalatse says that:

He also said, your parents want you to be taught "Yes sir, yes sir" [said in English]. You put pens behind your ears, but all this English and pens are going to destroy your families. You will be killing each other like animals because you want to imitate English people.[89]

But the Lutheran Church was, in fact, an institution with deep roots in the society, and Spooner appears to have been influential more in the education he offered than in any spiritual transformation he may have attempted — at least amongst the interviewees. No doubt his influence persisted amongst the elite who continued with their education and became community leaders. But few of the interviewees claim a long-term allegiance to his ideas — although they are, admittedly, not from the better educated stratum. Nthana Mokale points out that those who attended his school continued to attend Lutheran church services "because we were baptised by him and were thus affiliated to his Lutheran Church."[90] Another informant speaks bitterly of those who had been "disloyal" to Penzhorn:

> You know what, many people surprised me when they said they do not want Rev. Penzhorn's school. Honestly, they shocked me. They were committing a sin, do you understand? Penzhorn? When I think of him, the only church minister I had, I become heartbroken.

She affirms indignantly that Lutheranism had indeed penetrated deep into the community:

> The people who go around making a general statement that the Phokeng people were against Penzhorn do not know what they are talking about. Penzhorn's church was the main church here in Phokeng. It was the foundation on which all these churches were built. Even to date, I always argue with those who were against Rev. Penzhorn.[91]

Unlike Pentecostalism, Lutheranism was intertwined with such material factors as land, giving it a substantial moral hold over the community. The legitimacy given to the rite of confirmation by the society at large gave the Lutherans control over young people. Certainly, it was a means of drawing schoolchildren away from the influence of Spooner. Ernestina Mekgwe, a favoured pupil of Spooner, describes how

> Reverend Spooner got disappointed when I left his lessons for confirmation school, he said that I was intelligent enough to continue with my education. He could not do anything to help me out, I had to go to my church [the Lutheran Church] to enrol for confirmation lessons. That German priest was making it difficult for us during those years. At the age of sixteen, the German priest would collect all of us falling in that age group, to attend confirmation school on full-time basis.[92]

And indeed, Nkwapa Ramorwesi suggests that even amongst the elite it was not Spooner himself that saw to it that they furthered their education, but their own access to wealth and privilege:

> Spooner? There is no one whom we can point a finger and tell the people that he had been educated through Spooner's effort. Spooner sent none to an English college. . . .
>
> *Did Rev. Spooner not send Rangaka and Naboth Mokgatle to college?*
>
> No, they had been sent there by their individual mothers because they were rich.[93]

The Reverend Penzhorn's attitude toward Tswana culture, while it did not seek to impose on the Bafokeng a derived Western culture, was in its own way an attempt at control, in that it sought to preserve Tswana-ness perhaps in a context where other forces were attempting to destroy it. But clearly, even in the minds of the most ambitious and educated informants, he struck a chord of anxiety amongst the "ordinary" people which Spooner, with his more progressive Westernism, did not. "Is it not so, my child," said Mrs. Setshedi to Mmantho,

> young children today go to a cinema where they watch horrible things. There are books which show a very young child all the stages which an unborn child has to go through before being born. Young children have a tendency to reading this type of book. Today it is a joke to tell a young child that we get babies from a dam. [Laughter] Now, are we on the right track?

Mmantho replies "No, as far as culture is concerned, we are not on the right track," to which Mrs. Setshedi says, "I don't think it's fair to deviate from one's culture and follow another man's culture. My child, whites have taken our culture from us."[94]

Spooner's observations of the Bafokeng suggest an insensitivity to black culture that may have fed this perception. Having a black skin did not necessarily make for greater awareness of the nuances of African society: "I think that it can be truthfully said that the home life of all the Bantu Tribes of South Africa is about the same," he wrote, remarking upon "their many peculiar notions, their conservatism and fatalism, their extraordinary simplicity and childishness about some things, their exceptional duplicity, their peculiar point of view, their skill in some things and their ignorance in others."[95] His observations of the role of women were critical of Tswana orthodoxy, and unsympathetic to women's own perceptions of themselves as dignified people:

> The woman continues to be the beast of burden—a big jar of water on her head, another in her hand and the baby on her back is a common sight. She too must do most of the work in the fields and in the home. It is she who must build the walls of the house. When it is completed, my lord will see to the roof, provided there is plenty of beer.[96]

Little explicit acknowledgement of Spooner's specific concern with women's plight appears in the interviews; and yet it seems remarkable that, in spite of their generalised religious conservatism, the women are certain that Spooner both influenced them, and is clearly remembered by them. But what he had to offer was perhaps more in the line of an outlet for their already existing self-assertiveness, as the new generation of peasant daughters seeking to make their way in a new world.

The Lutheran Church remained the spiritual home of the Bafokeng—as we have said, the "establishment" church of the community.[97] Many of the women who, as children, attended Spooner's school, for example, did so while remaining Lutherans. Mahube Makgale says that "they spent most of their time at our place, and went to Spooner's for educational purposes."[98] They left the "Lutheran area" to attend school at Spooner's because of the English lessons given there, but "everybody" was confirmed.

The era of competition between the two missionaries continued throughout the period of Spooner's residence there. "His educational policy, being in striking contrast to that of other missions working in the same place, aroused great antagonisms."[99] In 1917, his school was nearly closed down, apparently through Lutherans' exerting influence over the local government education departments — to whom he, like many black American evangelists at the time, was a suspicious character likely to stir up revolutionary ideas. He was handicapped by "the fact of being classed as a native, the fact of his colour":

> From those at the head of affairs, attacks which caused him physical and mental unrest came to his school. Perhaps one of the greatest blows was that which came in 1936. The Education Department found some little excuse to deprive his school of its Standard 6 class. This cut at the root of his high school scheme.[100]

In addition, Spooner associated with white liberalism, also anathema to the authorities. He attempted to start a Joint Council for Europeans and Natives in the district in 1937, just before his death, and he was known to and indeed patronised by a local liberal, Eleanor MacGregor (on whose citrus estate some of the women were to work in their adulthood) and even by A. Lynn Saffery, a trade unionist, who attended his funeral. By the time of his death in 1937, Spooner was well known in the district and even in Johannesburg. Some twenty-five thousand people attended his funeral, and of these one hundred were whites from the local region. But his persecution by the authorities and the Lutherans persisted, and whether as a result of this, which Thomas Rangaka said "literally sent him to the grave," or the appendicitis that others said attacked him, the rivalry was ended altogether when Spooner died in Rustenburg hospital, some said of a broken heart. His death was followed by that of Penzhorn in 1940.

The deaths of both missionaries are vested with magical significance by the informants. Mrs. Mekgwe claims, in fact, that Spooner was bewitched by those who disliked him; and Penzhorn, it was claimed, died

> at a meeting which was called to decide on whether pupils should follow English or continue like previously. He just said "God help me," and collapsed. People got shocked and started asking, "what is the cause of this trouble, we want our children educated?"[101]

Mrs. Ramorwesi's account suggests that his death symbolised the depth of his commitment to Phokeng:

> When we were attending the confirmation lessons, you must listen to what I am going to tell you my child, Penzhorn used to tell us these words, "I pray to God that the day I die, I must die before the congregation, teaching them the word of God." I learnt later that we were not the only group which were told these words, those who came before and after us, were also told these words. Everyone knew these words. He said "I pray that the day I fall ill, I must be with the congregation. I don't want to be looked after at home and ultimately die there, away from my congregation." Are you aware that God received his prayers.... Indeed, he died before the congregation ... while he was delivering a speech at the opening of that new school, he screamed "Help me" and fell to the ground.[102]

If missionaries were not always the direct agents of imperialism in Africa, they were at least the representatives of a Western culture that aspired to a greater or lesser degree of hegemony over African cultures. As far as women were concerned, missionaries did draw young girls out of traditional homesteads into schools, where they were "educated for domesticity," the kinds of skills they were taught being at times quite extraordinarily narrow in conception. Young African girls were seen as potential housewives or domestic servants, and educated accordingly.

As a corrective to analyses that fail to point out the kind of sexism and puritanism that prevailed in late nineteenth- and early twentieth-century mission ideology, such interpretations are vital. They are certainly partly confirmed by an examination of the intentions of Penzhorn, who sought to teach the girls in his classes "the real and proper domestic science"—although even Lutheranism, much to the chagrin of the women, sought more to reinforce the peasant than the urban capitalist economy, for he also aimed

> not to make the young girls suitable as servants for the whites, but to make the young girls suitable as assistants in the house, and as future wives for their husbands, and domestic science of that kind teaches them to sweep in the corners and to build walls and to make a floor. They have to cook pap and fetch water and go to the gardens. That is domestic science, and the object is to make the girl a fit wife for her future husband.[103]

However, one of the things we have learnt about hegemonic visions is that they rarely attain the same meaning as that intended in the minds of those at whom they are aimed. If we examine the introduction of Christianity and all that it entailed "from below," we obtain a prismatic vision into Bafokeng society. Instead of the smooth imposition of ideas, we find that there was a struggle over the kinds of cultural symbols and material benefits introduced by each of the two missionaries in Phokeng; and we can see the ways—intended and unintended—in which they were being appropriated by the different strata of the local population. Neither missionary seems to have gained complete hegemony, and even Penzhorn's longer-lasting and more sustained influence seems to have failed to enter all the myriad areas of the consciousness of those whom he influenced. There was still space, room, for dissent and disagreement, and a sense that mission teachings could be used in some of the ways the Christianised population required. Furthermore, it appears that each type of Christianity had different meanings for the different emerging strata in the society, with Spooner offering a vision more appropriate to the ambitions of the aspirant elite, and Penzhorn representing the innate conservatism of those with more limited possibilities. But even this is a complex and ambiguous factor, for "ordinary" Bafokeng families also found it necessary and desirable that they should learn English, and rejected the neat functionalism of Lutheran ideas. The conflict between Penzhorn and Spooner thus seems to have reflected the divergent and perhaps internally contradictory needs of the community they sought to serve, as much as the philosophies and hegemonic ambitions of the respective men. The missionaries' cold war helps us to understand something of how the women acquired Christianity and what it meant to them, and its intertwining with their desire for mobility and modernity. We can also see something of the incipient stratification of the community, and begin to place the women as people who, whatever their ambitions for learning English, were to be largely excluded from the new, better-educated elite of Phokeng.

These latter insights are given even more depth when we examine a further significant aspect of Spooner's role in Phokeng. Whatever his effect upon the ordinary people's consciousness, he did partially succeed in inserting himself into the life of both the Bafokeng and the European community of Rustenburg. In his later years, he attended *lekgotla* meetings, for example, and "thus endeared himself to the chief and the people. On many important tribal matters he gave free advice." Molotlegi himself was attempting to embrace the forces of progressivism that Spooner represented, although his deeper interests lay with the Lutherans. The members of his *lekgotla*, however, were less clearly tied to Lutheran conservatism, and identified with the Westernism and mobility offered by Spooner much more clearly. So deep was Spooner's influence amongst this group that some have associated his influence with what the informants call the "Bafokeng Wars" of 1920–22, a conflict during which Molotlegi's hold over the Bafokeng was challenged by a significant "progressive" segment of the society, including the leading members of his *lekgotla*, and during which the values of Westernism, individualism, and democracy were posed as alternatives to the paternalistic and conservative communalism which the chief (and the Lutherans) represented. This was the time, according to Mokete Phalatse, during which the Bafokeng "were slitting each other's throats and fighting against each other like cornered rats."[104] This affair also made a deep impact upon the consciousness of some of the women, and provides us with a further prismatic insight into the workings of Phokeng in the 1920s, as well as into the women's own developing world views.

To those informants who have knowledge of the affair (and one, Nthana Mokale, says that "that was a men-only topic, and we as women never questioned or wanted reason for their decisions"[105]) this conflict is almost entirely remembered as having involved a popular challenge to the chief. It is seen as being about community, loyalty, and chiefship. The women are not critical of the *lekgotla* that had sought to depose the chief, who they claimed with some justification was frequently drunk and often corrupt, over his continued use of a grain mill which the community had decided to boycott:

> This mill was situated on the Indian's plot of land. The Indian was charging exorbitant prices for the use of his mill, and thus it was concluded after a discussion between the village elders that the grain mill should be boycotted.

The chief was caught disobeying what to the women was a higher authority — a decision of the community: "One of the chief's servants was caught while returning from the mill. When asked to answer for his actions, the servant said he had been sent by the chief." The response was complex, however. While the chief was "guilty," the question was whether or not he should be punished for it. What we know from other sources is that those seeking to depose the chief over the affair were in fact the aspiring elite, who had ambitions to individualised land tenure and a Westernised community. But to the women, it was simply about rebelliousness versus loyalty:

> This caused such a big uproar and divided the people of Phokeng. There became a group called the rebels who wanted the chief to be brought before the *kgotla* to answer for himself; another said no, a chief is like everyone of us here that makes mistakes and is usually forgiven.[106]

No informants remember that the conflict between the "rebels" and the chief was in fact about land as much as about mill prices.[107] The "Indian" mill owner, according to other sources, was on the land of a white farmer, whose high price for his land the chief was refusing to pay. The "rebels" were anxious for the chief to direct the community economy towards greater individualism of land holdings. He, in turn, was resisting this because it would undermine his authority, resting as it did upon a communal ideology. But to the women these abstract causes of the conflict were, perhaps not surprisingly, invisible. One informant suggests that "the rebels were arguing that they could not be ruled by a chief that broke rules agreed on by the village, and furthermore he was a drunk of an old man, they said."[108] Mrs. Setshedi also perceived the matter as one of chiefly disloyalty to the community decision. "Villagers had decided not to use that mill because the owner, Mokukiwa, was cheating them out of their produce." She shows an awareness that the landowner was white, but also brings an "Indian" into it:

Was the owner of the mill a black or white man?

It was a white man, called *Mokukiwa* [one who is carried]. The villagers said since we are boycotting the mill, the chief has no right to use it.... Also being boycotted was an Indian trader, whose shop was on land belonging to the white mill owner.

Mrs. Setshedi recalls it as having been something of a popular revolt:

The villagers arrived at the mill with intentions of stopping their chief from using the mill, and in the commotion that ensued the chief was held, though not assaulted, and reprimanded about his intentions to undermine them.[109]

Mokete Phalatse, too, remembers the role played by the villagers in censuring their chief:

The whole village had come together and concluded that the mill was not to be used because of its high expense. They placed a bell a little distance from the mill so that the village people could be gathered whenever there was an intruder or a culprit.

The chief's man, who in her account had been sent in fact by the chief's wife rather than the chief himself,

didn't know that and was amazed to see people coming to him and asking him why he used the mill. He tried to defend himself by saying he didn't know anything, but they wrung the truth out of him only to find that he had been sent by the chief's wife. They fined the chief's wife a cow, but she wouldn't take it. She fought them tooth and nail.

Not only does Mrs. Phalatse add several refinements to the story, but she suggests that the chief himself, and his family, were punished by the *lekgotla*. From then onward, the story, in the women's eyes, was about the restoration of community in the face of profound cleavages. The "sending" of the chief into exile was the first crisis in the community's "wholeness":

The chief's wife wouldn't hear a word about the fine. But people insisted on the fine being placed on Molotlegi because he didn't listen.... They were brought before the elders and were asked to give their views, but

Molotlegi's wife still refused, so ultimately they were sent off into the mountains to stay there until they had cooled off.[110]

Several informants remember the community having been split into factions given symbolic names and even uniforms: *Marabela* were the rebels; and *Matsielala* were the pacifiers or moderators.[111] The Matsielala eventually went to fetch the chief and his family from the mountains; amongst them was Mokete Phalatse's grandfather, and she invests the story with a certain colour:

How long did they stay in the mountains?

For a whole month, until they were fetched by a guard riding a white horse. When he arrived there he asked whether they still refused to pay a cow, and they stood their ground. My grandfather was with them. He called some of them to their homes, and helped them pack their things, and placed them on trucks and off they went.[112]

One man, Mokgatle Lekwapo, a "rebel" of royal blood, whose "comrades were more than his family, even though the family, was there," died during this episode, she says, and his funeral provided the occasion for a great meeting between the two groups:

The rebels were moving that side and the ruling party this side. On the way to the graveyard the trumpet was blown by the opposition.... They wore black colours, men were wearing a black cloth on their lapels and women wearing black doeks [scarves] and dresses.... Trumpets were blowing mournfully, and the day was bleak.

A ceremonial battle, the "Rebels' Battle," appears to have taken place between the two sides, with at least the Matsielala in full battle dress:

The Matsielala collected a lot of money and ordered horses from Johannesburg, which were fetched from the station by my uncle, who was wearing a manel [sic] jacket and a helmet. They were very regimental. My granddad was also wearing a new helmet and a field grey suit. My granny was wearing a black tartan dress, you would have liked the spectacular scene they made. When the horses came, a *Mogomokwane*[113] sounded.[114]

Setswammung Mokatle, with her royal connections, remembers what it was like being on the chief's side, where she experienced the pain of exclusion from the community:

We as relatives to the chief were ordered not to go into the chief's yard any more, Chere [her husband] and myself. Other people also stopped visiting us because as close people to the chief we were put in one camp.

She was forbidden by the rebels to visit her aunt, and her defiance of this led to her husband being "beaten up with sticks" the next time he attended a *lekgotla* meeting, and carried back home by a "mob of men." She was "pounding grain under a peach tree in our yard when I saw all of this."[115]

In the end, the chief invoked the laws of South Africa itself to back him up, defeating the "rebels" and destroying permanently, it appears, the power of his own *lekgotla* in the courts, which would always back chiefly conservatism against the emerging radicalism of the elite, which the authorities feared was part of a wave of Ethiopian-inspired nationalism sweeping the country. The "rebels" were expelled from Phokeng, and Molotlegi's rule continued. But to the informants, the rebels chose exile, rather than having it imposed upon them. Mrs. Mokgatle herself says:

> A secessionist move was formed led by Kagete Mokgatle, elder brother to Lebone, the present [1980s] chief. This new body went out in search of other places where they could live because they felt it unbearable to live under the jurisdiction of the old man.

They left not because they were chased away?

> No, they left because of the disagreement with the chief. They put Lucas Kagete Mokgatle as their new chief and cows were slaughtered for the celebrations that were throughout the village. Some days later, they went to Malebogo, where they built new houses.[116]

To Mrs. Mekgwe "the rebels were so dispirited with the chief that some left the village and went to a place near Luka called Malebogo,"[117] while Mrs. Setshedi says that the rebels,

> as they had already isolated themselves from all rulings under the chief, moved out of Phokeng and set up house on the hilltops outside Phokeng. There was real hatred between these two groups, and some emigrated to places like Malebogo and Bultfontein.... Even some relatives of the chief left to go settle in those places.[118]

Exile is interpreted by the women as being one of the most painful possible experiences:

Oh, was it that terrible?

> Yes it was. Even some relatives of the chief left to go settle in those places. They left their houses vacant and decided to move into places unknown to them. Those who couldn't stand the hardships of foreign lands returned to occupy their former houses, but the majority that left did not come back.[119]

Those who left experienced great sadness:

> Most of those who settled at Malebogo had left beautiful houses in Phokeng. After a long period of time, there were some who desired to return to Phokeng and reoccupy their houses but were advised that their intended action would lose them any credibility they had gained in opting out of the chief's jurisdiction.[120]

They moved nearer to home, to Chaneng, and called their home *Atamelang* (come near). "And though they returned materially rich, the majority were disappointed with life, their spirits were broken and their will to live was no more." Mrs. Mokgatle says they returned even closer to home, after some negotiations:

> Simon, a member of the secessionist group and a cousin to my husband came to our house and asked to see Chere. They said life was not easy at their newfound home and they would like Chere to plead with the chief to accept them back into the village and their former homes....

On a second visit they came "leading three cows with them, as a present that Chere was to give to the chief as part of their pleading effort." Chere must have relished telling them to go back with their cows because perhaps the chief might not accept them, and secondly, he told them that the last time he met with them at a meeting, these men had beaten him up, so it will not be easy for him to put their case without any prejudices against it.

The story is rounded off with these particular rebels, however, coming home:

Some days later the chief agreed to meet these men, and it was only after days of talking between the chief, elders, and rebels that they were finally accepted back. They were forgiven and asked to deliver cows and grain when they returned to the village. A big feast was held, meat was plentiful, and those rebels who came back were forgiven.[121]

To the women the interdependent worlds of Lutheranism and the chieftaincy had survived great challenges—from Spooner's influence, and from the elite he served, respectively. But their attitude to the forces of disruption was ambiguous. Their loyalty to and identification with the entity they conceived of as "Bafokeng society" was powerful—but its definition was fluid. Sometimes the "community" meant the home so deeply missed by the exiled rebels; at other times it referred to the conglomeration of individuals calling themselves "Bafokeng" whose personal lives and individual careers needed nurturing by church and school. In yet other references, they pose "the people" against the chief (when his disloyalty to a communal decision is at stake); while elsewhere they associate the chieftaincy, Penzhorn, and Christianity itself with the concept of "Bafokeng." Thus what to the outsider may appear to be mere "ethnicity" has an infinite number of complex, historically constructed meanings to the women.

As the women approached adulthood, Bafokeng society underwent further radical change during the 1920s and 1930s. These definitions of Bafokeng, self, and community were to be carried through and themselves to alter in the minds of young women whose ambitions to become educated were exceeded only by their ambitions to encounter the wider world for which Penzhorn and Spooner had intentionally or otherwise prepared them.

4

Leaving Home,
1920–1935

In this chapter, we examine some of the structural constraints that acted on the society and economy of Phokeng during the 1920s and 1930s, and which combined to make it almost inevitable that the young women of the time, like the young men of their own ages, would leave home and seek employment in the cities and towns nearby. Both sexes sought to leave chiefly and parental discipline and authority; and we shall see how in the case of the young girls, migration repre- sented at least a partial escape from the expectations of the patriarchal system that prevailed. But we should not fall into the simplistic trap of assuming that only young girls were subjected to patriarchal discipline. Indeed, a case may be made for its harsher application to young boys. Certainly initiation schools for boys persisted for longer than for girls, while birching and other forms of discipline were more harshly applied. *Lepaša* (tribute labour, controlled by the chief) expectations appear mainly to have applied to boys.[1] Boys left school earlier than girls and appeared more anxious to escape the society.[2] Patriarchy in its biblical sense (meaning the rule of older men over women and younger men) appears to have been prevalent.[3] However, it would appear that the rewards for accepting the system were greater for young men than for young women, for the former could look forward to the possibility of land and independence on their return, in contrast with the only option available to women — that of making a good marriage. This chapter explores the social and structural background to migrancy, both of men and women, and examines the experiences of the inter- viewees in that light.

That South African black rural areas underwent a progressive decline during the early decades of this century is well known. All over the country, rural economies that had until then been able to sustain themselves began to give up a migrant proletariat to the cities.[4] Regions that had at first sent migrants to work out of strength,[5] now did so out of weakness. In addition, white farmers, backed by a series of laws made in their favour, began to change the terms of the relationships between themselves and those who had sharecropped on their land,

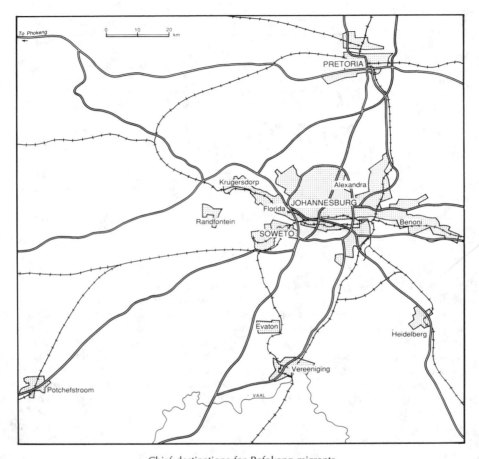

Chief destinations for Bafokeng migrants

so that the bargain between landlord and tenant shifted inexorably in favour of the former and to the disadvantage of the latter.[6] The progressive incorporation of migrancy and decline of sharecropping took place in a regionally differentiated manner. Some areas were forced to give up a migrant labour force early on, while others managed to hold out longer. In some places, fully fledged sharecropping continued far longer than in others.

However, the story of the establishment of both male and female migration in Phokeng does not fit an economistic picture of simple economic decline leading to the need for more migrancy. As elsewhere, a whole gamut of forces came into play, reflecting the complex interaction between the "tribal" and "capitalist" economies and social orders. That a distinction was made between male and female migrancy was not accidental, nor was it simply a result of the effects of capitalism and underdevelopment on African communities. It is also to be explained by reference to the "domestic struggles" that took place in each area, by the interaction of capitalism with households and domestic economies which had distinct "tribal" and patriarchal structures.[7]

In order to understand the way in which Phokeng experienced these particular forces we need to note its continuing relatively wealthy status. The Western Transvaal in general, and Phokeng in particular, had been able to resist "under-development" for a comparatively long time, as we have seen, and a fairly substantial and independent peasantry survived right up until the 1920s and 1930s. The three most progressive farmers in Phokeng in 1930 had bought land of their own, sunk boreholes, and were engaged in the use of sophisticated farming methods.[8] Most farmers in the 1930s used the double-furrowed plough, it was observed; and the Bafokeng were described as having "a considerable degree of advancement beyond other districts in South Africa."[9] This small community — numbering about five thousand families at this time, and occupying twenty-six farms, measuring about fifty-two thousand morgen[10] — owned fertile land, and this provided a basis for the wealthier and middle-level farmers. The community was healthy[11] and well served with schools.[12] Ernest Penzhorn himself noted in 1930:

> That old chief bought many farms for the community (volk). Earlier, through the missionaries, through my father and through other people, a great deal of land was bought for the natives. They bought farms for the community, and officially the farms were registered in the name of the missionaries or other white people... later the land was registered in the name of the native commissioner.[13]

As a result, even as late as the 1930s, he said,

> There are young natives who harvest between 100 and 200 bags, yes, and there are twenty-three who harvest up to 500 bags per year, and they bring more oxen in and more ploughs, and they go in for a very good sort of farming. This is a progressive people.

A few people, he also suggested, went even further:

> They see that they can make a better living by means of their farming, and not only a better life, but also an easier life. This is one of the big things that they begin to realise. There are some amongst the natives here in this district who try ... like Europeans to plant mealies, and these people have gone even further, and they plough with "skoffel" ploughs.[14]

Although these were few in number, so effective was African farming in Phokeng, that when the government sent a demonstrator, "a Fingo," to teach the locals how to farm, use seed effectively, and so on, "the natives laughed at that demonstrator; they said he could contribute nothing, he could teach them nothing. They had long ago perceived the things he told and showed them." They had learnt their methods from their observations of Boer agriculture as well as from missionaries, said Penzhorn.[15]

In addition, the community was producing a class of young artisans, mainly as a result of missionary tutelage. Penzhorn mentions one carpenter who did all his building for him, as well as shoemakers, highly successful bricklayers, and other "native tradesmen" working in the towns.[16] He bemoans the fact that these occupations, however, were less attractive to the rurally orientated Bafokeng than he would have liked.

Labour migration was there, but it was hardly symptomatic of the kind of deep and desperate poverty that characterised other areas. As one observer noted, "there is no poverty" in the Rustenburg area; the natives were "quite able" to sustain themselves economically, and migration was either unnecessary, or part of a strategy of improving the peasant economy:

> The original intention of the natives in going to work was quite a good one. A native went to Johannesburg after having got married. He went there with his wife to earn money in order to be able to buy a span of oxen and a double-furrow plough, and after he had earned enough money he came back in order to farm.... The aim and object of most of the natives is to go in for farming, for cultivating the land, and they go out to work in order to earn enough money to buy a team of oxen and a double-furrow plough and a waggon, and once they have got those they stay at home and they do not go out any more.[17]

For unmarried men, migration was for a rather different purpose — that of earning enough money — in those days about £40–50, to pay *bogadi* (bridewealth) and the costs of a wedding, in order to enable them to get married. By 1930 it could be said that generally all young men went to the city to work for this purpose.[18]

The tradition of male migrancy had long existed. Regiments of young men were sent out to work there by the first chief Mokgatle right from the earliest days of the Kimberley mines, as we have seen. The first men appear to have been sent in the 1860s, and some of the interviewees' grandparents or parents were among them. However, as in other societies of this type, this had not been an indication of the weakness of the Phokeng economy, but rather of its strength, its capacity to use the burgeoning cash economy as a means to peasantisation and land acquisition. Male migrants and even many sharecroppers were taxed by the chief, and as late as 1920 Setswammung Mokgatle records that her husband Chere, the chief's secretary, would visit the town to collect taxes there. As elsewhere, the particular domestic hierarchies within Bafokeng society allowed chiefly authority to be used to control young men's labour in this way; while at home, the domestic arrangements within families ensured that rural production did not suffer as a result.

By 1930, the society began to display features that threatened to undermine both the Bafokeng social order and its carefully developed relationship with the city. While August Molotlegi, after his challenge from the "rebels" in the 1920s, now appeared to be ruling over a tightly controlled and still-conservative community — or at least that was how missionaries and members of the royal clan presented things to the 1930–32 Native Economic Commission — this control was maintained at a very high price. Penzhorn's portrayal of the area is of one with people who were very law-abiding, with "very little crime; in fact, there is practically none."[19] A sense of powerful chiefly, state, and missionary control comes through his evidence:

> *Do you have any trouble with the Amalaitas[20] in your area?*
>
> No, not here. They tried to push themselves in and they influenced some of our natives. They troubled us a little for some time. It was the spirit

which troubled us here, but with the support of the Native Commissioners and the Magistrate we kicked them out. The Commissioners supported me very strongly there, and they even sent me native policemen and we put these people in Gaol. Especially at Christmas time we had some trouble with them, but we rounded them up and several of their ring-leaders were put into prison, and now we have chucked them all out.[21]

This control extended to the more important area of national political activity:

The chiefs here will not have anything to do with these native congresses, and these native meetings, of which we hear such a lot. When they come here they send them away, and they take up the attitude that these agitators are trying to spoil our people. The ICU will never come here. The chiefs would not allow them for one minute.[22] The chiefs do not want them, and they simply kick them out.

Penzhorn hints that radical thought, as indeed we had presumed in our discussion of the "Bafokeng Wars," had not left Phokeng completely untouched, although he underplays its effects:

They had meetings of native congresses here on one or two occasions, congresses of people coming from the towns. The natives in these areas at one time used to give them money, and they could never account for that money, and the result is that they do not want them now. As a matter of fact, our people here do not see the use of that kind of thing.[23]

But several forces served to undermine or contradict this conservative order. For one thing, in order to sustain that order the chief had to be able to dispense land to the aspiring elite. But the South African state, which had protected the chieftaincy during the Bafokeng Wars, and was sometimes seen as a potentially benevolent and paternalistic force, was not, in this period, quite fulfilling its obligations. The Bafokeng had from the very beginning strenuously objected to laws that imposed segregation upon them. They had petitioned against the 1913 Land Act, and in 1914, Molotlegi, acting as spokesman for fifteen chiefs in the Rustenburg district, had repeated their objections:

We humbly request you to record and report our protest to Parliament against the provisions of Act No. 27 of 1913, the Natives Land Act, which we consider as detrimental to the interests and welfare of the natives residing in this district, and to submit our humble but earnest request to the Union Parliament to repeal same.[24]

It was not as if the existing lands were included in the provisions of the act. We have already pointed out that they were not. But the Bafokeng needed more. Even at the early stage, he said, "our farms are getting too small for us, and if under this law we could buy more farms we should be glad. We would be satisfied with the law if it allowed us to buy land. We would like to buy land anywhere we could get it." These complaints were echoed throughout the 1920s, and by 1930 Mutle Mokgatle, brother of the then chief, was complaining that "we are all children of the government and we should be treated alike; it is wrong that some children should be treated rightly and others wrongly and that is a great grievance to our tribe." He added: "We have put our grievances to the government, but we have not had any reply so far."[25] The crucial grievance related to land:

The tribe is complaining about the buying of farms. We understand that there are two divisions: the one is reserved for white and the other for native people. The tribe is complaining because, whenever they want to buy a farm not in a native reserve they are not able to buy and precedence is always given to the white man. In the white people's reserve the black man is never able to enter.

Furthermore, "Even in our own reserves we cannot always buy, and even there preference is given to the white man."

Although the men who migrated in this period probably did not do so out of dire poverty, these restrictions on land acquisition must have affected them deeply: they sought to escape the burdens of a traditional order in which subservience to the chief could no longer be exchanged for a guarantee of economic mobility. The chief no longer had any power to extend his patronage to the young and educated, whose ambitions to land ownership in any case had run against traditions of communalism, as we saw in the case of the Bafokeng Wars, and the price of accepting harsh chiefly control was thus too high. "The people who leave their homes and go to the towns and never come back to their tribes are those who do not want to be ruled," said Mutle Mokgatle.

They do not want to obey their chiefs and they do not want to be ruled according to the laws under which their tribes have lived and flourished for so many years. They want to be free, as they say. When they are in the towns, they are their own masters and they do just as they please.... That is what they call freedom, liberty, because they want to be their own masters.[26]

They feared returning home, he claimed, because "they are afraid that they will be punished and reprimanded if they have done anything wrong." That young men felt the requirements of traditional obeisance to be too harsh was confirmed by Penzhorn at the time, who said that "they must look after the cattle for too long, they must work too long for their parents, and the parents do not give them clothes. They must run around naked; then they leave the cattle and they trek away, so that they will be in a position to earn money to buy clothes and to buy other things for themselves."[27] Increased "wants," the much-vaunted excuse made by white employers for the low wages paid to their migrant workers, did indeed appear to motivate the young and educated to migrate.

The chiefly hold over the rural young was also weakened by the lowering of the bargaining position of sharecroppers and labour tenants, first by the increasing capitalisation of white agriculture:

Do you find many natives coming back to the location to live there for good?

Yes, in these last years they are returning to the villages in numbers, and especially from the High Veld do they seem to be returning. That is only lately.

Why is that?

... I suppose that the white farmer is making more use than he did originally of his farm and the farm is becoming too small for himself, his children and the natives. The result is they are not giving the natives as many rights as they did formerly, and then the natives come back to the location because they feel with their restricted rights on the farms they must be better off in the locations.[28]

But black farmworkers were also being displaced by the entry of foreign "Blantyre boys" — men from Nyasaland who brought "ruin among the tribes in this country."[29] While local blacks had head and dog taxes to pay, "those natives from Blantyre come over long distances. They come here hungry and thirsty. But when they are here they do not have to pay anything and they have no expenses at all." Work on local white farms also became less desirable in the light of the growing and more highly paid spheres of urban employment.

As a result of these and other forces, what had begun in Phokeng as discretionary migration gradually gave way to something more permanent and functional. Some informants' grandfathers had worked at Kimberley, and as we have seen, the oldest informant's father and husband had done so. By the time the fathers of the majority of informants were adults, however, work in Kimberley appears to have become less common, and they worked in Johannesburg or other, nearer, towns. The few fathers of informants who had worked in Johannesburg had tended to do so as a means to accumulating sufficient cash to reinvest in their farms. But they had clearly moved one rung up in the status and economic hierarchy of the labour market. The sectors of employment that Bafokeng men occupied at the turn of the century were less arduous, and perhaps more highly valued, than mine work. No doubt this is because of the relative strength they enjoyed in the labour market, as a result of their more resilient and powerful local economy and nearness to Johannesburg.

Whereas for this older generation city work was still a means to other ends, by the time the women's own generation came to enter the labour market, male migrancy was undertaken for long periods of time and led more often to permanent residence in the city. Migrants of that generation continued to benefit from their fathers' hold upon occupations of higher status: "No, our people very seldom go to the mines. Our people prefer to work as kitchen boys, and store boys, and so on, and very few of them ever go to the mines at all," it was said in the early 1930s, although "some still go to the Kimberley mines."[30] They were often delivery men, shop assistants, or worked in dairies. This fact was to have profound effects upon the situation of the Bafokeng in town, on their cultural and political consciousness and their behaviour, as we shall see in later chapters.

The migration of men to town, according to Penzhorn, did not itself help the situation. A *de facto* system of privatising land that was *de jure* communal, appeared to have come into being. Land was often allocated to the young, even babies, in the expectation that they would eventually grow to make use of it. Although in many cases the women of the family would work the land, it also often lay fallow for many years. "The land lies there for years without ever being worked; and the chief allows it because it is bequeathed to Joseph [the presumed child]." This was even worse where migrants were concerned:

> There are people who have paid for their farms since 1888. They are still paying. They are amongst the first who paid, but they do not have land to plough. These are the people who trek away from the villages, and who go to the nearest farmer to work. There they obtain land to plough, even though they have their own land to work in the villages.

There were also those who "go to the towns to live in the city locations."[31] These people became victims of the *de facto* privatisation of land that had taken place in the community, for individual families would continue to lay claim to land of their own even though they might not be working it, leaving the rest of the community with less land than they may have obtained through strict communalism; such privatisation may have worked if restrictions on the further acquisition of land amongst the Bafokeng did not exist. But in the light of segregationist restrictions, the absolute amount of land available to the Bafokeng was limited, and this made the lying "ruined" of private land somewhat wasteful, in Penzhorn's eyes.

> There will, perhaps, be many people who are prepared to work the land, but the owner is away, and says, "This is my land and nobody can develop it." As soon as someone else comes and begins to work, members of the family come and say "Leave it; the land belongs to us"; "My son is going to build there, he is in Johannesburg, but he will come back and the land is waiting for him." The result is that the land lies ruined, and the village looks very bad.[32]

This state of affairs, according to Penzhorn, could be rectified by what he called "good administration" in the native reserves in general, Phokeng in particular. For part of the process of disintegration and decline had been, as he and many of the chiefs giving evidence testified, the loss of control by chiefs over their populations, brought all the more sharply into relief, perhaps, by what Penzhorn perceived as the good old days of chiefly control and the production of "good stock" amongst the "natives":

> The old stock in our location, that stock that has died off now — that old stock were not merely firm Christians, they were firm personalities as well. You could rely upon them, you could build on them. The young people nowadays, they are not only shaky Christians, they are shading from one corner to another on the question of what they are. They are doubting all the time, and there is no personality among them. The old native, the native of about fifteen to twenty years ago, he was a man, and although often a heathen, he was a man of self-respect, a man of truthfulness, but today's native, this young man of today, has not an atom of self-respect.[33]

There had been a moral decline in the communities, as a result of the fact that the chiefs had not decided whether to rule autocratically or democratically; as a result, their rule was ineffective. "With today's chiefs, they don't know how to rule. They either rule too autocratically, or they rule too democratically. They don't know what they must do."[34] And: "In times when no wars prevailed, in the past, democratic rule was the order of the day. But now the chiefs have given up democracy, and ceased to rule through *kgotlas* and headmen."[35] Perhaps Penzhorn might have recalled the time when he supported Molotlegi against his own *lekgotla*, who had joined (or even perhaps instigated) the "rebels." The crushing of the rebellious *lekgotla* had indeed given rise to a decline in chiefly legitimacy, and added to the forces pushing people into migrancy. As a result of this "bad administration," they "obtain no influence over their people," and people fled to the cities.

Today's chief thinks he must rule autocratically, and he will try to do everything himself instead of through his *kgotla* and instead of the elders of his tribe. This, in my opinion, is the greatest error of today, and it is the reason for great dissatisfaction, and for the breaking up of the tribes.[36]

This generalised sense of a loss of control began increasingly to apply to the wilful young women of the tribe, whose rapid Christianisation and relatively extensive education we have already observed. Parents and chiefs managed to exert control over them more effectively and for longer, it seems, than for the young men. "I have several families here where the parents do not allow their girls to go out to work. They say, 'Let the boys fight their own battles, let the boys see what they can do, but we do not allow our girls to go out.'"[37] Patriarchy and the chiefly mode of production worked together in harmony here, because keeping the girls at home meant that the bulk of agricultural and indeed other labour continued to be performed: "generally speaking the girls are ploughing and gardening and doing everything that has to be done. They specially look after the gardens," continued Penzhorn, and elsewhere:

Today in your location, do the women handle the cattle in ploughing at all?

Sometimes when the husband is dead or when the husband is working in Johannesburg, the women do it. . . .

Yesterday I saw quite a small girl driving the cattle. Is that the usual thing?

Yes; you see the boy leaves the cattle and goes to work, and then the father sends the girl to look after the cattle. That is what we find everywhere now. The boy runs away. The boys leave the cattle at the post.[38]

That such attempts at control existed is confirmed by Naomi Setshedi, who says: "Some girls were not given permission to go and work in the suburbs as domestics."[39] But they were increasingly unsuccessful.

Do young girls go from here to work as servants?

Yes, there are many who do that.

Are the parents not against that?

Well, the vast majority would much rather not see the girls going out, but they cannot prevent the girls if they decide to go. It would not help to stop them.[40]

These "girls" included the women who are the subject of this study. What underlay this rebellious attitude on the part of these adolescents, and what meanings did their move hold for them? As these peasant daughters became transformed into city matriarchs, we explore the worlds of work, home, and community, asking how the women perceived their unfolding engagement with a new, more complex world.

Because the system of migrant labour in Phokeng had at least part of its origins in the rebelliousness of the young against their elders, we shall see that the memories of their own migration by the women studied here are not unhappy ones. Migration is almost never remembered as having been forced upon them; it is seen and interpreted rather as something more or less willingly undertaken, or undertaken as a result of a sense of responsibility towards kin. For some it is a matter of prestige, of status. To say this is not to deny that deep structural forces, relating to encroaching segregation, capitalisation of agriculture, and the rise of urban labour markets were at work — we have seen that they were. But the crude functionalism that makes a direct link between the existence of these forces and the particular rural communities upon which they were acting is refuted by the case of Phokeng. Here, we see that each outside force came to be embraced by complex systems of meaning, hierarchy, and control, so that its significance for each individual Mofokeng was always filtered through the local significances of the patterns of social relations in which they were involved.

Leaving school and becoming confirmed were the two moments that signalled the beginning of adulthood, and for the young Bafokeng woman in the 1920s and 1930s this meant migration. Nthana Mokale, a bright, intelligent girl, whose mentors hoped she would become a teacher, left school at eighteen (she had only started at eleven) because she wanted to work:

> At school I was a bright student and it was my teachers who recommended that I go to Kilnerton and thereafter I could enrol as a teacher here in Phokeng.
>
> *You were not interested, I suppose?*
>
> No, I wasn't. My only desire was to find employment in Johannesburg.

She suggests that her sex affected this decision: "I never thought or believed that women could be teachers at that stage, and thus I regarded being a teacher beyond my capabilities."[41]

Ida Molefe might have wished she had Nthana's opportunity, for economic circumstances forced her to leave her studies: her aunt could not afford to keep her at school beyond Standard 5, even though she was at Spooner's school and could have continued. She too went immediately to town.[42] Mmadiate Makgale was luckier, because on leaving school in Standard 3, she was given the opportunity of working as a teaching assistant for two years — but she ended up working as a domestic in the city like most of the other women, and speaks regretfully of the education she never obtained.[43] Josephine Mokotedi, on the other hand, left school in Standard 5 because, she says, "Penzhorn did not allow us to go further than Standard 5, he even expelled one teacher that wanted to teach us further."[44] On leaving school she immediately went to town, and earned money to pay for her sisters' school and confirmation fees. Mahubi Makgale confirms this view of Penzhorn. She gets angry with Mmantho for asking her (again) why she left school. "Oh. So I am expected to stay in school, while my agemates and friends are making a living for themselves," she says. Mmantho asks: "Did girls, when reaching a certain age decide that working would be better than schooling?" She replied: "You say decide. We were ejected. Penzhorn hand-picked us according to our ages, and the oldest girls were put through confirmation classes, after that you are told to go and find a job. You have no hope of going back to school after that."[45] Mokete Phalatse, who was from a relatively prosperous family but only attended school for three years, left at eighteen and went immediately to work in town.[46] Most of the other women reflect similar patterns. Naomi Setshedi suggests that generally, educational attainment was sacrificed for wage-earning:

Granny, I cannot understand why you left school, because at home they were able to educate you further?

By that time I was now big enough to work. Do you hear me? I wanted to work because so and so were working. Furthermore I wanted to buy myself anything that I wanted. We were ignorant of the fact that education was important.... That was [the] time for me to leave school.[47]

Let us examine these kinds of experiences in more detail.

Ernestina Mekgwe confirms that migrant contributions to rural households had become significant by the 1920s. She went to work in Johannesburg in 1925, when she was seventeen years old. She had just been confirmed. Her mother had died in 1919, and the "aim of going to Johannesburg was therefore to earn some money so that I could help my aging father to bring up my younger sisters and brothers."[48] It was customary for young girls to work with this kind of aim in mind: "Those who attended school with me all left to work in the towns. They later were called from there to be married." I used to earn one pound, ten shillings per month as a domestic servant," she says; and she would go home to Phokeng twice a year—at Christmas and Easter—with her earnings. "Sometimes one would go home with at least thirty pounds. On our arrival it was customary to give your mother all the money you had worked for. She would then call your father and put the money before him. They give thanks and ask if you have a bus fare to go back to work. If there was nothing left for you, then they would give you something out of that money."[49]

But Naomi Setshedi denies that simple economic need underlay migration, in her case at least. When asked, "What prompted the idea of leaving your home and going to work in Johannesburg?" she answers, "Girls of my age were working in Jo'burg. I could not just till the land, unmarried as I was. There was nothing I could do with bags of sorghum I could have got from the fields since I had no children.... I looked down on the idea of going to the fields, young as I was."[50] Later, when prompted further:

Can you say your family was well off in those days?

We were not rich and among us being well off meant being able to live and feed your family without undue hardships. Our mother was a widow and had two married daughters, so she had no one to be responsible for. All she did was just see to it that she had enough to eat, and if possible eke out a living from the fields.

Mmantho probes this point:

Is that not the reason that made you to go work for cash wages in Johannesburg?

No, that wasn't the cause. Going to Johannesburg or any of these towns was like a means to an end, it also had some adventure in it. Even if I had stayed at home I would not have starved. There was a sense of freedom about staying on your own in Johannesburg, and things like furniture we had seen others bring as fruits of their work in the towns urged us to follow suit. We had all seen our older sisters returning from such towns with beautiful dresses, shoes, plates, cups and at times they would have lighter complexions too. Men always took notice of such girls and our sisters always had many boyfriends around them.

Mmantho continues to seek a more material motivation:

> *Was there never at any given moment a shortage of food in your house?*

> No. We always had grain sacks stored in our house, and this could be easily ground into a fine powder to make porridge. When there wasn't any meat to eat the porridge with, there was milk.

> *You mean there wasn't a time when your mother said she did not have money to buy sugar.*

> No, there wasn't such a time, and besides tea was not my favourite drink when I was a growing girl, although we always had sugar in the house....

Cash was available still without the household's having to resort to migrancy:

> We used to sell our produce from the fields, and the money derived from those sales would be used to buy soap, tea, sugar and other basic amenities.... We harvested about twenty bags and that was a lot.

But some needs existed that migrant wages did fulfil:

> When you were an elderly woman and had a child that worked in the towns, this child would send money for your maintenance. A slab of meat cost only six pence in those days.

> *Was there such a working child in your family?*

> My brother was working then.... He sold cloth and he made enough money from this business venture that he purchased a bicycle that had two carriers, one on the front, another on the back. He even hired a boy to help him with his trade.... During the day he worked at Stanley Dairy. He bought this bicycle so that he could sell his wares over a large area. He sent my mother enough money and we never went without food.

The value of this sort of income to the older generation does seem to have been important after all:

> It would be tough when you were an old woman but had children that worked but never sent you any money, you wouldn't even have porridge in your house if you weren't young enough to work in the fields. Every morning when you woke up you would walk to your relatives who would give you tea to drink and some food to eat, and perhaps if you were too old to walk around, they would cook and bring the food to your house, that's what I call suffering. That is poverty of the highest order, not having food in your house.[51]

However, many of the women are more anxious to remember the normative rather than economic aspects of their own migration:

> You could not sit at home doing nothing. It was the in thing in those days, and when you perhaps visited a friend in the village who had worked in the towns, you'd find her room stocked with all the furniture and that was all the incentive you needed as encouragement to find a job.[52]

Although Sophie Serokane was not born and brought up in Phokeng, she gives some sense of the status attached to working in the city. Her first job on leaving school was as a domestic servant on a white farm. But later, she decided to go to Johannesburg:

> All of my friends were already working in Johannesburg. It was a prestige to work in Johannesburg by then. One had to try one's best to work there. Our friends used to tell us about all the good things which were happening in Johannesburg. I also discovered that they were telling the truth when I was working there eventually.[53]

"Were you only interested in experiencing the good things or in better wages by going to work in Johannesburg?" asked Mmantho, anxious not to miss any possible material reasons which existed in Sophie's mind:

> It was a matter of prestige to work there. Our friends who were working there already used to look down upon us. At Christmas they would say our dresses are *tabarakwe* [a traditional floral cloth]. They used to have no time for us.[54]

Nthana Mokale reinforces this interpretation:

> *Was there a time when you had to go and work because of financial difficulties?*
>
> What do you mean? I can't comprehend.
>
> *I mean didn't you need money for household necessities?*
>
> We went to work on the Reef on completing school. It seemed . . . that if one finished school one had to go and work.

Later she categorically denies the economic motive: "We did not suffer. We had grain in the house and there was always milk from the cows. There wasn't a shortage of food, and this was the case with other girls."[55]

The link between male migration and the need to earn *bogadi*, or bridewealth, is well known.[56] But the women of Phokeng appear to have become involved in something of a reversal of this, for being able to bring furniture into the marriage seems to have been an important expectation for many of them. Bridewealth was obviously still being paid, but so, it appears, were informal dowries—a sign, perhaps, of greater female assertiveness and power. Nthana Mokale, the daughter of one of the wealthier peasants of the time, is asked if migration was "just a usual thing?" "Of course," she replied, "who would marry you if you were not working, being just a bag of lazy bones without a stick of furniture."[57]

Ernestina Mekgwe, for all her claims about going to work in order to help her father pay for the family's expenses after the death of her mother, implies elsewhere in her conversation with Mmantho that there was more to it than that: "During the fourth year of my stay in Johannesburg, I received a message from home that they have found me a husband." Working in the city was perhaps an excuse for the young Ernestina to avoid the obligation of an arranged marriage. "I refused that offer, arguing that I was working for my young brothers and sisters who were still at school." However, the demands of her rural family were relentless:

> That did not solve anything, because during my last year I received another message from home. There was no choice, they said it was not customary to give one a choice whether one wants to get married or not. I had to accept any husband they were in favour of. It was painful, because during those years most of us who were working in the Golden

City were being urbanised. We were beginning to look down on traditional marriage.[58]

Her grandmother, the stern upholder of tradition and arranger of the marriage, was unyielding, and Ernestina was reluctantly married to a man she was only to meet as a result of her more "modern" father's intervention. We pursue her story — and those of other women expected to marry those chosen for them — later.

To the young women whose very identities were bound up with the small community from which they had come, townward migration entailed some considerable cultural and ideological adjustments. By following their journeys to town and into labour, we may perhaps gain some ideas about how these adjustments took place, and with what resources to hand they were confronted. First, the journey. How would these young women travel to town? In some cases, and in the earlier times, partly by ox-wagon. Mrs. Setshedi remembers having to go from Phokeng to Rustenburg by hitching a lift with ox-wagons that were taking grain to the mill in town. Then from Rustenburg, she says, they would take a train to Pretoria, and then another from Pretoria to Johannesburg. Rosinah Setsome, although she was not brought up in Phokeng, talks of how travelling migrants would carry baskets of food with them on the train. Later, Ernestina Mekgwe took a train to Rustenburg from a siding near the chief's kraal, and from Rustenburg, she took another train to Johannesburg. Those who were not brought up right in Phokeng, such as Josephine Mokotedi, were less fortunate, in that they did not have a station right there. Josephine had to walk to the station at Boshoek, from Chaneng, and then catch the train to Pretoria. The journey itself was no doubt both exhilirating and frightening; tenuous threads connected the girl who was leaving with the place of her arrival. Nthana Mokale describes how

> I left Phokeng on 5th January 1927 for the Golden City. I was going there for the first time in my life. . . . I was all by myself. I had a piece of paper bearing the name and address of the person I was going to. Someone met me at the station. That piece of paper was fastened to my wrist [later she says it was in her pocket], with "here is Nthana, she will board a train to Johannesburg" on it.[59]

"How did the town appear to you when you first saw it?" another woman was asked. "It was very bright and scary in the evening," she replied. "It excited and also repulsed me. I didn't know where I was, or the direction in which Phokeng lay."[60]

If Phokeng was the centre of their world, then the places to which they migrated existed within a series of concentric circles surrounding their village. Indeed, patterns of migration often reflected a tentative "feeling-out" of places further and further from home, until Gauteng (Johannesburg, "the Golden City") was finally reached. Several young girls worked first on local farms and in Rustenburg; they then would move perhaps to Pretoria, before approaching the suburbs of Johannesburg. This hierarchy of occupations, hinted at in Mrs. Serokane's testimony, is reinforced by Mrs. Makgale: "After 1919, Granny, when you left school, where did you go and work?" asks Mmantho.

> I went to work on farms . . . the ones that are in Tlhabane, near the hills. We were making jam there.[61]

Who put you in the job?

There were many of us here in Phokeng who went job hunting, and this white man, who became our boss, usually came to Phokeng and Duiwelstroom during the orange season to look for people who would work for him.

Later, she went to Pretoria:

We were looking for green pastures . . . where we would get a job at the highest possible salary. Most of all, we wanted to work as domestic servants.

Did you enjoy working as domestic servants?

We enjoyed it very much.

Were the conditions better than those of your previous job?

Very much better. Don't forget that farm work is different from domestic work.

Following the hierarchy of occupations, she later moved from Pretoria to Johannesburg: "There were many reasons that made me leave Pretoria, including money. I wanted more money. . . . I earned more than I did at Sunnyside. My first payment in Johannesburg was three pounds, and that was a lot of money." Although Mrs. Makgale's father was also relatively well off, she places the earning of wages high on her list of priorities.[62]

Migration did not involve spending the long lonely periods away from home which the more distant migrant would experience. The surrounding towns and cities were relatively well known and understood, in ways that reflected the mental maps Bafokeng women held of their own rural universe. Just as the Phokeng area was divided up into sections, wards, areas, and villages, so was the urban domain. On the one hand, there was a clear perception of the different cities. On the other hand, there were suburbs within cities, which were perhaps the mental equivalent of the villages around Phokeng, and in each of which some cultural or historical connection with Phokeng needed to be made in order for it to be comprehended. So, the women talk of going to the area called "Malay Camp," an inner-city community, and of how this was where the Lutheran Church was.

However, while the city may have been mapped using mental symbols derived from the village universe, it was also very much a world "outside" that of Phokeng. The city—Gauteng—was definitely "different" from home. For one thing, the whites there were different. Ernestina Mekgwe says she was not afraid of whites, "because here in Tlhabane whites mixed and lived among blacks. We just took them to be like us and weren't working for them, but for the "big" whites in Johannesburg."[63]

In fact, if paternalism and feudal-like relationships were what Bafokeng were used to, then the women moved into the one urban occupation where these were most closely reproduced—that of domestic service, in the fledgling middle-class suburbs of the towns; places such as Parkview, which in 1925 was "just a very small suburb.... I think you are aware of that hill where Westcliff is located. Now, Parkview was just a small location next to that cliff. There was no place like

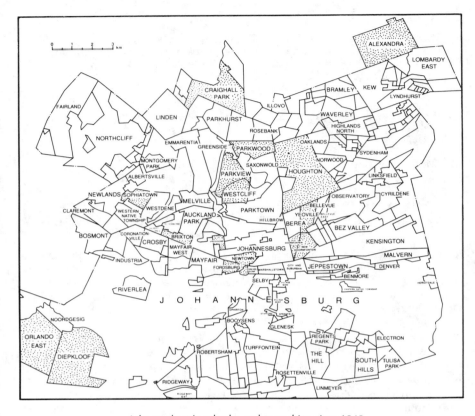

Johannesburg's suburbs and townships circa 1940

Forest Town during my first years in Johannesburg."[64] There, the women moved into small, backyard rooms in suburban gardens. Ernestina describes one in which she worked:

How big was their house?

From here to that tree. You could get lost if you did not know it well. It was behind mine. It was built like this [shows with her hands]. This is the white man's house. They have built a wall. This is my door, this is the laundry door, this is the door to the coal shed. This door leads to the boy's room. ... My room is facing the kitchen. It's not part of the house. I had a private door to use when I wanted to go into the white man's house. They said because I was a woman, if there is a surprise knock I must use that door.[65]

We should not assume that the choice of domestic service as an occupation was entirely accidental or a result only of the economics of the labour market. Important as larger structural forces were in steering women towards this type of work, from the point of view of their own consciousness of the situation, domestic service was a relatively good deal. For their vision did not appear to extend beyond the narrow choices society made available to them. We have already seen how teaching was mentally ruled out by more than one woman. It was a choice between one working-class occupation or another, and as one woman said, "firms" (meaning companies) were clearly "not for women." A number of factors reinforced domestic service as an occupational choice, ranging from their preparation for such work by missionaries to their acceptance of its paternalistic ideology. Domestic service was, according to Nthana Mokale, far better than farm work — and indeed it was perceived as offering a good income,[66] a means to the end of earning enough for the needs of the family, and for accumulating the protodowry that had come to be necessary to make a good marriage. The women's own instrumentalism was also at play here, and it served to retain their sense that they were coming to the city for their own reasons, and raiding it for the resources they needed for their own dreams to be fulfilled.

Raiding the city for its resources meant using what resources the women themselves could command to their best effect. Kin and community represented the most useful of these, and "home girl/boy networks" were the common means of actually finding a job. The process of providing a continual cultural universe in which the phenomenon of moving to the city could be perceived was structurally reinforced by the building of these networks, and they loom large in the women's consciousness, providing a vital and important part of their memory of the city.

By the 1920s, when most of the women migrated, patterns of closely networked migration amongst men and some older women had already been established. As Ernestina Mekgwe put it, "When one [man] found a job in Pretoria, he called his friends and relatives to follow him. The same applied to Johannesburg, Germiston and other towns."[67] Mrs. Mokale talks of how men "worked at Parkview or Parktown North [suburbs in Johannesburg, BB] because there were lots of dairies, butcheries, groceries, and blacksmiths. In fact they could be found all over the area. Some did gardening in the suburbs and others worked at firms in town."[68]

What began as male networking was later extended to women. Ernestina's brother had been the first in her family to migrate: "Was there any resentment towards his action [in migrating, BB] from your parents," asked Mmantho; "No, it had already been discussed among the elders at home, and it was decided that someone from the family should go out and learn the ways of the white man, as we couldn't all stay in our home and become ignorant of the things that go on around us," she replied.[69] By the time she herself went to Johannesburg, she had "some of my neighbours, who were older than I, already working in Johannesburg," as well as a relative: "I arrived at my relative's place of employment at Parktown and the following day, she took me where she had a job lined up for me."[70] She worked in Parkview for her first months, in 1925. She was nineteen years old. A cousin worked in the same suburb, and "we were great friends"; "one would have thought we were twin sisters, because we preferred to put on identical clothes."[71]

Naomi Setshedi's experience and that of her niece, Nthana Mokale, were linked. As Naomi said, "in most cases it happened that one had relatives working in Johannesburg already." Naomi's brother (Nthana's father) had gone to Johannesburg to work as a milk deliveryman in 1905, and clearly had a firm base in the northern suburbs, for Stanley Dairy, where he worked, was located in Parktown North, a middle-class white suburb. When Naomi decided to migrate, at age eighteen, her arrival was cushioned thus:

> When I arrived at Park Station, I asked people to show me a tram to
> Parkview. I found Stanley Dairy with ease, and my brother took me to
> one woman we were related to.... The following day I walked from
> street to street looking for a job. She directed me, otherwise I would
> have got lost in the maze of Johannesburg streets. I found that woman
> very helpful, because she also kept her ear to the ground, trying to find
> out whether there was a job for me. She ultimately got me a job.[72]

Nthana Mokale, who went in 1927 at nineteen, as we have seen, also used her
dairyman father, and now her aunt, as her network. With her piece of paper
attached to her wrist, she was met at Park Station by a young woman from the
village, Selina, another niece of Naomi's:

> Selina's younger sisters were Kentse, Monanki, and Nthanana. Some of
> them stay in this section of the village. Selina then took me to a place
> which was commonly known as Malay Camp, where we spent the night
> together. ... When I arrived there I was welcomed by Tswana-speaking
> people. Selina was also staying there. The next day we took *khepe* ... [a
> small horsedrawn carriage with a roof, owned by Indians, she adds
> later]. It took us to where my father used to work.[73]

Her father then took her to Naomi, who was by then working as a domestic in
Parktown North. "I stayed with her during that period when I was still looking
for a job." She found one around the corner, in Wexford Avenue, Parkview — the
suburb where many of the women from Phokeng worked.

Mmamatlakala Moje had similar experiences in Pretoria, where Roberts
Heights (called Voortrekkerhoogte today), a suburb where army personnel were
housed, became a key place of employment for Bafokeng:

> *Granny, how did it come about that you should first start by working at
> Roberts Heights in particular? Did you have relatives working there already?*
>
> There were many girls from our village who were working there
> already.... It happened one day before I could start working that one
> friend of mine approached me and told me that a certain white woman
> had asked her to help her to look for someone to work for her. I asked for
> permission from my mother, who agreed without hesitation. I therefore
> had to go with my friend to Roberts Heights when her leave was over.
> We finally arrived at her place of work.[74]

Josephine Mokotedi also worked in Roberts Heights, and was found a job by
friends and relatives from Phokeng.

What is striking about these women is that most of them seem to have used
these homegirl networks, building upon the good position in the labour market
that their male predecessors had established, in order to find jobs in the better-
paying suburbs. Their having learnt English was also important, and seems to have
given the work-seeking young women some bargaining power. Mrs. Mokotedi
gives the most vivid statement on this:

> *Could you write well?*
>
> Yes and easily.
>
> *You wrote in English or Afrikaans?*

In English. I can't write a single word in Afrikaans. We chose employers according to what language they spoke; if it was a Boer that spoke only Afrikaans, I would not chance employment under him because I would have problems conversing with him when employed. Even the Afrikaners when you went into their yard looking for a job and when he spoke to you and you said you didn't hear or understand what he's saying, he would retort "ons ook hoor nie"[75] and then chase you away. We were only interested in those who spoke [she switches to English] "come here," "you go there."[76]

Working in these relatively well off suburbs, the women seem to have been able to command reasonably high wages in many, if not all, cases. Mrs. Mokotedi was paid R12 a month (presumably she means £6) in the 1920s. Others got £3, and considered this to be a good wage. With these hard-earned wages, they bought furniture and other commodities, in many cases for purposes of investing in marriage.

You grannies were reaping off money in bulk weren't you?

Yes, and we bought kitchen cupboards, tables and chairs . . . from the Indian shops in Pretoria.[77]

Josephine "posted" them by train and they were collected at her home in Boshoek. Mrs. Mekgwe also bought a "lot" of furniture, clothing and lots of other things either at Indian shops or "in town."[78]

Because most of the domestic workers here seem to have occupied elite positions in the domestic labour market, hardly any of them were the only domestic in the household. "Women only cleaned and looked after children," says Mrs. Mekgwe. Male domestics, who had in earlier times monopolised domestic service and were still preponderant in the occupation,[79] often performed such jobs as gardening and cooking. Nthana Mokale says in one household in which she was employed, for example, "I was literally a monkey from Phokeng, I could only cook pap[80] and not casseroles." A Mosotho male did the cooking, serving, and gardening, while "I only cleaned house and looked after the kids, you know, like a nanny." In the evenings "he cooked the supper, set the table and dished out, while I would bathe the kids and put them to bed." He also washed and ironed the major laundry, while she did that of the children.[81] Mrs. Setsome was also a nanny in a household that contained a male cook and another Tswana woman.[82]

This did not mean that the work was not arduous. Mrs. Mekgwe talked of getting up at 5:00 every morning, and on Saturdays and Sundays at 6:00. The first thing she would do was make a fire, "on the coal stove since there were no electric stoves then." She then made breakfast, and packed sandwiches for the husband to take to work. Every evening she cooked a large dinner, washed the dishes, and then went to bed. Rosinah Setsome got up at 6:00, bathed and dressed the baby and gave her breakfast, and worked on general housework. She then took the baby to the park, and took him home to sleep. She left work just before sunset, after the employers had had supper. Nthana Mokale gives a grimmer picture, mentioning that on Fridays she had to get up at 3:00 in the morning to clean the coal stove, so that she could have tea and breakfast waiting for her employers before they went to work. On other mornings she would wake up at 5:00, and "there was no way you could oversleep because an alarm clock was set to wake you up every morning." Indeed, "The first thing you were provided with when you are hired as a servant is an alarm clock."[83] Mrs. Mokale, who later became a factory worker and lived in Sophiatown, resented what she experienced as the isolation of domestic service rather more than did other informants. She did not meet with friends, but would sit alone in the evenings, with a book or a bible, knitting or sewing. "There wasn't any other type of recreation available for us," she says.[84]

However, such loneliness was not always the case. Mrs. Mokale's rather solitary life seems to have been partly determined by the stringency of the routine kept by her employers, a German couple: "There were no leaves, no day off, nothing," she says; "When you worked for a white person he would keep you like his property or like his child." But others had different experiences, suggesting that what had begun as homegirl networks expanded into lasting friendships, which came to include Tswanas from farther afield than Phokeng. The isolation that domestic servants experienced, say, in Victorian England, appears to have been countered by the development of a rich suburban subculture, whose existence has been seriously underestimated in the literature on the subject.[85]

> *Were all your friends Tswanas from the same village with you?*
>
> Yes, we were friends from one village, and we regarded each other like brothers and sisters.
>
> *Did you have some friends from other places?*
>
> Yes, others were from Siega, Kgabalatsane, and other places.
>
> *That means they were all Tswanas?*
>
> Yes, Tswanas only.
>
> *Did you not have other friends who were Zulus, Pedis or Shoeshoes?*[86]
>
> No, they were not my friends. All my friends were Tswanas, talking the same language.[87]

These friendships embodied the older values of *gemeinschaft* that so many of the women remember nostalgically:

> Sometimes we visited our friends at their homes. We asked our parents' permission to visit those other villages. When arriving there I just feel at home because of their behaviour towards me. But now there is no love at all.[88]

In Mrs. Mekgwe's case, on Thursdays and Sundays she would work mornings, and then be "off."[89] She claims that the institution of "Thursdays off" was asked for by the domestics themselves, and was called "Shirley's day," a name introduced by the servants. "Each and every one goes out from the Kitchen and we are off. You sleep and start work [she switches to English] tomorrow morning."[90] On these "days" off, she would go to the Lutheran church at Malay Camp, to the Zoo Lake, or to visit friends. "Throughout Johannesburg and George Goch, there were people from my home town, there wasn't a place you wouldn't find them," she says.[91] However, she preferred her small circle of five or so friends, "we spent our time in the parks, just idle talking and sharing experiences." The self-perception of some of the women seems to have been that they and their friends constituted something of a social elite. Mrs. Mekgwe, when asked if she mixed with people in "Fietas," a mixed working-class, inner-city suburb, answers:

> I had many relatives in that place and also in Western Township, but what I'm telling you is this — we [she and friends] did not want to associate ourselves with them. We looked down on them as amoral and self-indulgent people, and thus spent our free time to ourselves at places like Zoo Lake.[92]

Time off was a time to dress smartly:

> *You must have liked church.*
>
> That was the only time we wore our best clothes. We strutted like cocks in our finery, the place was like a beauty competition, everyone seemingly intent on proving a point in fashion.... If you ever saw us dressed up for church you'd turn blue with envy. In those days Aunt Naomi was a real beauty, so light in complexion she looked coloured, and yes, she had an eye for clothes, that one. ... Her hair was pitch black, but it was not dyed.... We would plait and later loosen (our hair) and then comb it into various styles.
>
> *You must have been beautiful.*
>
> We were. Today girls are just breasts and armpits.[93]

If dignity could be retained in relation to the outer world of other working-class people, occupations, and living conditions, it was harder to sustain in the inner relationships constituting the white household. But once again, the memories of the women suggest that internal household relations were more complex than is suggested by a model of simple degradation. The discourses of paternalism — or in this case what might be called "maternalism," since it was usually with the white woman that most interactions were conducted — allowed room for employers to adhere sometimes more and sometimes less closely to the ideal model of protectiveness that the women appear to have held in their minds. Thus employers could be "good" or "bad." However bad employers were, they were still "yours":

> I went to Phokeng for Christmas only in 1927 and 1928, that was because my whites [*makgowa a ka*] had gone for a holiday those Christmases. Other than that you can work to your death without a break.[94]

We have seen how Mrs. Mokale perceived her employment for seven years as a domestic in rather grim terms. She shows considerable rancour: "You see," she says, "I spent the prime of my life cleaning white folks' houses and rearing their kids."[95] These were not generous liberals in her eyes. And yet, she seems to be constantly contrasting their employment practices with those of factories, suggesting that the flexibility offered by paternalistic employment practices were more compatible with the demands of the peasant economy to which she remained attached. You could get time off "if you found someone to replace you," she suggests; you could go home "if there was a funeral." Still, such occasions were rare:

So you only came to Phokeng when they either went for a holiday or when there was a death in the family?

During weekends she invited friends for teas, parties and you'd never get a chance to go anywhere.

Employers controlled everything. Even if you left work and tried to get employment with another white, your employer would "come and demand me back."[96] Employers, too, had networks:

Whites can get real fussy about such things. They will make it known to other whites in the neighbourhood that they are missing their nanny whom they would want to have back if her whereabouts are known. I naturally agreed to go back to him. His was a better place, and I was always given foodstuffs to send to my family at Phokeng.[97]

Mrs. Mokale seems to regret her failure to resist at the time, and she turns away a direct question about happiness:

. . . we never complained, just content.

Were you happy?

What we liked about being indoors was because our complexion lightened and turned very beautiful.[98]

Others relate tales of "good" whites. Ernestina Mekgwe worked for a liberal employer who "liked [black people] very much and was also involved in welfare projects in the township. They used to give blankets and food to old, destitute black people."[99] This liberal was regarded as "better" than most other "madams," because she respected her, in contrast with "other madams who shout at you constantly, showing you that you are nothing but a fool, a monkey. . . . She had such an easy attitude towards me that at times when she talked of her problems I would forget that she is my boss and regard her as my sister. I don't imply that they were always good to me but they did respect me and I respected them."[100] Sophie Serokane demonstrates a similar acceptance of the paternalism inherent in the idea of the good employer:[101]

I think I've worked for ten years for that family. I was their daughter. . . . Nowadays if you are working for whites, they make you feel that you are black, they are whites. We used to work for those kindhearted whites who treated blacks as though they were their children.[102]

Mahubi Makgale says possessively, "My family were kind and considerate,"[103] while Mrs. Moje says that even though she had to do almost all the domestic work, "I was very fortunate to be employed by that woman since she was very friendly. . . . I used to enjoy working there."[104] Ida Molefe speaks of the love that could arise in such situations: "My employers were good people who loved me very much,"[105] she says; they "kept her place" for her while she was away having a baby.

But some domestics combined the ideologies required of them by paternalism with a mentality of resistance that was facilitated by the difference between their language and that of their employer:

After learning English at school, is it not right that one should speak the language with its owners? Even if they don't care about learning my language it does not matter. She may think I am a fool for trying to speak as she does, but she is the bigger fool, because I sometimes speak about her or swear at her with a friend, in her presence, but she won't even hear us. I can plot with a friend to kill her and she won't suspect a thing.[106]

Paternalism and peasant rhythms of production appeared to be compatible in most households. Going home to see to harvests and to hand over money was the practice with these young women. Mokete Phalatse found an employer who would allow this seasonal work, even in Johannesburg. She describes an interesting transaction between paternalist and patriarch:

When your father wanted you home, did you just tell your employers that you were leaving and buzz off?

My father always informed me when the crops were ready for harvest.

Did he write you a letter?

Yes. I would take the letter to the employers and explain to them that I was wanted at home. My father usually wrote in June when I was to leave in July, so I served notice before I went home.[107]

However, while this may have suited the requirements of her family and community, it was not always to her personal advantage: "I couldn't adjust well in Johannesburg because whenever I was about to get used to the place my father would call me home."[108] Even Mrs. Mokale, with her grimmer experience, makes some concessions to Mmantho's persistent questioning:

Does that mean you spent seven years in that house?

The only time you left for home was when your employers went on holidays or when we attended funerals of our next of kin and friends, and that would only take a weekend.

Funerals took place during weekends?

Yes, you went early during the weekend and you returned before Monday. . . .

Didn't they allow you a chance especially during the summer months of the year when it's harvest time in Phokeng?

Unless when you found someone to fill your place, you couldn't go away.[109]

Thus Mrs. Mokale has had to concede that home visits were possible, although she certainly seems to have perceived the grudging way in which they appear to have been granted. This customary to-ing and fro-ing was not only important to the ongoing peasant economy, but would prove vital, later on, to women who wanted to have children and who found they could not afford to give up their jobs. Even Mrs Mokale says:

[I] would come home to deliver them. When they grew up and stopped suckling, I would leave them with my sisters and return to my work.

How long did you stay at home in those intervals? Was there anyone who substituted for you while you were at home?

Yes, and at times when I returned to Jo'burg I would go to a different white family for a job, but later my former employer would come and demand me back.[110]

Rosinah Setsome and Ida Molefe both talk of going home when necessary — either because of harvest or, when a replacement was obtained, to take a few months off to have a baby. Later in life, seeing children regularly became important, and women would go home two or three times a year to see their children, keeping contact with and an orientation towards Phokeng. Going home itself became a cultural institution:

We were taken by the bus *gaan en terug*. We went there [home] to help those whose relatives have died. At five you must be ready. The buses were two or three ... when the bus reached Tlhabane, we are at home. We visited the families which had had deaths.

The bus itself had a name — "diamond till."

When it approached it emanated the sound *Puuuu*. It rang, hit hard....

To announce that the people from the kitchens are coming?

Yes.[111]

Domestic work is normally cast as the ultimate experience of the colonised. Women who perform what is perceived by most as degrading work of a personalised nature, in the intimacy and feudal-like confines of the white household are, quite rightly, viewed by modern-day interpreters as victims of a system capable of inflicting particularly humiliating forms of subordination. We may ask whether these perceptions of domestic work accord with the self-concepts of these particular women, and how their memories of their first experiences of migration and domestic employment have been organised. The picture we obtain is far from simple. It reflects the fact that these young women were both wilfully independent, and caught up in the expectations of both the rural and the urban social institutions in which they were involved. Their consciousness reflects their desire to portray themselves as free agents, seeking to make sense of, and give cultural meaning to, their experiences, but also shows their awareness that their efforts were shaped and sometimes thwarted by the demands of their rural families, their own sense of duty, and the requirements of urban employers. It is not easy to characterise these women either as collaborators in their own oppression — the classic "deferential" workers of sociological tradition[112] — or as public, or even secret, resisters against it.[113] It would seem that actual, historically constructed consciousness is too complex for it to be forced into either of these two mutually exclusive categories, neither of which is capable of containing contradictions. In a later chapter, we continue to explore these themes, as what began for the women of Phokeng as a temporary adventure in the city unfolded into something altogether more long-lasting, and the world views of these peasant daughters and paternalists' servants required some realignments.

But what seems certain is that the moment of migration and all that it entailed was of crucial importance to the setting of a pattern of consciousness for the adolescents it affected. The historical circumstances of the coming of migrancy to Phokeng (which themselves had roots in a longer history) meant that people embraced it as much as they submitted to it; that they could, within admittedly narrow limits, choose occupations as much as have them forced upon them; and that they could think of themselves as actors as much as people acted upon.[114] These facts were to affect the women's evolving subjectivity over the next twenty years.

5

Courtship and Marriage, 1925–1940

Leaving home was, for the women, the first in a series of episodes of migration and city contact. Instead of seeing migration as a process of "oscillation" — an endless moving back and forth, with a cultural system constructed to suit — it may be useful to see it as a process that acquired cumulative meaning over time. Thus the women's own portrayal of their lives as migrants casts them as part of an evolving life strategy that passed through phases, each of which acquired a meaning which was built upon the one preceding it. The first of these entailed an escape from traditional constraints, but was also a means to accumulate the dowry they perceived to be necessary to make a good marriage. Once this marriage had been achieved, later spells in the city became the way in which the young family was to be supported. And finally, city work was a strategy through which women sought to accumulate sufficient savings to buy a house back in Phokeng. Central to these cumulative acts — although by no means the only motivation behind them — was the phenomenon of marriage, and the related activity of building a household. The attainment of marriage provided a goal for the first wave of migration, and the construction and maintenance of a household around the marriage a strong motivation around the second and third. All the time, however, the women sought to balance this core set of motivations against their other ambitions — for personal freedom and an escape from stifling traditionalism, for an income of their own, and for an encounter with modernity. We should not be fooled into thinking that these were simply traditionalists who saw marriage and nothing else. But the centrality of marriage to their conceptions of their life strategies warrants a separate discussion of the subject. In this chapter we examine the way in which the women experienced marriage, and how they handled the balancing act that was rendered necessary by their conflicting and sometimes contradictory ambitions.

Marriage itself, to the women, meant something quite different from what it meant to the protectors of the traditional order in Phokeng. In societies such as that of the Bafokeng, marriage alliances between lineages were a basis upon

which the power of patriarchal lineage heads were built, and the payment of
bridewealth by junior men a means of acquiring wealth by their seniors. Of
course once men became peasants, selling cash crops in a wider market, the
importance of bridewealth as a source of income must have declined. But its
symbolic and political importance did not. And when junior men and, even
worse, junior women, started migrating to town to earn their own incomes, this
forced chiefs and fathers alike to seek to exert new controls over them. As far as
men were concerned, tribal levies were imposed from the very beginning of
migrancy to Kimberley, as we have seen, so that men who earned money could
not use it as a means of breaking away. But the problem of independent women
was growing, so that by the 1930s, it began to be seen as a serious threat to
Bafokeng stability.

This only adds to the emphasis we have already made upon the assertiveness
inherent in the act of female migration. Although the city was at first both an
extension of, and an escape from, home for the young women in the first stages
of their migrancy—they kept their links with home, made and retained close
friendships with homegirls, went to the Lutheran church, went home frequently,
and sent money home—the very act of going to the city as Christianised young
girls who had already become relatively well educated, and who were avoiding
the direct control of parents, trying something new, earning their own incomes,
and accumulating their own dowries, was extraordinarily independent behaviour
for young women of the time. It contrasts quite strongly, for example, with the
situation in which their equivalents in Sekhukhuniland found themselves—a
region where Christianisation was less widespread, marriage ages were young,
and schooling of young girls was extremely limited.[1] Thus it is not surprising
that the phenomenon of female migration was deeply disturbing to the elders of
Phokeng and the guardians of its morality—who had anyway tried to stop it in
earlier times. Women were not supposed to challenge the traditional order at all,
let alone leave it. One chief talked of the "spoiling of our tribes" by the white
man, and this "spoiling" was symbolised for him by the fact that "girls" now
went out to work.[2]

To add to this, women at home were also quietly rebelling by not having as
many children as the community required. Amongst Christianised Bafokeng,
signs of the decay of this aspect of "traditionalism" in family life and structure
had begun to make themselves felt as early as the 1910s, during which time,
Penzhorn noted, a significant decline in birthrates had begun to appear: "the
birth figures are becoming less and less," he said to the Native Economic Commission in 1930, "There are very many households without children, and there
are many households with only two or three children."[3] Many Bafokeng families,
he noted, were smaller than those of neighbouring Boers.[4] He was unable to
explain this, mentioning that usually the "native," when he finds he does not
have enough children by one wife, simply takes another.

> I know the ordinary native. If he has a wife who has no child, then he
> will take a second wife simply with the idea of having children. If he is a
> Christian—well, he does not worry about that—he takes a second wife
> whether it is right or wrong. He does not care.... So, you can see, it is
> not voluntary, that they have small families. There is something wrong,
> and I cannot find out what the real reason is.[5]

Besides confirming the women's own perception that men were often fairly instrumental when it came to accepting the church's restrictions on polygyny, what his male-centred view failed to show was that while small families may not have been "voluntary" for the men, they might well have been for the women — and that the option of simply taking a second wife was less and less open to the male as women's assertiveness — and perhaps insistence on monogamy — increased. He himself mentions that rates of Christianisation were higher amongst women than amongst men ("There are many cases where the wife is a Christian, but the family is not; or simply the father is not a Christian"[6]), suggesting that the women perceived this as a means to independence themselves. Instead he attributed the decline in the birthrate to the "immoral" life led by many of the youth.

The theme of "immorality" looms large in this commission, concerning all who sought to understand why the rural order was under threat. Its prevalence suggests that female independence and assertiveness were threats not only to the economic and political order, but to the moral order as well. Women were redefining their own sexuality in ways not acceptable to those who would cast them as "reproductive" potential wives of respectable Bafokeng men:

> *Where do they [young girls] go?*
>
> To the cities. There are many of them who go to Pretoria and Johannesburg.
>
> *Could the conclusion be drawn that they fall into immorality rather rapidly?*
>
> Yes, the majority of them come back with children.[7]

Penzhorn's description was echoed by that of neighbouring chief Mamogale, who said, "It is a common complaint to all of us, that our daughters go into the towns and when they return some of them are pregnant. They have a child and they go away again, leaving the child with the tribe to be cared for, and when they come back again, they are in the same condition."[8] Mutle Mokgatle, brother of August Molotlegi, was even more outraged:

> All the boys and girls who are in the towns simply live to please themselves.... At their own homes they are not allowed to do as they like, but now where they are in the towns, when a boy meets a girl they will go and hire a room and they will live there as man and wife. They do not marry, but they simply live as man and wife.[9]

Another chief was shocked by the decline of the arranged marriage:

> In our *stads* [traditional Tswana towns], when a person marries it is his father or his mother who finds a wife for him. My father and my mother got me a wife. The woman will be my wife and I shall be her husband. Today, we are only hearing from the towns of what is going on there. We hear that in the towns, there are marriages that can be solemnised for six months. Now these bad people who like to stay in town please themselves, because they can marry in the towns and they stay a few months with a woman and then they can leave that woman and take another one.[10]

The parents of the pregnant young girl would, Penzhorn suggested, look for the *misdadiger*,[11] in order to punish him — a clear attempt to reinsert the role of seniors into sexual relationships:

I myself have seen many of those sorts of situations; I have said to the parents "you must find who it is and the 'misdadiger' must be punished." But they would say that it was almost impossible to find him, and they had given up, and so the "misdadiger" goes free.

The girl, it was believed, had invariably been "misled," usually by a "foreign kaffir, from another part of the country, perhaps from Pietersburg or Mafeking, or Swaziland; they meet in Johannesburg, or on the Witwatersrand, and so the thing happens." Some parents, in an attempt to find the youth, would travel to the city—but to no avail.[12]

The institution of *bogadi* had indeed ceased to play quite the traditional part in upholding orthodoxy. Not only do we see the emergence of a sense amongst the women that they needed to bring something into the marriage themselves (the furniture we have depicted as a form of dowry), but the peasantisation of the Bafokeng had transformed *bogadi* from its original purpose as a gift of cattle from the bridegroom's to the bride's father, which symbolised the commitment of both households to the marriage, to a more mercenary payment:

> I have been told by old natives, most of them are dead now, and we have only a few old men left, that it was a sort of a stamp to the marriage, a sort of cachet.... Originally, it was not a matter of trade at all, it was a matter of gift, pure and simple, and that is what all the old natives say.[13]

This commercialisation of *bogadi* meant that individual senior men could now use it as a means of private accumulation, and disrupt its functioning as a broader form of social cement:

> *I suppose it is the women you find who are most insistent on* lobola, *more so than the men?*

> .... Elsewhere it may be so, but here it is not so strongly the case. It is the father of course who is after the cattle. It puts him in a better position, and if he has a number of girls he will become a rich man.

More recently, young men would pay in cash, and suggest that their future father-in-law buy the cattle himself.[14]

But bridewealth prices had gone down in recent years, suggests Penzhorn: "Generally nowadays, it is about three or five [cattle]. In most instances it would be three," whereas "it used to be five or ten."[15] The institution's loss of legitimacy reflected the wider loss of traditional restraints upon the young, whether men or women. Neither the head of household, nor the chief, could sustain the kind of hold over young men which forced them to work for ever-longer periods of migrancy in order to pay their bridewealth. Attempts to make it higher or more stringent would only result in greater resistance. As one witness to the Native Economic Commission said, "*Lobola* is not compulsory here [as it then was in Natal, BB], but if the elders insist that it should be paid, and if the young men cannot pay it, what will that mean? It will mean that the girl and the young man will live in sin.... Many of our young girls will go to the goldfields and live with young kaffirs. There are many of our young men who are afraid to come home just because they are afraid of *lobola*."[16]

Things look different when viewed from the women's own standpoint— something which has been attempted relatively infrequently in the literature.[17] We have already suggested that to them, just as to the young men of Phokeng,

migration was not quite the flight into decadence that their elders imagined it to
be. Indeed, to a Mofokeng, marriage in most cases was one end (of several, it
should be reemphasised) toward which the first steps of migration were the
means. These were not women who sought to escape marriage altogether. Instead,
they sought marriage, but wished it to work in a way that fulfilled their broader
life ambitions. This is not surprising, in the light of the fact that marriage would
transform them from being people with junior status at home, working either for
their own fulfilment or to supply help to their parents' household, to increasingly
senior women with their own households to supply. But the elders and missionaries were right in one sense, for there was also a distinct intention on the part of
the women to alter the type and terms of the marriages they sought. How
were relationships entered into in the suburban backyard rooms in which the
young domestics lived, and in what terms were they understood by the women
themselves?

The women certainly did not perceive themselves as mere objects of exchange.
Nowhere in the interviews is there a sense that bridewealth entailed a simple
objectification of the women. And they did not accept the definitions of themselves
as "immoral" that missionaries, chiefs, and elders were attempting to impose
upon them.[18] Instead, they portray themselves as having been poised between
the obligations that lineage and community placed upon them, and their own
sense of purpose, subjective control, and justice in their personal lives.

Of course they were not the passive victims of seduction portrayed by their
elders. Even at home, the girls had been secretive about their real sexual
encounters:

> I was still growing up then but I was quite aware of changes in and
> around me. Boys used to write us letters proposing love to us, and I
> would go outside away from the prying eyes of my parents and read it
> there. Even at night, boys who were our neighbours used to come and
> spend the night with us, we slept with them in the same room, but our
> parents never suspected any of us to be promiscuous and thus, they
> didn't know anything.[19]

And when many of them moved to live in the suburbs of cities where the male-
female ratio was disproportionately high, and sexual advances from a variety of
men were likely, they sought to control the situation themselves. Yes, they were
now young girls in a situation where the "traditional" constraints on sexuality
were missing, and to their generalised fear of being in the city was added the fear
of unwanted sexual advances. But they evolved ways of defending themselves
against both—demonstrating considerable purposefulness, not to say feminine
solidarity, in the process. Like many of the other girls, Josephine Mokotedi
depended on her friends to keep fear and loneliness at bay:

> We always went to places where we had people that we knew from our
> homes and at times we slept with our friends in their rooms.

> *Were you scared of something?*

> Yes, after being used to sleeping with your sisters and brothers it was
> very scary to sleep in a room by myself.

> *Weren't you scared to walk around in the evening or stand with your friend
> on a path to talk?*

When we had completed our jobs for the day, we always waited for each other. We were about six girls and we slept in one room.[20]

Mrs. Serokane also speaks of the fear they felt:

I couldn't get used to the type of life of the Johannesburg people. I used to be scared of many things, you won't believe me if I tell you. All those girls who were from the same area used to gather in one room and spent the night together. At times one would find four women sharing one room. This would go on for some time until we got used to the place.

What were you afraid of?

We feared that people would break in the house and kill us.

I guess that by the time that you knocked off, it was late. Were you not afraid to move from your place of employment to that room in which you had to spend the night together?

We had to take rounds, collecting one another.[21]

Even in these early, relatively peaceful years the gangsters, who later were to become a more prominent part of city life, could be threatening. According to Mahubi Makgale, although "Johannesburg was not yet rough by then and we would travel from Brixton to Braamfontein at night without any fear," sometimes "we would come across *Malaita*[22] who used to do us no harm except to kiss us on our cheeks and then pass."[23] But these gangsters, "the real *Malaita*, from Pietersburg," were not dangerous:

They used to go around playing a "piano."[24]

Where?

At the "kitchens." They used to roam about in the suburbs and whenever they came across a woman, one of them would ask: "Choose the one you like best amongst us." One was compelled to make a choice and they would continue, saying: "Then kiss him." They usually left when one had satisfied them by kissing one of them.

Didn't you feel bad about it?

We did, but we knew that they would do us no harm if we carried out their instructions. Sometimes they would grab one's *doek* and go away.[25] We were afraid of arguing with them, but they were not as rough as those of today. Nowadays it is not safe to go alone during the night.[26]

Huddling together in suburban servants' quarters was also a means of protection against unwanted visits by men:

There were backyard rooms made especially for servants, that's where we lived. I used to spend the night with five other friends sleeping in one room, yet working for different families, but our employers did not mind. You'll find us packed on one bed like sardines.

What was it that you were scared of?

We believed that if one slept on her own in their own rooms, boys would enter our rooms at night and molest us.

Oh, that was very childish.

I still prefer that to little girls who act brave with boys at an early age and end up with unwanted pregnancies.[27]

Naomi Setshedi puts a feminist cast on this behaviour:

We used to enjoy working as domestic servants because we paid each other a visit. We had boyfriends but we didn't want them to sleep in our rooms. Whenever one of us knew that her boyfriend would be likely to pay her a visit, she would organise her friends to come and spend the evening with her so that the boyfriend could be inconvenienced.

What was the idea behind all that?

It was to make it impossible for the boyfriend to sleep with his girlfriend and to prevent pregnancy in a way. One would sometimes find ten people sleeping in one room.[28]

Friends provided solidarity even against more courtly male advances:

I remember one day after work I received a letter from a garden boy who worked near my employers. In the letter, he said so many things about love which I didn't even understand. It was so funny I showed it to my friends and we all laughed over that letter.... He was from Phokeng, he is still alive and he is a rich man with many buildings today. He is a distant relative and is a year older than I am. At last I bought an envelope and posted his very letter back to him.[29]

But the women's own high level of literacy was itself a formidable weapon. Thus Josephine Mokotedi:

We were taught English at Standard 5[30] and this came to be useful later when we were working.... Also when a man was pestering you and you didn't approve of his company, let alone his advances, you wrote him a letter in English, really telling him off.

How will he know that you are telling him off when he doesn't understand English?

That puts him off, because he wouldn't be able to read it, he would feel embarrassed to ask you to read it to him and thus wouldn't come near you again.

And when it's a guy that can read English, what happens then?

That's easier because he will know from the letter that you do not want his company and he will keep off.

The authority of the village supplemented the women's own armoury:

Didn't men pester you for your company in the towns?

They did try, but we weren't loose girls and if a man forced your company, touched your breast deliberately, you would cry and swear at him. And if perchance he came from Phokeng or Chaneng and you knew his home, you did report this insult to your parents and something would be done about it.

You would tell your parents that he held your breasts?

Yes. Even if he took your headdress, you reported this to your parents and a case would be taken to his parents.

Does he take your headdress to show that he loves you?

Yes.

In fact, Mrs. Mokotedi suggests, in spite of the presence of various types of threat, life was rather modest — perhaps as a result of the women's own successful barriers to unwanted sexual relations or assaults:

> We didn't have boyfriends.... These days you can't sleep twice with a girl when you are visiting her,[31] and a man doesn't come for her.[32]

Nthana Mokale also gives a picture of a time when new standards of decorum and etiquette prevailed, all channeled through the means of communication of the new society. Sexual relationships were still regulated — but by means constructed by the participants themselves, rather than their elders:

> *How were you able to meet with a man if he was interested in you?*
>
> He wrote a letter to you if he wanted to know you intimately. Didn't we go to school so that we could learn how to write? If a man saw you at the church or anywhere and was interested in you, he would write and propose to you through the post ... and if he didn't have your address he would find someone who did. He would find out everything he wanted to know about you.[33]

Nthana used to meet her lover every weekend, at a shop that sold the materials she needed for her sewing. But, she added, "Boys are problems, but we always declined the advances. We weren't as accommodating as you young ones tend to be." When her apparently chivalrous boyfriend was prevented from marrying her (by the fact of her arranged marriage to someone else), "he said he won't marry anyone else and he preferred to die unwed if he could not marry me." "Did he die before your husband's death?" "Yes, and he died a bachelor."[34]

In spite of this culture of modesty and chivalry, some of the girls did indeed become pregnant. Several of the interviewees had children by their boyfriends before they married.[35] But by the women's own standards of decency, as opposed to those of their erstwhile patriarchal controllers, this was fine if you subsequently married the father of your children, as did Mrs. Moje: "I only got married in church in 1940, but it was just for formality's sake, since we already had children together."[36] Mrs. Phalatse too says that she and her boyfriend "had been staying together for a long time and when we took our first son to be baptised at the church, they told us that our child could not be baptised in church because we had not married in church. Then we went to church and signed there."[37] Such patterns of delayed marriage were common and may have simply reflected the fact that marriage, in Tswana society, was more a "process" — a series of negotiations and manoevres, taking place over a number of years — than a single event. Still, this "processual" aspect of marriage was something which missionaries and administrators alike had tried to change in Africa,[38] and some of the women did internalise the stigma that they tried to attach to birth out of wedlock. Thus Nthana Mokale did not legalise her relationship until much later in life, and describes how "immorality" was stigmatised in the church:

> Can you see that I have a hat on [she points at her photograph, which was taken on her wedding day] instead of a headdress?
>
> *What is the significance of that?*

It means one got married after a fall.. ... At that time a woman who had no child was given more respect than the one who had a fall before marriage. . . . I had three children.[39]

But it is almost certain that much of what the patriarchs perceived as the "immoral" behaviour of the young women was in fact a way of delaying marriage itself; or of avoiding the imposition of an arranged one. Either way, it seems that the women were seeking to impose their own terms upon the marriages they sought. It is striking that for the fifteen women for whom the fullest information is available, the average age of marriage is as high as twenty-seven; and the highest age forty-three. And Nkwapa Ramorwesi, the one woman who never married the father of her children, suggests that this, too, had advantages — for the children remained "hers":

All of my children belong to one father but here in Phokeng it is not practical for a man to claim that he has children unless he has married the mother of his children. I think you practise the same thing too where you come from. One can't just give a man one's children. . . . Now these children are mine since he could not even afford to pay *lobola* for me.[40]

The strategy of avoiding or delaying marriage did not always succeed; elders and parents placed considerable pressures upon young girls still to conform to their expectations, and some succumbed. Ernestina Mekgwe's experiences are vividly recalled, in a way which brings to the fore her dramatic storytelling style. What is interesting about this story is that, although Ernestina eventually accepted her arranged marriage, she shows little sign of having any internalised sense that this was the right thing to do. Psychologically, therefore, she had freed herself from the acceptance of traditionalist definitions of marriage — a subtlety which it would perhaps be difficult to perceive from any other source than that of oral history. Ernestina, the independent migrant, is one day stopped from returning to Johannesburg after a visit home:

It happened that I went home with my cousin for a visit. We were great friends and we used to work in the same suburb. . . . It was during one of my usual Good Friday visits that my grandmother approached me and said: "You mustn't go back to Johannesburg, please remain behind because your father wants to talk to you." I realised later that they were through with negotiations concerning my marriage. My cousin went back to Johannesburg alone.

Ernestina's father, however, clearly balked at the prospect of this discussion, and handed the task back to her grandmother:

After her departure my father said to me: "Look, my daughter, I am your father and there is nothing I can discuss with you. Go to your grand-mother's place, she has something in store for you." I went there and granny, without beating about the bush, said to me, "Grandchild, you have no mother, she has long passed away, now you are old enough to get married. . . ."

Ernestina comments that, in fact, "I wasn't that old. I think I was about twenty-four years old." But granny continued:

"Now my grandchild, you have no choice to make, the only alternative that you have is to accept the man we are giving you. The mother of your prospective husband called here the one day. She told us that she has a son who is at present working in Benoni, and that she would appreciate it if her son could marry you. You have nothing to say, the man has been saving money with the intention that he will settle down as soon as he gets a wife."

Mmantho, somewhat appalled, asks "Was he someone you knew before?"

No, I didn't know him before. He was very much older than I was, in fact I was of the same age group as his youngest sister, Anna Mokua.

Ernestina protested:

I said to granny, "But I do not know him, how can I settle down with someone I do not know?" That did not move granny much, she was really stubborn, she went on to tell me that even if I did not know the name, they were through with negotiations. She said that they have seen the man already and were confident about him.

The young Ernestina was less confident:

Granny then exploded with laughter when I asked her "How are his eyes, does he have a squint?" [Laughter] She warned me not to mention such things in future. I said to her, "look granny, we are only two, there is no outsider, now how am I expected to react if that person has a squint?" Then she said that even if that man happened to have a squint, they were going to give him to me as a husband, they were sure that he was going to look after me properly.

He was being given to her, not her to him — and indeed, according to Ernestina, this form of arranged marriage was less harsh than that which had prevailed in earlier times. Her father tried to smooth the way:

After some few days, I think my father contacted my granny again. He suggested that since I was very young and knew nothing about that man, it was a good idea that I should see him. I guess we were better off those years, because our parents were not adhering very strictly to custom. We had the privilege of meeting our prospective partners before marriage.

The meeting was not as informative, however, as Ernestina hoped:

We greeted each other and sat at the table. Fortunately, there was a vase with flowers on the table. I could hide behind those flowers because I was very shy to look at the man who was supposed to be my husband in a month's time. His elder sister had to leave the two of us so that the man could express himself.... I felt uncomfortable in his presence, I could not speak freely with him.

She felt that there was little point in saying anything:

The only words I could say were yes and no. I really felt that I was a bore, but, with them everything is alright, even if you curse him, trying to show that you disapprove the whole thing.

Ernestina's real feeling about the marriage emerges at this point in the story:

He doesn't get worried?

Nothing, he believes that a woman who tries to insult one, is a potential housewife who is going to look after the house. Time and again I would hide behind that vase.

It came to your rescue.

It really came to my rescue, but, he was busy peeping at me, and hell, he made me feel very shy. I concluded that he was a playboy, he had learnt all those tricks of peeping at women in Johannesburg.

But her suitor then emerges as a more courteous — even romantic — figure:

He said, "my young sister, I received a message that you do not know me and I think it is true because you were very young when I left for the Golden City. I think you may be as young as my youngest sister. When my parents were telling me about you, I felt that I love you. I got attracted to you before I could meet you again even after such a long period. I have come home to marry you."

Ernestina remained unimpressed:

During his lengthy speech, I was very quiet, I could not utter a word. We were served with tea but I was even shy to have it. I was prepared to have my meal after he had left. As he was bidding me goodbye, he told me that he would be leaving for work the following day.... He said "Look, do you know where the bus stop is? Please stand at the corner of the street next to the bus stop so that I can see you, even if it will be at a distance." I got surprised. I could not understand why he wanted to see me the following day. When he finally said goodbye I did not allow him to touch me or kiss me. I even refused to open the door for him. You know such wild behaviour did not infuriate him.

Ernestina resigned herself to marriage, which, she insists, was not all that bad in those days; but her standards of comparison were low:

Even during the existence of a marriage, it was very rare to find a man beating his wife very horribly. Parents used to reprimand a man if he happened to beat up his wife. Sometimes he was given a severe punishment.[41]

Mmantho, after this interview, felt obliged to prompt Nthana Mokale on the same subject — and found psychological acceptance rather than rejection:

What happened when you have a lover around the area you are working at, and your parents had already earmarked someone to marry you. Did you object to your parents choice and opt for your choice?

Nthana insists arranged marriages had a purpose and meaning, which was why young women obeyed their parents.

We never went around looking for mates, if your parents had found someone to marry you, you stuck to their decision.

Even if this man they chose was disabled, say he had only one eye?

That was not important.

It must have been very tough on women.

No, it wasn't. Parents found a mate for everyone. There weren't many spinsters in our time.[42]

Nthana's traditionalism (which matches her political and social conservatism) is echoed in that of Mrs. Moje, who, however, manages to suggest some resistance to the whole system even while acknowledging its immoveability:

> *Granny, you have said that by 1930 you were chosen already as Mr. Moje's future wife.*

> In 1930! Jesus! It was long before that year, although I can't remember the exact year. It happened immediately after I had left school.

> *So you went to Pretoria knowing very well that you had a "husband" somewhere in Johannesburg?*

> Definitely. I knew very well who was going to marry me although it took him quite long before he could manage to marry me. I could not understand what was preventing him from marrying me. However, we eventually got married to each other, but it was at a time when I had lost hope of any marriage proposal from him.[43]

Mmadiate Makgale's experience was similar to that of Nthana, but her response was more ambiguous:

> My parents sent a message that I should come back home while I was at the Golden City. They had found me a husband who was one of my mother's aunt's sons.... I used to know [his mother] because she was still alive during my school days. But I didn't know the man who eventually became my husband during those years when I was still attending school.

This marriage had been arranged many years before:

> I was told that my husband once approached my mother concerning our marriage. Things became easier for him since he was a relative of ours. There is a story which goes that [when] I was about twelve years of age, my prospective husband, accompanied by his mother, once visited our family. His mother then chose me among my sisters to be her prospective daughter-in-law, but my husband was not satisfied about that choice. He wanted to marry my elder sister. My mother-in-law then advised him to get married to me since my sister was already a grown up and she argued that my sister was already more clever than he was.... Our parents advised him and said: "This one (my elder sister) is old enough to get married ... you can't choose her because you will be wasting her time. You better choose that one — referring to me — because she is still very young. He couldn't accept the situation, he said "But the one that you are talking about is still very young, she still uses her hand in cleaning her nose, she doesn't use a handkerchief or something else." He was then made to understand that by the time he could have decided to settle down for marriage I would have grown into a woman. So it happened that several years after their visit, he came back again and proposed marriage to me.

She was forced to give up other relationships:

> Now when I was already working at the Golden City I had a boyfriend from this village but I had to leave him because of pressure from my parents who wanted me to get married to that man who eventually became my husband.[44]

Mrs. Setshedi's marriage was not an arranged and loveless one, by contrast:

By the way, in which year were you married?

Not very long ago, in 1935, I was quite old at that time.

This man who married you, was he chosen for you by your parents or you met on your own?

We went to the same school and that's when he proposed love to me and we've been mates from that time until we married. He was staying and working in Kimberley.

Parental approval was important:

If getting married was easy as it is now, we could have wed just after we completed school, but my parents did not approve, and there was nothing I could do, only bide my time.[45]

Their affection was deep, and her mother did not impose an arranged marriage upon her:

At times we spent a full year without seeing each other, and I was waiting for him, I reserved my affections for him and awaited his arrival patiently ... we wrote often ... and I received a lot of offers for marriage while working in Johannesburg, but I turned them down. Some even sent their parents to negotiate with my mother, but she in turn declined their offers.[46]

Her mother's liberal attitude was far-reaching, even controversial for the time — and perhaps it is no coincidence that Naomi turned out to be the most politically active and radical of all the women in later years:

Had your husband's mother been to see your mother yet?

She had, and my mother told her that someone had promised to take my hand in marriage, so she was waiting for that person. One woman came in the same week that mother died, and my mother said to her, "even though its been a long time I've been waiting for my daughter's suitor, I am not in a hurry to marry her off to anyone. If that suitor does not fulfil her promise, my daughter shall find herself a man, even among the Matabele people."

Explaining this rather extraordinary statement, Naomi says: "Well, naturally, the Matabele are the Tswana's worst enemies, so what she meant was I could go and find myself a man anywhere in the world, even among my enemies."[47]

Although the women may have balked at, and at times escaped from, the requirements of their parents, in an attempt to delay or control the actual marriage, the institution of marriage itself is respected by most informants. The symbolism of marriage included other matters besides bridewealth — the clothes you wore told how you had moved from the protection of your own family to that of your husband — and Ernestina respected these:

Was it a compulsion to wear long dresses?

You had to put on a *doek* on your wedding day and leave all your old clothes and move to your husband's home with only your wedding clothes on and nothing else to tag along. Then you start afresh and buy new clothes of a length befitting a married lady [i.e., long].

But then you arrive at your in-laws without a wardrobe, do they buy you clothes then?

You first receive clothes from your in-laws as well as your home initially, from there you become your husband's responsibility.

But first you receive clothing from both sets of parents?

You receive a *doek*, an overall, and some blankets from your in-laws and wear them as what the English people call going-away clothes, and a suit for your husband too.[48]

Further traditional customs were imposed after the women had married, when it seems to have been expected of many of them that they would return to Phokeng, or to their husband's particular place, and live there as housewives; or return to the city either with or without their husbands, to work; or in the case of some, even live in the city as housewives. Whatever the particular configuration, it seems that marriage did imply that Bafokeng society expected something of the young women — typically, an increased recognition of the power and role of their newly acquired mother-in-law in the women's lives. Nthana Mokale says "I had to go stay with my in-laws.... I stayed with [her mother-in-law] for several years."

But a vision of a future household not under the strict control of seniors did exist. The furniture that these young women had worked so hard to accumulate was brought into the marriage, but was intended for the couple's future household rather than for that of the parents-in-law:

You worked so as to buy yourself all things that you would need for your new house if you got married. You could instead buy such basic utensils like pots and dishes until such a time that you're married, when you could then purchase the furniture to keep your utensils in.

When finding that your in-laws have such furniture, where will you keep your items, because they tell you explicitly not to touch articles that belong to them?

That means a jumble of household articles will accumulate in the house because each occupant must have their own things. Every male member of the family who is married and lives in his parents' house together with his wife will eventually have to go and build his own house; when such a time arises they will take their belongings with them.

When coming to your in-laws with your own furniture, were you provided with a room where you could keep it?

If you had such a room you kept your things in it. In most cases your in-laws will have a house with many rooms including a room where all cooking is done and thus the room that you sleep in together with your husband, will be the room where your belongings are kept.[49]

Where this future household was to be situated was crucial. Since most of the women were working as domestic servants at the time of their marriage, and since most of their husbands were also in city work, the question arose as to whether the new household would be based in the city or in Phokeng. The women split into two groups at this point. For the smaller group, marriage entailed a move home and a permanent engagement with the declining peasant economy. For some this was because their husbands forbade them to continue working. Thus the apparently liberal employers of Josephine Mokotedi, who worked in Roberts Heights, Pretoria, were formally informed of her marriage and the likely attitude of her husband:

> In 1929, when they left on a three months leave, I came home and on the third month of my holiday I got married; now since they were sending me my pay through the post I wrote them on that third month and told them stop the payments. I also advised that I might not becoming back after those holidays because as I was now married I was not sure whether my husband will allow me to go back to work or prefer me to stay at home and raise a family.[50]

And indeed, she did stop working, for a while at least. But her relationship with employers entailed more than a simple, breakable contract:

> I only went there again later after giving birth to my first child in 1930 and that was because my former employers wanted to see me and make sure that I was truly married and not staying away because I had a grudge against them or something like that.... They received me with open smiles and gave me presents and money.

But servanthood prevailed: "They then asked me to do their laundry while I was staying at my husband's quarters."[51] Josephine does not make it clear whether she thought this request was further evidence of their kindness.

Mahubi Makgale also stopped working around the time of her marriage, but does not give that as a specific reason for stopping:

> I didn't work for many years. I only worked for three years at Carole Street and after those three years I had to go home to get married. I did come back and worked only for a year. My mother passed away after that year and I had to go stay at home.[52]

She too suggests that such departures did not always signify the end of a relationship with employers, for she describes how her employers thought she would return—but in the end she did not.[53] Nthana Mokale also "had to" leave her job when she was about to get married when she went to stay with her parents-in-law in Phokeng.[54]

However, very few women became rural housewives and farmers. A far larger proportion, having had a taste of the city and of some of the relative freedoms it provided, did not want to give it up. Mrs. Moje puts it thus:

> My employer told me that I should go home for a while and then come back after six months to see if they were back. I did go home and stayed for some time.
>
> *Did you enjoy your stay in the village after spending several years working in the white area?*
>
> I could not enjoy that life any more. Before long I approached my mother and told her that I was leaving for work.[55]

For women such as these, a commitment to marriage, usually to a man with urban connections, was not perceived as simply a commitment to the role of the traditional Bafokeng wife. Instead, they sought to build their marriage and their households in the urban setting itself—and thus to pursue the independence they had already obtained through city work. One woman was asked:

Granny, you said that when you left school, your intention was to help your father in building a comfortable house at your place. Where was that house then?

Since I was married, I couldn't go back to it. I had tasted already what it was to be independent, therefore I couldn't go back home and be under my parents' authority.[56]

Of course, rurally based and fully traditional marriages had been rendered unlikely anyway by the 1930s, because of the limits to Bafokeng expansion outlined in Chapter 4. By the time of their marriage, few husbands or wives were in a position to envisage a permanent return to the land. Not only had their mentalities become transformed, so that cash incomes and urban life styles were considered normal, but the Bafokeng economy proved increasingly unable to support the children of the once-rich peasantry. Bafokeng traditionalism may have succeeded in drawing at least some of the women back into the village for the brief period immediately after marriage — but in the longer run, it was mainly as urban mothers, wives, and matriarchs that the women were to build their households.

Still, the women did not have to live in the cities. They could have remained on the land, as thousands of wives of migrants have done throughout South African history, living off remittances from their husbands as the peasant economy declined, and constructing *de facto* female-headed households there. Those women who became urban wives and mothers had exercised at least some choice in doing so. Thus in this, as in other respects, the women themselves asserted their own interests in the making of their marriages. How they built households, found a place in the city, and continued to balance their various conflicting personal goals in a volatile situation, is the subject of the next chapter.

6

Respectable Matrons, 1930–1945

For a number of the women marriage was followed by a second phase of living in town. This was something specific to their generation. Older women such as Setswammung Mokgatle had either never worked in town at all, or had, as in the case of Mmadiphoko Mokgatle, only worked for a short time until children were born. Mmadiphoko was, in fact, appalled at the idea of the city mother:

> Who could have looked after my children whilst I was working in Johannesburg? Tell me, who would have been prepared to carry one's load, carrying one's children piggyback style whilst one is away on employment? ... Am I a fool to abandon my children whilst I am still living? A person who neglects her children and deserts them for employment is an idiot. What does she think about them? I find such people's actions to be mind-intoxicating. What does such a person think about her own flesh and blood which she has given birth to? When God has given them to her to look after them and care for them? My children were all raised here at home.... With you young generation of today, it is quite different—you employ people to look after your children whilst you are at work, isn't it?

Mmantho asks whether it is perhaps "not due to lack of finance that we go out from home and seek employment?" But to Mmadiphoko this is itself caused by living in the city:

> Correct. When one is living in Johannesburg, there is nothing that one can do about this issue because one is living in a rented house, one is obliged to pay rent, buy household items, groceries, all those things need money, so that one has no option but to enlist the help of a person who will look after one's children. But, what can one do when one is living in a village? Where can one get a person who is prepared to take care of one's children?

Mmadiphoko does not see the point of working in the city at all, revealing a distinct absence of any internalised ideology of the value of what she sees as simply monotonous and alienated urban "work":

Now, granny, did you not go back to Johannesburg?

Here I am, you can see me where I am. What could have prompted me to go back to Johannesburg.

Did you not go back for employment?

Working for what reason? Working in a job that is perpetual. In the end I benefit nothing, I end being wasted physically.... One works until one has grey hair. I find that women who are working here in Tlhabane are better off because they are able to spend some time with their children. Employers nowadays are a bit reasonable because their jobs afford their employees time to be with their families. Those who are not live-in servants are ones strained by travelling to and fro, to their places of employment during hot days.[1]

But Mmadiphoko's premodern philosophy was inappropriate for several of the younger women, who had little or no means of survival on the land. By the 1930s, the Bafokeng peasant economy had been prevented from expanding, and this ensured that those born in the 1900s, unlike their parents, could not build and support a household without engaging in a relationship with the city. Their world views had, accordingly, to change. To the women who had sought an urban sojourn as an end in itself, and who had met and married men with similar ambitions, it became both desirable and necessary to work in the city.

So far, the city had been, to the women, a series of white suburbs, each containing white households of different economic and cultural standing, whose social meaning was mediated by the "homegirl" nexus. Largely black townships, such as Vrededorp or Marabastad, had been places to visit. They had some cultural landmarks—the Lutheran church, the relative's house. But they were not seriously engaged with. Now these places—where most urban blacks who did not have a room in a suburban backyard were required, by the laws of urban segregation, to live—came into focus. Each woman lived for varying lengths of time in one or more of a variety of different townships, including Alexandra and Sophiatown (the two freehold townships in Johannesburg)—Fietas (Vrededorp), Meadowlands, Emdeni, Dobsonville, Twa Twa, Marabastad, Julia Location, Kotiti, Vergenoeg, Malay Camp and even Nyanga in Cape Town.

In analysing the structural position that the women and their families came to attain in the city, it is useful to divide the women's sojourn there roughly into two eras. In the first, that of the early and mid-1930s, the period during which the women established their families, a process which had begun much earlier continued, and the Bafokeng families we are examining became part of it. This was the process of the establishment of a "respectable" stratum of the urban working class, which appears to have originated in the early part of the century from better-off sharecropping and peasant economies in the Transvaal and Free State, and some parts of Lesotho.[2] In the later period, which began in about the mid-1930s and continued right up until the Apartheid government of 1948 called a halt to it, the social configuration of the townships was substantially altered with the coming in of new waves of far less "respectable" immigrants, from the weaker strata in Lesotho or Natal,[3] whose situation had often been undermined by the more complete destruction of precapitalist productive and social systems[4] and by more far-reaching migracy by men, the analysis of whom has dominated the literature. As we shall see in the next chapter, the women who saw themselves as "respectable" could not adapt to the arrival of the "disreputables." At first, they expressed dislike and anxiety at the violence and decay which the new urban influx had brought. Later, when the 1948 National Party government compounded the situation by attacking some of the social bases of their livelihood, the women who had chosen to stay in the city adopted more defensive positions, as their phase of compatibility with city life came to an end.

The cities into which the women now moved — roughly in the 1930s — were segregated, although less strictly than under the post-1948 government. Blacks — sometimes alongside whites, "Coloureds" and Indians — lived in designated free-hold "townships" not particularly far from the city centres, such as Alexandra or Sophiatown in Johannesburg, or Marabastad in Pretoria; in less formally defined areas, such as the slumyards of Doornfontein; or in the racially much more heterogeneous inner-city suburb of Vrededorp (Fietas). Large, distant, and entirely African townships such as came to constitute Soweto, were a later creation. The distinguishing feature of some of these earlier townships, compared with later times, was that blacks were often permitted to own stands within them. The black population was thus rapidly divided into those with the wherewithal to buy these stands — and we shall see that at least one of the women had aspirations to do the same — and those less well off residents who rented backyard rooms and shacks from the standholders, the group to which most of the women belonged. But often ties between standholders and tenants were complexly mediated by kinship relations in ways that made it difficult to identify hard-and-fast classes.[5] Furthermore, as we shall see in the case of the women and their husbands, often the decision not to buy a stand was less a matter of lacking the financial strength to do so, than of lacking the desire to remain permanently in the city. Many Bafokeng with fairly good incomes chose not to buy in Johannesburg because they envisaged their long-term future as being back in Phokeng.

The tenant population itself came to constitute the two strata discussed above — the "respectables" and the "disreputables." Like many inhabitants of the black townships of the 1920s and 1930s, the families from Phokeng occupied a particular structural, cultural, and moral space. While they were not generally standholders, they did form a group with distinctive characteristics. As we have seen, they were drawn from a less than completely undermined rural economy, from which they had brought fairly high standards of literacy and education, and very clear-cut notions of Christian respectability. Their proletarianisation had not taken harshly gender-distinct patterns, as it had in the case of migrants, say, from Lesotho.[6] The occupations they or their husbands undertook were not those of the lowliest proletarians, but rather tended to revolve around service industries and the less sleazy end of the informal sector. We shall see that their marriages appear to have been relatively stable and often took a Westernised form. They sought educational advancement and social mobility, if not for themselves, then for their children. And their ideological and cultural perceptions of city life reflected these things. In addition, city and state authorities in these interwar years tended to want to promote and support the values of "respectability" embodied by these families.[7] It has been suggested that "respectables" such as these constituted the backbone of prewar township political and cultural life, including providing the key constituency of support for ANC or Communist

Party politics.[8] Certainly it is obvious that they constituted a very different political constituency from, say, that which supported the populist pseudotribal and charismatic politics of squatter leaders such as James Mpanza in the 1940s.[9]

Tswanas in general, and Bafokeng in particular, appear to have regarded themselves as something of an urban elite, and even though these women did not envisage staying permanently in the city, they had connections with standholders, and with the aspirant and actual middle class of the black city, some of them Tswana, who did. Frances Nameng suggests that Tswanas were leading standholders in Alexandra: "In Alexandra things were a bit tight. Most of the people staying there were Tswana-speaking and most of them were standholders."[10] Rosinah Setsome had an indirect relationship with a standholder:

> We didn't pay rent because we occupied one of my sister-in-law's backyard rooms.
>
> *How did your sister-in-law get a house in Alexandra?*
>
> She got married to a Northern Sotho man whose family lived in Alexandra.
>
> *Did they have a plot on which to build their house?*
>
> Yes, they had two plots, one in Alexandra, and another one in Sophiatown.
>
> *How could one own a plot in those areas?*
>
> They were not so expensive then. One could buy a plot and build some houses for tenants. It was common to find a big house belonging to the owner of the plot with several rooms in the yard for tenants.[11]

But Mrs. Setshedi suggests that although the Bafokeng regarded themselves as an elite within the city, in fact they did not own stands to any significant extent. Tswana strength and confidence lay in their continuing links to comparatively viable peasant economies:

> We argued that we had our permanent homes at Magaliesberg; therefore, we could not buy plots in Johannesburg as if we were Coloureds who did not know where they belong.... The Xhosas, Southern Sothos, Shangaans, Ndebele, Pedi started buying plots except Tswanas. Very few Tswanas bought plots because most of them argued that they have villages where they belong. They looked down on other ethnic groups when they decided to live permanently in Alexandra.[12]

Several other women make it clear that they did not imagine that they would stay in the townships forever. A strong perception was that while it was acceptable and even desirable to live in townships for a part of one's life, township life was immoral, violent, and corrupt—and became increasingly so as time went on. Many families assumed that their stay in town was temporary, and that they would ultimately return home:

> *You had always intended to return to Phokeng?*
>
> Yes, even when I was at Twatwa, I knew that we lived there because he was working there, later we were going to return to Phokeng.
>
> *What was it that made you to prefer rural life in Phokeng and dislike town life in Johannesburg?*

I did not like the people in towns.

What did you not like about them?

Life was not pleasant in townships, you'd find a man and his wife drunkenly fighting and swearing at each other in the street. The next day another man is beating his wife because she had slept next door with another man. Being in the midst of such decadence is just not for me. I come from Phokeng, it's a small community where people are friendly and respect each other.[13]

Rosinah Setsome echoes this perception:

When you were still working in Johannesburg, were you still prepared to come and stay here in Phokeng?

Yes, I was prepared, because I preferred staying at the village than at the location.

Was there anything that annoyed you in Johannesburg?

Nothing annoyed me, I just did not like it from the start. Another thing was that the Johannesburg people were fighting, so I was dissatisfied.[14]

High rents were also to blame for this strategy, as we shall see in Chapter 9. We shall also see that the line dividing those who stayed from those who set their sights on going back was a thin one.

Perhaps it was their good position as respectables, plus their self-confidence as former rich peasants, that led many of the women to remember their early years in the townships as a relatively happy time, in spite of their cynicism about the city as a permanent home. This contrasts with their later perceptions of the coming of violence discussed in the next chapter. Mrs. Setshedi and her husband rented a two-roomed house in Alexandra for £1 per month, as, she says, did many from her village. She speaks with nostalgia of her life in the freehold township:

Alexandra was a very good place for poor people. We used to love it for that. When a youngster from our villages wanted to work in Johannesburg, it was usual to find him going to Alexandra to get himself a "pass" so that he could look for a job. Almost all youngsters who went to Sophiatown on their arrival from the villages would finally get a "pass" in Alexandra. It was very simple to get a pass. All we had to do was to go with the boy to the Help Committee[15] offices in Alexandra. We then had to introduce him to the committee which gave him a "pass" without any fuss.[16]

Nthana Mokale echoes this nostalgia when talking of Sophiatown:

Sophiatown could be compared with Phokeng, it was "England." [Laughter] Life in Sophiatown was very enjoyable.[17]

Frances Nameng also had experience of Sophiatown, and is able to make a favourable comparison with Alexandra:

Now in Sophiatown the Tswana-speaking people were scattered among whites. They were in houses built by the same company that built for whites, but whites had to make themselves comfortable first.

Were you getting on well with your landlords, that is, the standowners?

They were limiting water for us, and our toilets were flushable. The place was clean, believe you me. It was not in the least as dirty as Alexandra. I disliked [Alexandra] mainly for the soiled water that flowed from broken sewerage, thus emitting a terrible smell all over the place and moreover their rooms were too small.

Was the five rand you were paying for electricity, water, and the like?

Electricity was excluded because we didn't have one inside our homes. Electric lights were out in the streets. We used paraffin as a substitute for electricity. . . . That was for the standowners only. They rented quite a lot of rooms to different people, and you would find that people were clustered around the stand.[18]

Her standowner landlord, a Mr. Nhlapo, was a Swazi who was "clean and tidy," and did not allow his tenants to use a *paola* (brazier), but insisted on a proper stove, because "a primus stove and a *paola*" would soil his ceilings and walls.[19] He was alive at the time of the interview, and his story seems to confirm the argument of some that standholders were the basis for an emerging bourgeoisie,[20] for he became a coal dealer who stayed in the elite Soweto suburb of Dube. "He owned many stands in Sophiatown while he himself stayed in a very big house with lots and lots of servants.[21]

Nostalgic memories of freehold townships are mainly evoked when the women are asked to remember their lives in relationship to the lives of other settled, respectable, family-living blacks — a common way of recalling things to Mmantho. In these terms, Bafokeng city dwellers were not the worst off, and had a certain status. What the interviews allow us to explore is the way in which this respectable working class constructed itself, how its members distinguished themselves from the later "disreputables," and how their notions of their own respectability affected their political and cultural consciousness. The main arena for such an exploration must be that of the evolution of household and work.

While the nature of work and the construction of the household were inextricably intertwined, in the women's minds it was the construction of the household that took pride of place. How did this process evolve in what was often a hostile environment, and how did it draw women into an engagement with a wider world?

It is useful to see the women as active participants in the construction of their own households, rather than as passive victims of the arbitrary requirements of "reproduction." Of course, the process of household construction took place within clear structural constraints, provided by the economies of the city and of Phokeng, by the needs of children, and a variety of other factors. But the women worked and schemed to overcome or find ways around these constraints, to operate the system to suit their own requirements. Although their designs were not always successful, their own self-image is that of people who regarded the city as a place that provided resources which they could use, albeit inadequately and often at a price.

It was the bearing and rearing of children that was at the very heart of the women's household strategy. Wanting to have children and bring them up themselves was what had drawn the women out of domestic service; actually having children to look after led them into informal sector activities whenever possible; and seeking social mobility for their children was a key motivating factor in the women's assessment of the good and bad sides of urban life. Later, their desire to give their grandchildren a "proper" cultural heritage also shaped their decisions. How did this core strategy emerge and become enmeshed with the other institutions with which the women were surrounded?

Having children often preceded marriage, as we have suggested, and certainly followed it. And almost every woman stated that she had wanted children. In part, this desire must have been shaped by the socialisation process in Phokeng. From their girlhood, the women of Phokeng had been taught how to care for babies and children, and were expected to bear them. Sophie Serokane, talking of her childhood, says:

> We used to carry babies on our backs whenever our mothers went to church or to work at the fields.

> *Did you not have an instance where you had to look after babies who are still being breastfed?*

> There was. The mother would leave the baby and some milk for him. When the baby is hungry one would feed the baby with the milk.... We had no feeding bottles by then. Mothers used to hold milk in their mouths then they would feed the babies through their mouths. It is as though one is kissing the baby.

> *Is that in a case where a baby is difficult to feed with a mug?*

> Yes, that was also to facilitate faster feeding of the child so that one could attend to other chores. Feeding bottles were not yet available by then.[22]

Ernestina Mekgwe also describes how

> our mothers looked after them [young children] but we carried them on our back throughout most ... of the day, and periodically during the day you gave it some boiled milk to drink. If it was an infant, your mother took it with her on her back while going about her other jobs. Those of two years stayed with us at home. We fed them and carried them on our backs.[23]

Nthana Mokale reinforces this interpretation:

> If you are the eldest you have to look after them [younger brothers and sisters].

> *What did the mother do if you had to do all these?*

> She attends wedding ceremonies and funerals whilst the eldest child looked after the smaller ones. My mother once went to Johannesburg for one year, and I had to help rear the younger children.

> *Does that mean you were left along with other kids to look after?*

> I stayed with them so much that I learned how to shave a head. I shaved them with a table knife, their hair was running beserk on their heads and something had to be done, so I tried the best I could.

> *With a table knife, granny?*

> Of course. An eating table knife. I sharpened it and tried my luck.

Fortunately all went well, and when my mother returned in 1926, she was surprised to find a barber in her house.[24]

She was still at school at the time, but in the protected environment of Phokeng, this did not matter.

How did you manage with all the responsibility?

I left the little ones at home and went to school. The main advantage was that our houses were clustered close together and people from one yard could see what was happening in another. So I prepared their meals for the day and went to school. . . .

You had quite a difficult time?

It was enjoyable, though, I cooked them vegetables and fed them very well with so little, mainly with *kgodu*[25].

But one cannot ignore the extent to which the bearing of children was an expressed goal of the women themselves — something more than a predetermined effect of socialisation. "I wanted more children, but my husband died," said Ernestina Mekgwe,[26] and in adulthood, the women interviewed bore many children, at least by modern Western standards. The average number of children born for the married women for whom information is fullest, was 5.6 — although this appears to have been low compared to the numbers of children borne by their mothers and grandmothers, as we have seen Penzhorn suggesting. But the average disguised large variations. Dikeledi Makgale had twelve children, of whom seven died; another woman had ten, of whom four died; and two had nine, of whom four and six respectively died. Certainly high rates of child mortality must have motivated women to want more children, if only to ensure that some survived to assist them in their old age.[27] Of the average of 5.6 births, an average of 2.5 died, although some of these deaths were not in childhood. But this instrumental view of childbearing must obscure its more complex meaning to the women. What were some of the individual experiences disguised by these mechanical figures?

Women were symbolically valued in terms of which children they had borne. Indeed several of them are primarily known by Tswana naming custom as "mother of" (Mma-Diate is mother of Diate; Mma-Diphoko is mother of Diphoko).[28] Barrenness was stigmatised. Mmadiate Makgale's first child was born retarded, and she waited a long time — eleven years — before having another. During this time, her husband's family made it clear that steps would have to be taken if she did not fall pregnant again soon, an attitude Mmadiate accepted:

My sister-in-law was complaining. . . . She was encouraging my husband to adopt the children of his brother, and marry his brother's wife as a second wife. His brother had deliberately left his family here in Phokeng and was staying with another woman at the Golden City. What made things more difficult was that even the woman who was left behind here in Phokeng was not lawfully married. He didn't pay *bogadi* for her, the only thing that he did was to build a house for her. My sister-in-law, therefore, wanted my husband to pay *bogadi* for that woman so that she could rightfully belong to our clan. . . . I would say that my sister-in-law who acted as my mother-in-law was getting worried about my being infertile.[29]

Becoming urbanised did not mean the women accepted "modern" ideas in this sphere of their lives. A number express the view that traditional ideologies and practices were much better suited to giving birth and rearing children than were modern ideas—and most went home to Phokeng to give birth. Mrs. Mekgwe was asked of her children:

> *Were they born in the traditional Setswana manner?*

> Yes, not with pills or injections. The injections condemn a person's health.[30]

Her belief in traditional medicine and childrearing practices is strong. All her children were healthy "because I breastfed them, not bottled milk. You'll find a child playing with the milk bottle, prodding the teat into the ground then putting it in its mouth, and that is unhealthy because there are a lot of germs in the soil and sooner or later that child is going to fall ill."[31] Ernestina denies—to a disbelieving Mmantho—that in those days there were any serious illnesses.

> *Things like small-pox, measles ...?*

> There was nothing like that, *niks*. Those sicknesses came with whites and their type of life. We were just ordinary people living in our grass-thatched houses, without heaters, sheets, or cough mixtures, but our children were always healthy.[32]

The children were seen as the bearers of the lineage or the broader ethnic heritage. They should, for example, preferably be born of relationships that were identifiably Tswana. Mmadiate Makgale mentions with some fascination that "sometimes people have children who are not completely Tswana," and that in extreme cases these might even be the children of white fathers. This, she suggests, could only be a result of some sort of immoral behaviour (so the women, too, had their own criteria for immorality), or perhaps a liaison designed to test out barrenness. She tells this extraordinary tale: "When we were [coming] from work during our times, you would find a Jewish man standing on a street corner with his organ out, having lump sums of money in his hand ...." If you thought you may be barren, "You would then agree when a white man says "hey, here is money":

> *Now granny, did it ever occur that people should conceive white children during those times?*

> Yes they did. Those who were still novices in the profession begot such children.... At my birthplace Chaneng, there was a woman who gave birth to a white child. She was an elder sister to ... you know ... they are just imbeciles, those folks.

She mentions another at Luka, suggesting that such births were to be ashamed of:

> When the child was born, the mother was asked who the father was. It was found that the father was a Jew. However, the child passed away after birth. We were then saved the disgrace.[33]

It is not surprising, given the generalised patriarchy of the society, that boys were valued more highly than girls. Mrs. Mokale suggests she was fortunate that all six of her children were boys, not because of any concern with the lineage, but because boys were off one's hands sooner than girls:

> When I looked at girls of the same age as my boys, I found many of them having five, three, four, or even six children, but still staying with their parents. Many of them were not married.... Sometimes one would come across a girl having five children, each of them having her or his own father different from that of all the rest. I was so grateful that I had to look up and said "Thanks, God, for having refused me with baby girls." I thanked God for not having given me baby girls, otherwise I wouldn't have managed to build this house.

But in old age, what were the advantages of early distancing now become the disadvantages of a lack of contact:

> *Granny, didn't you have a negative attitude towards the idea of having boys only, without a single girl in the house?*
>
> No, I never looked at it as a problem. It is only now recently when I have to kneel down with those swollen knees and clean that I have begun thinking that it would have been better if I had a daughter who could be helping me.[34]

Most of the women describe times when their children had suffered serious illness or had died; these descriptions often reveal feelings of helplessness, particularly in the context of Western medicines and hospitals. Jacobeth Lekalake talks of the pain she felt at the deaths of her children — and of her need for the church:

> I was having a lot of children, boys and girls.
>
> *How many were they?*
>
> I do not remember well, some of them died when they were already mothers. Some died when they were also fathers. Even their children are also not all here, some have died too; their graves are all here in Rustenburg.
>
> *Do you still remember them all?*
>
> My first child was Hendric, he just disappeared from home. Another one was Daniel; he had an accident, was knocked down by a car and broke his hand; another one is Francinah, younger than Daniel, another one is Petros, named after his father, he was a very sickly person. Actually there were seven in all. Nine died, and I am only left with two, Francinah and Petros.[35]

She left Spooner's church, although her children had gone to school there, because

> At Spooner's church they did not care about me and my family. My children got sick and eventually died, not even one of the church members ever came to see me. Only pastor Spooner visited me. Then, I decided to leave.[36]

She joined the Catholic church, who now care for her and bring her a sacrament.

Unlike the households of the "disreputables," the Bafokeng urban households into which children were born were sometimes structured in recognisably "Western" ways. The women's husbands were often the main breadwinners.

They had full-time jobs, in the entrenched "soft" positions the earliest Bafokeng migrants had established for themselves — as shop assistants, security guards, dairymen, butchers' assistants, policemen, or delivery men.[37] Naomi Setshedi's husband, for example, first worked in a bakery, and then worked in a grocery shop, weighing food and packaging it.[38] Another was asked:

> Where in the towns did most of the menfolk find employment?

> When one found a job in Pretoria, he called his friends and relatives to follow him. The same applies to Johannesburg, Germiston and other towns. They worked in grocery shops, chemists and so on.[39]

Patriarchal concepts from home were easily transferred to town. Ernestina Mekgwe said that at home she had been taught that "the husband is the head. You must not trade words with him."[40] Although most of the women worked, as we shall see below, housework and childcare were mainly, although not exclusively, their responsibility. Only one interviewee, the exceptionally independent Mrs. Setshedi, gives detailed descriptions of internal household arrangements, and even in her case, substantial cooperation between herself, her husband, and her children did not exempt her from taking primary responsibility for the running of the household:

> Did your husband ever try to help you whenever you were busy making dresses?

> With what?

> I mean with domestic work like cooking or cleaning the house?

> No, it never occurred to us that men can help with domestic work when a wife is around.

Mmantho tries to probe the underlying beliefs:

> In other words you didn't like him to help you, or did he argue that the work was yours?

> I felt that I had to cook for my husband,

However, Mrs. Setshedi does acknowledge what contribution her husband made to the home:

> But there was something I could not cook very well, thick porridge. What I would do was to boil water in the saucepan and wait for my husband to come home and ask him to mix it for me.... Most of our men can cook good thick porridge.

> Granny, did he also help in looking after the children?

> Yes, as far as looking after the children was concerned, he used to help me. But there was nothing much he could do because he always came home tired after working hard at work.[41]

Mmantho's questioning goes further:

> But both of you were working hard?

> He always found children clean, only waiting for their supper so that they could go and sleep. I used to wash them everyday before supper.

> Was he used to playing with the kids?

You know what, my husband was a religious man. Every day when supper was over, he would gather the family to the table, read the scriptures, and explain to the children. He was also fond of teaching them arithmetic and helping them in reading English.... When he started working he enrolled at night school. He attended lessons until he could read and write English.... He was therefore able to help children with English and arithmetic. Every evening he would ask them to show him what they had been doing during the day.[42]

Ida Molefe's husband appears to have been exceptional: "I would usually come home to a lit fire and cooking pots with delicious fragrance drifting through the air," she said, adding, "He was not the macho man sort who would like to make his wife his prisoner."[43] Ernestina Mekgwe's husband sometimes also helped with the housework; he would sweep, cook, and generally treat her "well." But all this was within strict limits: "when a child starts crying, he helps me by making up the bed, but he said that if he can sweep he will turn stupid."[44] Children also provided household labour:

I was very fortunate to stay next to a butchery. What usually happened was that before leaving for work I would give my son, a firstborn in the family, some money to buy meat so that I could find everything available at home. I used to say to him: "When you start cooking, your father should find pots on the stove already when he comes back from work." When I arrived home, I would take over from him and finish up cooking.[45]

She was primarily responsible for cooking:

I used to like well-prepared food. [Laughter] Even on Saturdays I would go personally to the butchery to look for tasty meat. Under normal circumstances I would buy short rib to be cooked the following day on Sunday. I never made a mistake of leaving out potatoes and rice. On Sunday morning I would order the children to make a fire, we had a coal stove, and in the meantime get busy peeling potatoes and whatever needed to be peeled.

Did the kids not help in peeling?

No. They too, were busy cleaning the house.[46]

She taught her firstborn how to cook eventually, and to clean the house before school on mornings when she went to Dunkeld to do washing. "We had no problem because the house was very small, he could finish cleaning it in good time." When she arrived home from work she would check their cleaning, and "do some washing since they could not wash their clothes very clean . . . sometimes I would even iron them in the evening if they were dry."

One or two of the women talk about the internal financial arrangements within the household. In Mrs. Setshedi's case, a joint financial strategy seems to have emerged, a sense of income pooling:

Granny, who in your household had a greater say on how you should spend your earnings?

What we used to do was that my husband would give me his earnings to save. It happened, on many occasions, that I felt I was being extravagant. I would then complain to him that we were not saving enough when money was in my hands. The following month I would shift responsibility to him, giving him all the money in the house to take care of. My husband would take care of that money while it was still in the house.

Did you not deposit money at the bank?

He used to deposit it at the bank but he preferred to keep it at home until he had accumulated enough to deposit it at the bank. However, whenever he felt like shifting the responsibility of taking care of the money back to me, he would do it without any problem.[47]

Actual daily spending seems also to have been Naomi's responsibility: "I would buy everything I needed and go home. We women were made to understand that a woman should see to it that there is enough food in the house." Taking financial responsibility for food went along with taking responsibility for its type, variety, and preparation:

[A wife] must know the type of food she is going to entertain her husband with when he arrives from work.... In my household I was free to buy any type of food I wished to buy, unlike in other households where the husband was very strict on food and would go all out buying food for his wife.[48]

However, the overwhelming impression this gives of a "nuclear" family structure needs at least some modification. We know that the women had already shown wilfulness and independence from patriarchal control at home. We should remember that constructing the household was very much presented as a task that women both wanted and needed to undertake themselves. There are times in the interviews when the women suggest that the powers over the children which the Tswana marriage relationship gave to the husband were too great for them to tolerate, and where they express the view that the children were morally, if not always legally, "theirs." After Ernestina Mekgwe was widowed, she was reluctant to remarry, because, she suggested, her second husband would not necessarily pay for her children's school fees, and indeed his presence may have prevented her from supporting them herself: "I stayed alone. I took them to school. If I had another husband, who would have paid for their schooling? I hated a man like a prison. I wanted to look after my children."[49] Perhaps it was because she "hated a man like a prison" that Mrs. Mekgwe delayed her second marriage so that her children could see for themselves if the second husband "was not good for us. When we have a fight in the middle of the night and I am forced to make a fast exit, I just pick up my things and go, I don't have any babies to carry."[50]

It was the priority given to the household strategy that shaped the relationship of the women to the economy and the township. For the women, previously engaged in domestic labour, the choice of living in the township, and the desire to construct and maintain a household meant a change in the nature and purpose of earning an income. Working as a young domestic had been about breaking free, accumulating some sort of dowry, and supplementing parental income at home. Work now became necessary to help construct and support the women's own households. Building and maintaining the domestic economy was an activity often undertaken jointly by man and woman, and work outside of the domestic domain was seen, at least by the women, mainly as a means to this end. The instrumental attitude towards work which they had displayed in their earlier days continued.

However, constructing and maintaining a household economy in the city could not be undertaken without the establishment of a far deeper relationship with the city itself. Protected as they were from the desperate proletarian condition that led poorer immigrants into the city into prostitution and the sleazier side of liquor brewing, even these women now found themselves having to confront the city far more boldly. Like Naomi, those who wished or needed to work had to find forms of employment that could be combined with housework and childcare. To understand why this requirement usually landed them in the informal sector, let us examine some of the other employment options open to them, and explore their compatibility or otherwise with the women's wider goals.

At first glance, domestic service appears to have been suitable. We have already seen how it had adapted to the peasant economy to which the women were still attached. Many women had an experience similar to that of Ida Molefe, who benefited from paternalism when her first child was born, because she went home to Phokeng to give birth in 1936, and her employers held her domestic job for her: "My employers were very good people who loved me very much. I was very much at home with them," she says.[51] But this system depended upon the commitment and economic security of kin at home, a factor that certainly worked for some. Nkwapa Ramorwesi, for example, worked in Cape Town for thirty years, and her children were brought up entirely by her mother. She left when they were small, and came back "to find them married." When asked "How do you feel about that," she simply replied, "I used to send them clothing and money to buy groceries."[52]

But most of the women did not place such expectations upon mothers and mothers-in-law for long. Perhaps the decreasing viability of Phokeng, plus their own notions that they should themselves care for their children, drew them into focussing on creating a fully fledged household in the city, rather than a divided migrant household. This inevitably entailed leaving full-time, live-in domestic service. Mrs. Molefe says, for example, that she eventually moved to the township, where she became a washerwoman, because "My children were still too young for me to sleep at my place of employment."[53] As Mrs. Mokale put it, it was those who "had kids" who "stayed at their homes brewing liquor to sell." Anyway, the township permitted them to live in ways that were inconceivable to the live-in domestic or to the Phokeng peasant. Even Mrs. Mokale, who lived an unhappy life as a factory worker, talks about some of the freedoms provided by town life — she "couldn't tolerate stay-in":

> One Sunday I had to be off, while the next one I had to look after the children while their parents were out at night. That was not the condition I wanted to work under. I wanted to be off every Sunday so that I could attend the church service at Malay Camp. There was a Lutheran Church there.[54]

Becoming a full-time housewife was a rare possibility for one or two of the women. Ernestina Mekgwe and her first husband, Thomas, got married in 1930 and lived in Benoni (Twatwa) where he worked in a grocery shop, for the seven years of their short-lived marriage. He died in 1937. In those years they had three children, and Ernestina stayed at home. "I used to do domestic work, clean the house, cook or do some washing," she said.[55] "He didn't want me to work while he was working." All three children were born in Phokeng — she went back home for each confinement. "When I was pregnant, I came back home and the old women looked after me and helped me deliver."[56]

But generally speaking, neither of these options was compatible with the women's other goals. If one wanted or had to live in the townships, the choice was between factory work, and engaging in the informal sector. The former type of work had its own set of compulsions and problems. Ongoing kin networks helped. One woman, Dikeledi Makgale, who continued to work after marriage but stayed in the orbit of Phokeng, worked in Rustenburg, where she and her husband lived with his parents. Her husband worked in Bewelspoort, and she worked at a tobacco factory in Rustenburg; her children were cared for at home:

> I stayed for a long time looking for a job, and afterwards I found a job at a tobacco factory in Rustenburg. I worked there for twenty years.... I was packing tobacco into grades and as time goes on I started teaching the newly employed staff how that work was done.

> *When did you leave that job?*

> I do not remember well which year it was, the only thing is that I worked for twenty years. I retired because my feet were no longer strong enough to stand for a long time, and so I was afraid I would become crippled.[57]

But if kin were not available, who was to care for the children? For some in the township, people could be found:

> *Now, with whom did you leave your children when you went to work?*

> They were of schoolgoing age by then.

> *I mean when they were still [too] young to be admitted to school.*

> I used to leave them with a childminder, just as it is being done in the townships nowadays.[58]

But the experience of those who went into factories — and such jobs were not easily available anyway[59] — was not a happy one. Nthana Mokale had six children, and benefited neither from a husband at home, nor a mother or mother-in-law in Phokeng. Three of her children were born before marriage (she was the woman who "fell") and three after marriage. At first Mrs. Mokale, like many other women, alternated between working as a domestic and returning for childbirth and breastfeeding on the one hand, and staying at home in Phokeng as a housewife on the other, until she was widowed in 1946. She returned to domestic work, leaving her children with her mother-in-law in Phokeng. But when her mother-in-law became too old to care for the children in the village, she had to change jobs. She left domestic service, and took a job in a factory: "I worked for twenty-one years at H. Jones and Company, processing jam, tomato sauce, and other things.... I used to earn five rand a week when I first joined the company," a salary that, she says, was far better than any earned in domestic work.[60] If she included overtime work, she could earn up to ten or twelve rand a week.

But in spite of these economic advantages, factory work was far more grinding than either domestic work or work in the informal sector. It lacked the cushion of paternalism, for one thing. Nthana, for example, felt the boss was mean:

> *Granny, were you sometimes given some fruit to take home?*

> No, we never got anything unless we bought some. Our boss was very strict on the workers. For instance, he could even go to an extent of

dismissing a person when he finds him or her licking his hands at work.... One of our duties was to peel fruit, and we were not allowed to lick our hands in the process.[61]

Besides the absence of gifts, the small flexibilities that paternalistic arrangements in domestic work allowed the women were absent. As she said, "At H. Jones and company there weren't any Christmas or New Year holidays."[62] Thus the harsher factory environment made no concessions to the peasant economy as domestic service had done. Domestic service adapted to migrancy, whereas proletarian labour did not.

Factory labour also entailed what were perceived as far longer hours — perhaps because the long hours of domestic work were tempered by their location in the suburbs and the youthful and migrant status of the women, who had no children waiting for them at home each night. Nthana said that she had no time to look after her children:

> Honestly, I had no time. At Christmas I used to look for someone to bake for them. I would give them some money for groceries and leave them behind. I never enjoyed staying with my children.[63]

When she worked overtime, it would be from 5:30 A.M. to 11:00 P.M. and her children would be left with friends. "If you had friends working as servants in the nearby white suburbs you asked them to look after your child until you returned from work. If there was no one you knew then you had problems," she said, adding:

> It's long that I have been struggling.

You really struggled, of course.

> Having to wake up every morning and leave behind my children still asleep.

In 1948, the family moved to Sophiatown, where they all lived in one room, at a cost of fifteen shillings a month. But being a factory worker cut Nthana off from township events:

> When those Sophia gangs were caught by the police, I was at work. I had been working since December and I worked until the next December without stopping; there wasn't anything I saw myself.[64]

Nthana also lacked the social support of kin and community, which appears to have given both domestic servants and informal sector women comfort. She was a lone Mofokeng on the assembly line, and gives us a rare glimpse of her experiences there:

> I worked on the canning machine.... The machine had a conveyor belt and after foods were put into the cans, they were moved by the belt and emptied into some pots where they were to be processed.... I packed them onto the machines, on other days I offloaded them from the machine onto trays and on other days I worked in the sauces section. I washed tomato sauce bottles after they were bottled so that they would be in a clean condition when they are sold; we also cleaned the labels printed on them and all.

Did you also stick labels on the bottles?

Yes, we did that too.

Were there Coloured workers?

They were only time keepers.

What did the white workers do?

They mainly worked in the offices. There were some Boers, namely Koos and Billy, who worked with us when cooking the pots.

Women were in control of the line:

Who were your foremen?

In the women's section we had Agnes, Dorah, and Grace. One supervised the tables where food was processed, another supervised the canning machine while the other looked after the tomato sauce section.

To which nationality did the foremen belong?

Grace was a Mofurutshe, Agnes was a South Sotho, and Dorah was a Swazi woman.

There was a Mofokeng national there, by any chance?

I was the only one among some four thousand workers.... I was the only Mofokeng person, and even when I left that company I was still the only one.[65]

We shall examine the effect of her structural position as a factory worker on Nthana Mokale's consciousness in a later chapter.

It is not surprising, given the disadvantages to them of domestic work and factory work, and the economic impossibility of becoming full-time housewives, that the most adventurous and secure women established a place for themselves in the less formal side of the urban economy. Rejecting the constraints of both servanthood and factory labour, neither of which were particularly profitable, and both of which prevented them from engaging fully with their own households, they moved into the activities of petty entrepreneurship that the volatile urban economy and burgeoning working class culture opened to them.[66] For example, becoming an independent washerwoman rather than a full time live-in servant — one of the most common options for township women — meant that you could build upon paternalistic expectations to expand your commitments to the household. One woman says that while employed (by various employers) as a washerwoman, she could maintain her household in the city with some flexibility:

I would never go to work when my child fell ill. I would send a message by one of the women who worked in the same area that I worked to tell my employer about the child's illness, and that I wouldn't be able to come to work ... they would say nothing against it. My child, whites were reasonable enough during those years. They were not like whites of this century who would have said "Go back and stay at home as long as you like," having got an excuse for employing a new servant. Our employers would wait for their servants until they had solved their problems.[67]

There were numerous other ways of making money, each of which entailed finding a market, a cultural and moral rationale, and a degree of compatibility with the household.[68] The most independent and entrepreneurial of the women, Naomi Setshedi, seems to have experienced most of them. While living in Alexandra Township, she undertook dressmaking, finding a market amongst the peoples and cultures around her:

> At weekends I would do some cuttings in the evening, and wake up at six o'clock the following day to sew. I had a sewing machine. I used to make dresses for babies and sell them.

> *Did it earn you a lot of money?*

> Yes, enough to keep my family going.... They were very cheap. I used to sell those the size of a four-year-old for twelve shillings. Bonnets were very reasonable, I used to sell them at two shillings. ... I didn't follow any pattern from the book. Later on I started making dresses for old people also. I began making blouses and dresses for women who belonged to a particular society. Our traditional aprons used to sell for twelve shillings if one had brought along her material.

> *In other words, it was not compulsory for one to bring along her own materials?*

> It wasn't. In most cases I had to buy material and sell the dresses to who happened to like them.[69]

Mrs. Setshedi did washing as well ("My washing days were Monday, Tuesday and Wednesday"), and she also used to sell apples in the streets. This drew her into the company of women who were almost, but not quite, homegirls:

> I used to go and sell apples with a group of women from Bethanie, a village near Brits. They are the ones who introduced me into that business of selling apples, mangoes, and other fruits.

This time, she found a market amongst the middle classes:

> Do you know where Market and Commissioner streets are? We used to sit down on the pavement with big bales of fruit beside us.... Madams would also buy something when passing by. When all of the fruits had been sold out, I would go back to the market and buy again.

This was a relatively profitable activity:

> Sometimes I would bring home five pounds a day.

> *I guess it was more than what you earned from doing washing.*

> Yes, it was. But sometimes one could only bring three pounds home and we never complained. We consoled ourselves by saying that God would give us more in future.

Mrs. Setshedi emphasises that it was to the end of supporting her family that she did it: "On Saturdays we used to knock off at twelve o'clock. It was then that we were able to buy groceries for our children."[70]

Engagement with the informal sector did at times contradict the women's own self-image as respectable people. However profitable it might have been, selling fruit on the streets was not considered dignified for the young Tswana woman, who, perhaps for the first time, was drawn into the consideration of the different "ethnic" characteristics of those around her, and of what it actually meant to belong to the category "Tswana":

Ndebele, Pedi, Shangaan, these groups were not cooperative.... Jesus, they were more cunning than the Tswana group, they used to sell bananas, cabbages, and some other vegetables and fruit at the bus-stop terminus. The Tswanas were shy to stand in the street selling fruits or vegetables.... It was scandalous among Tswanas to listen to people saying "I have seen so-and-so's mother selling fruits or vegetables in the street." When I started selling in town, I had to sit down and think before I could venture into that business. One day, when I was busy selling, one man I was acquainted to shouted at me and said "Mma-Josefa, why do you stand there selling apples in the street when on the other hand Joseph is busy working to support you and the children?" I felt so humiliated that I could not even answer to that. Most of the people excluding Tswanas were not even ashamed of it. They continued selling vegetables and fruit even after they had moved to Soweto. We were ashamed of doing that.

Later, however, some thought it was somewhat squeamish to have felt such shame:

We realised later that we had been wasting our time, we could have been making profits out of selling fruits or vegetables like any other ethnic group. They used to go to the station selling coffee, tea, cigarettes and other things in what we used to call "coffee carts." The law was not strict with people who sell on the street by then.[71]

Much more proper was the effort of Mmadiate Makgale, who used to supplement her income as a domestic by crocheting in the evenings:

Where did you go whenever you were off duty?

Sometimes I would visit my relatives, but I preferred staying in my room crocheting. People used to buy my crocheted articles.... Dressmaking also was not a problem to me, but nowadays I do not do it any more because I am suffering from asthma. Dressmaking earned me a lot of money while I was working at the Golden City. I was so interested in dressmaking that I could not even try the business of liquor brewing. My parents also didn't like brewing liquor for sale. In actual fact, they hated liquor.[72]

Once she left domestic work, she returned to sewing as a more substantial means of earning a living: "When I left domestic work, I then relied on my hands. I started sewing aprons for people." In her old age, she still crocheted collarettes for Anglican church women to wear over their uniforms. Women would order the collarettes, pay for the cotton and then she would charge them five rand for labour.[73]

A great variety of informal sector activities was available thus, some respectable, others less so. Moketi Phalatse made money through selling "fat cakes" (a Boer delicacy, *vetkoek*) possibly while selling liquor.[74] Mrs. Moje, like other women, earned money in the semi-legal sphere of Chinese gambling, or *fah-fee*:

I was also involved in gambling. One day I was arrested for having something to do with the "China gambling...." Jesus, I used to try my luck almost anywhere. I was acting as a "second runner."[75]

Were you lucky with that sort of gambling?

My people used to be fortunate and I was also lucky in predicting the correct number. It happened on many occasions when the numbers of different "bags" were called out, that Mrs. Ackerman would ask: "Wie is nommer twee?"

Who was Mrs. Ackerman?

She was the woman who was ranking at the top of the gambling.

Was she Afrikaans-speaking or what?

She was Coloured. My "bag" used to predict her correct number on many occasions.

In her case too, this was an activity strongly based on the need to support the household:

Did you find gambling helpful to you?

To a large extent. The money that I earned from gambling was enough to keep us going. I didn't feel the strain of maintaining the family when my husband was ill in hospital.[76]

Mrs. Setshedi confirms that *stokvels*[77] were also a marginally immoral means of raising money, if not making it:

I used to sell apples anyway and the profit that I made out of that enabled me to be able to contribute something whenever we had a *stokvel*.

Yes?

But I was doing it against my conscience.

How did you run your stokvels?

A *stokvel* was usually formed by more than two people. I was very often involved in a *stokvel* having eight to ten members. Each member was expected to give a specified amount of money, for instance four or five rand, to a member in whose house the *stokvel* happened to be held. We used to make sure that each member of the *stokvel* had a chance of having the *stokvel* in her house before we could start the round all over again.

Did you say that stokvels *were helpful to you?*

Yes, I found them very helpful.[78]

Undertaking liquor brewing and selling — by far the most profitable home-based activity[79] — was not for every Bafokeng matron. While finding a market amongst the burgeoning black township population was no problem, of all the informal sector activities, it required the most robustly flexible morality. Nthana Mokale, for example, the factory worker who had professed decorum and modesty in her relationships with boyfriends in the suburbs, was asked:

In the suburbs, did any of you brew liquor?

We didn't touch liquor, we hated it, and even to this day we didn't drink it.

She expresses a general hostility to the township culture into which most women were drawn:

Weren't there any women's clubs or places where women met for recreation?

We did not attend *stokvels* or clubs. Only women who didn't mind to have their names degraded by being participants in such lowly gatherings attended these clubs. Drinking and being merry in this fashion wasn't our line. We were only interested in working and keeping our jobs, and not at things we didn't come out here for, like what was happening at places like Malay Camp and Fietas.[80]

Ernestina Mekgwe, the stay-at-home housewife, also finds the brewing of beer morally unacceptable:

Didn't you brew liquor?

No, we were against liquor. Very much against liquor.

She contrasts the structured discipline of "traditional" drinking with the decadence of more modern times:

Even at home we did not drink liquor. We did not brew liquor. If a boy sees you he wouldn't marry you. Even the boys did not drink.... A boy of about nineteen or twenty years old did not drink liquor. When he reaches the age of thirty he can drink at home. You will hear the old man saying today this boy can start drinking liquor. He is given liquor and he goes to drink whenever he wants. They respected him very much. He calls his friend, same age group, and drinks with him. You sit far away under a tree and drink with your friend. They were not like these of today.

Today, she laments, these standards have declined: "You find a woman sitting and drinking with young boys," she says.[81] She suggests that the subversive liquor selling that was to prevail in later times had not yet penetrated suburbia:

At that time the women were very scared to venture into such practices, but today they sell homebrews and bottled beer and spirits; there are *shebeens* all over the white suburbs though the madams don't know it.[82]

She even suggests that "we didn't even think of doing such things, because we had never done them where we came from, so why should we start now when we are supposed to be concentrating on our jobs?"[83] But in fact, she gives a vivid description of the part played by young girls in the provision of liquor in her childhood. During the "Rebellie"[84] in 1914, she says, when "English-speaking people were fighting against the Boers," a group of English soldiers settled near the Phokeng post office. At one stage they passed through the village on horses:

We were aware that they were asking for something and the only word we could understand was beer. They said, "we want beer." That sister took a calabash and gave the soldiers home-brewed beer with beer foam pouring out of the calabash.... They were really enjoying it, one gulp was enough to make a soldier ask for some more beer. They called other soldiers and in no time, the yard was full of soldiers on horseback. We could not ask for payment since we did not understand their language. We thought they were going to drink our beer without any payment. When all of them were satisfied, they took a number of half crowns from their pockets and paid for that beer. They even overpaid us.[85]

So in spite of Mrs. Mekgwe's earlier denials, liquor brewing was indeed a traditional skill. Rosinah Setsome learnt the art of beer brewing as a child. Her mother, she said, did little "except drinking beer with the elderly people."

This beer was, however, not sold unlike today.

Did she not drink beer when there was a ceremony only?

No. People from several houses used to brew beer. These elderly people would first start drinking at a said house. They would then move to the next one and so on. This was their work.

After Rosinah's mother taught her how to brew beer, the mother no longer brewed it. "It became my responsibility to brew it. I used to hang sorghum to dry. After this, I would grind it."[86]

According to Mmadiate Makgale, in fact, it was the idea of selling liquor rather than brewing it that went against the grain for the older generation. "I was so interested in dressmaking that I could not even try a business of liquor brewing," she says, "My parents also didn't like brewing liquor for sale. In actual fact they hated liquor.... At home, my mother never brewed beer for sale. The only occasion when we brewed beer was when threshing was being done."[87] Later she described such occasions:

There would be about five truckloads of maize from one field only. There were no harvest machines during those times! These bags would then be placed under a tree at home. We bothered little about cows eating the crop. We just went to bed after shooing stray cattle away. Beer would be brewed. An old lady would be responsible for that. Old men would come to remove the maize from the cobs. They would then drink this beer. However we had to cook for them first. They would eat whatever they fancied. They would use sticks to thresh the corn.[88]

However, some women's mothers or aunts had themselves already been city brewers. Ida Molefe reported that her mother had sold beer in West Roodepoort in the early 1900s, and she later became a brewer, as we shall see. Her aunt too had been well known in Randfontein Location for selling *barberton* (see below). As we have suggested, the traditional skill of beer brewing was soon put to good use by the women's own generation — or at least those who overcame their moral qualms — in the city. According to Rosinah Setsome, drinking in the early years was a social occasion, and was not illegal:

Women were mostly present. I still remember that I was not yet drinking when I was breastfeeding this boy. Many people used to be present because they did not have any work to do. Even the police went around on horseback. Beer was not illegal thus we were not arrested for it. That is why I told you that this and that house used to brew beer at the same time. The next morning the women and grannies would go there to drink.[89]

Mmadiate Makgale was asked:

Were you not employed whilst staying at Fietas?

No. We just stayed at home and brewed beer in a tin.[90]

She says she made *skomfana*.[91] This was not brewed: "You just mix the ingredients with water, then add sugar.... We used yeast, ... sugar and water." But "the strongness of the brew kills people," she adds. Various types of liquor were brewed or distilled, of which "Barberton" was "the most dangerous . . . to human health":

> When you were found selling *barberton*, they fined you more. . . . It was made out of bread, yeast, brown sugar, and water. It was again known as *sebapa-le-masenke*. My maternal aunt at Randfontein was well known for selling *barberton*, even at the police station she was known.[92]

Sophie Serokane, the Pedi who married a Mofokeng, lived in Julia Location, as we have seen. There she sold brandy and *barberton*, with the assistance of a local Chinese man: "His bottle store was at Newclare. When you arrive at the bottle store you just peep inside so that they can see you, then the Chinese workers come and serve you."[93]

Frances Nameng also brewed, in her years in Alexandra and Sophiatown, and ran a strict house:

> *So you were brewing beer. Would you tell me what happened in a nutshell?*

> After brewing, I would take the beer and lock it up. If you got drunk, I didn't give you any more beer. Some people behaved themselves, some didn't. After getting drunk, they would start making noise, which I couldn't tolerate because above all it drew the attention of the police.

> *How much was a litre?*

> It was sixpence.

> *How big were the pots in which you brewed?*

> We made African beer which we called *hobbs*, or *skomfana*. We mixed sugar, *malla* and leave to boil. With *hobbs* we used more complex contents. That is why it was dearer than normal beer.[94]

Mrs. Moje also brewed, though she, like many of the interviewees, showed a certain reluctance to initiate a discussion on the subject. Later, she opened up:

> *So, granny, during the day when your husband was away, what did you do?*

> I used to do all the domestic work and I was not used to visiting people.

> *Did you not sell home-brewed beer?*

> Beer, I used to brew plenty of it.[95]

At that time, she was staying in Ferndale.[96] After an arrest, the owner of the yard in which she and her husband stayed forbade the brewing of beer—but its economic importance was too great for them to accept his strictures:

> I agreed with my husband that we should leave the place. I said to him: "Do you think we should continue to stay in this yard whose owner does not want us to brew beer? How are we going to earn a living?"

They found a room in Gibson street, Sophiatown:

> I stayed for some time before I could start liquor brewing. One day I said, "Am I going to stop brewing beer?" On that particular day I went into the shop and bought *momela* and all the necessary ingredients. I brewed beer on that day.[97]

Important as it was to supporting the household, the brewing of beer seems to have been perceived as an activity the women undertook themselves, one that gave them a certain independence, not to say income, of their own. It was not a "family" activity, or a way of earning "pocket money." It was an income-generating business. Ida Molefe, who sold liquor to "the Coloureds" amongst whom she lived in the Randfontein Location, portrays herself as an entrepreneur with the interests of her household at heart. "I managed to buy and sell liquor," she says, even though it was illegal.

> I bought it in a bottle store in town. The bottle store owner was in favour of me, that was why he did not report me to the police. My customers did not drink it at my house, they just bought and left. I was also careful not to sell liquor to strangers. I was once arrested because of selling homemade beer known as *mqomboti*, in our language, and fined three rand.

> *Were you able to make more money by selling liquor than by working for whites?*

> Yes, I made more money, and I was able to buy furniture for my house.[98]

Thus most women do not express extreme moral reservations about liquor brewing. But there is evidence in several of the interviews that having undertaken liquor brewing was in fact a source of some degree of shame, whether because it transgressed certain rules of respectability, propagated by church and tribe, or because it involved the seller in confrontations with the police, as the activity was illegal at the time. There is some hesitation on the subject in the interviews, for example, and in one case, the interviewee denies altogether that she was a liquor seller, although she had told Mmantho about it in an earlier discussion. However, the economic necessity for the activity, as well as its compatibility with their individual ambitions and their wider household strategy, combined to make it a key part of most of the urban women's lives. We shall explore its deeper implications for the women's consciousness in the next chapter.

With the exception of Mrs. Mokale, the women avoided becoming fully fledged members of the Johannesburg working class. The informal sector here appears to have operated as a defensive mechanism — both against full proletarianisation, and as a means of protecting the less-than-traditional household, by avoiding work that involved long absences. As washerwomen, liquor brewers, and hawkers, the women continued to exist at a distance from the disciplines of time, productivity, and monotony that the more deeply proletarianised sections of the work force were experiencing. (These sections did not seem to have included Bafokeng men either, but consisted of those who worked on mines and in factories.) Thus the women could be present at the making of their own urban family structures. But the women's lives and consciousness were transformed by their experiences as married mothers and working matriarchs. While extending their sojourn in the city they established and sustained relationships with husbands, bore and nurtured children, and lent essential economic support to the households in which they laboured. These activities led them into an engagement in relationships with people of other classes, races, and ethnic groups; into expanding their ability to make strategic economic decisions; and, later, into confrontations with the police and the government. We shall see how in these cases they showed a considerable capacity for defiance, but were also led into a further confrontation — one with their own existing moral universe. The chapters to come explore how particular resolutions were reached by each woman, against the background of the volatile and increasingly politicised townships in which they lived.

7

Subjectivity and Identity: Tales of Violence and Persecution

This chapter deviates from the roughly narrative and chronological format taken by the book so far, to examine some of the ideas expressed in the interviews in more detail. It looks at certain aspects of the consciousness revealed by the interviewees and, especially, explores the storytelling in which they engage at certain points. For it is in the telling of stories that the women give us insight into their subjectivity. Tales about the horrors of urban life are particularly revealing. What forms of consciousness emerge in the context of discussions of city life, and what do they show us about this incompletely urbanised or proletarianised population? The discussion builds on the preceding chapters, which have already outlined the central features of the women's own historically emerging subjectivity[1] — their respectable peasant backgrounds, their Christianity, family ideology, rebelliousness and so on — to explore their evolving perceptions of the world outside themselves.

We have seen how their core self-definitions as respectable householders forced most women living and working in the city into an interaction with and consciousness of a far wider universe than that encompassed by Phokeng, paternalism, and the intimate homegirl networks that had characterised domestic work. In talking about their lives in the city, the interviewees often suggest that they, like most migrants, adopted a variety of categories for thinking about themselves and those around them. Just as had been the case with the back yards, their first concept of the city was concerned with the place therein of the Mofokeng or the Tswana. Their own selfhood was placed at the centre of their interpretation of the meaning of the city. Nthana Mokale's first port of call, and later, her place of marriage, in the city was "Malay Camp":[2]

> Malay camp used to be situated at the place where the pass office now stands. Do you know those offices where marriage vows are being

conducted? That is where I made my marriage vows with my late husband. It used to be a black township.... When I arrived there I was welcomed by Tswana-speaking people. Selina was also staying there. The next day we took *khepe*,[3] ... a small carriage used to transport people during those days.[4]

Another woman:

Did you stay at "Fietas"?

Yes, I did stay there.

I have been under the impression that Fietas was meant for Indians and Coloureds only.

No, many people from this village used to stay at Fietas, Tswanas were familiar with that place. I stayed there for a long time, for about seven years.[5]

Central to the evolution of the notion of the "respectable" woman, thus, was the existence of symbolic connections between her and her place of origin. But there was also a world outside the Mofokeng self. Both work and domestic life brought these peasant daughters into an ethnically and racially mixed world. The comprehension of this required some reorientation.

One means of comprehending the new world was through transferring their own historically based experiences of other groups from the rural to the urban context. And they also transferred ideas of the boundaries of Tswana-ness to apply to the boundaries that defined other groups. As a result, to the informants, something akin to the academic concept of "ethnicity" was a key category through which the world was understood.

As the women's sense of themselves as Tswanas was consolidated, so outsiders were often thought of in terms of categories such as Swazi, Zulu, and Xhosa, representing the other ethnicities in black society. Many memories of township life are cast in elaborations of ethnic categories. Ida Molefe got married in 1937 and moved with her husband to Randfontein "Old Location," or "Kotiti."

Was it composed mostly of the Sotho-speaking people?

There were mixed tribes, but I stayed among Coloureds. I sold liquor.[6]

There were also "Xhosas, Ndebeles, and Amampondo."

Were there any faction fights?

No, only at the beerhall. People used to fight there. Especially the Amampondo were troublesome, but one day they were attacked and most of them were killed.[7]

Nthana Mokale too, as we saw above, used ethnic labels to describe the foremen in the factory in which she worked: "Grace was a Moforutshe, Agnes was a South Sotho, and Dorah was a Swazi woman." A variety of other similar conceptualisations are given in other chapters.

At times, these concepts operated as ways of thinking about class. People in the township were divided into two categories:

Some were rich, others very poor.

How did you judge the rich ones?

They had beautiful brick houses, their children were well dressed. The poor ones lived in houses made of mixed patches of corrugated zincs, cardboard boxes and plastics, their manners and morals left much to be desired, and you could see that they were poor.[8]

But Mrs. Mekgwe, on explaining what she disliked about Twa Twa, invests these apparently economic distinctions with an ethnic content:

I also didn't like to see my children growing up in such an environment. Twatwa was full of Sotho [Bashweshwe] people, and the Sothos are the dirtiest and most unruly people I've ever lived with.[9]

Incipient classes were not categories that existed outside of ethnic ones. If Sothos were poor, then Tswanas were not. We have seen how, in the minds of the women, it was Tswanas who were connected to standholders, if they were not themselves standholders, and who constituted the "respectable" stratum. Ethnic stereotypes of the differences between respectable and violent, or rich and poor (stereotypes to which researchers have been able to give some credence,[10] not because of any inherent "ethnic" differences, of course, but because of different regional and "ethnic" experiences of peasantisation and proletarianisation), appear to have been firm in the women's consciousness.

Of course such a category as "race" existed: "There was nothing like [smallpox, measles]. Those sicknesses came with whites and their type of life," said one woman,[11] echoing a hundred different statements about the "character" of whites. Whites were good, bad, kind, unkind, had brought Western civilisation (variously conceived of as a "good" or a "bad" thing), were "different" from Tswanas, "different" from blacks, rich, cruel, or thoughtless. But the childhood experiences of the women had been complex and their memories are filled with ironic twists of interpretation. Several of the women distinguish between German missionaries, who were white but behaved "just like Tswanas," and the black man, Spooner, who was "a great man, he behaved himself like a white man. When he was moving in the streets of Phokeng in his car, American style, everybody used to turn heads."[12] Simply identifying whiteness and blackness (or Tswana-ness) with skin colour was clearly an inadequate way of conveying the meaning of the category. "Whiteness," like "class," rather, operated as an empty category that needed to be filled by a typification with some historical and cultural resonance for the women themselves. While in Rustenburg, for example, "whites mixed and lived among blacks. We just took them to be like us and weren't interested in working for them," in Johannesburg, there were "big whites" or "rich whites,"[13] for whom one would work.

Like black-skinned people, white-skinned people were not always thought of as a monolith, but were broken up into various "types." Jews, Germans, Boers, and English-speakers, for example, represented the ethnicities of white society. These were all categories drawn from peasant experiences, where Boers had farmed alongside Bafokeng; Jewish traders (as well as Indians, who were also conceived of as "special") had operated throughout the Western Transvaal; Germans had been missionaries; and English-speakers had increasingly penetrated commercial life in Rustenburg district. "Was it Indian traders you traded with?" Mrs. Mekgwe was asked of her childhood memories. "Yes, and some Jews, but here in Phokeng it was mainly Indians. Boers were farmers just like us."[14] Such notions were transferred to the city: "They were Jews," said one woman of her employers. "They had difficult Jewish names as a result."[15] Mmadiphoko Mokgatle talks of how "Jews used to pay us one pound ten per week, and ten pounds per month," but "the English-speaking whites" were preferable because they paid more.[16]

Thus the women's "selves" were, on one level, constructed racially or ethnically, and those surrounding them were the mirror image of their own racial or ethnic being. But we need to distinguish between the labels given to the inner and outer worlds, and the reality of how they are handled in social settings. People may label themselves and others as Irishmen or Afrikaners, Jews or Catholics, whites or blacks in ways that do not actually reflect their mode of existence and interaction. Further insight into the operation of the relationship between the women's "selves" and the forces outside the self may be gained by examining their responses to the things that threatened them. We shall see that these threats were only conceptualised in terms of ethnic or racial dichotomies at a very basic level. The "forces without" were black gangsters from Lesotho, as much as white policemen from Pretoria. But a more complex set of interpretations is given than is indicated by these labels. The self was multiple and layered, defined as respectable, Bafokeng, black, female, in the process of building a household and many other things; and the forces outside themselves were defined as disreputable, of other ethnic groups, white, male, official, and so on. The women's anecdotes about their experiences are based on cultural motifs about the self/community and the outsider/threat, which are given a different metaphorical and historical content depending upon the situation.

When, during the late 1930s, the liquor business was increasingly defined by the authorities as illegal, and thus came to involve both subterfuge and brushes with the law, the women experienced threats to both their livelihood and their sense of themselves as "respectable." At the same time, they were subjected to the increasing violence of township life as "disreputable" people flooded into the cities. These two processes were not unconnected. The "respectable" liquor sellers were, perhaps, persecuted increasingly by the police because of the authorities' dismay at the "immoral" activities of the newly urbanised "disreputable" women — and also, of course, because municipal authorities wished to control beer brewing themselves, in order to raise revenue for local housing and other costs.[17]

For people aspiring to living an upright life in the townships, these events created great tensions and contradictions, and it is not surprising that tales of arrest and harassment by police, and of brutal attacks by gangs, are legion in the women's testimonies. While in the 1920s and early 1930s, townships were remembered as places where modest and ordered lives could be led, they were increasingly to become the more violent and unstable places that the women's own Christian and basically peasant vision had feared them to be, as urban classes without a stake in Christian morality and respectability emerged. One woman said wryly: "Jesus, do you think blacks can stay in one place without quarrels?"[18] The central motif of these tales revolves around the fact that things began to "happen to" the women, rather than the women acting as the central agents in "making things happen" themselves.

Using the language of violence and victimisation, the women talk about townships as places where gangsters crept out at night, and the innocent, normally living peacefully, suffered. Ernestina Mekgwe, who married and went to live in Twa Twa with her husband after marriage, speaks with fear and dislike of both that township and of Alexandra:

> I was afraid of that place.
>
> *What were you afraid of?*
>
> A person can't live in a dark city. There were no lights there. They used to terrorize us in the streets.[19]

Terror and darkness were also associated by Frances Nameng who, when she was asked: "Was it not rough in Sophiatown?" replied:

> The gang of people called *Malaita* were the only ones who murdered and robbed people of their possessions, but generally it was peaceful. They were the night wolves that caught their prey only in darkness.
>
> *Didn't they break into your homes to steal?*
>
> I can't say that because I didn't hear of anybody whose house had been broken into, but there were thieves who swept anything that you forgot outside at night.[20]

The theme of terror is developed by Naomi Setshedi. Living in townships required courage, and appealing to notions of respect accorded to age helped:

> We used to be brave during those years. Groups of delinquent children used to stand at the corners of Alexandra streets, but I was never afraid of them. When I met them I would say, "My grandchildren, let granny pass." They gave me no problem. Alexandra was a rough township during those years.

She still insists that life was good, though:

> *That place has long been known to be the roughest of all the townships.*
>
> Yes, but life was still better during our stay there.

The culture of brutal gangsterism was imported — from Sophiatown — together with its own cultural motifs, mainly to do with threatening-looking automobiles:

> *I think most of the gangsters were from Alexandra, originally.*
>
> No, most of them originated from Sophiatown, the Americans. The Americans and Sprawlers [Spoilers] were originally from Sophiatown. They came to Alexandra to wake Alexandra gangsters up. They used to go around the township in their car with all the windows wide open and their revolvers sticking out.

The gangsters terrorised everyone, even the women's own enemies:

> *Why didn't the police arrest them?*
>
> They were also afraid of them ... there was nothing they could do.[21]

But it was "the people" who were most threatened by them:

> Msomi gang used to kill people in Alexandra. They broke into our houses, robbed people of their money, and sometimes stabbed them. We had to buy strong doors to guard against them, otherwise they broke into the house very easily.

They must have been very rough people.

They were very rough. I am afraid of those people. We used to live a
miserable life because of them. During the night we became used to
hearing screams of people being terrorised by Msomi gang. The police
were also afraid of them.... They could not just come near to Msomi
gang without tight security, because they were quite aware that they
would be risking their lives also. They would take cash, and beat the
occupants of the house up. One woman who lived a few houses from
ours lost her eye during one of these fights.[22]

Several of the women relate personal anecdotes of their experiences of
gangsterism. Attacks upon their homes and their persons are paramount in their
memories. Mrs. Setshedi tells a riveting story of the day the Msomi gang tried to
break into her house. In the story, it is she, rather than her husband, who shows
the initial alertness to danger:

I think it was in 1939 if I'm not mistaken.... It happened while we were
sleeping. I said to my husband, "I hear some voices outside." He dismissed
the topic and said that there was no one outside, I was just imagining. I
had to wake up and sleep far from the door. The next thing we heard a
very loud knock on the door. They started knocking at the door.... I
knew immediately that it was that gang. They had come to kill us. We
woke up and tried to hold the door very firm. We did not have expensive
furniture, because the idea of building a house here in Phokeng had
always been in our minds. I therefore thought that they would kill us
because we had not furniture to give them and save our lives with.

The two of them tried to hold the gang at bay:

We held the door very firmly, my husband and I, but the people outside
were very powerful, they were pushing it from outside.

Neighbours should have helped, but did not:

I tried to scream for help, but people were asleep already. No one came
to our rescue. Then they broke the window, the wooden window frame
was also broken into pieces, leaving behind a very big opening.... I
looked at the window for anyone who could force his way through it.
My attention was drawn to that window. We heard one of them saying.
"Get in through that window."

But Naomi confronts them when they get inside, and finally drives them away:

When he landed inside he found me ready for him. I pushed him to the
stove, trying to burn his hand on the stove.... he jumped, but my nails
still held at this throat. They were deep in his throat. I did not know
before that I was that strong until that night. Now, during that struggle I
prayed to God that he should accept our soul because it was clear that
they were going to overpower me eventually. I gathered strength and
told myself that I had to open the door, no matter what could have
happened. I left that man on the floor, pushed my husband away from
the door, and swung it open. I said, "People, why do you want to kill
us?" One of them then said to the others, "Let's go."[23]

Her courage is at the centre of the story. Furthermore, she seeks revenge, and,
poignantly, compensation. Alexandra was not such a big place that one did not
know how to find the perpetrators:

One of those guys came to our house one day. Before that boy could enter into the house I had a vision in which that boy appeared to be one of those people who broke into our house.... That boy stood at the door, he was hesitant about entering into the house. He couldn't even look at me. I then asked, "What do you want here, can I help you?" He said that he was looking for a man by the name of Moatshe. I looked at him very closely and saw that he was wearing the same clothes he had on during that terrible night. My neighbour knew the boy and she told me that he was not living far from our place.... I did go to his place, but I could not find him. They told me that he was a robber and went out at night in most cases. I left a message that he should pay for my broken window, but he never turned up to pay for it.[24]

Maria Mathuloe confirms that Alexandra changed during her stay there:

At first it was a nice and cool place but afterwards life changed because of gangsters. There was the Msomi gang and the Spoilers gang. These gangsters were dangerous, they robbed and killed people.... They roamed the streets during the night.

Her story is one of fear — for herself, her husband, and her daughter — of the protection-racketeering Msomi gang, which is described using vivid imagery:

Did they ever come to your cafe? [They lived in a room next to a cafe.]

They did come, it was in the afternoon, and they found my daughter Mantwa in the shop. I was in the back room. I heard the voices and realised that the communication was not in a good manner, and it seemed those people did not want to pay. When I opened the door I saw their car parked in front of the shop. When I saw the car I then realised that those people were the Msomi gang.

The symbolism of their cars loomed large:

Their cars were like hearses, they were black and very broad.

They, too, were not completely unknown to local people, however:

I knew one of them, even my husband knew him. They told my husband that he should pay a protection fee because they wanted him to join them. It was about a hundred rands, and he should also do the same thing they were doing.

This time, it was her husband who showed defiance:

He was so furious and not interested in talking to them any longer. They told him that they were going to take him along with them by force, and he was to pay that money. I was so frightened, but after they left he told me that he would rather die fighting. I told my child Mantwa she should pack her clothes and go to stay at her in-laws in Potchefstroom.

Her story ends in the arrest of the gangsters, whose flamboyant leader and den of evil were now exposed, to the delight of those whom they had oppressed:

The Msomi gang came to our shop on Tuesday and on Thursday they were arrested. I heard people singing happily saying that the Msomi gang were arrested, and their leader Shadrack Matthews was among them.... He was from Zambia. He was chained around his waist and feet, his arms tied together behind his back.

The evils perpetrated by the gang were symbolised by dress and bizarre acts:

> He was still wearing that gown he used to wear when roaming around.... It was red in the front and on the other sides was navy blue. At that time the Msomi gang was taken to the place where they stayed. It was far from other houses, the police found a lot of money in tins and clothes full of blood stains. The gangsters used to bank some of the money.... They got that money when robbing people. These gangsters buried their dead victims in the cemetery on top of other graves. They did not dig other graves because they did not want people to realise their movements. You could look for a lost person in hospitals, prisons, and mortuaries but never find him because it was possible that he was buried by those gangsters in the cemetery.... The Msomi gangsters had a priest.... He was chosen by them.... His work was to pray and to influence people to join them, and if you refused he promised to kill you.[25]

Even the memory of gangsterism was too much for Maria. These traumatic experiences, she says, drove her back to Phokeng:

> This story of Msomi gangsters is too long, I cannot go on any longer.... When I talk about these stories they frighten me a lot. After that I decided to leave Alexandra and come here to Rustenburg. I wished and prayed that I should never meet these kind of things any more. I do not want to live in the city again.[26]

Mrs. Moje's story is of a vicious assault on her husband in Alexandra in 1941, this time in the street rather than at home, and by a more anonymous gang:

> He was assaulted by hooligans one day ... in 1941 during the period when I was breastfeeding that girl [she points to her daughter].... On that particular day he went to work as usual, and, as usual, came back home. At dusk he said to me, "Mother of Matlakala, I do not have snuff, let me go and buy some." He went down the passage, but he couldn't get it from the nearby house where we used to buy snuff. He proceeded further and fortunately he got it. Instead of using the same way on his way back, he decided to take a different direction.... He came across them at the corner.... I don't know who they were. They assaulted him at roughly about 8 P.M. and they left him lying there, thinking that he was dead.... He was terribly beaten up. His eyes were probably beaten up with the chain of a bicycle. Oh. He laid there unconsciously from 8 P.M. to 3 A.M. He only recovered at 3 A.M., and he could not see his way home because his eyes were bleeding.

In his helplessness he sought help from the community:

> Fortunately, the street in which the assault took place was the only tarred one and he could guess which avenue it was. He crawled up to the corner and decided to sit down and shout for help. We were staying in the house which was standing opposite to his sister's place. He shouted my name and that of his sister, but both of us could not hear him as we were fast asleep. Fortunately, one of our friends who lived a distance away from us, heard him calling and she recognised his voice. She woke up her husband and when they were convinced that it was my husband who was calling for help, they rushed to me. The wife woke me up while her husband went to my husband to help him. She said "Your husband has been killed." I couldn't wait for the explanation.

She too, showed courage, where kin and neighbour should have been available to help, but were not:

> By then, I was seriously ill in bed, my mother-in-law had to send a telegram to come and look after me.... On that particular day my mother-in-law was not with me. That friend of mine said to me: "Do not wake up, my husband has gone to fetch him." After some time, he came with him. His eyes were swollen. He could not see where he was. The man dropped my husband in the house and went away.

Did they not help you to look for transport to take him to the hospital?

No, I had to wake up and warm water so that I could wash his wounds.

Why didn't you wake up other people?

> On that particular day there was no one in the house. My aunt and my mother-in-law were not in. My mother-in-law had gone to visit her daughter, who was also staying in Alexandra. She had said to me, "Let me go and spend the night with your sister-in-law. It is long that I have been here with you. I will come back tomorrow." I washed his wounds and prepared where he could sleep. I then took him and put him in between his blankets. When the sun was about to rise, I took a walking stick and went to my sister-in-law's place.... I had to go there because my mother-in-law had spent the night there. I knocked at the door, and they were surprised to see me at that early hour of the morning, weak as I was. I told them what had happened and before I could finish relating the story, my mother-in-law was already up and on her way to our place, leaving me behind. My sister-in-law and I followed her. After sunrise I asked my sister-in-law to go and look for a boy who could take my husband to the clinic. She didn't struggle and in no time my husband was at the clinic. He was attended to and asked to report again the next day. The next day the boy came again and took him to the clinic. They decided at the clinic that he should be hospitalised. He spent about a month in hospital.

Did he eventually regain his eyesight?

He received an operation on one eye and he was asked to come back after some time for the other eye to be checked. He never went back to the hospital.[27]

In these anecdotes the women portray themselves as beings at the centre of a range of evil forces, some anonymous, others less so, composed of brutalised gangsters, who lack any moral concern, and who are associated with darkness, ruthlessness, and lack of guilt. They, on the other hand, are supported in their struggles against these forces, it seems, by a variety of elements that represent "goodness." These include their own courage and moral respectability, their families, Bafokeng or Tswana virtue, or the communities in which they live. The police, interestingly, are cast as helpless, and the burden of responsibility for seeking revenge or compensation rests upon the women themselves. In the theatre of the anecdote, these layered complexities of being are revealed.

It is interesting that in the case of the second set of anecdotes, those relating to the experience of arrest for illegal liquor brewing, the police figure more prominently, this time as the "evil" force themselves. But in these anecdotes a broadly similar conceptual structure to the "gangster" ones may be detected. In both cases, there are attacks upon the respectable, just, and innocent, by the uncaring, brutal, or evil. Of course the detailed symbolism of each differs.

It was difficult for the beer-brewing women to portray themselves as "just" and "innocent" unless the worlds of the church and the shebeen could be reconciled. This was virtually impossible, and it seems that all that could be done was to keep them as distinct and segregated cultural universes. Sophie Serokane relates how her only experience of arrest nearly caused a calamitous meeting of the two institutions:

Tell me, granny, were you never harassed by the police?

We used to run away when we saw police.... I, personally, was very lucky. Look, I stayed for many years in Johannesburg, but I was never arrested. It was only once that I was arrested for selling liquor and funnily enough, I was still wearing my Manyano [a women's church group] uniform when the police arrived.... I belong to Manyano women. On that day they came to my house immediately after I had arrived from church. It looked as though they had been waiting for me. But, because God is great, I didn't go as far as the cell. I cried to God for help and he answered my prayer. I knew very well that I would have to pay a fine in church if ever the church minister could have known of such an offence. Fortunately, they never knew of such an offence, otherwise I could have been fined.

The symbolism of the two realms had to be physically separated:

Did you go to the police station in that Manyano uniform?

No, my child, you can't go to the police station in those clothes. But I paid a small amount of money as fine.

What could have been the reaction of the church minister if he could have known that you were arrested for selling liquor?

It could have been an embarrassing situation.

The embarrassment was as much for her husband as for herself:

I guess you never thought of selling liquor any more since that day.

Yes. My husband is well known in the church, it would have been awkward for his wife to engage in liquor selling.

Is he an evangelist?

Yes. You can imagine such a great man being arrested for selling liquor.[28]

But stories of arrest like this one are in nearly everyone's testimony, providing as they do a colourful focus for a pointed anecdote. Having been arrested might, in other examples of oral history, be passed over by the informant, especially one laying claim to respectability, leaving one of the "silences" that tells us so much. But there are no silences about arrest here. Naomi Setshedi, who brewed home-made beer from her very first years in town, suggests with a sort of pride that the police were regarded as enemies, to be feared, outwitted, or avoided. Their capacity to induce shame, although present, could be limited or controlled. She had lived, in her younger days, "in a certain place in Rustenburg called Madikampa":

But I did not stay longer there. I was having one child only. We were also selling beer, even if it was not to our satisfaction, because we were still afraid. When were busy draining beer some would be watching the police. If they see the police, they say something loud, they may say "The pig," so we can be aware that police are near.

The police themselves appear to have fed this perception by behaving with callousness:

> *What were the police doing if they found you having some beer?*
>
> They did not care what you were trying to tell them, they will just spill the beer.

Naomi also brewed in her years in Alexandra township, and is certain that her motives were highly respectable, thus making any act of arrest itself immoral: "We were arrested many times and bailed for a certain amount. That was the only way we could earn a living by selling beer. We were making a reasonable sum," she says. If the women put out spies for the police, then the latter retaliated:

> We used to pour beer into about three tins which contained twenty litres each, and put the tins into a small hole.
>
> *What did you do when a customer came?*
>
> I had to uncover the soil and the lid, so that I could serve my customer.
>
> *Were you sure that the person you were serving was not a spy?*
>
> Yes, I made sure that he was not a spy. Sometimes when you were still busy serving your customers a spy may be watching you and arrest you.[29]

This type of attitude towards the police amounted to something of a culture of subterfuge, which was fairly far-reaching. Subterfuges involving the obtaining of yeast — which was both expensive and illegal — were a major part of the brewing process. Frances Nameng said that yeast cakes cost thirty cents each, and in those days "you would buy a dress for thirty cents." She sold liquor every day, and made more for Sundays, while her husband was at work. People could not drink openly:

> *Did all the people who came to drink sit in the room? Was it not possible for them to drink outside?*
>
> It was illegal to sell liquor and we had to make it a sure case that we were not caught by the liquor squad.
>
> *What if the children wanted to sleep?*
>
> We did not sell as abundantly as you do. After drinking everybody went on his own way.[30]

The subversive culture involved the use of networks of communication and support set up with friends and neighbours. That acts of subterfuge involved community support is revealed by Mrs. Moje's tale of her arrest in Sophiatown. The story begins with an evocation of the virtuous context in which the arrest occurred:

> One of my homegirls invited me to a wedding. We had to attend the wedding since the bride was from Phokeng. It happened that while we

were still there, the police raided our house.... They searched the room. When I arrived home, one of our neighbours said to me: "Your beer has gone down the drain." I just kept quiet.

In every tale the community shows the capacity for great solidarity. In this case, on the following morning, Mrs. Moje's friends educate her about how to handle things:

While we were drinking tea, one woman came to me and said: "Mother, the owner of this yard would be angry if he found all this *mtombo* splashed over the place." I asked, "What do you usually do when things are like this?" She replied, "You ask two people to stand on both sides of the passage and watch for the police while you clean the place quickly." I did as she told me....One person stood at the gate while the other stood at the opposite side. I was pregnant at that time.

But just as frequently, there is betrayal:

While I was busy cleaning up, I saw a policeman coming straight to where I was kneeling down. He came to me and stood next to the water tap. He found me still busy, with my hands full of *mtombo mela*. Next to me, there was an empty tin which indicated that there was beer in it. I realised later that the woman who advised me to go and clean the place had brewed *white horse* (hard liquor), which was hidden in one of the tins which were scattered around the water tap. The white policeman started to look around and unfortunately he discovered white horse in one of those tins. He was infuriated when he discovered white horse. He said "I am not worried about the beer, you are busy cleaning the *mtombo* off. I am going to arrest you for this white horse which you have brewed." I told him that I knew nothing about that white horse, but he insisted that it was mine. He arrested me and I followed him to the police station.

The arrested and pregnant woman pleads with the hard-hearted policeman:

On the way to the police station I tried to plead with him, but he was unreasonable. He demanded six pounds from me. I said "Please reduce the fine...." When we arrived at Newlands police station, I was told to go in and I found several women who were also arrested.

Was there no sympathy because you were pregnant?

No.

But by her noble stubbornness she resisted the policeman's attempts to question her:

At intervals a policeman would bounce into the cell and ask me the place where my husband was working. At that time he was working at No. 3 King George Street in the city, but I didn't want to give the policeman his address. After some time, another policeman would bounce in and ask: "Woman, where does your husband work? We would like to know." I insisted on saying that I had no idea about my husband's place of employment. I had to remain in the cell until it was dark.

Were you not aware that they wanted to get hold of him so that he could be notified that you had been arrested?

I was quite aware of that but I wanted to be stubborn.

Why?

I didn't want them to know his address. Late in the evening, one of the policemen came and said to me: "Woman, do you want us to believe that there are some women who do not know where their husbands work? It is amazing." I kept on saying, "I do not know."

The penalty was inflicted — more time spent in jail:

He continued: "When you go to sleep, make sure that you put a number of mats on the floor, one of top of another, before you put blankets on top. You must make sure that you are warm and comfortable during the night." When it was time to go to sleep, I did as he told me. I slept in the cell that night.

She was finally rescued from her plight, after some complications:

The next morning, a policeman bounced in and shouted, "Come on." All of us went outside. Fortunately my husband and one woman I knew were standing outside. However, I could only talk with that woman, who even managed to give me some food they had brought along. The woman asked, "Are they still insisting on a fine of six pounds?" I told her that they had reduced it to two pounds. On hearing that the fine had been reduced she immediately went back to the gate to go and tell my husband about it. Before she could come back to me, the policeman ordered us to go back to the cell.

That was terrible.

When we arrived at the cell I invited all the women to share the food with me. After some time another policeman came in and shouted my name. He said, "Take your belongings and go home." I hurriedly took everything that belonged to me and went out.[31]

Rosinah Setsome sold beer in Alexandra, while her husband was at work as a deliveryman: "My husband was working for a white man popularly known as Thorontoro. He was delivering goods. He was later transferred. He delivered post. Later on he delivered liquor and sweets."[32] She sold liquor and portrays the police who persecuted her in personalised terms. She was, she said, "repeatedly arrested by a policeman popularly known as Skepere."[33] One of her arrests was described in detail. It too involved innocent pursuits at first:

I was busy washing the dishes at my sister-in-law's house when two women arrived. They bought *sekala* [a tin used as a measurement of beer]. They offered me a drink. Then Skepere came in and found me red-handed.... Only those who were found drinking beer were arrested. They did not bother about the owner of the house.

In Alexandra, her intelligence system was highly developed. In this case it was based upon connections in the police force itself, the racial composition of which did become important:

We were fortunate because we knew when the police would raid us.... They used to raid us towards dawn. The black policemen did not arrest us. They told us when the white policemen would accompany them in their raids. Thus we knew when to expect them....

Black policemen occupied a place that straddled both the inner community and the hostile world, becoming part of the culture of subterfuge themselves at times:

> The black policemen did not bother us because they used to drink at my sister's place. These black policemen would normally pretend that they are searching. Thereafter they would come out and tell their counterparts that there was no liquor here. The liquor was however hidden in the wardrobe.... They knew that they would come back later to drink. They drank hard drinks also. They would sit and drink in the dining room. They would then leave hereafter and arrest our neighbours instead. This was not always the case. Most of the time they did not arrest people.[34]

But such intermediaries, who provided the illegal goods, protective cover, or the means of leaving jail, all of which were essential to the effective operation of the business, did not have to be black. In Mrs. Setsome's time at Boons,[35] the white owner of her rented room had promised it would be alright to brew beer, saying that nobody would arrest them as police would need his permission to enter the premises. And, as her story reveals, his protection was important when the day of reckoning came. One day, she says, opening the tale on an innocent tone once more, her husband requested her to make beer. "I reluctantly made it." She had hidden the beer

> in a hole especially dug for the purpose. We copied this thing from Johannesburg in Alexandra. Spears were used to search for this beer.... The police arrived unannounced. Before I could realise that they were standing next to the door, they had long seen me. When they told me that we should go there I obliged. That liquor was spilt on the ground. My husband was looking at them from a distance. I was arrested. Many more people were arrested along the way. We were in the company of one lady who was very drunk. She was singing. She did not have any problems. Oh, liquor is very evil indeed. As it was approaching Soutraville, the van stopped. The door was ajar, thus one could easily slip away if one wanted to.

> *To which police station did they take you?*

> Boons. They offloaded us and we were closed behind the bars. Thereafter the van went back and collected others who were coming on foot. Oh, the police have once tortured us. When my husband arrived at home, he took fifteen pounds from the drawer and off he went on his bicycle.

Conditions in the cell were poor, and only the drugged could stand them:

> There was a bucket for passing urine on one end of the cell. There was also a bucket for faeces next to it. The porridge was brought in a very big dish. Would you eat? No, you would not.... In the cell there was one girl who was drunk.... She was just singing. She was not worried about anything. When she was arrested, she was busy baking bread for her employers. Some of it was in the oven, and it burnt as a result. Her employer secured her release. One other woman was released. Hereafter my husband and Charles Pieters arrived. I was then released.

The police were corrupt, she suggested. They would confiscate the pots and then sell them cheaply at Koster police station. Perhaps this justified her various acts of subterfuge:

> *How did you evade the police?*

We knew the day on which they would raid on us. We hid it. After brewing beer I used to hide it at the mountain top. One day there came a boy who was a farmhand. My husband requested that I should pour him a *sekala*. I told Magdeline to use a bucket so that there should be enough provision for the others. When she reached the top of the mountain she saw a *khwela khwela* from Boons. She ran to the farm where she hid herself. The police began searching. They asked me where the beer was hidden. I told them that I did not brew beer.... They continued to search but to no avail.

She again personalises the police, while showing that they could be outwitted:

Amongst them was a policeman known as Botha. He was very cheeky and looked like a greyhound. He went to the hilltop. He had a spear in the one hand which he used for searching beer. He was not, however, successful in his endeavour.[36]

In Mmadiate Makgale's case, the culture of subterfuge had extended to architecture, which had been altered to cope with beer brewing:

These policemen were not aware that there was another hiding place in the house. We had a pillar that supported the house. Around that pillar there was a wall that was cleverly built around it. This pillar was very big and it was directly opposite the main door. One could not tell that behind that pillar there had been built a small room.[37]

The evolution of a culture of subterfuge and defiance did not prevent the women from experiencing their arrest as painful and humiliating. Arrest was not to be taken in one's stride. Those who loved Mmamatlakala Moje were desperately worried:

My mother, who was staying here in Phokeng by then, heard about the incident and she fell ill immediately.... She knew that I was pregnant and the idea that I was arrested in that condition worried her extremely. She was heartbroken. She even died of that illness in 1936.

In spite of the gravity of this incident, Mmamatlakala carried on brewing. "I guess you never had anything to do with liquor brewing thereafter," asks Mmantho:

Jesus, I couldn't have lived without it. I continued with liquor brewing even during our stay in Alexandra.

She recalls that she was arrested once at Ferndale, once at Sophiatown, and twice in Alexandra. The first of these latter two times she paid the fine; the second, she spent the night in a cell again.[38]

Mmadiate Makgale was arrested during her years in Fietas. At first, she had pretended to Mmantho that she never brewed. But then she described her experiences, including those above, concluding with the fact that her arrest put her off brewing forever:

I tried to brew beer for sale, but I couldn't go far with that business.... It happened that one day I got arrested for selling beer. That particular day all of my beer was sold out except a small quantity which the people in the house were busy drinking. It was only a small quantity in a calabash, and it was in the hands of one of my customers. I think that policeman [was] looking through the window, and said "They have a calabash in their hands." He knocked vehemently at the door.

Her bitterness over the event was greater than most, because she saw her husband as her betrayer:

> My husband, who was fond of behaving like an Englishman, stood up, went to the door, and said, "Somebody is knocking at the door, he says I must open the door." He went to the door but the person who was holding the calabash in his hand persuaded him not to open the door before he could finish that beer. My husband refused to wait for some time. He opened the door, and with lightning speed, the policeman pushed my husband aside and went straight to the man who was holding the calabash in his hand.... The man said, "Your husband did a foolish mistake to open the door knowing that it is the policeman who is knocking at the door." I was arrested for the first time in my life.

She does not recall the memory with pride; but remembers the help given by kin:

> My firstborn, who I said was mentally handicapped, rushed to one woman I was related to ... and made her aware that I had been arrested so that she could hide whatever liquor she had. She said she took the calabash full of beer immediately and threw it away.... I was escorted by policemen to the police station. I sent one child to go tell the granny that I had been arrested. She was also afraid to come nearer to us because she had a feeling that the police would go to her place also and discover the liquor which her husband used to keep in stock. It was not home-brewed beer we were used to, but it was liquor that was bought from a bottle store.

She showed her naivete as a first-time arrestee:

> All the way to the police station I was swearing at those people who were arrested with me. The policeman asked whether I was being arrested for the first time because they could see that I was not used to it. When we arrived at the police station my husband and some other people arrived a few minutes later.... We left the police station after he had paid the fine....

Although her husband secured her release, she never forgave him:

> I was furious. I couldn't brew beer any more. My husband asked me to brew beer for his own consumption only, but I refused. What angered me most was that when he was asked by the police whether I had brewed beer for selling, he agreed with them. I tried to deny it, arguing that I had brewed it for his consumption and not for sale. So, whenever he asked for home-brewed beer, I would refuse to do it, and I would tell him that he was afraid of being arrested but he wants me arrested.

Her humiliation was made worse because, she said, it was public — "before whites":

> *Was he not on your side at the police station?*

> No, he wasn't. Whenever I wanted to make him angry, I would tease him by referring to that incident. I would say, "You disappointed me before whites at the police station, I have no hope in you. You tell those whites that I have brewed beer for sale because you were afraid of arrest." He would get very angry with me and stop talking. I told him that if he could have agreed that I had brewed that beer for him, I

couldn't have paid that fine because the police could have been convinced by that since there was no evidence.[39]

In an earlier interview, Mrs. Makgale had described her experience in an entirely different form. Her first portrayal is starker and more bitter, the language more dramatic, the story more developed. This may be a result of the fact that the first telling took place during one of the more spontaneous interviews, while the second one — the blander one — was during the administering of the more rigid "questionnaire," an interesting example of the different degrees of evocativeness and subtlety obtained by different research methods. Here is the original version:

> The policeman stormed inside the house. Whilst this man was still agape, the policeman bellowed, "Yes, you are under arrest, man." This man [her husband] then started to protest. "No, no, no, don't arrest me, my brothers, when it is my payday I will ... repay you." I then said, "You keep on saying you will repay these people, are you guilty about my beer? And besides, it is finished." His friend then said, "Man, tell the police that the old lady had brewed the beer for our own consumption, she did not sell the beer to you, so that they should not arrest her." He replied, "Who must say that? They are going to handcuff me, I do not like to be handcuffed." His friend continued, "For Christ sake, you now want them to arrest our mother?" He said "Yes, they have to arrest her."

Her fine was only ten shillings, sometimes one pound. "Life was relatively cheap," she says, "Selling beer was not that high a fine. We never used to distil."[40]

The construction and varying complex meanings of these tales of innocence, subterfuge, arrest, and defiance are of interest to us in a variety of ways. In these anecdotes what on one level appears to be a simple case of whites attacking blacks is cast in more complex moral terms, similar to those used to describe gang attacks. Again each component of the "races" is given a historical content. The forces of good — the housewife and community-spirited woman brewing her homely beer — are starkly posed against those of evil — the uncaring South African police. And around the entire event is constructed a series of cultural and social expectations, symbols and forms of behaviour, involving the woman herself and her particular character, her family and their characters, the wider community, the "audience" who witnessed the arrest, the inner structure of the police force, individual policemen, the jail and its inmates, and the law. Thus while of course the racial dimensions of these occasions are always implicit, the dichotomy is not usually overtly presented as one between "blacks" and "whites." These crude categories were unable to capture the more subtle meanings of the interplay between beer brewer and policeman, which had a deeply social content and were shot through with the complexities of collaboration and betrayal.

In both the gangster and the liquor stories, ethnic and racial discourse did not provide an overarching vision, but interlocked with other aspects of the women's subjectivity — key amongst which were their urban adult selves, which had been built upon their rural childhood selves: the Bafokeng daughters of a once wealthy and self-confident peasantry becoming women with notions of "respectability" and "household building" that they had evolved in the cities. "Race" or "ethnicity" as categories were intertwined with these definitions of their inner and outer world, and only at moments were they the primary discourses through which the women thought of themselves. Understanding this fact may help us to interpret the women's later responses to the more overt political repression they were to experience in the late 1940s and the 1950s.

In addition, the stories reveal that the point of arrest represented something of a crisis of consciousness in the women. Their alternative (to those of the state) definitions of status and respectability were to an extent punctured and some convey pain and embarrassment at the experience. But, interestingly, the women resolved this contradiction by concluding that breaking the white man's law was not itself something which placed them beyond the pale of respectability, painful though it might have been to be arrested. That one could go to jail and still be "respectable" was an important perception, lent legitimacy by the "culture of subterfuge" that appears to have been prevalent, which was to stand a number of the women in good stead in the years to come.

8

Resentment and Defiance: 1945−1960

The Nationalist government of 1948 did not invent segregation or social engineering, nor did it have a monopoly of brutality. Previous governments had had their share of all of these things. But during the 1950s, by which time the initially rather uncertain Nationalist government had begun to evolve a surer plan,[1] the women came to experience white power in ways that were fairly new to them. It is clear that they had not really been subjected to the brutality of direct rural dispossession in their youth. The forces that had driven them to town had been indirect, and were hardly perceived as societal or political forces anyway. Similarly, in their initial years in domestic service and in townships the women had succeeded in finding for themselves a place in the city far stronger than that held by other, newer, and more vulnerable black immigrants, their main reference group[2] for comparison. The main changes they remember from earlier years, as we have seen, were the increased arrests they experienced for beer brewing and the decline of stability in the townships. But they and their households appear to have survived the disrupted period of the Second World War intact,[3] and at a distance from the squatters' movements that arose amongst the newest migrants to the cities during the 1940s, and which rocked the Rand.[4] They were part of the relatively stable and secure urban working class, which local and state authorities could afford to tolerate—particularly in times when a less stable and more threatening urban working class was coming into existence.

But the situation of urban workers worsened with the ending of the war, and then the coming to power of the National Party. Economic conditions in the country deteriorated after the war. Workers found their wages inadequate, while residents found rises in transport costs, a central part of the segregated household's budget, too much to bear.[5] Strikes and bus boycotts were commonplace. And then, an uglier and more direct interface between themselves and the new holders of power developed. This brought a fundamental transformation in consciousness and behaviour amongst at least some of the women.

It was not as if the National Party wished to destroy the stable urban dwellers. Their pure segregationist rhetoric did claim the need for "all" Africans to reside in the cities only insofar as their labour was needed—and thus for their status as urban dwellers to be temporary. The logic of this would have been to make most of the women under discussion redundant, since they did not work in the formal sector, and to force them back to Phokeng, their "traditional homeland." But in fact this pure segregationism was not fully implemented. Indeed, it has been shown that the National Party's actual practice, if not its ideology, included the retention of the position and many of the rights of the stable working class, although there is debate over whether this practice was itself forced on the government by the sheer strength and immovability of the stable working class or by the resistance of local municipal authorities to pure segregationism, or whether it constituted a Manichean hidden vision of their own.[6] Thus it was under National Party rule that the majority of the large, outer-city townships were built in which hundreds of thousands of settled urbanised families were housed, and schools built for the education of the envisaged black working class.[7] However, this necessary correction of previously rather exaggerated notions of the National Party commitment to an ideologically driven segregationism should not draw us into ignoring the very real social engineering in which the new government did engage—albeit for reasons that were perhaps more economic than ideological. The fact that they were to be tolerated and even housed did not alter the fact that the coming of the National Party entailed considerable hardship for the women of Phokeng. For while full territorial segregation may not have ever been possible, segregation within the urban areas themselves was. The new government sought to do what previous municipal authorities and national governments had never been able to[8]—remove blacks from proximity to whites, and settle them in townships far afield, where they would be cheaply housed, physically controlled, and politically contained. Furthermore, while in practice the settled urban working class was not to be forced to return to the rural areas, the new government sought to entrench in law its *right* to so remove it, by legally extending pass controls to all sectors of the black population. This, for the first time, included women.[9] Thus new and brutal impositions of state power fell upon the social setting in which the women had entrenched themselves. Black urban dwellers were forcibly removed from inner-city townships such as Sophia-town in the mid-1950s and freehold property rights were ended.[10] Maria Mathuloe, who lived in Alexandra after her marriage to a man she met in Johannesburg, says of her time there: "At that time whites were still provoking blacks. They did not allow us to have our own houses. We struggled hard to get ourselves just a little shelter."[11] And passes were imposed, for the first time, upon black women. Of all the measures introduced by the Nationalists, it was these that were experienced the most directly by the women.

But another new element—new to the women at least—entered their lives at the same time, in response to these and other oppressive measures. This was the rise of popular township political mobilisation.[12] Some, if by no means all, of the women found that what until then they had perceived as personal and inner experiences, became during the late 1940s and 1950s the objects of concern of black intellectuals, politicians, and social organisations. The ANC, black trade unions, and the Communist Party sought to make overtures to the ordinary township resident in ways that had never been undertaken before. Popular working-class and township issues such as rents, wages, bus fares, removals, housing, and the extension of pass laws were the subject of widespread township and factory campaigns. This was outside the previous experiences of the women. Never before had their own, humble grievances been anybody's concern. (And it may be argued that social movements became stronger because never before had so wide a range of grievances come into being at the same time). Phokeng itself had remained untouched in the 1920s by the one popular rural movement that might have affected it—the ICU[13]—while the women's relative sense of security and mobility in the townships of the 1930s and 1940s had made them less likely to respond to earlier political overtures in any case.[14]

The women's responses to the new social movements were varied and complex. Many remained apolitical, or even antipolitical, their resilience and defiance continuing on a personal level. Others went along with political and social action, but later claimed that their hearts had not really been in it, or that they had become disillusioned by defeat; a third, tiny, category was entirely captivated by the political and social ideology of the movements concerned, and appears to have undergone a personal and intellectual transformation as a result. Here we try to dissect the reasons why different types of political consciousness developed in different women. What made some women militants and others conservatives, when all had come from more or less the same "cohort"? This is the subject of this chapter, which does not pretend to be an exhaustive examination of the history and nature of the various protest movements involving women in this period. Rather it attempts to provide a series of qualitative insights into consciousness and its mainsprings. In it, the women's responses are examined and ordered. They range from conservative conformism, through expressions of bitterness and decisions to register protest by leaving the city, to overt forms of protest of a variety of types.[15] Few women evolved a consistent response, and some attention will be paid to the changing and varied patterns of consciousness displayed by particular individuals. Some attempt is made at the end of the chapter to explain the sources of the different types of consciousness which, it is suggested, lie in the structural, historical, and ideological backgrounds to each woman's experience, as well as in her own personal biography. The analysis in the preceding chapters, then, provides a basis for exploring the different forms taken by consciousness when it coalesced into ideology. Because we understand something about their pre-existing consciousness, we are able, through examining their responses, to obtain some impression of the ways in which the "derived"[16] ideologies of popular organisations intersected with the "inherent" ideas of the women themselves, in times when they had much to protest about.

In the period after the National Party had consolidated its power[17] (the early 1950s) and attempted to implement its far-reaching segregationist vision, pushing black urban dwellers out to the periphery of the cities, imposing pass laws, and segregating races and even ethnic groups, great bitterness was felt by the women. It is this expression of resentment that constitutes the basic stance of the interviewees, and this will be explored first. Such resentment was bred by a number of factors and took a number of different forms. Sophie Serokane is the least clear-cut in her response. She lived in Julia Location, Roodepoort, for twenty-five years. She and her husband built their own house in the location, and she brewed and sold liquor while he worked "at the electric house next to the police station."[18] They were finally removed, as part of government plans to clear inner-city, older townships, in 1967. She is ambiguous about the removals. On the one hand she says: "We were taken by the government against our will." However earlier in the interview she says:

> We left Roodepoort when houses in Dobsonville had been completed.

Did you leave the place voluntarily?

> Yes, we wanted to occupy those new houses.... We appreciated the idea of moving to Dobsonville since we were staying in single rooms at West Roodepoort. At Dobsonville we were going to occupy four-roomed houses.[19]

Her testimony confirms the reality of class distinctions in the townships. As so often in these kinds of situations, tenants were often less hostile to removals than were standholders. When asked "Were those who owned the stands also willing to move to Dobsonville?" she answers "No, they were not willing to go. They wanted us to stay so that they could receive rent from us. However, when we arrived in Dobsonville, the municipality built big houses for them."[20]

But in the long run, removal could not be tolerated, even by tenants, for economic or cultural reasons. For example, the trauma of moving to the outer-city townships of the embryonic Soweto was interpreted in moral as well as practical terms. Frances Nameng even suggests that gangsterism was caused by removals. It was not, but this does reflect something of the evil with which removals were identified:

> It [Sophiatown] was a nice and cool place, with its share of misfits, but otherwise okay. The peace was disrupted when the government ordered them to move out, they bundled them like cattle and took them to Meadowlands. It was then that they became wild.[21]

For several of the women, removals to more distant places meant the end of their commitment to city life. Sophie Serokane recalls that some removed from Julia Location were taken to Meadowlands, in what was to become Soweto, and her own family to Dobsonville. Julia Location was demolished. They stayed there until 1975, when

> We were old and could no longer manage the location life. Life in locations was becoming too expensive for us, and we got less money for our pension. We stayed with our grandchildren here in Phokeng. Their parents send money and food.[22]

Although many of the women had always planned to go home, it is not difficult to connect the retreat to Phokeng with the hardships the women experienced in their new situation, as well as with their increasing age. Government strategy may not have been directly aimed at getting the more settled Bafokeng back into their "homeland", but this was one of its unintended consequences. We shall examine the move back to Phokeng in more detail in the next chapter.

As traumatic as removals was the imposition of passes upon women, something which none of the interviewees could accept. The personal independence that so many of them had sought and won was at stake. As Josephine Mokotedi perceived it, things were easier in her youth "because we didn't have to have passes to obtain a job. There was free access to jobs."[23] The women's existing independence had been possible because previous state policy had regarded their status as housewives and mothers as important — had wanted them to provide stability for the urban working class. They may have provided this stability, but they also used this status to pursue their own personal and economic interests. The new regime, on the other hand, acted as though it wished to treat urban women like urban men — as the mere providers of labour power for the industrial white economy. The overt ideology of Nationalism claimed that reproducing families could be undertaken in the rural areas, while cities would be for work alone. In this order, there would be little or no room for the independent woman, whose household and family could be run fairly competently while a satisfactory income could be earned through informal sector and other independent activities. Nobody would obtain a pass for selling apples or washing laundry — let alone brewing alcohol.

Not surprisingly, the women took this ideology at face value. According to Naomi Setshedi, "Women refused to apply for passes because they argued that they too would have to be registered when employed somewhere. Were they telling lies? ... We tried to avoid some of those problems that you people are faced with when looking for a job." As it turned out, the "grand apartheid" vision of a fully migrant male and female workforce, with all reproduction being undertaken in the rural areas, was never fully implemented.[24] Many of those urban black families, like those of our interviewees, which had obtained a place in the city in the earlier decades, fought long and bitter struggles to ensure that they remained in town;[25] while state and municipal authorities came into conflict over how far-reaching the removal attempts should be. But the women of Phokeng were not to know that — and anyway, the imposition of passes was oppressive in itself. Even those remaining in town had to prove their eligibility under the notorious "Section 10" of the Urban Areas Act, and all would have to carry passes. As Ida Molefe said:

> We couldn't understand why women had to carry passes. We had already accepted the fact that these things were meant for men. You can just imagine how we felt when we had to carry these burdensome things, to and fro, forgetting them along the way only to be arrested for not carrying them. They were a real problem to us. You can imagine carrying a child on your back and rummaging in your bag for a pass with the contents spilling from it. That's why we hated them so much.[26]

And Naomi Setshedi gives the more material argument that "women argued that they needed no pass because with that pass they would be forced to pay some money on registration as a worker. Our employers used to pay two pennies for our registration but that money was deducted from our wages."[27]

Hostile as they may have been to the measure, not all of the women joined the Federation of South African Women's protests against it.[28] There was a distinct gap between awareness of hardship and willingness to join a social movement. Sophie Serokane — married to a Mofokeng, but herself a Pedi — responded in an extraordinarily conservative fashion, showing considerable fear. Indeed, she was reluctant to talk about the matter, even to Mmantho:[29]

Did you start to stay in Dobsonville before or after the pass campaign?

We went there before women could be forced to apply for passes.

I learn that many people did not like the idea of applying for a pass. What was your opinion?

Some people used to refuse passes. I couldn't understand why they were refusing to carry them since they had no reasons for refusing.[30]

Mmantho prompts her by saying that "some of those who refused them were residents of Alexandra," and this draws out Sophie's conformism:

You are right, I used to hear people talking about a group of people which was not prepared to carry passes.

In other words, in West Roodepoort people accepted passes without a fuss.

Yes, that is why we never experienced unrests.

Granny, I guess you hated to be involved in unrests.

I hate them wholeheartedly. I don't even like to talk about them.

But there were grannies who were not in favour of passes, who. . . .

They didn't know what they were aiming at. If there is a group of people which has accepted the law, there is no alternative for the others but to accept it also. We don't own the land, it is theirs [whites]. I am basically a coward, I think I can die if I can be confronted with that situation. I think I can pray to God that he must accept my soul before these unrests start. For what will I be living?

Later she suggests that her fears were justified: "I had no choice. I had to take a pass because I feared a possibility of being killed by the government."

When action was taken against this order, why did you not participate in the strike?

I have already expressed my opinion on the matter. One has to conform like a cow. If a cow runs away, it is herded into a pen and always has to toe the line. We had to conform so that the issue should be quickly done away with without any farce [fuss?]. One has to obey authority and do according to its bidding.

Mmantho disagrees:

Is one supposed to conform even if it is against one's convictions?

Yes, of course.

Doesn't protest help one against coercive conformity?

We do not rule the country. We had to take those passes because we did not know what would have happened to us if we had not taken them. Furthermore, maybe that would have meant more misery for those who have not taken them.

Is it that factor that made you resign yourself into taking a pass?

Yes, the country did not belong to us, we had to do as instructed by our masters.[31]

Maria Mathuloe, who lived in Alexandra and worked with her husband in a cafe they appear to have owned, was similarly anxious to obey the law — but again, it was an act of resignation rather than willing compliance:

Were you still in Alexandra when people were rioting against the law for forcing them to have reference books?

We were still there, but I was not interested in the strike. I did have a reference book, but other people were still fighting not to have them.

What happened to those who were arrested at No. 4's prison cells?

Others were fined and released on a certain amount. It was useless for the people to go on strike against the laws, you cannot fight against the law. The day when I went to collect my reference book I met the demonstrators, they sang and said, "We would not have reference books, *Mayibuye.*"[32] I was with another friend of mine, we saw the police disperse and arrest them.[33]

Nkwapa Ramorwesi was not overtly hostile to political mobilisation, perhaps because she lived in Cape Town at the time, where pass resistance was minimal. She simply accepted her pass:

Granny, I guess you were still in Cape Town when passes were issued to women for the first time....

I was in Cape Town by then. Clerks from the Transvaal went as far as Cape Town to issue passes to Tswana-speaking people who were living in Cape Town. I can't remember whether those clerks were from Johannesburg or whereabout but they were from one of the offices in the Transvaal. They could speak undiluted Tswana, the same way that I could speak it.

Were they concerned with Tswanas only?

They were concerned with Tswanas only, since the Xhosas also had their own people who were issuing them with passes. Their officials were from Transkei.... The only things that they wanted to know was the name of one's chief, the parents, and the place of birth.

In other words you didn't give your officials any problem; like, for instance, you never argued why they were issuing you with passes.

No, we never argued with them.[34]

Some women's lack of involvement in this particular campaign may have been a result of their structural position in society. Nkwapa Ramorwesi gives the strong impression, in her later years at least, that her domestic employer put pressure on her not to join protest movements such as the 1976 strikes and boycotts:

There was once a powerful strike in which three men were killed.... Three men died at the Cape and we learnt that a number of schoolchildren also died in the Transvaal.... I am not sure of what was happening since I was working as a domestic servant by then and I could not understand what was going on in the township.... Sometimes we would meet a crowd of people marching in the city and we would learn that they are on strike. My employer used to advise me not to join the people who were on strike.

Were those people who went on strike workers or ordinary people?

I am not quite sure. I think that strike was the same type of strike in which some of the people ended up in Robben Island. It was that type of strike. However, I can't tell you how it had started and how it ended because I was away in the suburbs and my employer was not in favour of the strike.... My employer didn't like the idea of being involved in that type of thing. They would say, "You didn't come here to involve yourself in strikes." They couldn't even allow me to go and see what was going on.

She did break away at times:

However the day when the three men were laid to rest, I managed to attend the funeral since I was off duty on that particular day. They were buried in Langa Township. A big crowd attended that funeral because the death of those three men had touched many people. They were shot to death on their way home from work. The shooting took place when they were about to enter their flats.... It was during that time when white policemen were busy shooting people. I guess blacks were stubborn, they didn't want to surrender.[35]

Ida Molefe, who did domestic work but was also a beer brewer, and lived in Randfontein, is at first keen to discuss the pass campaign. She tells Mmantho that she was involved with and committed to it:

We had quite a struggle with passes, we did not want them at all. We even struck against them....

So you kept on going to the offices.

Yes, we persisted together with people from the Johannesburg locations. There were thousands of us going to the municipal locations.

She describes the organisation of protest:

Where did you get the guide of how and when to march?

We were told by our leaders that there would be a procession on such and such a day, sometimes we would meet the crowd marching from the Soweto locations and join them.

What about those who did not want to hear anything about strikes, did you punish them?

We didn't do them anything, not even lay a finger upon them for some were even going to work amidst all the unrest.

Her defiance of the state was taken into the personal realm of defiance of her employer as well:

This pass business was a real problem. We once had a raging row with my boss over it. He said if I didn't want to register the pass I'd rather leave. We were already carrying them but we were dead set against them. I hated them very much.... He said I must go and register it, if not so I was to leave him immediately.

You refused?

Yes.

Why?

The pass business was still on discussion. We had taken them but still were hoping for the best, that is why we sat on top of them. By so doing I was carrying the struggle forward and trying to show my employer that I was not interested in the pass.

He ended up too powerful for you?

He defeated me. He said I was the one to be arrested, not him. If I did not register, I was going to end up in jail.[36]

The pass campaign's ultimate defeat was because of the greater power of whites, and the betrayal of some blacks:

How did it come about that you gave up your struggle against these passes?

We were defeated because they were too powerful for us and the ultimate blow was that some of us went and took the passes and we had to follow suit.

In the end she, like all the others, had to take a pass, a document she still keeps:

I don't remember the year in which I took it and it's quite far, otherwise I would hunt it down for you.

Was it not somewhere in the late fifties or early sixties?

Hmm, somewhere there.... That's when I started working with a pass.[37]

These variations on the theme of resentment provide an important backdrop to the understanding of the consciousness of the three individual women— Nthana Mokale, Ernestina Mekgwe, and Naomi Setshedi—who became directly or indirectly involved in political campaigns and social movements. These individual women displayed complex configurations of belief and behaviour, which changed or developed according to time and place. The most differentiated response was exhibited by Nthana Mokale, whose political views changed substantially over the period of the 1950s. At first, she joined overt protest against her removal from Sophiatown. In her conception, life in Sophiatown had been relatively happy. But:

Then a white man intervened and pierced our hearts with a spear.

What do you mean by that, granny?

By demolishing Sophiatown, and removing us from that rich land. Sophiatown was like a chief's *kraal*.[38]

The destruction of Sophiatown was a disaster for Nthana, who already had considerable transport difficulties. She makes a direct link between the actual act of removal, and the onset of poverty: "Then, we were resettled in places like Naledi, Moletsane, etcetera, where poverty was the order of the day," she says. Clearly part of her objection was material: transport to Emdeni (a distant suburb of Soweto), where she was settled, was considerably more difficult than it had been to Sophiatown.[39] When working overtime, she would come home very late:

I used to arrive at home at Emdeni at one o'clock at night. At twelve o'clock midnight I would board the last train to Soweto at Park Station.

Granny, were you not scared to walk alone in the dark?

There was nothing that I could do. However, there were other people also who were working overtime, therefore we used to walk in a group. I used to start work at 5:30 A.M. when I was staying at Emdeni and whilst at Sophiatown. But in Sophiatown it was better because I could catch a bus at 5 A.M. and arrive in good time at my place of employment, whereas when I was staying at Emdeni I had to board a train at 4 A.M.[40]

She joined the ANC-organised resistance:

You were one of Mayibuye *people? What were you actually doing?*

We were protesting against resettlement. We had leaders who could speak English and Afrikaans, saying, "Ons dak nie."[41]

What?

They used to say, "Ons dak nie, ons phola hier."[42] We had confidence in our leaders, with the hope that our protest would succeed.

She describes how the protests were repressed, and how their supporters resorted to subterfuge. In her description, a major theme, present in many testimonies, is that of the role played by the police, the main interface between township dweller and state power. The women who had previously developed a strong consciousness of the need and their ability to stand up to the police in the case of liquor raids, were now confronted with the same powers, but in a far more unequal contest, with far higher stakes. Once again we are forced to acknowledge that the coming of National Party rule did mean a transformation in life as experienced by ordinary township dwellers — even those technically allowed to remain on the Rand. What in the case of beer brewing had been mainly a culture of subterfuge here became something far bolder. People would resist or escape arrest:

Granny, were you ever harassed by the police during your evening meetings?

Oh, they did. People used to run for their lives whenever police arrived on the scene. However the police were looking for our leaders in particular.

Only the leaders?

Yes, most of them were imprisoned. Many of their supporters were left alone.... It was for the first time in our lives that we were asked to produce permits in Sophiatown. Many of us were arrested and the only alternative left for us was to hide ourselves in a hillock which was next to our township.

In other words you deserted your houses during the night and ...

You talk of houses, we were staying in shacks because the houses had been demolished.

What happened in the morning then?

In the morning we would go back to those dilapidated houses and prepare ourselves to go to work since many of us were workers.

In the evening when you came back from work, what did you do?

We would go back to the hill and spend the night in the cold.

But such techniques of resistance were, it seems, fragile in the face of a determined and highly bureaucratised police state. Eventually, she says, the people were worn down by the removals:

> They set dates on our removals, like on a certain date the occupants of a whole street would be moved to Meadowlands or other designated places. They would move down each street until the whole area was vacated. We had to be very cautious about how we moved or what we did in their presence, for they would not have hesitated to shoot anyone whom they thought was resisting the removals. They could easily beat anyone and leave him dead.

This was why, interestingly, fear had to become translated into a show of subservience:

> They did not mind people passing along the street on their ways but you had to show humility, walk like someone who is afraid, knowing that survival was guaranteed if you showed those soldiers that you're scared of them.... We lived real tough then. When you stayed at Sophia and it was not your turn to be moved, you never ventured out in the evenings to a distance away from your home. Even when you went to work, there was always this feeling that someone would pounce on you. Your mere existence was questionable, the place was like a ghost town.[43]

Mmantho asks for more detail, and is told that added to the power of the police was that of the army:

> *I understand that residents were forcefully removed from Sophiatown; was it painful, I mean sad?*
>
> There were soldiers from Pretoria... led by Roberts Heights.[44] It was a dreadful sight, there was a whole division from Auckland Park and they pushed their way into the township early in the morning.
>
> *Had they given you a date by which you should all have been out?*
>
> Yes, we were all supposed to move out. They would stop at one end of the street and order everyone out of the area.
>
> *Waiting for you to move out?*
>
> That's when it became hell, some people refused to move.

Finally, the people registered their names, thus allowing themselves to be moved — the leaders as well:

> We were called upon to approach the municipal officer. He wanted to help all those who were stranded. We therefore went to him to have our names registered. That was a sign of despair. Our leaders, Steve Ramokgadi, Segale, and the rest, followed suit, they also went for registration.
>
> *Granny, what was the municipal officer's intention when he was asking you to have your names registered?*
>
> His intention was to look for houses at Emdeni, Naledi, Moletsane, etcetera, for us who were stranded.
>
> *Did the police stop harassing you then?*

Yes, we were not arrested any more since we were in the hands of the municipality.

She suggests that the government removed the more militant people to specific suburbs of Soweto, an observation which is made by other women too:

> Granny, I tend to believe that Tswana-speaking people were resettled in Meadowlands. Why, then, were you not resettled there?

We were supporters of *Mayibuye*.

For her, as we shall see, the defeat of the protests was intolerable and led to a transformation in her consciousness, from defiance to pessimistic resignation:

> We realized later that there isn't a single black who can defeat a white man. . . .

And later:

> What else could we have done? A white man cannot be defeated by a black man. He [the black man] can be how educated but he will be a liar if he can say that he would defeat a white man. A white man is the God of the earth.[45]

This conservative strand in Mrs. Mokale's thinking is evidenced by her response to the antipass campaign. Here, Mrs. Mokale suggests that being a factory worker made acceptance of passes necessary, and resistance against them extremely difficult:

> Granny, I guess you were still staying in Sophiatown during the pass campaign.

Yes, I was staying there.

> Were you keen to apply for one?

I had to apply for a pass because it was going to be difficult for me to find jobs without a pass. Is there anyone who would be happy to stay at home, unemployed?[46]

Independent women had the time and freedom to protest:

> I learn that your Aunt Naomi went to the extent of marching to the Union Buildings.

Yes, it is true, because she was not employed by then, she could go wherever she wanted to. At that time she was selling apples on the street and, obviously if one is one's own boss, one can free oneself when it suits. I was employed by then.[47]

Her own schedule made political involvement difficult:

> Granny, couldn't you manage to attend meetings which were held in the township?

In the evening?

> Yes, or at any time of day?

I couldn't attend meetings because I used to work till late in the evening, at eleven o'clock I would knock off. The next day I would start work at five o'clock. Therefore there was no time for meetings.[48]

Elsewhere she says:

While people were busy marching to the police station and to Pretoria, I couldn't go with them because of H. Jones and Company. We used to have no holiday or Christmas at that factory.[49]

Her hostility to the pass campaign was also born of her earlier bitterness about the defeat of the resistance to the removals from Sophiatown:

When passes were burnt, I kept my family's passes in safety. I just convinced myself that we would never succeed even in the pass campaign since we had failed already in Sophiatown, our protest couldn't help us in any way because we moved to Soweto eventually.... It happened that one Sunday while I was at work, people collected passes and burnt them. The following day on Monday when everyone was going to his place of work, police stood at every street corner demanding passes. Many people were beaten up on that particular day.

Whereabout, in Soweto or in town?

Naledi, Emdeni, Newclare, all over the place. Rumour had it that passes were being burnt all over the country, therefore, police were demanding passes even in the Free State.

She attributes the defeat of the campaign to police brutality:

People were beaten up to an extent that the next day almost everyone rushed to the offices to apply for one.[50]

Later, as we shall see, she suggests that the people were betrayed by their leaders as well.

Nthana's third encounter with direct acts of defiance was during 1958, when she joined a strike at H. Jones and Co, the firm for whom she worked such long hours. In this case, she joined in. In fact, she is the only Phokeng woman who displays some sort of working-class consciousness. Here she presents an entirely economistic viewpoint:

Did you have a trade union or an organisation you could take your complaints to in that company?

We had a representative called Mr. Levy when we were put in jail for eight days.

Why were you put in jail?

We were jailed for money, we wanted more money.

Oh, it was a strike.

Yes, it was a strike.... We struck for more money, we wrote on placards demanding a minimum of three rand per week, and other demands were written on placards. We were being paid one cent for overtime per day. Others got two cents, all these we were told in court.

Who suggested that you should strike for more money?

Our supervisors started it all, telling us that they too were cheated, not only us were short paid.... We were shocked, they worked us like we were cows. We started work at 7:30 A.M. and most of us knocked off at 11:30 P.M. doing overtime and boarded the last train going to Soweto at 12 P.M. This train was full of thugs wielding pangas and the like, it's God's wonders that we are still alive. We're shocked at the end of the week when we were paid ten rand, others nine rand or eight rand. We then took this complaint to our supervisors who told us to stand on our feet and do something about it. We decided to strike and the Union agreed that we should strike but advised us not to fight but should only speak our case to the finish. We then stopped working.

You stayed at home?

We went to work, when a bell was rung to begin work we just stood outside the firm near the gate with our placards. The whites came out of their offices and asked us what was wrong. They asked our supervisors and they told them the works. Lastly the whites decided to call the police.

And so, the ever-present police intervened here as well:

The police came led by a scrawny sergeant who stood in the front and told us to go back to work because the food will get rotten. We told him we have been cheated for a long time and were not intending to step inside the firm until our demands were met. We told him we had kids to support, wives to feed and cripples to look after, and therefore demanded some better pay than what we received. After this exchange of words the police moved in and took us, we did not run away....

They were held, tried, and won their case. Mrs. Mokale relished the victory:

You did not have to plead your case?

We did. We appeared at the magistrate court for three consecutive days and the court was filled to capacity....

Were you ultimately given more money?

Yes, we did get it.

Did they also stop beating you up?

Yes, we stopped knocking off in the middle of the night.

In fact, it emerges that the workers' grievances had not simply been economic:

After the strike, conditions changed considerably, this time when you spoke to a white man he listened, not kicking you on the buttocks and calling you *kaffir*. Even the owner of the firm, Jones, looked at us in a different way, not with contempt as was usual but with respect, we had really taught him a lesson. We were paid more than the shocking one or two cents per hour.

However, her conservatism was still evident. She says that she had not been wholehearted in her support of the strike:

We really behaved like mad people with not a single care in the world. I was worried really and I told my fellow trialists that if they called me to give evidence against Jones I would blunder and lose the case for us. In the first place I did not understand why we were supposed to strike, but I did join in the strike for fear of being called a sell-out.

So, they had forced you into it.

They had reasoned that since we're complaining about work conditions we should join in the strike. And anyone who did not join would be killed because then they would be selling out.

Were there cases of intimidation on those who had wanted out?

Yes, they did. During the strike some wanted to run away or opt out of the strike when the police came but they were pulled by their clothes and told to go inside the awaiting police vans. They reasoned that if any of us stayed at Jones and carried on working while others were on strike, this would jeopardise their bargaining power.[51]

Although they had won their case, Mrs. Mokale remained deeply uncertain about the efficacy of social protest.

Ernestina Mekgwe's position and consciousness differed in many ways from that of Nthana Mokale. She was not involved in the pass campaign, but is altogether more circumspect about relating her views and experiences to Mmantho. It emerges in the course of the interviews that this is because her views are militant ones, and her sympathies for nationalist protest deep:

Grandmother, you said that day when they were wearing things, "Away with the passes." Can you relate that incident again grandmother?

So that I must be sent to jail?

No. Please, grandmother.

So that I must be sent to jail.

If Nthana had been excluded because of her employment as a factory worker, it was Ernestina's situation as a full-time domestic that cut her off from the ambit of most township protests. Domestic servants were generally outside of the information networks which mobilised wider protest:

Were you still in Johannesburg when they struck for a pound a day?[52]

Yes. We were still in Johannesburg but we did not take part.

Did you support them?

You mean us?

Yes, from the kitchens?[53]

Yes. . . .

That old lady relates much about that pound-a-day strike. Did you also get pamphlets? Those papers which inform you on when it is going to happen?

No.

You did not get them?

No.

. . . like for instance if there is a meeting in Alexandra reflecting something, they inform you with written papers that there will be a meeting tomorrow. They throw them in the streets because they could not distribute them, being afraid of the whites.

No. We were working in town.

You did not notice so many things that happened?

We did not notice many things.

But one of the ironies of domestic service was that it provided access, for literate servants, to other media:

> Only in whites' newspapers. Whites had interest in that. We even got what happened from them.

So Ernestina knew a great deal of what happened, from the papers bought by her employers, and from the tales of her friends, like Naomi Setshedi. And she gave symbolic and practical support to the protesters and suggests that domestic servants were included in campaigns, even if just as supporters. Kinship and experiential links joined the servants to a wider community:

> *While in Johannesburg, did you take part in the ANC's Women's Pass Campaign or any other political activity?*
>
> I only saw the bus boycotts, when they said "A zi Khwelwa" [we don't ride]. But I didn't join. It was our people. Some of them were relatives who lived in the townships, we also sympathise with what they were doing. They used to write us letters saying that whenever we came into town we should pass at Noord Street near the station and give donations to their members who will be wearing green, black and gold clothing.[54]
>
> *But you never attended some of their meetings?*
>
> No.

Interestingly, it was stories of the brutality of the police that were conveyed most vividly to her — but the women's defiant attitude comes through as well:

> *The other lady was once locked in No. 4.[55]*
>
> Yes, she told me that. She said she was locked there for four days.... A big police van, *khwela khwela*,[56] arrived and there is confusion. They surround you and say, "Ride, ride." They hit you with a *sjambok*. They pack people inside.
>
> *They push women in?*
>
> That's right. Women fought, they did not care. They did not care.

Ernestina collected food and money for those in jail, and Mmantho draws her reluctant story out:

> I said all the people who were concerned about their people were collecting money so that they should feed those who were in No. 4. They must feed them with food, those who were arrested. Are you satisfied then?
>
> *No grandmother, I am not satisfied. What happened after they had collected?*
>
> After you have collected they stick a paper written "away with passes" on you.

Her situation as a domestic servant rendered her vulnerable, but her more liberal employers do not appear to have tried to control her as did Nkwapa Ramorwesi's:

> After that I went home. I went back to work. I left that place. When I went to the kitchen to work, the son to the white man came in. The son to the white man asked me, "What is that badge for, Dorothy?" I told

him "This is your language, read it." He read it. "Away with passes." He told his parents. His parents came. They asked me "What's away with the passes?" I told him we don't want passes in our land. They gave us passes, both men and women. Passes are for men. Even then if it's a pass it must be a relevant pass because the pass is able to identify the person. You must not be arrested for it. They forced blacks to carry it.

It should be like the one carried by whites?

It must be like the one carried by whites. They must move around and no police should be asking for it in the streets.

Her employers quizzed her, but she stood up to them:

They said to me, "You are now safe, you got away, if you can be arrested you will be in trouble." I can rather be in trouble. I don't want a pass in my own country. What can I say if I am arrested? I was born without such troubles but now I have troubles. I am going to try to get rid of these troubles with my people. I am trying to fight for my own country.

That's what you said? Did they not get angry with you?

No. They were not party to these things, they were from England. They were new here. They told me that things will get better. "They will get better, there is still time." I told them nothing will get better, [in English] "no way."

Her sympathy for protestors in such situations is cast in deeply nationalist language, evoking land, womanhood, sexuality, and race pride in the process. Besides her linking of the struggle for passes to "my country," she relates her version of how the protesting women spoke to the Boers:

You would hear them say a bastard cannot be afraid of another bastard. It's alright, let the bastards finish us in our country. They said we are bastards, we don't know where we come from, let them tell us where they come from. Where do they come from, because we have our roots here in Africa?

They were telling that to the Boers?

Yes. We originate here as blacks. Then this land belongs to blacks. Black Africa.

Women have the power to say things that men do not:

They are looking at these women. Policemen are looking at these women. These women are insulting them. Although they are insulting them, they can't do anything.

They did not know what to do with them?

But if a man can talk like that they will say he insults them, they will shoot him he will die. Women said whatever they wanted to say. You would hear them saying in Zulu, "Let us go, let us go, don't be afraid."

In what must have been an extraordinary scene, which overturned the conventions of paternalism, militant "Dorothy" tried to convey these very ideas to her "baas" and "missus," starting with the notion that while they, her employers, might be of pure race, coming as they did from England, whites in South Africa were "half-castes":

I asked "Where were you born, Baas." He said "In England," I asked "Where were you born, Missus." She said, "In England." I said, "If I insult you I can say to you, you bloody European. But what will I say to these bastards? Who are they?"

Because they are not white Europeans?

They are half-caste. They are half-caste, what can they tell me? I can say, "You bloody European, go back to Europe." But these other whites, where do they come from?

She says this is why Europeans "love their fathers, they don't love their mothers." Black women were not ashamed of their bodies, and took pride in having nurtured children, and therefore the nation. Whites were "bastards" because they could not not acknowledge their connections to womanhood. Thus when black women were angry with whites, "you could get amazed":

They could take out their breast. . . . She takes it and holds it like this. Whites are afraid of the breast. She takes it out, big as it is. Whites surprise me, they hide their breasts. Women said, "You were fed from these breasts." She takes out a big breast and says, "You were fed from this breast. You were fed from this breast." They meant Boers were bastards.

It was better because then they could tell them that.

They told them and did not care to be taken to jail.

Her Nationalist sympathies extend to an understanding of the symbolic importance of history. The past had been falsified, and this was why whites could rule, a proposition with which Mmantho heartily agreed:

Blacks have fought wars here in South Africa.

They fought?

Yes, they fought. They had a reason to fight. By the way, what year was it? When a fight started that there should be no Dingaan's day. The Boer said, "Why should Africans celebrate this day when they killed our people?" . . . He wanted to keep his throne. At twelve o'clock they said, "Kill the wizards, you were supposed to be already asleep."

Mmantho says encouragingly: "They gave us those books. It was not the real history. They hid the real truth." And this triggers off Mrs. Mekgwe's beliefs about the hiding of truths, indicating the presence of a subculture within black society which is sharply aware of the "real" news:

Even today they don't want to publish the deaths which occurred in Meadowlands.

Which deaths?

Power.

Oh. That one which occurred in 1976?

The way children are so ill-treated, they do this and do that. I don't know whether that will appear on the TV.

No, they won't televise it.

Yes, they won't because people died. Buildings were burnt.

Mrs. Mekgwe's support, she says, was that of a rural person who had no place in urban struggle, but who recognised oppression:

> We were essentially rural people with strong ties with our background, while they [the bus boycotters, etc.] had chosen to be townspeople and had thus severed their ties with their rural origins.

Did you foresee any problems if you had joined them?

Yes, because how could I participate fully in these organisations when my origins still heavily influence my direction in life and not the municipalities that ruled over the township?

But do you think it was good that they stand up and speak up for what they thought to be good for them?

Of course, they had to. They were determined to live with their children where they worked, so they had a right to secure a future for their children.[57]

Naomi Setshedi embraces the most militant ideology of all the women. Naomi, living an independent married life in Alexandra Township, and subsequently removed to Meadowlands, supported the ANC's Pound-a-day campaign,[58] the Alexandra Township bus boycotts,[59] the potato boycott, and the pass campaign. Her early participation in the potato boycott of 1953 was motivated by a belief in the profound evil of certain "Boers," an evil so great that it was even manifested in the potatoes themselves:

> Rumour had it that the Boer who farmed with potatoes had the habit of knocking down his lazy labourers with his tractor. He did not bury them, instead, he used them as compost in his potato farm. We were convinced that what we heard was true because even the potatoes themselves were shaped like human beings. They were not completely round.... In every township, potatoes were boycotted, we argued that eating potatoes was the same as eating human flesh.[60]

Later, In 1957, she boycotted the buses of Alexandra, walking to work every day for six months, saying "we didn't even feel the distance from home to work going on foot." The 1957 strike was assisted by whites who gave lifts to workers, sometimes out of a sympathy born of their work relationships:[61] "They felt pity for us, they somehow supported us in the struggle because we were working for them."[62]

She describes the pass campaign and her own involvement. First she describes how the organisers required people to hand over their passes if they had applied for them:

Now granny, were you still at Alexandra during the pass campaign?

Yes. ... Men used to go around collecting passes from those who had them already and they tore them apart. One would find people collecting passes at a bus stop from those who happened to be waiting for a bus. Passes were set alight.

Did they collect women's passes only?

They collected from both men and women, anyone who did apply for a pass had to hand it over to those people....

She acknowledges that the campaign was unsuccessful, saying it "worked out to be a futile attempt." But, in contrast to Mrs. Mokale, this does not lead her into cynicism about political protest itself. Instead, she links the pass campaign to a much broader conception of black rights to land and liberty themselves:

Now, were those women who staged a protest against passes crazy? They said, "We are fighting for our land, the Transvaal."

Her involvement began in Alexandra, where the decision to take part was democratically reached:

Granny, how did you in particular, end up in No. 4?

I also joined the campaign because I couldn't imagine a woman carrying a pass like a man.

Did you march to No. 4?

No, residents of Alexandra Township got together and discussed the pass issue. We resolved that we were not going to apply for passes.

She interprets the campaign in protofeminist terms:

Women only?

Men also were in the struggle but women were in large numbers as compared to men. My child, we really protested against passes and ended up at No. 4.... Yes, women were furious, no one could stop them from doing what they thought was right. I started to realise that women are militant sometimes. If they could have been sent to war during that time, they would have carried their arms without hesitation. Police vans came in large numbers to the scene, and women packed themselves therein. They instructed the police to arrest them because they were not willing to apply for passes.

Did you reach No. 4 also?

Jesus, I did.

She speaks with pride of the role of leaders and followers alike:

My child, police vans got busy, people were arrested and taken in police vans to different places.

Were the leaders arrested also?

Leaders? They said, "Bus boycott, we don't apply for passes." Rumour had it that nine hundred people from Sophiatown were taken to different police stations that morning, those who staged a protest against passes. Marshall Square, No. 4, Jeppe, Pretoria, Krugersdorp, Nancefield, and Randfontein police stations got busy. They had no accommodation for all those who were arrested.

She remembers the great march to Pretoria:

During the strike, we didn't pay for the bus services. We just climbed on the bus and demanded that the bus driver take us where we desired.

When we went to the Pretoria Union Buildings we took buses which we found at the bus ranks and after asking the passengers to climb off or go with us to the Union Buildings we climbed the buses and the driver drove us to Pretoria.[63]

Elsewhere she describes how meetings were organised — and crushed:

How did you come to know that a meeting was to be held on such a date?

You know what, they used to distribute pamphlets wherein it was stated the date and place where the meeting was supposed to be held. Meetings were held at No. 3 square[64] in most cases. During the meeting concerning the issuing of passes to women, it was resolved that we should throw away passes, those who had applied for them already. The reasons were that we would be faced with a problem of having to register with each and every employer that one desired to work for. Another reason was that women would have to carry passes wherever they wanted to go. The protest then started and *khwela khwela* started filling up the streets of Alexandra. Policemen in uniform forced people into those police vans. The policemen argued that we were holding meetings with the intention of rioting. Meetings were subsequently banned.

Did they ban meetings?

Yes, they no longer allowed public meetings. Then we went into police vans which drove us to No. 4, some were taken to Randfontein, Krugersdorp, and to other police stations. All of us were arrested for allegedly refusing to apply for passes.

The cause was betrayed by other blacks:

Unfortunately our effort was eventually rendered futile by some of the women who went to apply for passes.

I pity you.

Policemen said to us, "You should not anticipate problems, because you have chosen this course yourselves."

The campaign was, she suggests, particularly powerfully supported amongst Tswanas:

Which ethnic group formed a large number of the group that was resisting?

The Tswana-speaking people. Most of the Tswana people hated the idea of registering when getting a new job.

In fact, she says that "Xhosas and Shangaan women remained behind, selling vegetables on the streets." Tswanas taunted them, portraying their indifference to the protest as a generalised indifference to black suffering and dispossession. But in fact, her discussion suggests that a difference in class position and gender relations underlay the differences between ethnic groups (if they existed — we must remember that Mrs. Setshedi is strongly pro-Tswana in her entire testimony, and that her radical nationalism does not seem to be incompatible with ethnic chauvinism):

One Tswana woman went to them and said, "Hey you are busy here making profits because you don't care for what happens since your land has long been taken away from you by whites. Your chiefs have sold

your land to the whites, now you have come here to work for your
children and you don't care to join in our struggle. You are satisfied
when you rent a house, we [Tswanas] rent houses with the hope that we
would go back to our villages and settle there eventually. Do you think
we should fight for your rights while you are here making profits? Let's
go, join the struggle all of you, Pedi, Shangaan, and Xhosa.

But such pleas fell on deaf ears, she suggests, and the groups who would not join
ultimately betrayed the protest:

> To which ethnic groups did these people who were applying for passes
> belong?

> Ndebele, Pedi, Shangaan, these groups were not cooperative.[65]

Mmantho pursues this point:

> In one song that you sang for me you say that Mapedi, Shangaans, and
> Xhosas didn't want to join the strike. Can you elaborate?

> Yes, Shangaans and Pedis didn't want to strike. When we went to
> demonstrate the issuing of passes to women, we passed these women on
> their hawkers' stands selling vegetables and asked them to join our
> procession. They joined us and we left for Marshalltown Square police
> station, where we entered the police yard and sat in civil disobedience.
> Towards sunset, these Shangaan women told us that they had to go back
> to their homes because they had left their houses locked and their
> husbands expected them home to cook the evening meal. We told them
> that we also had husbands who expected us home but because we had
> responsibilities beyond our homes which we were presently attending
> to, we couldn't go home, so how could they go home. They should not
> expect themselves to go about their hawking business while we did not
> work but took part in demonstrations which if proved successful would
> benefit them as well as us. In other words, we could not struggle for
> them.

> Does this mean that Batswana women were prominent in the strike?

> Yes, the Batswana women had given themselves up for the cause of
> women and if the white people had dropped bombs on us it wouldn't
> have mattered.

> What other nationals were prominent, other than Batswana?

> There were other nationals like Basotho, Zulus, some Bapedi and little
> Shangaans, and so on. We all joined with the determination to stop the
> issuing of passes to women. If we had been assured that white women
> will also be required to carry passes, it would have made sense but as it
> was, only black women who would carry these passes.

The strike was betrayed by these ethnic groups, and the police gloated:

> If every black woman in South Africa had joined the demonstration, we
> would have got our demands. While in jail we asked some policemen to
> bring us newspapers, but they refused, and one Afrikaner policeman
> told us that we were just wasting our time in jail because a lot of women
> were coming to police stations around the Reef and were registering for
> the passes.

The women appeared in court, but were defeated. The reasons were, she suggests, white power, and black betrayal:

Who represented you in court?

I do not know their names but they said that Mandela was one of them, he is still in jail to date.... When we were protesting against passes we predicted a situation in which we would have to go around carrying passes and this is exactly what is happening today.... The following day while we were waiting outside the court one policeman came to us and said, "You *Mayibuye* Africa [those fighting for Africa] you have lost the struggle, because the Shangaans, Ndebele, Xhosa, and Southern Sothos are busy applying for passes. You are busy with the struggle, you are not going to win, the problem lies with these other ethnic groups who are busy applying for them. It is going to be a fruitless effort to continue with the struggle. One of you can read aloud this leaflet to confirm what I am telling you." One of us read it and we were very disappointed to learn that we fought for nothing.[66]

One of the consequences of defeat was that militant Alexandra residents were removed to Soweto. Without leaders present, this was easy:

If the whites had not put our leaders in jail, they would not have succeeded in removing some Alexandra residents to Soweto. They also succeeded in removing us because they had brought soldiers from Roberts Heights to help in the removals.

Later she adds:

Immediately after all these strikes, most of us were forced to move from Alexandra and Sophiatown to Meadowlands, Orlando, Diepkloof, and other townships. We think the aim of the government was to make us less militant.

But, were you genuinely supporting them?

Yes I was. All those people who are presently staying at Emdeni and Naledi are those whose parents were supporting "ons dak nie, ons phola hier." They are those who were for "we can't carry passes." They were those who were ultimately defeated and sent to Emdeni and Naledi.

But, as she says, the legendary courage of the women could not be crushed. "We were very brave to stand in front of the machine guns at the Union Building. There was no fear whatsoever, we were determined to die for Africa and for our nation.... During that time many Batswana women were militant and people remarked that they had eaten fire that is why they were so brave." So in spite of defeat, Mrs. Setshedi describes a surviving tradition of militancy.

Were you not afraid of the police?

No, a policeman could never even think of standing in front of a *Mayibuye* woman. We were militant. Even in town, the bus drivers used to clear a way for us so that we could go in without having to stand in a long queue. They used to say, "Make way for *Mayibuye* women." ... Then we would go in without any problem.

I think you enjoyed being so militant.

Yes, we enjoyed it.

Later, when she finally and reluctantly applied for a pass, several years after the deadline for applications, she takes pride in this:

> My child, do you know that I applied for a pass here in Phokeng in 1963?

> *Was it for the first time that you were applying for a pass?*

> Yes, it was. One of the clerks at the magistrate's offices said to me, "Granny, are you applying for the first time? People here have long been applying for passes, where have you been?" Then I said to him, "*Mayibuye Afrika*. I also took part in that struggle so that you could work as a clerk in the office like this one. I was not satisfied to see Boers only in the offices." He laughed and I continued, "Now that you are an office clerk, you are going to be my mouthpiece. [Laughter] I do not think you could be sitting on that chair if it were not because of our efforts."

She wishes she could carry the militancy of those days into her life today:

> You know at times I get discouraged when Rustenburg Bus Service keeps on increasing their fare and people saying nothing about it. If it were during those years we would be boycotting them. Nowadays we pay fifty cents for a single trip to Rustenburg, a distance we used to make on foot without any problem.[67]

The women's testimonies give us insight into the forms and distinctive patterns taken by their consciousness. They also reveal the interface between the "organisations" that were attempting to mobilise them, and the individual women themselves — the very stuff of the ability of social movements to operate. We are able to gain some insight into the workings of leadership, local organisation, and the social movements' own cultural and political symbolism, the means whereby disparate individuals are drawn to act together.

Although the organisations that mobilised the protests were often national, the consciousness of the more militant women appears to have been transformed by their very local and small-scale experiences of organisation. It was through the actions of local leaders — the "organic intellectuals" of the movement, perhaps — that people became mobilised and committed. Thus the national or broader organisation behind each act of defiance is hardly mentioned in any of these testimonies. Ida Molefe, like most other women, remembers individual organisers instead. She praises the courage and presence of one of them:

> *Who was the main force towards your organisation of the striking force?*

> There was a certain lady who was as brave as a lion, but she's late [dead] now. She was tall in height and heavily built. She could grab a policeman by his collar and shove him out of the way.... Her first name was Mojanku and her middle one was Fenny, which people preferred. She was a Gabashane, that is, her surname.

> *She was the one who led you in Randfontein?*

> Yes, and she was a born leader with a flair for efficiency.

The courage of leaders was always an inspiration. Mrs. Gabashane's courage was legendary:

No, if anybody had to be detained, it was Fenny and her subordinates. Every time there was a march there would be a rumour that said she was wanted by the police, and she would vanish into thin air, only to appear again later.[68]

Naomi Setshedi also remembers individual leaders vividly:

"Fish" was the man who was very active in organising meetings in Alexandra. I think his name should have been written down in many books because he was very popular.

Mrs Setshedi suggests that she understood black community leadership in ways that had meaning to her as someone from a village: "The committee members of Alexandra township used to represent us, like in any other village you will find a group of men acting as representatives."[69] White leaders, on the other hand, such as those from the Black Sash,[70] were well-intentioned outsiders but were still accepted. Nthana Mokale speaks of the white leader in the H. Jones strike, in this case "a Jew":

Who spoke to the whites, who was the leader?

We spoke all at once, and then one would translate what we said to them.

Who was it that spoke to the whites?

Members of the trade union, especially Mr. Levy.

What nationality was he?

I think he was a Jew, but he wasn't a black man.

Nthana Mokale was proud to be able to say that, besides Robert Resha and Peter Nthite, one of the leaders she remembered best from the antiremovals campaign was actually from the Rustenburg area—in fact from Mmantho's home village:

Who used to chair those meetings?

People like Steve Ramokgadi.

Ramokgadi! I am familiar with that surname.

You should be. He was originally from Mabeskraal. Steven was referred to as our *sebonda*.[71]

Don't you recall his other name?

No, I can't remember his Tswana name. He was called Steven Ramokgadi.

National leadership also played a vital symbolic role. Later Mrs. Setshedi mentions that "we had Mandela, Fischer, Mthembu, and lots of other leaders," and that "even today Mandela is still in jail":

Did you see him with your own eyes?

Yes, he used to address meetings in Alexandra.

Mandela had special powers feared by the whites:

During that trial Mandela was sentenced to jail, he is still in jail. Some few years ago there was a rumour that Mandela was going to be released but whites changed their minds seeing that Mandela is very intelligent. They argued that he would confuse us when he comes back to us.

Whites as well as blacks could be leaders; but both required the English language in order to be effective, said Mrs. Setshedi:

> *You have said before that there were some whites in your group. Were they acting as your mouthpiece at the Union Buildings?*

> Yes, we were just one organised group of women. All that we wanted to know was an explanation of how the pass system would work out finally.

> *So you had a number of blacks in your representative committee?*

> Yes, they knew English well.[72]

Mrs. Mokale also associates the speaking of English with effective leadership: "Nkosi and Segale were militant because they could even speak the English language more fluently." But to her, the militancy of the leaders disguised their deep duplicity, and those who supported them did so simply out of ignorance. By the time of the pass campaign, "I had no more confidence in our leaders. So, during the pass campaign, I dug a hole in the yard and buried all our passes therein." She talks of the leaders of the campaign as "they":

> They came to my house demanding passes to be handed over to them. I told a lie and said that my pass was burnt in Newclare some time ago. I am still having that pass with me to date.

> *Granny, you have said that many people joined the pass campaign when they arrived in Soweto. What did they actually do?*

> They burnt them, fools burnt them only to discover that people like Steven, our leaders, never burnt theirs. They deceived many people.... I, for one, couldn't agree with the majority when they were burning their passes. I felt that it would be the same as [the] Sophiatown protest. There is no black man who can defeat a white man. I repeat: a white man is God of the earth.[73]

The experience of prison — not unfamiliar to the beer brewers among the women — gave a central motif to the memories of protest. It acted in two contradictory ways. It was a means of consolidating consciousness and creating solidarity amongst the women. But to the police, it was a way of creating tensions and divisions within the protestors. Going to jail was common enough in those times to have been predicted and planned for my some, such as Nthana Mokale:

> *While you were in jail who looked after your children?*

> They were old enough to look after themselves. Remember I said Ndona was going to Tigerkloof; and I gave him a hundred and forty rand on the understanding that if I was given a long spell in jail, he would take our belongings to Phokeng and then spend the rest of the money as fees at Tigerkloof. Fortunately we were discharged.

It was unpleasant in prison — but not crushing:

> *Can you tell me how it felt to be in jail?*

We were taken to No. 4 prison after we had been demonstrating at No. 3 square against the ruling that women should carry passes. We were put into police trucks are taken to No. 4 prison where we were jailed.

I mean what was it like inside jail, what type of food were you given to eat?

The usual type of food that is given to prisoners. Semicooked porridge eaten with carrots, also not properly cooked. All food that is given in jail is not properly cooked, perhaps with the intent of dissuading us from participating in strikes.

While in the cells were you allowed to speak to each other?

There were policemen planted among us, so we didn't speak about the strike, for fear that they might use it against us during trials as evidence. We only spoke about our everyday life in the townships.

Were you not impatient about when you'd be released?

No, we were just waiting for the trial day and we knew that after paying fines ranging from ten rand to five rand we would be released.

Granny, how many days did you spend at No. 4?

I spent four days at No. 4, and I was granted bail after those four days. Some of the women I was arrested with were also bailed out. The court kept on remanding our case, but in the meantime most people were also being arrested. Boers were very cruel those days.

The imprisonment of women had specific implications:

Granny ... you said that some of the women who were expectant gave birth while they were still at No. 4. What did the policemen do concerning such cases?

They were taken to hospital and were later sent home with their babies.... We had a very bad experience, we were miserable every day of our stay at No. 4.

Domestic responsibilities could be used to undercut militancy:

No, the pass campaign was not successful because while we were in gaol, some of the women resolved to apply for passes because they argued that they had the welfare of their children who were at school at heart. They had to work for them.[74]

A factor that encouraged solidarity rather than division in the face of such hardships was the culture of protest, which, if it was built on what was called above the "culture of subterfuge," was certainly a more developed cultural form. Rich in song and symbolism, the women describe it as having been rooted in the crowd. Ida Molefe was asked about this:

Where did you learn all these choruses?

I can't tell you where the songs sprang from because I really don't know. I just heard them from the masses of people who were gathered to defy the pass law. You know it's easier to learn a song from a group of people than when you are being taught how to sing it. We went along with the rhythm until we knew them by heart.[75]

Naomi Setshedi breaks into song at several points in her testimony:

> Then we started singing: "Hei Verwoerd, Hei bula teronko; hei, thina si zo ngena zimankosikaze; Mazulu, Maxhosa, Sotho, Shangana" [Hey, Verwoerd, open up the prison cells. Hey, we women, we are going to enter therein. We are Zulu, Xhosa, Sotho, Shangaan].

Songs made one brave, even reckless, at times of crisis:

> Yes, we got into police vans all of us. We were locked up in prison cells and given porridge to eat. We started singing our "Verwoerd" song even behind bars ... we didn't care what could have happened to us. Whites lost hope of ever being able to control us. Vans took us from Marshall Square to No. 4, where our names were taken down. Some of us were then beginning to fear the consequences of the campaign. One said, "I've got the key of the house with me, I must go home, otherwise my husband is going to be stranded." However, we didn't listen to such stories.

Militancy was widespread:

> When we returned from court, we came on buses, singing "Hei Verwoerd, open up the jail."

> *What other songs did you sing?*

> There were many songs that we sang, the popular ones being "We the women shall enter," "Zulu, Xhosa, Sotho, let us be one thing." Do you hear? ... We also sang "Nkosi Sikelel' I Afrika" and "We are going to shoot them" ["Sizo ba dubula"]. Our people were really militant then and if anyone had supplied us with guns, we would have wiped out these whites.[76]

Ida Molefe remembers Randfontein's own particular version:

> We had a song we usually chanted when we went to the Randfontein offices.... we sang thus, "Ga re di tsee, ga re di tsee mone Randfontein dipasa" [We won't take them here in Randfontein, these passes]. That was our main chorus.

The women's heritage as Christians gave them access to this language of protest: "We had another one in Zulu that went as such. "Jesu sezinikela kuwe, a si a fune amapasa" [Jesus, we give ourselves unto you, we don't want these damn passes]."[77]

Nthana Mokale remembers that even the act of imprisonment was grasped symbolically in song by the strikers at H Jones and Company:

> They loaded us into *khwela khwela*, the whole lot of us, and we sang, "Ha e tsamaya e a nyanyatha" [This car has no wheels, when it moves it wobbles]. At that time we were being taken to Strydom police station, singing different songs in different trucks.... We sang, "Unzima lomthwalo uwis amadoda" [It's a heavy load that we carry, it even topples men]. It was like a wedding celebration. The car flew on, we fell inside, stood up again and continued singing until we arrived at Langlaagte where it was decided we should be driven to Newlands and the trucks turned for Newlands.... Thousands, not a few hundreds, thousands were taken away and at Newlands we filled the place to the seams. Men and women, some beautiful and others ugly, it was a mixture.

After they had appeared in court, they sang again:

> In court it was too full, but when we were out of the court room we did sing, saying "Igazi lendodana liwu lomthwalo unzima" [The blood of the Son; this is a heavy load].

She disliked the patronising voyeurism of white observers of this strike and its singing participants. Songs were not frivolous or quaint:

> We were released and whites were buying newspapers wanting to know all about us. Some asked us to sing and taped our songs, they said "Oh you sing so nicely." There was no singing nice about anything we did, it was painful.[78]

Naomi Setshedi indicates that the symbolism of protest extended beyond singing, into the spheres of dress and comportment. She interrupts Mmantho, who was interviewing her on an entirely different subject, to tell her of her participation in the greatest symbolic occasion organised by the Federation of South African Women during the pass campaign of 1955—57—the march to the Union Buildings in Pretoria by twenty thousand women:

> My child, I forgot to tell you about our march to the Union Building. We marched to the Union Building protesting against the issuing of passes. Our leaders had black dresses trimmed with yellow and blue on.... On that particular day, unfortunately I can't remember the exact date, we took buses from Johannesburg to Pretoria. When we arrived at the Union Buildings, people were running around, surprised at seeing so many buses. Most of them had an idea of what was going on because they got the information from the newspaper. We parked our buses and marched to the Union Buildings. We demanded Verwoerd, we insisted that he should come our and explain the pass system to us. We sang "Nkosi Sikelele," followed by its Tswana version. They were looking at us through the windows.

> *Who?*

> The policemen. Some of them even went outside to watch us. Besides the "Hei Verwoerd" song, they sang:
> Koloi ena, e ya nyanyatha
> Koloi ena, e ya nyanyatha
> fa sa suto ya go thuila
> [This car is moving very fast, if you don't move out of the way, it will knock you down].

This display of anger and unity had a devastating effect upon Verwoerd himself,[79] she believes, even though its immediate impact was dissipated:

> Did he live long thereafter, he didn't. We told him that we were going to bewitch him so that he could be knocked down by a car. We waited for him outside but he never turned up. Finally we received a message which said that we should go home. Verwoerd would hold a meeting with us some few days thereafter. All that they were telling us was lies.[80]

What makes a peasant woman, perhaps from a comparatively wealthy background, whose orientation may be towards going home in the long run, whose self-perception is that of a respectable and upright Christian, and whose concerns are those of family, home, and community, enter into political campaigns? While we cannot make sociological generalisations on the basis of the experiences and subjective memories of a few individuals, it is possible to make some modest interpretive statements about the consciousness of the women we have looked at. In the case of the two women most directly involved — Naomi Setshedi and Nthana Mokale — their relative and absolute deprivation was at stake. In Naomi's case, it was her livelihood as an independent informal sector entrepreneur that was rendered vulnerable by the pass laws; and in Nthana's, her transport costs or her meagre wage, long hours, and daily humiliation at work. But when it comes to explaining consciousness, as the introduction to this study points out, the material realm is a necessary but far from a sufficient explanation. How, for example, does sheer material necessity explain Ernestina Mekgwe's feelings of solidarity, Naomi Setshedi's involvement in broader political campaigns, or some of the women's conservatism in the face of threats to their livelihood? In describing each woman's responses, I have tried to convey the presence of a whole nexus of historical and biographical factors that contributed to them, and there follows a discussion of at least some of these factors.

Naomi Setshedi is the most unequivocal about the meaning and importance of her political past. As a long-standing resident of Alexandra and a woman who never totally became absorbed into the domestic servant sector, she appears to have adopted a "township" ideology and orientation. Her identification is with the township, her ideology militant, populist, and "black," with a strong tinge of Tswana chauvinism accompanying it. White men are the enemy. She talks to Mmantho of "those whites." She is a sensitive and intelligent person, who plans and makes her life opportunities work for her, showing a strong entrepreneurial streak.

Ernestina Mekgwe, her friend, is also rebellious — she is the woman who unsuccessfully resisted her arranged marriage. In her earlier testimony, she emphasises her happy childhood, the "golden age" of the past, the virtues of preindustrial society — crafts, self-reliance, creativity and respect, plenty, a rich and varied diet, and the virtues of breastfeeding. She is overtly sympathetic to the ANC, "power," bus boycotters, and so on. It is perhaps precisely her conception of a previous "better life" that gives her the capacity to value actions which seek to improve the present situation. However, she sees herself as an outsider to these things. She is essentially a rural person, who distinguishes herself from urban-oriented people or township dwellers. Again, the word *populism* springs to mind — both women embrace modernising ideologies that blend nostalgia for the old values with a desire to grasp the new. Mrs. Mekgwe sees herself in a supportive role to people like Naomi, but is far more reluctant to talk about her views. Mrs. Mekgwe's fear at being somehow discovered to be a fellow-traveller is in contrast to the bold statements of Mrs. Setshedi, whose fearlessness appears to be unique. The more common response, however, is ambiguous and timid, fearful that overt displays of resistance should be seen as signs of disreputable or irresponsible attitudes.

Nthana Mokale is interesting because she is the only woman with any experience of factory work, and yet, contrary to any expectations one might have that the proletariat is always in the vanguard, she is the most conservative of them all. Her experience of a lifetime of labour, of harsh work conditions, and poor treatment by employers and government officials alike has left her with a sharp political and social awareness. She is cynical about whites, employers, hours of work, and suffering. But she is not happy to translate this awareness into social and political action. She has, indeed, participated in two events of some considerable significance — the resistance against removals from Sophiatown, and a strike of workers at H. Jones and Co. However she is at pains to emphasise the fact that neither of these two events has an inspirational meaning for her. Neither of them acts as a memory towards which she will turn with pride or nostalgia. Rather, they are seen as painful, difficult events. In the case of Sophiatown, the failure of the resistance is etched deep in her memory — she says "we failed" and "whites cannot be beaten, they are the Gods of the Earth."

While acknowledging that individual personality differences must account for a significant portion of the different political responses of the women here, there are some connections between the patterns of resistance they display, and other factors. Their childhood at home, for example, may well have helped shape their responses in town. Mrs. Setshedi and her friend and supporter, Mrs. Mekgwe, were two of the most independent young girls from Phokeng, and the former had made it her business to go to Spooner's school. Mrs. Mekgwe had actively, although unsuccessfully, resisted her arranged marriage. Mrs. Setshedi had a mother enlightened enough for this resistance not to have been necessary. Mrs. Mokale, by contrast, had shown a tendency to conform even in her younger days. She was the daughter of rich peasants, and displays a high degree of awareness of this. She appears to have had an unduly strict upbringing, and was highly intelligent at school — her teachers wanted her to teach. But she left school early, and showed, rather, an interest in escaping from her repressive home, and in material things such as the acquisition of furniture, a means to helping her find a husband. Her attitudes towards Bafokeng custom are also conservative — although she played the role of boy in a family of girls, she shows an acceptance of patriarchal rules, such as the exclusion of women from meetings, the fact that women tended not to become teachers, or the arranged marriage, and is indeed extremely anxious to please. She overtly expresses an admiration for Penzhorn as a teacher.

The type of employment in which they were involved in town also affected the women's capacity to resist; domestic workers, particularly live-in ones subjected to the paternalism we have already explored, were more vulnerable to employers' attempts at control. Living in the township, as a corollary, exposed the women to the discourses of protest — but not if they, like Nthana Mokale, spent much of their day in the factory, excluded from township activities, and without the time or space to take part. Her adult life drew her into painful and exploitative situations. Her domestic employers appear to have been harsher than most, and her early widowhood forced her into the hardships of factory labour, with its long hours and overt racism. The more independent women who found their way through the complexities of the informal sector and independent domestic work had both the mentality and the time to join in.

The few women who had some experience of organised protest give us an idea of how they perceived it symbolically. For them, practical and immediate gains and victories were, not surprisingly, far more important than the abstractions of populist and nationalist symbolism. Local worlds of meaning appear to have been more compelling than those drawn on a larger map. But their mobilisation as participants in collective acts of defiance would clearly have been impossible without the presence of a more abstract discourse that could transcend their personal and immediate concerns, realised through the leadership to whom they related, and the symbolic languages of song, Christianity, and defiance. Obviously in their mature years they no longer identified themselves as simply Bafokeng. Conceptions of themselves as Tswanas, Blacks, or township-dwellers provided just some of the alternative self-definitions which the city had conferred upon them. Notions of womanhood, too, which embraced the virtues of courage, boldness, independence, and defiance, were blended with the more domestic conceptions of themselves as mothers and providers. The most powerful and political of the new self-definitions that emerged during the 1950s is probably the notion Mrs. Setshedi espouses of the *"Mayibuye* woman" — an all-encompassing identity which proves powerful enough to transcend time and space, and which is recalled as a means of identification even in Phokeng thirty years after the events that gave rise to it. But such a transformation of self was rare.

It is an interesting fact that few informants are concerned to portray to Mmantho the stark contrast between the life they lived in the townships and the life lived by whites elsewhere, particularly in the wealthy white suburbs of which the women were well aware. Perhaps they take for granted that Mmantho knows of and is aware of these realities — but perhaps they also indicate the extent to which the "reference group" that held most meaning to the women was represented by other township blacks, or by their own past experience. What seems to have mobilised them was not a sense of injustice vis-à-vis whites, but a sense that whites were imposing upon them an order that was an intolerable contrast to that under which they had made their modest lives before. It was white power, rather than white wealth, that was at stake — power to dispossess, to cause "relative deprivation." As Ernestina Mekgwe said, "I was born without such troubles, but now I have troubles." We have seen that the women are voluble when it comes to their experiences of authoritarian control and official imposition upon black life by the state and the local authorities. It is no wonder, then, that the police figure so prominently in their consciousness. The women thus display all the ingredients of a nationalist, rather than a class, consciousness. Their awareness is less of black economic deprivation than of their enemy as the "white man," embodied in the police force primarily, but also the state, government, or officialdom. Perhaps this analysis of the mainsprings of their consciousness, then, can give us some insight into the nature and origins of African nationalism in South Africa, and its particular resonance for women.

It is also in this area of their testimony that the interviewees show a sharp awareness of the fact that they were not fully free agents, and that there were distinct structural limits to their capacity to realise themselves as independent beings. It is here above all that they speak about the presence of larger structural forces shaping their lives. But, in acknowledging this, they do not acknowledge submission. Small and large acts of defiance continue to define their stories. While the balance between structure and agency may change over time and space, both appear to persist in every epoch. The significance of this lies in the fact that although Sophiatown and other townships were removed and Soweto created, strikes and trade unionism were illegal, and passes were indeed imposed upon the women, the presence and depth of African protest in the 1950s did set limits to the capacity of the government to impose its will upon all,[81] and created a cultural reservoir and set of memories of defiance that were to provide inspiration for later, more successful, protestors.

As far as the women of Phokeng were concerned, while the moral victory of government over governed was not complete, their situation was permanently changed by the implementation of apartheid in the townships. For it was after the years of protest and defeat that most of the women came to the decision to return to Phokeng. We now turn to examine the closing stages of their stories, and see how the women continued to make decisions to act, within limits set by history.

9

Leaving the City,
1960−1980

In their later years all of the women who had migrated returned to Phokeng after decades in the cities. Many of them perceived their return as something they had chosen. But here, as the apartheid system made itself felt inexorably throughout the country, we should understand their "choice" as having been powerfully constrained and shaped by a whole range of factors. Now, more than ever, their ability to act independently was weakened, and they sought to maximise their own visualised life strategy in circumstances ever more closely shaped by political, economic, and social realities. In this chapter we ask what contributed to their decision to go home, examining the return to Phokeng as a combination of "push" and "pull" factors, the mirror image of their decisions, decades earlier, to migrate.

These push-pull factors were broadly located in the changed political economy of the South Africa of the 1960s and 1970s, the era of high apartheid, when the state sought to implement as much of its segregationist vision as possible. We have already seen how government attacks on inner-city black suburbs had deeply affected the women at the urban end. At the same time, the state was reconstructing the "homelands" — the black "reserves," based upon the land originally allocated to Africans at the time of the 1913 Land Act. These, in the logic of "grand apartheid," were to be given a spurious political independence, in order to try to defuse the power of African nationalism and divert it into ethnicity, and their economic viability was to be encouraged (within limits). But they were also to act as "dumping grounds" for hundreds of thousands of blacks, removed from cities, white farms, and the few "black spots" in white areas which the 1913 Land Act had failed to eliminate, and as labour reserves, places to which the unemployed could be banished in times of recession, and from which new supplies of labour could be drawn when it was needed. Phokeng was located in one of these "reserves" — an area which became the "independent state" of Bophuthatswana, a peculiarly scattered series of bits of land in the Western Transvaal and parts of the Free State.

A home in Phokeng, as photographed in 1990
(Other houses are shown on pages 201, 203, 205, and 207)

By exploring the various factors that led the women of Phokeng back home during this era, we are able to look at the way in which "grand apartheid" affected not only those at whom it was specifically directed—the cities' overflow, the surplus of labour on white farms, the residents of "black spots"—but also, and mainly, at those who had supposedly escaped its tentacles—the relatively settled, respectable, black working class. These people, as we have suggested in Chapter 8, were not actually meant to flee to the homelands. Townships, however humble and inadequate, were built to house them. But the gravest failure of the Nationalist government lay in its policy for "urban blacks"—for whom not even the half-truths of homeland "ethnicity" could be invented, and we have seen how alienated even some of the most upright of the Bafokeng women became during the implementation of urban segregation. It is perhaps not surprising, thus, that the "homeland" came to exert a strange and unintended magnetic pull upon people such as the women of Phokeng. Both the "push" of urban alienation and the "pull" of home found expression in the consciousness of the women, and to each was added a whole range of different variables originating in the women's histories.

Those migrants from Phokeng who had lived in the city for longer periods had always envisaged an eventual return to their home village.[1] But their decision to go home in their later years was never a simple one. Some inherited a house in Phokeng, presumably a strong incentive to return. Mrs. Moje, for example:

By the way, why did you decide to leave Alexandra for Phokeng?

My mother-in-law had passed away and there was no one to come and stay in this house. Therefore we decided to come and stay here.[2]

For others, the completion, and in some cases perceived success, of their strategy of household building and child rearing marked the end of the time it was thought necessary for the women to spend in town. Some of their families had, in fact, achieved social mobility. All of Frances Nameng's four children ended up living in Meadowlands with their "own" houses.[3] This is a common pattern, and in fact it may be argued that it is the children of better-off migrants such as these who form the secure resident population of Rand townships today. In terms of occupations too, several, but by no means all, of the women's children reached middle-class occupations, such as those of nurse or teacher, or became at least occupants of the same upper-working-class position held by their parents. To retain or improve upon one's class position in the repressive period of the 1950s and 1960s was not as easy as perhaps it may have become by the 1970s and 1980s, when new opportunities for black middle-class people were opened up, so this is an important factor.

If the city could no longer offer anything to the women, Phokeng could — it appears to have exerted a powerful pull. Mrs. Mekgwe returned home because she considered Phokeng to be more secure than the city, and says that she always has done so. In fact, she hardly wants to set foot in town again.

> You see when a person is old like I am, he doesn't like to be running around Jo'burg visiting because there are lots of thugs in the townships and they are bound to kill you.[4]

She claims always to have nurtured a deep suspicion of the intentions of white authorities in town:

> One day while visiting them [people in Sophiatown] I heard my aunt shouting "Ons phola hier." I asked her what is "ons phola" then she answered "here we are staying." I told her "it will be one day," you are not clever both of you, you should instead go and built yourselves houses in Phokeng and let those houses to teachers who will pay you rent every month. Sometime in the future when they throw you out of this township [Sophiatown] and you are not able to find other accommodation, you could always go back to your house in Phokeng. I gave them good advice, but none of them used it.[5]

But many of our chief informants will have agreed with her, as they are quite clear that the aim of building a house was paramount in their minds during their working years, particularly towards the end of the 1950s. This coincides quite uncannily with the period of township removals, and the firmer implementation of apartheid. It could thus be seen as a form of resistance to (or, in a less romantic way, a retreat from) the apartheid order. Mrs. Setshedi, for example, discusses her strategy of house building in full awareness and consciousness of its implications for household strategy. At first she outlines how the situation in Alexandra declined:

> My child, whites take what belongs to blacks free of charge. Look at what has happened to Alexandra Township. They had forced people to buy plots, peri-urban. Peri-urban built houses in Alexandra.... The peri-urban people are the ones who moved soldiers from Pretoria and built them houses around Alexandra, on the land that blacks could have occupied.... Then blacks were moved to Diepkloof, Meadowlands, our solidarity was destroyed in this fashion. The Shangaans and Pedi were moved to Chiawelo.... Those ones had policemen who moved from house to house asking for a permit in the evening. We never had such

things as "permit" in Alexandra before peri-urban could take control of that township. The only document we were familiar with was the receipt we were issued with when paying rent.... Accommodating strangers or visitors was no problem then. No one could ask who those people were, but with peri-urban our doors were often swung open during the night when their policemen were raiding for "permit." ... All of your children should be on the permit otherwise you were in trouble. What had been happening prior to peri-urban was that a representative from the offices where we used to pay rent normally made visits to different houses and asked how many people were occupying each house. No one was ever arrested for permit during those visits. We used to help many people who were stranded.

Had they bought plots before the coming of the oppressive "peri-urban" board, the first attempt by the Nationalist Party to control the ever-wayward Alexandra, they would have benefited:

During that period Alexandra was under the administration of Campbell ... an English woman. We could have bought a plot during Mrs. Campbell's time if we wanted to, we would be living comfortably now. People used to buy plots, make bricks and build houses for themselves. A plot was very cheap then, fifty pounds, and twenty pounds being a deposit.[6]

She makes a direct link between this and her strategy of returning home. She at first, as we have seen, expresses feelings of regret that perhaps she missed an opportunity:

Jesus, we misused the opportunity. We argued that we had our permanent homes in Magaliesberg, therefore we could not buy plots in Johannesburg as if we were Coloured so did not know where they belong. But, till to date we regret why we didn't buy plots, we really behaved in a stupid fashion. A friend of mine from the Free State once advised me to buy a plot of land. It only cost one pound to get one's name on a waiting list. It was possible to get a plot with a house built already.... Most people used to build big houses and reserve rooms for tenants. But it was possible to find a house built already, since the place was occupied by the Italians before. Whites didn't like to go and stay in Alexandra because they said it was filthy. Mrs. Campbell then advertised it to blacks. We were promised an amount of money as compensation whenever we wanted to move out of Alexandra, those who bought plots of land I mean.

How much?

Four hundred pounds. The Xhosas, Southern Sothos, Shangaans, Ndebele, Pedi, started buying plots, except Tswanas. Very few Tswanas bought plots because most of them argued that they have villages where they belong. They looked down on the other ethnic groups when they decided to live permanently in Alexandra....

They thought those groups were stranded?

Yes.

However, it emerges that her desire for a plot did not contradict the long-term aim of returning to Phokeng — it would have been a means to facilitating it:

We realised later that those people were very clever, they wanted to make a profit out of their plots. I wanted to buy a plot also but my husband didn't want to hear anything of that kind. My friends used to persuade me to buy one but my husband was very stubborn. I almost went mad because of that. What I had in mind was to buy a plot and sell it again after five years for four hundred pounds. I thought I would then take that four hundred pounds and build a house here in Phokeng.... Again, plots were being sold at Winterveld near Pretoria during those years. People flocked to that place, my husband kept on postponing to buy a plot there until it was then difficult and expensive to get one. Then, one could get a plot for thirty pounds.

Was the place previously occupied by whites like Alexandra?

No, it was not. People from Alexandra used to organise lorries to take them to Winterveld to buy plots. Some of them built houses there to let. One woman bought a plot in Winterveld and later sold it for three hundred pounds. With that money she was able to buy another plot in Alexandra and she built rooms for tenants on that plot.[7]

Her husband worked all his life with a house in Phokeng as his ambition. But:

Now my child, my husband worked for that employer of his until we were able to build this house. One day he decided to go home to see whether the house was completed. He went there on a weekend and on a Monday after that particular weekend he couldn't go to work because he was not feeling well. He died eventually.... It was in 1962, we had to move into this house during that year, but he was unfortunate to move in here dead.[8]

She links their planned departure explicitly to what she claims were the politically motivated removals of activists from Alexandra (which had escaped Sophiatown's fate of total destruction) to Soweto:

> Now, when they started building up houses in Soweto, the government undertook the project of resettling us with the hope that strikes would be curtailed. People who lived in Sophiatown as well as those living in Alexandra tried to resist resettlement, but they could not go much far with it.... When they said to us, "Go to Meadowlands," my husband then said, "Both of us are getting old. Look, you have some washing to do in Dunkeld, it is going to be strenuous on your side to catch a train from Soweto to Park Station and a double decker from there to Dunkeld in the morning and in the afternoon. I don't think you would make it; let's build a house at home and go stay there." I then agreed to his suggestion because we had some money at the bank to enable us to start building a new house.[9]

Although her decision was puzzling to some of her urbanised friends, Naomi is certain that it was the right one. The cities are now not only poor, but life there is so difficult as to render its inhabitants deprived in every respect:

> It is only now of late that I find people struggling in Soweto to make ends meet. When I decided to leave Alexandra for Phokeng people started criticising me, saying, "How can you spend so many years in an urban area and then decide to go back to a rural way of life?" I then said to them, "I was born and brought up in that rural area, I know the type of life those people are living. I won't let myself be fooled by the type of life that the township offers because I am quite aware that there is going to be a stage where most of us would be struggling to make ends meet."

I used to observe those who were much older than I was, how difficult it was for them to pay rent every month. Most of them had children, but these children would leave the household after getting married. What happened was that the poor parents had no one to pay rent for them. . . . Now I couldn't imagine myself exposed to that situation. I said to myself, "Is this the type of life I am faced with when I grow old? No, let me go back home where I won't have to pay rent, and where if I may happen to stay in a dirty place, people would condone it by saying that I have grown old." . . . Yes my child, the Golden City is a place for whites.

Her decision is vindicated, in her eyes, by this poignant story:

Nowadays when I visit that place, I meet old people that I know. A female hostel has been built up at 4th Avenue Alexandra, on the site where our house used to stand. . . . We used to stay there but our houses got demolished and a female hostel has been built up there. Recently I met one old woman at that hostel. She used to rent a house in Alexandra, but she was originally from Bethanie near Brits. . . . My brother's daughter stays in that hostel and one day while I was visiting her I saw a very old woman walking past us with a walking stick in her hand. I recognised her immediately and began to ask "Is that woman so-and-so from Bethanie, she looks much older than I expected. Where does she stay? Why does she walk towards the hostel's entrance?" One woman then told me that the old woman was staying in that very hostel. Her children got married and left her. She had to leave the house she was staying in because she could not pay rent every month. She then decided to go and stay in that hostel. It would appear that rent was reasonable at the hostel. I continued asking, "Now what about her property, to where did she send her furniture?" I was made to understand that she sold all her belongings except her clothes and blankets which she brought along to the hostel. I looked at her with a broken heart and thanked myself for having gone to Phokeng to stay there while I was still having some means to build a house. I don't think she had money to go home and put up *matikiri* [a house with iron roof and walls]. . . . I looked at her for a long time with sympathy. I felt a pain raging in my heart like as though I had lost one of my children. I realised that she had no hope in life, she was a deserted woman. When I look at most people in Soweto I tend to pity them because I know that most of them would like to have houses at home in the countryside but they can't afford it.[10]

She is not, she says, simply referring to economic circumstance. "Life is expensive wherever you are," she says. But having remained in the city has deprived women such as her Bethanie friend of dignity, community and hope. She was "a deserted woman."

Some women had indeed been forced, or, like Mrs. Setshedi, driven by the threat of force, to move to Phokeng, in an era where forced removals of blacks from townships, white farms, and "black spots" were common. Rebecca Phiri came to the town as a result of being removed from a different village, Magokgwaneng, in Rustenburg:

We were then moved from that place to another in Rustenburg by whites. . . . At that village it was even better than this one, because we were having mealie fields, cattle and sheep. Here there are no fields so we are struggling to live. . . .

When you left there did the government help you to remove your goods?

Yes, because they were the ones who were removing us from our village to a strange one. They did not even give us damage money.

Even those who had beautiful houses were not paid anything?

They were only paid a small amount. When we arrived at Rustenburg, we were told to pay for walls which were said to be ours, but there were no roofs. We roofed with our own zinc.... We were badly treated, they told us that the place which we were at was not a good place for us. They moved us to another place and we had to start building all over again. Then after some time we were told again that the place which we were staying at was going to be used as a road. So we moved back again where we started.[11]

Lydia Phiri also had an experience of removal, this time from a white farm, where she and her husband had been sharecroppers. As a returning Mofokeng she was made to feel welcome in Phokeng:

What made you decide to come and settle here?

We came here because the whites were chasing us out.

Are you referring to the whites from whom you bought that land?

No. I am talking about the whites who were controlling us after we had bought that land. We were farming together with them. They came later. It was the whites who chased us out.... They chased us away, by hook or by crook.... Chief Lebone provided us with trucks. He brought us here. By the way, we are children of Phokeng, my child.... He provided us with tents temporarily until we received proper accommodation. After receiving proper accommodation we took the tents back. Where we were staying at first, we had beautiful houses. We were under the providence of God. Now they spoilt everything. We are suffering here because we have no fields. We are, however, still waiting for a word from the chief. We are here to stay, there is nothing we can do.[12]

Elizabeth Morobe is not a Mofokeng, but she and her Tswana husband moved to Phokeng in 1969. She had lived in Pretoria, but was under threat of removal: "We were not interested in the place they promised to take us to ... in Pretoria. We liked Rustenburg. We were removed by the government,"[13] she says. Maria Mathuloe was not born in Phokeng, but lived in Rustenburg for a long time, and subsequently in Alexandra township. She left Alexandra in 1962 because of removals: "It was on 6th March 1962. We arrived at my mother-in-law's house, and afterwards I built my own house here in Rustenberg."[14]

Not only did Phokeng act as a refuge for some of the casualties of apartheid and of the capitalisation of agriculture, but others married into the Bafokeng, and were grateful for the opportunity to move into one of the few economically viable regions in the homelands. Sophie Serokane, the Pedi, and her Mofokeng husband went to Phokeng in 1976. For her, it was a new place, not "home": "We came to Phokeng in 1976, during the year of the unrest. It looked as if we were running away from the unrest, but we came here a few months before the unrest could start."[15] They sold their house in Dobsonville and according to Sophie: "I think we made a wise decision to come here."[16] Later, she says that

We were old and could no longer manage the location life. Life at locations was becoming too expensive for us and we got less money for pension. We stayed with our grandchildren here in Phokeng. Their parents send money and food.... These days life seems to be too expensive compared with the time when we left Dobsonville.[17]

She talks about how they used to visit Phokeng regularly during their years at work in town; and how they were "always kept informed about conditions at home, news about so-and-so having passed away and so-and-so being married, and so forth."[18] They used to visit Phokeng "occasionally," and now they live opposite her sister-in-law, who also returned to Phokeng after her husband died.

The pursuing of their originally urban household strategy was not incompatible with the retention of a rural vision as well, epitomised in the aim of every woman, and her husband too in most cases, of building a house back home. Not only would the house in Phokeng provide security in old age, but it could be viewed as an extension of the household-building strategy of earlier times, for children and grandchildren could regard Phokeng as a resource for their own use, and the ongoing rural connection would, the women believed, assist them in keeping alive kin and cultural networks which might otherwise be under threat. The city could eat away at the resources necessary for these cultural projects, and whatever surplus resources were available should, many of the women believed, be ploughed back into the village. Mrs. Makgale recalls the day she decided to build a house in Phokeng. It was after she had lived in Fietas for about seven years, and thus early on in her time in the city:

One day I sat down and calculated the money I had lost through paying rent and I was shocked to discover that I had lost more than a hundred

pounds. I happened to come across a book in which the rent that we used to pay was recorded every month.... I was shocked to discover that I had lost so much money through rent.

She suggests that she was the initiator in the decision to redirect their focus:

I then said to my husband, "Look, with the money that we have lost so far, we could have built ourselves a house at home." ... I was about to build this very house by then. There was a small hut out there where that "tin house" (house with iron walls and roof) now stands. That was allocated to my husband and me after we got married, but it was so small that I had to bend whenever I wanted to go in there. The wife of my husband's brother, the old *ngwetsi*, used to stay in the main house, which had one bedroom, a dining room, and a passage. I was the young *ngwetsi* because I got married long after she got married. My husband had bought building material, but his brother made use of it while they were building the main house they used to stay in. My husband and I then had no alternative but to go stay at Fietas. During our stay at Fietas, the idea of building a house at home was still in my mind. So it happened one day while I was busy counting the amount of money we happened to have spent on rent that I decided to go back home and persuaded my husband to allow me to. When he arrived home I said to him, "A man of God, take this book of George Bai and count the amount of money that we have spent on rent." George Bai was an Indian ... to whom we used to pay rent. He started counting the money and he was shocked to discover that we had spent quite a lot of money on rent. I asked him, "Don't you think that we could have built a house at home with that money? A man of God, I want to go back home, when you have received your wage I want to go home." He replied, "Now what are you going to eat when you get there?" I said to him, "I am going to eat just what the Bafokeng are eating." We agreed that I should go back home and it was then that I started packing up my things. I took along my firstborn who was born in 1923, but he was about four years old during that time.... We went home and I started building a two-roomed house, the very one that we are now seated in.

Having had urban experience did not preclude her from undertaking the traditional job of house building:

Did you build it all by yourself?

Yes. I used to mix soil with water and try to form bricks which are used to build the walls. I never dried my bricks, I used them raw as they were. My firstborn was the only person who helped me when I was still building the walls. When I was through with the walls, I asked one man to help me with roofing. There was one dilapidated hut next to this one and I asked him to take all the poles which used to support that hut and use them for roofing my house.

Was that hut already falling?

Yes it was. Some of my clay pots got broken when it was falling. I managed to roof the house with relatively little expense. When everything was over, I asked those men who were roofing my house to put a hut so that I could have a place to make fire.

In fact, she built two houses, and ruined her health in the process:

Has that house over there been built by you?

Yes, when I was through with mine. I started off building it as soon as I had finished building mine, but it took me three years before I could complete it. One day I fell down while I was busy building up the wall. I had to go to hospital where I spent five months.... I had to walk with a pair of crutches for three months.[19]

She interprets the incident as an example of witchcraft:

I was alone at home on that particular day and when I was going through the door, I had a fracture. I was at the door of the house that I built where I fell, I got convinced that my fractured leg had something to do with witchcraft. When I was about to close the door behind me, my foot slipped and I fell to the ground. I took the incident very lightly, but later on I discovered that it was a serious case. I went to a witchdoctor who told me that after I had fallen while I was lying down, a *tikoloshi*[20] came and twisted my leg.[21]

Mmadiate says that she could not stay in the city because of its "misery and poverty." However, it is not certain whether this refers to a spiritual and moral deficiency rather than an economic one:

Seeing that life was a bit better in the cities, why didn't you buy a house and stay there in Johannesburg?

No, no, not me. Even now I do not desire the place.... I do not want to hear even mention of the place. I only saw that we were staying there for misery and poverty. There was no progress in life, but only poverty. I then concluded that it was only wise for us to come back home....

She is proud of the immense labour she put into her house:

> You can see the evidence of the thorough job which I made here at home. I built this house with my own hands. There was a very big house over there that belonged to Mathure's mother-in-law, the house had been fine when I was married, but when I came from Johannesburg, it had fallen apart. Before, my sister-in-law had a separate room in it. I also had my own hut which had been built near that little stairway. On my return, I took the poles from that ruin and erected a tin shack. I then started rebuilding the house. I also had built a small tin roofed house over there. I used earth to rebuild the main house.... I then sought the assistance of a certain man for the roofing. I paid him ten shillings. They were still cheap by then.... He was only a man whose trade was roofing.... We used zinc material that had been taken from that flat-roofed hut which was over there, that is the tin shack that I had constructed. We then roofed the house. The roof stripped hut was now used for storing a stove. When I was from my sister's funeral in Johannesburg, I then continued with extending the house. My son used to hoist the soil forth for me. The house had partly caved in due to high showers of rain which had taken place.... My son used to sleep therein before his marriage. Presently I am busy plastering this one which has been built by bricks.... I have not rested. I have done that task for two years.

She financed the operation by crocheting in her spare time, and with the help of her son and husband:

> We would often take breaks from the job. We would then do some crocheting because there was a demand for these articles from the people. I would then earn some extra cash so as to help my son. He is responsible for buying all this building material. When the bricks have been used up, I would tell him. He would then order some when he is on his way to work. It was on the third year when the house is completed when he announced that he is marrying.... I went on with this task for two years. There was a shortage of water during that time. However, I used to obtain it from the local shop owner. However, shopkeepers during those times were not as sharp as they are nowadays. They now charge one rand per drum. Things were still cheap. I would then take breaks.

Is it during the period when your husband was in retirement?

Yes. He used to help me in mixing the soil.

Her husband, too, was proud of her work:

> At times he would find that I had demolished a certain part for revamping. He would say, "Had you not had the guts to do the job for yourself, a person assisting you would be angry and quit the job." Whilst I was busy, there halted a motor car with a load of zinc sheets. I was amazed at their numerousness. I then woke up the next morning, I demolished a certain part and extended it. I went on steadily with my job. I then smeared the interior with a type of soil known as *kotokoto*.

She describes a second injury:

> When I was busy with the exterior wall, I fell. I was about to climb down from the table and bench which I was using as stepladders; the bench collapsed. I fell onto the bench with both feet. I then said to myself,

"Today, I have broken both my legs, this is my end." Even today there are visible gash marks where both had been hurt. It is long that I have been sustaining injuries. Some of the scars have disappeared. When a man comes to take a look at this house, I then came up to him whilst he was still amazed and asked him whether he thinks that it is only men who are able to build houses.[22]

Mmadiphoko Mokgatle never worked in Johannesburg except for a short period before her children were born, when, as we have seen, she chose not to work and mother at the same time. So she built a house when she went to settle in Phokeng after the birth of her first child. House building for her, and for many of the other women, was a personal responsibility, with roots in traditional expectations, and she gives us some idea of how closely the creation of a house — and hence a home — was tied up with her sense of self, as well as how much sheer hard manual labour went into it:

> *Now granny, when you came to settle over here, did you not assist in erecting the walls for the huts as it was the usual practice for women here in Phokeng?*
>
> What kind of a person would I have been without building? What could I have ... called myself? I have built that house with my own hands. I have built three rooms with my own bare hands in that house that is at the back.... My husband did the foundation. He used to build the foundation on Saturdays whilst he was still employed. Me and my grandmother-in-law used to erect the walls until the walls were this high.... We used mud bricks and wattle. We made three rooms.... On Saturdays he used to climb to the top to fasten the rafters and to thatch the roof.[23]

Mrs. Mokale, in discussing her reasons for returning to Phokeng, gives some idea of why it was considered important for women to have their own homes. She returned on her retirement, and like several of the women, did not want to become a "township granny":

> I felt it was about time that I returned because I was old and not working any more.
>
> *Were you already receiving pension by then?*
>
> Other than getting pension, my children were working and having their own families, so I thought it best to come back here instead of staying in the locations where I would soon be a burden on my children or become a township granny.

She gives a cynical and grim picture of the fate of such people, suggesting that village culture provides protection against the abuse of the elderly by their own children:

> *Why didn't you become a township granny?*
>
> No ways. When you're too old your children don't have time to look after you. They have their lives to live and at times they don't feed you, they beat you up, you know, generally mistreating you.
>
> *They say you disturb them?*
>
> Yes, they want you to stay in your room and they in theirs. And if it's in

Phokeng, you'll be able to have order, since it's your house, but out there in the townships many sons beat up their mothers, evict them from their houses, now here in Phokeng it would not happen because the villagers are around to help you and the chief is also present.

Her views appear to have been drawn from her own experience. She left her house in Emdeni, Soweto, registered in her name for her son to occupy, leaving him the right to it when she dies:

It is still in my name because I still receive my pension in Johannesburg. The municipality doesn't prefer old people to register their houses in other people's names because they fear that those people can decide to push the old people out of their own houses.[24]

But this strategy of self-protection failed. Her son evicted her, and appears to reject her:

Do you ever visit him and his wife?

They would bury me alive.... Just because they are staying in an urban area they see me as an interfering old lady.[25]

She built her house in Phokeng herself, saying that she regretted that because her husband died in 1946, he had not been able to build one for her:

Granny, were you solely responsible for all the expenses incurred in the building of this house?

I am the one who worked for it. I couldn't do otherwise once my husband left me staying with my in-laws.

I thought your sons helped you to a large extent.

No, I worked for many years in Johannesburg. I started in 1927 and came back in 1930. From there I worked from 1947 to 1973.... This house was built in 1973 after a long period of stay in Johannesburg, since May 1947.

In spite of her bitterness over her son's behaviour, she suggests that the house was part of a new household-creating strategy — that of holding her extended family together, and of giving them a sense of the meaning of being Bafokeng:

I guess you were really determined.

I was. I knew that if my children were to start working and without a home of theirs, they would be tempted to go stay with the families of their girlfriends.... So I had to try my best to provide them with a home so that they could bring their wives here when they are married.... I hated the idea that one of my sons would be taken by his wife to Boons, the other to Swaziland, to name the few, since I was aware that they would soon forget their place of origin. They grew up in Johannesburg and [it] would have been, therefore, easier for them to forget everything about Phokeng.[26]

But the decision to leave town was a hard one, and she may have exchanged security of residence for economic hardship:

Granny since you stayed in the township for the better part of your life, what can you say about township life as compared to life in the village? Which one would you prefer?

You know what, I am beginning to think that life at Emdeni can be far more better than here. Oh, things are very expensive. I guess it could have been better if I were to stay with my children, sharing with them the little that they can get, because groceries are very expensive nowadays.[27]

But Naomi Setshedi confirms the generalised perception that children in the townships may treat their parents with some cruelty:

I have seen girls your age leave their parents in a rented house and going to live in a shebeen queen's house, brewing and selling liquor for that woman. I've seen boys kicking their mothers out of a house that is rented and registered in the old woman's name when they wanted to bring girls home to sleep with them.

She remembers one such woman:

There was once an old woman who lived next door to our house and she had eight children; three of them worked but didn't live with her nor did they come to visit her. This woman had an irresponsible husband who worked in the white suburbs and came home only when he desired. One late afternoon when returning from work I see this old woman sitting on a small stool, her shoulders bent inwards and her face clasped in her hands. She was sitting beside a brazier fire and on the fire was a boiling pot. As the fence dividing our yards was broken, I crossed into her yard and stood beside her.... I discovered that they hadn't had a meal for three days, and the pot on the brazier was just filled with water.[28]

Leaving the city was, for most of the women, a result of a combination of circumstances and beliefs. High apartheid had undermined their sources of stability and income where it had not actually moved them. They also showed a perceptive scepticism about the capacity of the anomic cities to support them in their old age. Phokeng, on the other hand, was still there, and those with foresight could plough urban incomes (together with a large amount of physical labour) into the construction of homes for their old age. These homes would provide security, as well as the possibility of continuing to develop the household-building strategies that had for so long motivated the women in the cities. But the Phokeng to which they sought to return was a very different place from the village they had left. We conclude with an examination of some of the ways in which this "homeland" town was experienced by the women, as they settled into retirement there.

10

Grandmothers and Pensioners, 1980–1983

The "homeland" to which the women returned was indeed apartheid's dumping ground, the place to which people were either directly forced to return, or indirectly manoeuvred if they would not accept the city on terms dictated by government policy. And yet Phokeng in the 1980s was also able to offer the remnant of a meaningful community and culture, a sense of place to the women. But this was not the old Phokeng. The village itself had changed beyond recognition during the absence of the migrants, who themselves had reached the closing stages of their lives as working people, creators of households, and reproducers of culture. "Going home" to the women meant constructing a life in entirely different circumstances, for entirely different purposes, from those which had guided them as young girls. The interviews give us some idea of the dimensions of their new lives, in a changed community.

Mmadiate Makgale sums up the new Phokeng:

> Phokeng today is a rough place. Nowadays it is not safe to go alone during the night.

> *I guess Phokeng is one of the roughest villages around Rustenburg.*

> Yes, Phokeng is a rough village. It does not differ much from Tlhabane township. Recently a white man had shot dead my nephew in town.[1]

We have already mentioned how when Chief August Molotlegi was succeeded by his son, Edward Lebone Molotlegi, in 1964, the declining peasant economy gave way to one far more dependent on revenue from the Bafokeng-owned platinum mines. These mines were opened during the 1940s and, together with remittances from migrants, provided the community with a consistent source of income. The ending of the nostalgically perceived peasant past is given, by some of the women, as the symbolic moment of the coming of the platinum mines to the area. Bafokeng agriculture may have begun its decline long before the 1940s. But it was the establishment of the mines — with their compound-dwelling migrant

213

A scene from modern Phokeng
(See also pages 215, 217, and 219)

labourers, who were perceived as "foreign" by the people of Phokeng — that is remembered as having marked the end of the "golden age" of the peasantry.

Valuable farming land was given over to the mines, in a deal which was perceived as having excluded the people:

> It was in 1940.... That was the time when mine diggings were in action, and it was dangerous for us. Then after some time, the mine diggings took over our ploughing fields.
>
> *Did they pay you for taking over your fields?*
>
> No, we didn't get anything because it was an agreement between them and our chief.[2]

The mines, says Evelyn Rakola, were "situated exactly where it used to be our fields."[3] And it was the chief, not the people who benefited from them.[4] That the mines brought "danger" was a widespread perception:

> We benefited a lot from (farming), especially before these mines, Bafokeng mines, were put up. The mineworkers then started terrorising us at night out in the fields. Most of us had to quit farming because of terrorism by mineworkers.[5]

These views are echoed by Naomi Setshedi:

> When the mines started we left farming in fear of mineworkers. A woman would not have dared walking alone to the fields.... We were scared of the mineworkers who used to roam about. The mineworkers

had a habit of getting into any field and reap maize or sorghum. Some of them thought that sorghum was the same as sweetreed.... My child, one could not move freely. It was so dangerous that one could not even imagine going to the fields alone.[6]

These notions reflect a great deal about Bafokeng perceptions of outsiders, and about the perceived importance of the isolated fields where women and children had farmed. Hardly anyone ploughed any more. Josephine Mokotedi talks about how "farms that were taken by the mines are those at Phokeng. In Chaneng and Luka people still plough their fields. It's only in Phokeng where they have stopped."[7] Dikeledi Makgale says that farming is impossible now:

Do you have any mealie fields here in Rustenburg?

There are some, but they are of the clayey soil.

Do you plough anything there?

We are unable to plough something because the mineworkers spoil our fields, and they are dreadful people.

Although several of the women mention that they had access to, or even ownership of, fields, none of them farmed. Nkwapa Ramorwesi was unable to farm; she had no fields, and anyway,

I would not be in a position to do that. I am now past my prime years. I can only go there if I were to be transported there by a motor vehicle. I would only be able to look after children here at home. And when it is time for the workers to return from work, I would make fire at times, I would just sit.[9]

The Serokanes had land when they came back to Phokeng, but never lived as farmers in their later years:

Did you have any land to plough when you came here to Phokeng in 1976?

Yes, the land belonged to my in-laws....

Did you plough the land?

No, We have never ploughed the land.... There was no impelling need for us to do so because we used to buy what we needed and besides that we used to have a small patch of land that kept us well supplied with maize.[10]

The decline of agriculture, many of them suggest, had led to a change in the moral order as well. The mines had led to the "spoiling" of the chiefship, says Mrs. Phalatse, who, although she is related to the chief, is highly critical of the direction taken by the Bafokeng under his rule:

This boy [Lebone] behaves in a naughty manner because of the revenue he gets from these mines. He is now building a clinic near his house ... a very big one.... The old clinic will be demolished, those who want clinic services will go to the new one near the chief's house.

Isn't it going to be difficult for those living far away?

It's their problem; buses are available.

But buses cost money, you know.

Yes, it costs money. It's also your problem to get sick. You think that boy called Lebone cares about that.[11]

Later she adds to this theme:

> Maybe ... he's scared people will kill him for his riches. No, he's just too rich and these riches make him feel above everybody. "Hy is te ryk"[12] and he is very young. There are four mines in Phokeng and he receives revenue from all of them. When he became chief, he said he doesn't want white people in Phokeng. When you hire a white farmer to plough your land, he chases the farmer away, but right now his soldiers are white men, his house is guarded by white men, yet our children don't have jobs. You hear me. At the post office, the top jobs are occupied by white people. So is that not uppityness?

> *Perhaps there are not any educated black people to fill those positions.*

> You don't need a degree to guard a house and beside there are lots of children who can fill the posts at the post office. If people want to kill him they would long have done so.[13]

Mrs. Setshedi, too, expresses some resentment that the mines, which were owned communally by the Bafokeng, were actually in the personal control of the chief:

> *The mine that you have been talking about, does it belong to the tribe?*

> Yes, that mine belongs to the tribe, it is Bafokeng mine. Now, can I, as an individual, spend money that they get from that mine? No, I cannot. We as the Bafokeng tribe spend that money through building schools for our children. But we do not have direct control over that money.[14]

Mmamatlakala Moje, who left Alexandra relatively early on in her marriage, says that she and her husband ploughed right up until the 1950s, but that this source of income dried up in later times, leading, she suggests, to a generalised decline in Bafokeng health

some years after 1950. We were ploughing our fields and we had no
problems with so many illnesses that are so problematic nowadays.
Since we stopped going to the fields, we have become prone to illnesses.
I suspect it is due to the fact that we no longer do hard work.[15]

One of Bophuthatswana's wealthiest communities, Phokeng was (and is)
distinctly a mixed blessing to the homeland government. The revenue it supplied
to the homeland was of great importance to the "national" income. However this
was accompanied by an assertiveness, in keeping with Bafokeng tradition perhaps,
which did not always prove palatable to the leaders of Bophuthatswana. As we
saw in Chapter 1, the Bafokeng have in the past threatened to secede from the
homeland; and in more recent times Phokeng was named as the place where the
plan to mount a failed coup against Bophuthatswana's President Mangope was
hatched. The subethnicity of the Bafokeng appears to have become both a means
to develop the boundaries within which the social and economic standing of the
community were improved, and the means whereby the Bafokeng could wield
their political muscle more broadly in the context of Bophuthatswana politics.
This had consequences for the inner politics of Phokeng itself, where there
appeared to be a growing ethnic chauvinism that had spread beyond resentment
at the presence of the miners. It was not easy, for example, say the women, for
those defined as outsiders to gain permission to live in Phokeng. As is the case in
most "homelands," increasingly scarce land and other resources may only be
allocated at the discretion of the chief, who seems to have developed an ideology
of ethnicity suited to the task of deciding on allocation. Outsiders who settled, or
were forced to settle, near the village were spoken of with either hostility or
anxiety. Mokete Phalatse talks of Phokeng in the early 1980s, and the sense of
ethnic exclusiveness that had emerged:

> [Here] the chief has lots of fusses and is jealous.... He said here the
> other day, everyone who is not a Mofokeng should leave Phokeng, only
> people born here should stay. Those who like our husbands were not
> born here should go away.[16]

Sophie Serokane—herself a Pedi who married into the Bafokeng, but who is
sensitive to the problems of being the "outsider"—talks of the exclusiveness of
the Bafokeng:

> Some people came here because their grandfathers were born here, but
> when they arrived here they were ordered to give the chief two to three
> cattle. Then the chief just decided that he does not want them any more.
> He actually chases you when he could find out that you are from other
> tribes.[17]

Ida Molefe too talks about how the chief tried to rid the village of foreigners:

> He said the village was full of foreign people and there was no place for
> his people.... Men came to stay in Phokeng at their wives' homes
> instead of women staying at their in-laws. Those foreign people were
> not allowed to be buried here. There was a North Sotho man who was
> buried last month, the chief was against his burial but the time he came
> to stay here he was told to give the chief a cow. That day the chief was
> just impossible towards his burial, forgetting what he was given. He
> told the wife not to tell him about a dead man, his family was also
> chased away.[18]

Mokete Phalatse says, however, that the chief found this hard line difficult to hold:

> So a question was put to him — because foreigners should leave Phokeng, is your wife also going to leave because she does not come from Phokeng but from Botswana? So what can he say to anyone, while a culprit is in his house?

Does he not say that only men should leave?

> Do you expect a man who has a family here in Phokeng to go and leave it behind? He will take all his family, wife and property included, and go where he will be accommodated.

Did anyone leave eventually?

> Who? No one left Phokeng. They told him he should have stopped us from entering Phokeng in the first place. The people around here have hard heads and in the end it was him, the chief, that conceded and said, "I never said you should go, I didn't mean it, I was just joking."[19]

But Chief Lebone, she claims, had even tried to exclude his own brother from the area:

> After that he chased his younger brother ... Mokgwane.... Mokgwane was a manager at the mine until perhaps the chief did not like it that a kin should know the riches of the mine.... He was explicitly told to leave Phokeng and not to be seen here again. Mokgwane did not care, he went to Hysterkrand where he bought himself a house. He's living there now, with his wife and children.

Where in Phokeng did he stay before he was chased away?

He had a double-storey house just behind the Civic Centre.

So he left it empty?

It's their father's house, it was given to him by his father.

So why should he leave his inheritance behind?

He couldn't take the bricks with him to Hysterkrand, so he bought a house when he arrived there. He is a nice man, he receives visitors from Phokeng, even old people, like they are his friends. Not this Lebone who won't see you when you come to his house but [will] send a messenger to talk with you.[20]

Sophie Serokane and another stranger to Phokeng, Rosinah Setsome, talk at greater length about their situation. Mrs. Setsome, who was born in Klerksdorp and lived in Botswana with her husband for a while, moved to Phokeng in 1969. They were forced by a white farmer to move from the farm they had occupied. The regent chieftainess of Phokeng invited them to live there, and they transported their goods there by oxwagon, and also moved their cattle to Phokeng. There, her husband sold their cattle, as he had no land and "could no longer look after them." He died shortly afterwards. Her main difficulty with living in Phokeng is that "foreigners cannot be buried there." But otherwise, she appears to be well integrated in the life of the village, belonging to several church organisations and groups.

In spite of the fact that her husband was related to the chief's household,[21] Sophie Serokane feels her foreignness more deeply. She relates that:

I started to lose weight here in Phokeng. Look how thin I am nowadays. Some people think that it is through hunger that I am thin. They say, "She thought that Phokeng is the same place as Johannesburg where she used to have enough to eat and drink." I pray God that I regain my weight.[22]

Later she says that "I came here being so big ... look at me now. It is not these people who are responsible for my condition. It is illnesses. However these people here bewitched me and I became semiparalysed. I used a walking stick to aid me when walking."[23] She finds Phokeng a difficult place with strange traditions and customs.[24]

Within this increasingly bounded community, where private agricultural pursuits were limited, the women depended on incomes from a meagre range of sources. Most of them had become "homeland grannies" rather than "township" ones. They cared for their grandchildren, living on money paid to them for this task by their children, who tended to remain in town to work. They provided a bridge between the peasant life of their own early twentieth-century parents, and the city life for which their grandchildren were no doubt destined. Some of them grew a small amount of subsistence crops in the backyard of the house they had built, while a large number of them receive a tiny state pension.

Most women found living on a pension extremely difficult. Evelyn Rakola, who moved back to Phokeng after marriage, and continued as a rural housewife and farmer, lived on a government pension: "We are just in poverty, we rely on pension."[25] Mrs. Moje, too, found it too little to live on, especially as she had no grandchildren to care for:

The only source of money is the pension. I wonder where would I get money from if it were not for the pension.

Don't you have grandchildren to look after?

No. I am staying in this house with my daughter Sina and my two sons.[26]

Mokete Phalatse was partially paralysed, and cared for six grandchildren on very little money. She describes the hardships she experiences:

I am earning my pension now and these children's mother sends us some money every month. Although we are struggling we can still try and make a living for ourselves.... We only feel the strain when the little money we have is finished before the month, and it is then we struggle. Don't forget that there are six children here.

Are they your grandchildren?

Yes, there were nine of us when my husband was alive.

Do you mean that it is you who looks after them, the whole bunch? I don't think you can still make it.

They look more after themselves than I look after them.

I mean the younger ones; if another baby was brought would you cope?

I wouldn't take another baby. What would I do with it when I need to be looked after too? I am a cripple to add on to that, so you can just imagine what a burden a child would be.[27]

Mrs. Mekgwe is less negative, talking of her home and her life in more matter-of-fact terms:

Now what are you doing for a living presently?

I am on pension.

Is the money that you get from the government enough to keep you going?

Yes, that is my main source of income.

Your houses have been very beautifully decorated. Who decorated them for you?

I decorated them myself. I just used water paint and a roller because it is expensive if you ask somebody to paint for you. When I was working at the Golden City, whites used to tell me that painting is a very light job, women can do it.

Your daily work is domestic work now, I think.

Yes it is.

Do you go to the bush for wood?

No, we do not do that any more. We buy wood and coal nowadays.[28]

But her phlegmatic approach is exceptional. One of the women hints that in fact, pensioners have protested against their situation. Mmadiate Makgale raises the matter herself, in a roundabout way:

What worries me nowadays is that my memory is not as good as before.

Fortunately, I can still write and my handwriting is still legible. I think Mangope himself is going to be surprised at the letter which I wrote him.

What were you complaining about?

Mangope said that we should voice our grievances whenever we are not satisfied with pension. One woman once wrote him a letter because she spent several months without getting her pension.

Does he encourage you to write to him?

Yes, he said that we should contact the nearest council in our respective areas, but now if one doesn't know of any member of the council, one has to direct a letter to him, Mangope. I once read from *Morongwa* magazine that one woman complained to Mangope, but he didn't ignore her letter. He considered the matter but said that there was no further step he could take since the name of that particular official who refused her pension was not known. He said that he was sorry because the money that we are being offered is so little, that he finds it unfair for the officials who earn more than we do to take it for their own use. The name of that particular women was not announced, fortunately, so the officials do not have any grudge against her.... I wrote in Tswana. Look here is *Morongwa* magazine. I am going to read it to you and you should tell me whether I interpreted it correctly or not. They say "the other agreement was that all pensioners in the whole of South Africa should continue receiving their money." Do you understand? "The Prime Minister has made it clear that if there is anyone who does not receive his or her pension any more because of being a Bophuthatswana citizen, [that person] should contact the office of the Bophuthatswana consulate." Now what does that mean?

It means exactly the same thing that you have been saying.[29]

Later she talks of "Thandabantu," the white man who relieved their plight, to some extent at least, telling us something of the humiliating and inefficient system of distributing pensions in such places as Phokeng:

He was a white man.

When did he pay you pensioners a visit?

I don't know exactly when it was, but I think it was round about 1964. I didn't take note of the year during which he paid us a visit. I used to get four pounds prior to his visit but I received increments until I was given ten pounds because of Thandabantu's efforts.

Was he concerned with pensioners only?

Yes, he used to go around listening to the complaints of pensioners. Administration at the offices where we used to receive our pension was very poor. Pensioners used to come from as far as Masosobane, Lemenong, Pududu and Lenatong, and they would spend three days waiting for their names to be called out. It was a pathetic scene. I used to accommodate some of them in my house. After Thandabantu's departure we were divided into small groups which makes their administration far easier.... We pensioners nicknamed him Thandabantu because it was due to his effort that conditions were improved.[30]

The more active women undertook other means of earning small amounts. Nthana Mokale, for example, was, as we have seen, a healer. At first, she does not consider this to be worth mentioning:

What type of life do you live in Phokeng?

I just sit around, live my life, and keep to my business.

Don't you attend clubs? Are you a member of an organisation?

I do attend societies, but other than that I don't do anything. I don't sell anything, even liquor. I am just an old woman who smokes her snuff.[31]

But under more persistent questioning she opens up:

So you are a doctor.

My healing powers are with water, not with herbs.

How do you heal with water?

I have my patients drink this water, which has been blessed by my ancestors, and then force them to vomit it; in this way I cleanse their spirit and this usually removes any evil spirits that may be in them. I also use a *spuit*[32] if the vomiting process does not work.[33]

The women's paltry incomes are supplemented by money sent to them by their children or other relatives, to help them care for youngsters. Ida Molefe, on the day of one of her interviews with Mmantho, was looking "after her grandchildren, who are still too young to attend school. I found her with her husband and two grandchildren. She was busy baking bread—she baked dough on the plates of her coal stove and not in the oven. She said that she wanted the children to have something to eat when they came back from school," wrote Mmantho. Mrs. Mekgwe also cared for her grandchildren:

I am looking after my grandchildren. I am helping my children. When one bears a child, she brings the child to live with me ... they stay with me and help me. They cook. Others go out to fetch water. Others, whilst [I am] talking to you are now in Makapan, where they attend school.[34]

However she complains that

we are very old now. Their mothers must now take over. We cannot do it any more, looking after their children. They bear children and say, "Grandmother, look after this child of mine." Just like the other one who is now older. I took the child while she was small.... His mother works in Johannesburg. When his other grandmother died he was brought here.... We did not agree on payment, but they gave me twenty rand a month.... Yes. We did not say "I am paying you for your job." It was a gift.[35]

Sophie Serokane says she came to Phokeng because "my children asked me to look after their children":

Do you like looking after the children?

It is hard work because one has to cook for them, wash their clothes. Like I am doing now.

But she was able to offer to her grandchildren the advantages of the good schooling provided in Phokeng, partly as a result of the platinum revenues accruing to the tribe:

Do they attend school in Phokeng?

Yes, all of them.... They are five and all of them have passed their exam last year. I respect Phokeng schools. I think I came here late in my life. If I had come earlier, my children would have qualified as teachers and nurses. I like Phokeng mainly for its education.

How is this place as compared to Dobsonville?

It is very much better than Dobsonville. I wish I had stayed here ever since.[36]

Caring for grandchildren was more than simply a physical task. It involved seeing to their moral welfare as well. Nkwapa Ramorwesi talks fondly of the grandchildren she cares for, placing a great emphasis on the need for education, and showing great pride in each member of her family and the level of education he or she has reached.[37] So the women saw themselves as fulfilling an important cultural and social role as well. This was part of their ongoing ambition to be constructors and protectors of the domestic realm, and the community. By returning to Phokeng as mothers and grandmothers, women of mature age and high status, they were able to find new ways of realising this ambition.

Their maturity and increased status appear to be an important part of their older selves. As a member of the royal clan, Setswammung Mokgatle's status grew with age, and she values the respect she is given in her nineties:

Chief Lebone respects me and when he sees me he refers to me as his mother. Only the other day he brought me some new blankets and wrapped me with them before he took a photo of me. He was in a company of some whites who took the photos. After our snapshots he said, "These photos I am going to frame and hang them up so that you can look over me, even tomorrow when I am dead people will see the photo and know who my grannies were."[38]

For some, their mature and more conformist selves appear to clash with the more rebellious side they showed in their youth. Thus Ernestina Mekgwe, who had resented her arranged marriage, says nostalgically, "Today it's bad. We old people say that marriage no longer exists. It is because we know what a marriage should be."[39] Nkwapa Ramorwesi, also hardly a model conformist in her youth, played this protective role when her son died in more recent times. She actively encouraged her daughter-in-law to marry Seantlo, one of her other sons. Her suggestion should be followed, she says, not only because her daughter-in-law is obliged to listen to and respect her but because Seantlo's marrying her will ensure that children are protected against an "outside" man marrying her and "ill-treating" the grandchildren.[40]

Mmadiate Makgale expresses similar, deeply felt views about the need to continue operating domestic relations along lines that reflected both traditional values and "common sense." Her husband's brother had married twice. His first wife he had married in church, and paid *bogadi* for. But when he left her for another woman, from town, he did not pay *bogadi* for her, leaving her in a social limbo after his death. At first it was suggested that Mmadiate's husband pay *bogadi* for her as a second wife. But he argued

> that he had no money and that the house that his brother had built for
> that woman was expensive enough to be treated as *bogadi*. However, we
> tried our best to order her to a gathering of our clan members so that she
> could be introduced formally.

However the woman refused to go,

> on the basis that she was not married legally and as such her relatives do
> not recognise her marriage.... Now that he [her husband] is no longer
> alive, who can take pains trying to sort out that issue? The person who
> wants to introduce her to our clan must pay something to the woman's
> relatives before he can be allowed to do that. No one is prepared to make
> that sacrifice because even her late husband argued that he had built her
> a house.[41]

Mrs. Makgale was outraged at the woman's assumption that the Bafokeng should,
by recognising her, deny the legal and ethical validity of the first marriage.

> We were shocked by the news that she demanded *bogadi*: "You demand
> *bogadi* from that man knowing quite well that you took him from his
> wife. How dare you? We are trying to ignore such things because we
> argue that the legal wife stays in Johannesburg, therefore you are free to
> join our clan here in Phokeng. But you keep on demanding *bogadi*....
> You know quite well that the man you stay with maintains you and your
> children only. He doesn't care a damn about his legal wife. But we, his
> relatives, won't forget everything about that family, we will always be
> on their side."[42]

But the idealised kinship networks and community respect and support the
women defend, and hoped they would receive in Phokeng, had not materialised
for all of them. Nkwapa Ramorwesi feels strongly that the old order, where elders
were respected by the youth, has gone:

> The world was not yet corrupt like nowadays. One looked upon every
> elderly woman as one's mother, gave her all the respect. It happened that
> whenever an elderly woman came across children having a fight, she
> would intervene. As school children we used to quarrel and our fights
> were usually fought after school on the way home. Whenever an elderly
> person intervened, we used to respect her and gave her the same respect
> as we would to our parents. Nowadays when an elderly person reprimands
> a young person, he or she is likely to get a raw deal from a youngster....
> Each and every man was respected as a father. This shows how obedient
> children used to be during those days. Nowadays it is not strange to see
> young lovers walking hand in hand. They do not even feel ashamed
> when they meet elderly people in the street. At times if an elderly person
> continues looking at young couples passing by, one would hear a male
> voice saying: "Why is she looking at us, we have nothing to do with her,
> her days are over." That is today's child, you can't reprimand him or her
> whatsoever. Even those who attend school, once they are about fourteen
> years of age, they think that they are old enough to be regarded as
> "ladies." The rules that governed our lives when we were young were
> good ones, nowadays we, who were able to taste what those rules
> contained for us, still cry for them. We still long for that strict discipline
> under which we were brought up.[43]

Mrs. Phalatse is inexpressably angry at her betrayal by a younger brother, who took some of the cows she had inherited from her husband, a sharecropper on a white farm,

> telling me that he was going to herd them in Kamelsboom. Then one day I sent a child to see how they were coming up. When the poor child arrived there he found a pile of hides and no cattle. When he asked where the cows were, they told him that they were dead and only three were alive. They then instructed him to fetch them and move out even if he died on the way, it was still OK. . . . I hated him so much that when I thought of him at night I would wake up and sit on a chair. . . . He will not enter the Kingdom of God. Before my husband died he would ask me to fetch them so that we could sell some and get money, only to find that there were three left. I always had a premonition that they were dead and my husband would ask me how I knew and I would tell him that my father left me with an iron rod that could tell me everything. . . . He doesn't have a cow in his life. He was rich with my own cows. He robbed me of my herd, telling me he was going to look after them only to find that he was going to eat them. I told him when he was here that "you've eaten them fair and square and they are going to eat you too."[44]

She planned to go to court to obtain restitution, and to use old paternalistic networks to justify her case. The white farmer, Mr. van Heerden, whose nanny and cook she had been in his childhood, would, she said, testify that the cattle were hers, from her husband's labour on his farm.[45]

Perhaps because of their experiences of the failure of kin and community, the women's religious beliefs took on a new meaning, and their participation in religious and semireligious social groupings appeared to be far more important to them now than in their middle years — indeed, in their testimonies about those years, very little reference is made to religion.[46] A concern with death, and its attendant rituals, is present in all the testimonies. The moment of widowhood is remembered clearly by all who experienced it, with alien and inexplicable medical practices featuring high on the list of difficult memories. Mokete Phalatse resents greatly the hospital treatment given to her husband (and herself):

> He became ill but was not bedridden. After some time he was admitted at Moruleng hospital for observation, where he died. At Moruleng, when you don't have any relatives you are not likely to make it.

> *When you don't have nurses who are relatives, or what?*

> Yes, and they don't care about patients, they play around with them. You can ask a nurse for a chamber pot and she'll tell you to wait she is busy. How can you wait when you are pressed and cannot go to the toilet on your own accord, tell me.[47]

The experience of hospitalisation was traumatic for patients and their families. Mrs. Mekgwe remembers vividly how her second husband died in 1970:

> He had a bad cough and I took him to Kruger Hospital, they told me it wasn't TB or asthma, but no one was telling me what it was that was wrong with his chest. When I asked the nurses they just evaded me and my not knowing what was wrong with him was frustrating me. At last in desperation I asked one of the white doctors that had been examining him. I said, "Doctor, may I ask you something?" and he said, "Yes you

may." "I want you please to tell me what my husband is suffering from."
He told me that its not TB or asthma but his lungs are jammed and he
cannot breathe properly.[48]

But the technical rituals of Western medicalised ways of coping with death
are kept at bay. This is done through more than one means. Strong and continuing
Christianity — the resources which the women had treated as both useful and
meaningful from the very earliest days of their Christianisation — provides spiritual
comfort and a more acceptable means of coping with the deaths of loved ones.
Through church groups and societies, the women also retain a sense of their own
dignity, and are accorded respect by their fellow worshippers. In addition they
display a robust capacity to face up to the inevitability of their own deaths,
which, they insist, must be marked by appropriate burial rites and a funeral
which adequately expresses the community's respect for them.

Ida Molefe is one of the stalwarts of her church. On one occasion, when
Mmantho went to interview her, she found Ida "in the middle of a large church
congregation at her house. It was an independent sect church, and after I had sat
for a while, I discovered that Ida was one of the first members of that church in
Phokeng and thus held an important position in the church." And the oldest
informant, Setswammung Mokgatle, values the social, welfare, and cultural
contribution of the church:

Are you a member of the women's league at church?

Yes, we still wear those white clothes. We meet periodically at our
homes and pray and also read from the Bible. At other times they bring
me gifts and food parcels.

Would you say the church has been beneficial to your life?

Yes. For instance during some days when the government does not pay
out our pensions, the women at church bring me and other old women
like myself food parcels and linens to tide us over until the next pension
pay. They also select passages from the Bible which I read when I am
lonely and in need of company. They really look after me, those Germans. I
am thankful for what these Germans did for us in Phokeng and I am also
glad that the chief renovated the old church; he put in pictures on the
wall and provided new benches for the church.[49]

Mmadiphoko Mokgatle regards her religion as a far more personal matter.
She does not attend mothers' union meetings and does not sing:

*Do you usually go to the priest and tell him about your problems so that he
should help you?*

Why should I tell the priest about my problems? In any case what is he
going to do about them? I only communicate my problems to my unseen
God. I do not communicate them to a person who is made of flesh and
blood just like me. I communicate my problems to Jehovah so that he
should minimise them. I am telling you. I keep my distance away from a
person who tells me that he is able to cure problems. God, the unseen
one is the one to whom we communicate everything. I am not the one to
be duped by a flesh and blood person who says "I remove problems."
No. How can he remove them, he being the same species as I? The only
one who can remove them is the one we cannot see.[50]

Mahube Makgale is also committed to a personal religion:

When you are troubled emotionally, can you go to the church for help?

Yes, because they will pray for you.

Are you able to tell your problems to the church congregation?

You don't have to say anything to anyone, prayers are enough to alleviate your problems.

So who listens to your troubles, the church or the congregation?

...you cannot tell anyone about your problems. Family and personal problems are for you to keep, not to bandy about in church.... Do you go about telling people of your family problems, even in church?[51]

Josephine Mokotedi shows a more wavering set of beliefs — it seems she believed too literally when young, and was later painfully disillusioned:

We believed in Christ then [when she was young], not like you young ones who just don't care.... We liked and believed it [church] to be the place to meet our Creator. Nowadays we have given up faith because we haven't met him still.

Oh, at that time you believed that God was alive in the flesh?

Yes. When it was nearing Good Friday we would be called to church to come and see Jesus rise from the dead. We really believed we would see him rise half-dead. We spent the whole evening in church and the following morning we would be told that Jesus rose from the dead last night. So we don't care much about such things any more because we know that there is no God, otherwise if he was alive we old ones would long have seen him.

So now you believe there is no God.

Yes, there isn't. At times we were made fools by these churches, we spent a night out in the graveyard, awaiting Jesus' resurrection ... waiting for him to wake up, yet we wouldn't see him even if he did wake up. We were also told to watch the sunrise, it would be dancing when it appeared, apparently overjoyed at Jesus' resurrection.

Did the sun really dance?

No, but we believed it danced. We did not have to see it dance to believe it.

But now you think it's better to believe after seeing?

Yes, in fact, it's you children who say you will only believe in God after him. Have you ever been to a night vigil awaiting Jesus from the dead?

No.

You see. Now we believed, we went to wake Jesus up but yet we didn't see him and still we believed that he had woken up.

Do you believe that the church helps you?

No, I go there just to respect.... One must not complain, just pay your church dues even though you get nothing, only sitting and prayers. We have resigned ourselves to go to church because we don't want to be heathens, nothing more.... We don't know if we will live again. There isn't one person who has returned from heaven to tell us anything like that. All these priests who tell us of life after death have not been there, so it is just lies.... What is the reason for death if you are going to live again? We could instead stay here on earth forever among our kin, rather than die and go off to some place we don't know anything about its hardships.

Does the church help you when you have problems in your home or whatever they may be?

No, they don't.[52]

Sophie Serokane is a more dedicated churchgoer, an Anglican, whose church minister

always brings me sacrament here at home because I am handicapped by my leg. He usually sends someone here to inform me that I should prepare myself for Mass.[53]

Until her illness, she had never missed church:

It is only now that I have started absenting myself from the church due to my illness that has affected my leg. However I receive my sacrament monthly. People do turn up to my house to watch the colourfully clad Anglicans who come to administer the sacrament.[54]

The church will see to it that her burial is appropriately handled:

Do you find any significance in the church?

Yes. I will get a Christian burial in the event of my death. Do you think that my coffin would be taken to the cemetery without the presence of a minister? ... I won't hire a priest for my burial. I was born and raised by my parents in a Christian fashion.... I have been confirmed in the Anglican church. I will die being a member of the Anglican church. My last Mass will be conducted in the Anglican church. My father was a member of the Anglican church. I also will remain being a full member of the Anglican church.

She will never desert her church for pagan ideas:

What would you do or say when a person tells you to change your Christian views and attitudes, to believing in your ancestors?

I wouldn't listen to that person because I know nothing about ancestry worship.... Can one live without attending church? We have been brought up in the church. We are supposed to die doing our church roles as prescribed by the church norms. I am firm in my conviction. I will never desert my church.[55]

Mokete Phalatse sees the church more as a welfare than a spiritual institution. She changed religions:

I was born in a Wesleyan family, grew up and married a Lutheran, now in this present moment I am in the Roman church.

Why did you leave the Lutheran church?

There wasn't a black minister. The one that used to be there was chased away by the congregation.... He was accused of dividing the church. I then stopped going to church after he left, so when the Catholic church was opened in Phokeng I joined it. . . .

Does he come occasionally to give your sacraments?

Yes, he comes every Wednesday.

Do you believe the church has been helpful to you?

Though they don't give me many things, it does help me and the people close to me. For instance Dorothy's daughter attended school and her mother could not pay her fees any more because she wanted to build a house. This child was forced to leave school and find temporary jobs, but eventually she couldn't stand the fact that her age mates were attending school while she was idling. So she went to the Catholic bishop and asked for a bursary. This they did. They paid her school fees and bought books for her, she still had her uniform so she went back to school.[56]

Mrs. Mekgwe holds a broad and liberal conception of religion:

The church helps and guides us to find God. It is only when you believe in Jesus Christ, what the Bible says, will you be able to find God. I prefer to have the knowledge and awareness of the presence of God than to be ignorant. . . . The Christian is better off because the Bible teaches you that all people are the same, there is no one who is better than the other, be he green or yellow. This should give any black person confidence and they must not feel inferior when speaking to white people.[57]

Her beliefs are of mainly personal significance:

The church helps you especially if you believe that it helps, but if you have no faith it can't do anything for you. It is also not necessary to bring out your problems during church sessions. The church faith and belief should all be in your heart. You don't need a nice building or nice altar. You can make your own church in your house and pray in a small little corner where your mind and purpose won't be disturbed. . . . I attend St. Paul's apostolic church. I have this belief that I can see through the spirit, I make prophecies.[58]

Nthana Mokale attends church on Sunday and Thursdays if she can walk there:

I can try to waddle down there. I did attend a fortnight ago. I limped until I got there, I was with this small child, he carried the books for me. After the church service the minister saw me. He then told the owners of the shop that is located there at the top of the village to take me home in his car. It was hot. You know when it is too hot I cannot walk.[59]

She also sees the church as the means whereby her soul will be transported to God after her death. In fact one of her main criticisms of Penzhorn had been that

he was too rigid and had many strings attached to the carrying out of his duties. For instance, he would not pray for dead people when they were buried if he felt that you were not a regular church patron or that you've never helped in the maintaining of the church and its school. . . . He would comment like "How can I transport your soul to God when I never knew you in flesh." . . . I supposed unless the priest prays for the delivery of your soul to God in the higher heavens, you would wallow in the fire of hell. . . .

Is that what you like most about the church, to be delivered in heaven?

All of us would like that.

Earthly problems would be solved in the afterlife:

> If you have any problems you must go to church and pray. Whatever complaints or disturbances you might have, you merely ask God in prayer to help you. Any other matters will be solved when you go to the kingdom of God.

She goes to church every Sunday:

> I have nothing to do with people. I go mainly so that I can hear for myself what is being said by the priest and perhaps be told when will we be taken to the kingdom of God.

> *Now, if you were told that the kingdom of God is no more, how will you take to this news?*

> I will stop going to church, there won't be any need for it anymore.

> *I mean because as the priest is the one who tells you that there is heaven, what if someone enters the church building and declares that there is no heaven, God is no more?*

> If he has a way to prove it, then we would all discontinue going to church. If he has no proof, we shall take him to task for his blasphemy.[60]

The women's deep concern to ensure that their deaths are appropriately marked, and also to help their bereaved friends cope with the grief and expense of funerals, is expressed in the fact that many of them belong to burial societies — more than one, in fact — to which they subscribe. Mrs. Molefe, living on a tiny pension, says she is a member of three societies:

> They are all over Phokeng. There is one at Katse's, one called Kutlwano and another called Nkolomane. This Nkolomane was a Ndebele by birth but he stayed, died, and was buried here. His grave is in the village.[61]

Nkwapa Ramorwesi belongs to several societies, and all of them are for funeral savings. She indicates their social and economic, as well as spiritual meaning to her:

> *Granny, how many societies do you attend?*

> I attend a number of them.... I attend a society of the Matshwane, which is usually held on the fifteenth of every month. Another one, Mfapha society, is usually held on the third of every month and again on the twentieth when we gather together to contribute towards buying mielie meal the day when one of us is in death trouble. Again I attend the society which is usually held on the twenty-first. This one is specifically meant for paying a sewing machinist who would be responsible for sewing black clothes for a bereaved person.

> *Now what is the procedure when death has occurred in one of the society members?*

> When death has occurred, we give the bereaved family money for the coffin and contact the mielie-meal society so that we can be able to buy mielie meal and sugar.

Do you buy a ready-made coffin or do you must buy planks and make it yourself?

It depends on the individual, because we only give him cash and it is for him to decide on the type of coffin he desires.... They only give you money. We have also the society for transport. There is no specific amount given to the bereaved family for transport, the transport cost varies from day to day and the amount that a society gives out is the one that the bus company asks for. The society gives the family an amount of seven pounds to meet the expenses of a special car which is hired specifically to transport the bereaved family.

I guess it comes out cheap when one has affiliated to a number of societies when death has occurred in the family.

Yes, even the local people contribute something. One would contribute about twenty-cents, another thirty cents, fifty cents, and so on. Sometimes even your society members do contribute as ordinary local people. It is quite a lot of money because one may find that contributions from local people have amounted to eighty pounds.[62]

Josephine Mokotedi, who had expressed such grave doubts about the existence of an afterlife, belongs to ten burial societies:

Ten! What are they all going to do for you?

They are going to bury me.

All of them?

Yes.

You must be paying a lot of money in fees.

There are different fees for all these societies. The fees I pay range from fifty cents to twenty-five cents, and they in turn will contribute for my funeral monies ranging from seventy rand to twenty-five rand and so on.... In this way you are guaranteed not to have a pauper's funeral. When we say someone is poor, is when she has only two societies. When I die I don't need my children to pay for my funeral expenses, my societies will buy my coffin, food that will be eaten during the funeral, and also pay for my mortuary expenses.[63]

Dikeledi Makgale also belongs to ten:

How many societies have you joined?

There are about ten. I spend most of my pension money at these societies and am left with a few shillings for food. I started joining three of them, at Punodung, Radiale, and Dibua. I again joined the other at Rustenburg location, "Bana bu basadi," Mothloding having two divisions, meaning at Mothloding and Lekgonyaneng. The other was the bus society, which had three divisions.

What was the advantage of the bus society?

It means if I die or anybody in my family, the society is supposed to hire a bus for the funeral. We paid for three divisions every month; twenty cents for a bus, thirty cents for groceries, and ten cents for water — that came to sixty cents a month.

Is it possible that the society could run short of money when they are supposed to provide condolence and needs?

If it happened that the society ran short of money we are supposed to contribute again so as to cover all expenses.... Sometimes we found that we spent a lot of money in contributions for the funerals because there were many deaths. The treasurer is supposed to tell us so that we can contribute again.

Then you are sure that if something should happen to you there will be no financial problems, because you belong to ten societies?

Yes, I even manage to attend all their meetings because they are not on the same days. The days are as follows: on the third, the fifth, the seventh, the tenth, the eighteenth, and on the fourteenth. The location society's meeting is on every Saturday, all these other meetings are also held during each month. Concerning the location society we contribute three rand.... The contribution is once a month, that is thirty-six rand a year, and that is divided into two groups — two rand for monthly contributions and one rand for bus contributions.[64]

Frances Nameng, who belongs to three societies — two in Luka, where she was born, and one in Phokeng — talks of the need to join these societies early, illustrating their function as a means of setting and even policing boundaries to the community, and the way in which they prevent abuse:

Granny, if somebody wants to join your society, how does she go about doing it?

Firstly, we only allow you to join if you are a newly married somebody or if you are new to our place. It's because we have a clause that says punishment to all who have been in the place but have not joined.... You spend a certain period of time without getting the benefits of the society. There was a certain lady who decided to join all of a sudden because her husband was late [dead] and she could not cater all the expenses alone because she had no security. We couldn't help her because she had to be dealt with accordingly. I understand it was not the first time she joined, she usually came back when she felt she needed the services of the society at her own convenient time. Ultimately she was expelled from the society.[65]

Surplus burial society money is placed in the bank: "We long learned to take any surplus to the bank, because members used to borrow it only to retain it for keeps."[66]

Thus burial societies fulfil several purposes. They help distinguish "genuine" community members from others; they provide community networks and support; and above all, they provide assurances that death will be properly handled. As Mrs. Moje says, "Societies! All my hope lies in societies.... Jesus, I attend several of them."[67]

In this chapter the women present us with their perceptions of what Phokeng meant to them in their old age. We see the new Phokeng as a more violent and fragmented place, where cynical constructions of ethnicity had created a new edge to old community boundaries — a process that was exacerbated, in the women's eyes, by the presence of foreign mineworkers; and where the old peasant order had given way to a new one based upon more powerful chiefly based, exclusive, and hierarchical accumulation than was the case under earlier chiefs. These facts give substance to claims that the government's homeland strategy is designed to make the system the focus for a new ethnicity; and here we see the fact of being a Mofokeng and a "Tswana" beginning to acquire an entirely different meaning from the "Bafokeng-ness" of earlier times. The women appear to resent these aspects of the new order, which represent a deviation from the Bafokeng values which they saw themselves as protecting.

Amidst the increasing failure of kin and community, the women give us a sense of their strategies of survival in their old age, and of their own social contribution to the village, their households, and their communities. Grandmotherly care had become a fragile way of protecting and reproducing the values for which the women had stood for so long, as well as a means of supplementing tiny and inadequate government pensions. They had ended up poor, in ill-health, and hardworking. But characteristically, their hardships still tend to be seen as challenges or problems that need overcoming, or that can be kept at bay by spirituality as well as by remembering. The very oral histories that are the stuff of this book become resources for aiding spiritual and moral survival in the present. Their past successful creation of household and family, their defence of community, and of their own personal independence are achievements of which they speak with pride—in some ways, this whole study is testimony to the meaning of history to the women in their old age. Their final return to the village, even in cases where it was more or less forced, thus is not seen as a defeat, although their attempts to preserve old values is sometimes felt to be futile. Looking back, they consider themselves to be fortunate to have experienced the things they did during their earlier lives. Some even think that the encroachments of "Western Civilisation" have deprived their children's lives of great meaning and richness. Sophie Serokane captures the nostalgic tone which permeates their testimonies:

> Yes, that was a joyous way of life. You know the old order's way of life surpasses the current way of life. Nowadays life is that of thuggery. There were no policemen and troubles during the olden days.... Nowadays children are struggling, their education is costly. We are the ones who have been fortunate to have lived in an era when things were unlike now. I think we belong to the last generation of that era.[69]

Conclusion:
Life Strategy and
Social Identity

The women of Phokeng had lived through the years of South Africa's great industrial revolution. But a bare handful of them had actually engaged with capital itself. Their dispossession was not directly forced, nor indeed was it ever complete. The transformation of their community from one based upon peasant production to one on the periphery of the new industrial and harshly segregated economy was gradual, and their lives in town were never as harsh of those of the compound-dwelling migrants who produced the gold on which the new order was based. Nevertheless their stories convey the fact that large, inexorable forces were at work throughout their lives, forces that were no less effective for being indirect. The centrifugal power of the massive social and economic revolution in the society at large flung Phokeng into a new era, changing everything from church to childhood, and releasing the women from the hold which their community had had upon them.

They, in turn, were pulled to the centre of the social revolution — the Rand — and it is not surprising that they experienced these early changes as exhilirating and challenging. Their resilient spirit, formed in these first decades of change, helped them survive the next, more crushing, period — when they finally felt the full force of the increasingly powerful state, which sought to engineer the emerging social order in ever-harsher ways, affecting both the cities and places such as Phokeng itself. Their descriptions of their departure from town and their old age in Phokeng are poignant because they reflect the fact that their earlier optimism had never quite been realised. But their life stories rarely convey an sense of despair at this fact.

It is against this background that we need to assess the findings of this book — to draw together the strands of consciousness it reveals, and to attempt a historical explanation thereof. A basic argument of this book is that the consciousness of these women of Phokeng is organised around what I have called their "life strategy." It appears that each woman views herself as a decision-making existential being, who has pursued a strategy of her own. The strategy is not an independent one, but is linked to and dependent upon the possibilities open to the woman, which are provided by the changing material world in which she has lived. Furthermore, it does not develop evenly over time. By a blending of "materialism" and "Africanism," the book shows how both the identities and the strategies of the women have their origins in their childhood in Phokeng, and then suggests that each woman has shaped her strategy in terms provided by the realities of pre-capitalist and peasant society under the impact of mercantile colonialism; and has elaborated upon it according to the exigencies of life on the fringes of urban industrialism, and, later, within a regionalised "peripheral" economy.

That a straightforward materialism is not enough is demonstrated by the fact that at the same time as the peculiarities of the early Bafokeng "mode of production" came to shape her choices, so did race and gender relations impose their own structures on each woman's experience and consciousness — indeed, in each period of her life her choices were the choices of a black and a woman, not only of a peasant and an urban worker. A key institution that shaped the women and which they in turn shaped — the household — embodied at least some of these forces in different ways at different periods of time, and if located within systems of production and power, provides a useful means of understanding the operation of gender in a broader context. Let us explore the overarching arguments of the book in these terms.

The first three chapters of the book cover the early part of the women's lives, when identities were forged and basic strategies conceived. They show in some detail, given the crucial importance of this period to the forging of consciousness, how in the early part of their lives, the young girls were socialised within the chiefly patriarchy into which they were born. They were given particular feminine identities, but were also offered new choices by the peasantisation of the Bafokeng economy. Their parents' households were transformed by Christianisation, education, and the rise of markets, and they could make use of the opportunities this opened to them. Their enthusiastic embracing of Christianity and schooling and of the opportunity to work in the cities should not be seen as evidence merely of their colonisation or eventual impoverishment as blacks. They were also means whereby the struggles within the precapitalist household, over age hierarchies and gender relations, could be tipped more in their favour. A concept designed to allow a further refinement of simple materialism, the notion of "domestic struggle" attempts to capture both aspects of the process at work here. On the one hand, it could be said, the preindustrial household as a whole was locked in a struggle with outside forces. Male and female household members, young and old, would here regard themselves as members of a unit whose generalised interests they were attempting to advance, under the aegis of a sympathetic chief. This they did by transforming the household from a subsistence into a peasant one, through the investment of wages, or the reshaping of family labour power (girls were placed in previously male jobs where necessary, for example). From this point of view, the work of young girls, or the Christianisation of the family, could be seen as a household strategy designed to make peasantisation possible, in which

the interests of the household as a whole, and even that of the Bafokeng themselves, superseded those of its individual members.

At the same time, in tandem with and often in contradiction to this first
struggle, however, the household and indeed Bafokeng society itself was engaged
in an internal struggle between its own members, a struggle which took the form
of conflicts between generations and genders, and between royalty and commoners. The members of each household sought to use the new forces at their
disposal to further their own individual position in the household and in the
community, in contestation or collaboration with other household members and
other Bafokeng. Thus the young girls saw education and city work as the means
to the end of advancing their own position in the household and community,
escaping the requirements of strict gender roles (such as arranged marriages), or
simply pursuing their own personal goals. The chief, in attempting to harness the
forces of colonialism and merchant capital to the "common" (i.e., patriarchal and
chiefly) goals of creating a "tribal" peasantry, found that strata had been created
that would not accept subordination to communal goals, and his strategy floun-
dered on the rocks of internal tensions within his own society, and the encroachments of harsh outside forces. Men and women, parents and children, chief and
commoners came to clash as a result of the tensions produced by their divergent
strategies, with complex results.

It was the period of their adolescence — and particularly the period discussed
in the pivotal Chapter 4, which coincided with the period during which precapitalist expectations were loosened — that saw the formation of the basic life
strategies of the women. They appear to have adopted what may be called a "life
stance" during this time, one shaped by the changing and contradictory institutions through which they passed in their youth — church, school, family, and
the cash economy. Their adopted stance was reinforced by their peers, who may
be seen as the link between the individual and the wider group to which she
belongs. Their strategies were a mixture of assertiveness and conformism. They
sought freedom from certain precapitalist controls; but they set out to use this
freedom to establish themselves as active participants in and creators of households that embodied some of the values drawn from their youthful upbringing. If
any one aspect of their life strategy could be said to have dominated, it was that
of "household building," by reference to which a great deal of their subsequent
behaviour and evolving consciousness can be explained.

In these first chapters, thus, the book examines the ways in which various
strands of consciousness were forged in the rural areas. The interpretation of the
material through such notions as life strategy, household, and domestic struggle
has provided greater refinement than the initial simple materialism. And the
focus on the whole lives of people has revealed something about the origins of
consciousness — suggesting that to understand urban people, one has to know
as much of their social and cultural origins as of the synchronic forces operating
in the city. As the book moves towards examining the urban experiences of the
women, it begins to interpret them in terms of their already-evolved basic "life
stance," seeing them as already-formed people whose contribution to the culture
of the city was derived from an interplay between what they had come to see as
their own purpose in life, and their experiences there.

The women's first interaction with urban institutions was as domestic servants in other households — those of white suburbia. To them, the white house-hold represented a paternalistic institution which provided them with the means to pursue their own ends — which they had by then defined as the need to earn an income for the purpose of ploughing back into their parents' households, and investing in their own future ones — and was only secondarily perceived as a place of exploitation and humiliation. Within the confines of paternalism, both employer and employee existed in a state of only partial understanding of one another's aims; but the mutual incomprehension that characterised domestic service in other times and places appears to have been absent in this case. It was around this time that the women began to construct their own households — bearing children, marrying (if possible avoiding their parents' choice of husband), and in some cases, securing a base in the city upon which to build, while retaining certain rural connections essential to the embryonic household's survival. Domestic service proved an unsteady base for the pursual of this process, in spite of its capacity, as a paternalistic institution, to work relatively harmoniously with the women's ongoing connection with Phokeng. It was compatible neither with the stable marriages the women sought, nor with the child rearing they valued. In the relatively free-moving times of the 1920s and 1930s, it was possible for a number of the women and their families to move into the townships themselves, where their husbands had often secured a base, where they could free themselves of the constraints of paternalism and preindustrial patriarchy, and where they could earn their own livelihood, outside paternalistic constraints, with the continuing growth and maintenance of their households as a central concern. The urban households that the most successful women constructed — within the culture of respectability that prevailed in some townships at the time — were remarkably Western in form, institutions in which women as well as men contributed to incomes, made decisions, or initiated discussions about future family strategy, and fought off external pressures of a variety of sorts. At the same time, they maintained rural links to ensure suitable backgrounds for their children, and concerned themselves with investing in education for the next generation, in an attempt to ensure their social mobility.

The high point of this strategy was reached in the 1940s. Whilst the women's households appear to have survived the upheavals of the Second World War, their life strategy was brutally turned around soon afterwards by the encroachments of capitalism and underdevelopment on the hinterland of Phokeng, and by the closing down of most of the urban avenues through which the strategy had been pursued. Removals and pass laws in particular strangled the household's economic and social base. Not surprisingly, some of these otherwise "conservative and respectable Christians" were drawn into political protest, as the central tenets of their life strategy were attacked. They displayed a variety of ideological and cultural responses to this disastrous encroachment upon their worlds, with a major one being the reorientation of their strategy towards building a house back in Phokeng, rather than remaining in the city.

In their old age, which they spent back in vastly changed Phokeng, the women saw themselves as having only partially successfully realised their aims. Many of their children achieved the social mobility they had sought for them — but sometimes personal relationships were acrimonious. They had relatively secure homes in Phokeng, where the cultural values they treasured were at least less eroded than elsewhere; but the old peasant economy had died and they depended on meagre pensions and grandmotherly incomes for their survival. In this latter role — that of rural grandmother — they continued to pursue their household and cultural ambitions, as well as earning a little money, seeking to imbue in their grandchildren the values they treasured and to ensure that they too obtained a good education. It is not clear whether they would have succeeded better had it not been for the coming of the Nationalist government in 1948, or whether they were destined to achieve only partial success anyway, because they existed mainly in the interstices of the increasingly capitalist economy.

This study has attempted to question two extremes of approach: the "victimology" that caricatures black South Africans as the somewhat pathetic objects of colonialism, racism, oppression, poverty, patriarchy, and capitalism; and the converse of this — the "rah rah" approach, which makes romantic, celebratory, and teleological assumptions about black South African consciousness and struggle. The women whose lives are explored here fit into neither of these categories. They are not permanently colonised and dehumanised victims, deprived of their humanity and selves. But they are also not the fully class-, race- and gender-conscious subjects of the struggle for liberation that perhaps some would hope and wish them to be.

Do these black South African working women see themselves primarily as blacks, workers, or women? Again, this study rejects the false dichotomies this type of formulation presents. Born of essentially structuralist notions of determination, formulations such as these see society as consisting of a variety of neatly encapsulated, if intersecting, systems. Here we have "race," there "class," and over there "gender." Add them all together and you get the much vaunted "triple oppression" — a vacuous concept with no inherent capacity to explain the relationships between these forces. Discovering the nature of consciousness thus becomes a matter of deciding which of these structures is the primary one; the type of consciousness that will evolve will be a more or less automatic result of the determining effect of the appropriate structure. In fact, neither the structuralism nor the concomitant determinism of such approaches is acceptable. This study shows that at the more intimate levels at which meaning is constructed, even such seemingly obvious concepts as "race" are ambiguous, forged through a series of processes and shot through with both class and gender attributes. It suggests that consciousness is formed historically, within a nexus of structures (yes, structures), experiences, relationships, and events, all of which are seized upon by the self-aware woman seeking to pursue her own life strategy, and that it cannot be understood using a purely structural or synchronic method of analysis. Organic intellectuals who seek to mobilise the poor by appealing to their consciousness are perhaps more aware of this than are the academics who study them. When the really successful symbols of social movements are analysed, they express these elements of historicity, complexity, and ambiguity, and do not in fact reduce experience to one structural component or another. It is the unsuccessful intellectuals who confine their vision of popular consciousness within the straitjackets of theoretical determinism, and who find themselves resorting to more-or-less subtle forms of social coercion, perhaps, when people do not respond to their overtures.

The book also examines the anecdotes told by the "best" informants, which often emerge as existential statements. The "I" is defined through them, as though it were at the centre of a series of concentric circles, each of which represents a layer of experience. The individual self appears to be primarily defined by the family or the village, which constitutes an encircling world, within which identity is realised. So lasting is the concept of the "village" in fact, that it has its homologous structure — the "suburb" or "township" — in town. Within the village, there exists an accepted sense of hierarchy, in which each person's place is given a particular meaning. Between villages and regions, too, there are differences of kind and of culture. The "Bafokeng" way of doing things is distinct from that of other groupings, even those which are also Tswana-speaking and of the Bakwena branch. The women apply such structures of identity and of ethnic difference to a variety of situations. Townships and suburbs in the city are thought of as the structural equivalent to villages and regions back home. Whites are, at least in the memories of the women's early peasant days, not so much a "race" as a series of ethnic groups—Boers, Germans, Jews, and so on, each defined by virtue of its characteristic relationship to the Bafokeng. (Boers are also farmers, who know about crops and seed; Jews are traders; German missionaries have a whole series of special characteristics.) Even on their first move to town, the women think of whites in terms of their individual characteristics as employers (they were "good" employers), also often linking these characteristics to ethnic background. (English employers are "better," "Jews pay well".) These essentially village and peasant ways of seeing things are transformed to some extent, even by this generation of women, by city experiences. Ethnic perceptions persist and new ones are recreated in the town, when the women first encounter the need to distinguish themselves from a whole range of other "kinds" of people whom they had previously not encountered. New concepts of class (the "poor" who live in "dirty" townships), of race (whites "in general" come to be discussed more frequently), and of power (the police who raid, control, remove), for example, are added to the original conception of the world as a place where a series of villages create a series of unequal but basically not incompatible identities.

In the interviews, many of the women reveal a sense of personal ambiguity about their situation. They were the creatures of segregation, poverty, and sexism. But they were constructivists — the creators of family structures, worlds of cultural meaning and work patterns as well. Not all of them have the wry, sturdy humour about their memories that idealistic middle-class interviewers might hope to find amongst the poor. There are those who are turned inward and bitter. This study tries to avoid stereotypical and fanciful characterisations of consciousness, and to understand rather than to pigeonhole.

By treating the interviewees as historical subjects, and thus avoiding the static format of "synchronic" sociologists, this study attempts to confront the question of the historical and structural formation of consciousness. How and when it is formed is seen as a process, located within time, place, and material reality. In particular, it asks about the fact of gender, and its place in the determination of being.

The consciousness of the women is explored in the context of their origins in the village and community of Phokeng. This focus on one particular village has a number of advantages (besides that of having enabled the interviews with Mmantho to take a particularly rich form). The women form a "cohort" who convey narratives that "spring from a common landscape,"[1] allowing us to identify with greater precision the mainsprings of the common and diverging patterns of consciousness each displays, and to give a "thicker" description of meaning and culture.[2] While not pretending to be comprehensive on this point, the study attempts to point to some of the sources of each element and type of social identity displayed by the women, and to show that these are shaped historically, within the limits set by the material world, and are not arbitrary. Each fragment of identity — involving the women's perception of themselves as Christians, as Bafokeng, as Tswana, as women, as mothers, wives, "respectables" or whatever — has a history, and a link with a prevailing discourse. Each fragment is an inherent tradition which was once derived from a particular past situation, socially created, and yet brought into idiosyncratic and individual expression by its incarnation in the character, the "self" of each particular woman.

In addition, the focus on Phokeng made it possible to develop a common historical and social context within which the question of gender could be approached. It is a common myth of some practitioners of womens' studies that gender, as a category of analysis, can stand on its own.[3] What the choice of Phokeng as a focus has shown is that factors of gender are profoundly intertwined with those of class, region, ethnicity, economic circumstance, and broad social process, an intertwining that cannot be understood through an examination of randomly selected topics, whose claim to relevance is that they involve "women." If "women" are abstracted from their context, a series of supposedly universal statements are made about them with little or no examination of the balance between the universal and that which is peculiar to the women of that region, class, or time. But the women in this study show themselves to have been influenced by their own regional, ethnic, and class backgrounds, in ways that cannot be divorced from their gender.

The analytical structure of this book as outlined above takes two forms. In the first place, it involves setting the women alongside what is already known about the kinds of things that have impinged on their lives. It is useful to see that they were daughters of the kinds of peasants that Africanists identified twenty years ago; that some of their parents engaged in the sharecropping of which we more recently became aware; that their lives as servants resembled those portrayed by others; and that as city dwellers, they were part of a culture of "respectability," as well as being the archetypal beerbrewing inhabitants of Sophiatown, and so on. It is interesting to compare and contrast their experiences with those of other, better-known groups, and to decide where they were exceptional and where exemplary.

But in the process of setting the women in these and a hundred other contexts of which we are already aware, something new and different emerged: the fact that the women's own depiction of their past and present constituted a version of history itself. They too had a conception of context, of the broad sweep of things, of which were the important classes and groups surrounding them, and which were not, of which events were significant and which less so. Not all of these historical conceptions can be dismissed as the result of the accidental emphases emerging from interviews, although something like that was no doubt happening as well. The result is that the study portrays their lives as a complex mixture of these two aspects. At times, the women are structurally located in terms of the literature that already exists; at others, perhaps the more innovative and exciting side of the book, they are allowed to soar—their own vision is given precedence, and their own particular balancing of what is important against what is not, is allowed to prevail. We are often told that the "great men and great events" theory of history is inadequate, but we are not often allowed to see what the alternatives are. Here the women give us their version of how things look from below, how history is constructed in their eyes. The reader may find this jarring on occasion. Why, for example, are the activities of two obscure missionaries in the Western Transvaal given more weight than the First World War? Why is the experience of arrest in the city given greater priority than the "forces of proletarianisation and class formation" to which we have become so accustomed in the literature? This is not because the author of this book is unaware of what is "really" going on. It is because this is how things look to the women—and if we seek to understand consciousness, then this is where it's at. And if some would deny that such subjective versions have any importance, or that they are all "false consciousness," then they should tell that to the woman who prays, retreats, marches, boycotts, or strikes to protect what she perceives as her world and interests. They would not receive a particularly open hearing.

NOTES

Introduction
Oral History, Consciousness, and Gender

1. The work of Anthony Giddens, for example, appears not to make this distinction, and his fruitful and useful concepts of structuration and its relationship to human agency, which have indeed influenced the conception of this book, are weakened by his failure to locate them within a comparative view of power and powerlessness. See Anthony Giddens, *The Constitution of Society: the Outline of the Theory of Structuration* (Cambridge: Polity Press, 1984); and Maurice Roche, "Social Theory and the Lifeworld," *British Journal of Sociology* 38, no. 2 (1987).

2. This book is very much a companion to an earlier study I did on the nature of ruling class ideology (B. Bozzoli, *The Political Nature of a Ruling Class: Capital and Ideology in South Africa 1890–1940* [London: Routledge and Kegan Paul, 1981]), which analyses dominant, capitalist ideologies in South Africa. See also, for an exploration of broader social ideas T. D. Moodie, *The Rise of Afrikanerdom* (Berkeley: University of California Press, 1975); D. Posel, "The Language of Domination, 1978–83," and S. Greenberg, "Ideological Struggles within the South African State," both in S. Marks and S. Trapido, eds. *The Politics of Race, Class and Nationalism in Twentieth Century South Africa* (London: Longman, 1987), and S. Greenberg, *Legitimating the Illegitimate* (New Haven: Yale University Press, 1987).

3. This is the subject matter of many studies, both in a broader context and in South Africa. Those that have influenced this book the most have been George Rudé, *Ideology and Popular Protest* (London: Lawrence and Wishart, 1980); and James Scott, *Weapons of the Weak: Everyday Forms of Peasant Resistance* (New Haven: Yale University Press, 1985). In South Africa a variety of studies attempts to engage with the "view from below," including S. Marks and R. Rathbone, eds., *Industrialisation and Social Change in South Africa: African Class, Culture and Consciousness, 1870–1930* (London: Longman, 1982); B. Bozzoli, ed., *Labour, Townships and Protest* (Johannesburg: Ravan Press, 1979), *Town and Countryside in the Transvaal* (Johannesburg: Ravan Press, 1983), and *Class, Community and Conflict* (Johannesburg: Ravan Press, 1987); P. Bonner et al., eds., *Holding Their Ground* (Johannesburg: University of the Witwatersrand Press, 1989); A. Sitas, "Moral Formations and Struggles amongst Migrant Workers on the East Rand," *Labour, Capital and Society* 18, no. 2 (1985); T. D. Moodie, "The Moral Economy of the Black Miners' Strike of 1946," *Journal of Southern African Studies* 13, no. 1 (1986), and many others.

4. See, for example, C. Bundy, "Street Sociology and Pavement Politics: Political Aspects of Youth and Student Resistance in Cape Town 1985," *Journal of Southern African*

Studies 13, no. 3 (1987); C. Glazer, "Students, Tsotsis and the Congress Youth League 1944—55" (history honours dissertation, University of the Witwatersrand, 1986); K. Jochelson, "People's Power and State Reform in Alexandra," *Work in Progress* (November—December 1988); and J. Seekings, "The Origins of Political Mobilisation in PWV Townships 1980—84," in W. Cobbett and R. Cohen, eds., *Popular Struggles in Africa* (London: James Currey, 1988).

5. This essentially Gramscian point has been drawn, particularly, from G. Larrain's exposition of Gramsci's view of the nature of popular ideology, and has also been influenced by the work of George Rudé on the subject. See George Larrain, *Marxism and Ideology* (London: Macmillan, 1983), as well as C. Boggs, *Gramsci's Marxism* (London: Pluto Press, 1976).

6. See Raymond Williams, "Base and Superstructure in Marxist Cultural Theory," in R. Williams, *Problems in Materialism and Culture* (London: Verso Books, 1980); and D. Hebdige, *SubCulture: the Meaning of Style* (London: Methuen and Co., 1979).

7. I have chosen to focus on the Gramscian concepts of "hegemony," "consciousness," and "ideology," rather than the Foucaultian idea of "discourses." Using three concepts, each with a particular meaning and purpose, and located within a framework that acknowledges the presence of historically located power, interests, and exploitation, rather than one catchall notion, seems to offer a way to a deeper understanding; while the humanist thrust of this book makes it imperative that the element of human will and purpose, contained within the notion of "consciousness," be embraced. This is not to say that the notion of "discourse" could not be applied to the material here, as a means of describing ideologies that attain something of a life of their own, and as a means of drawing the analysis into questions of symbol, language, and meaning; and the concept does appear from time to time.

8. In the South African context there is something of a positivist tradition which seeks to interpret consciousness through the use of such methods. See, for example, W. Hudson, G. F. Jacobs, and S. Biesheuvel, *Anatomy of South Africa* (Cape Town: Purnell, 1966) and a variety of studies by psychologists and sociologists that use questionnaires.

9. See the classic historical studies of E. P. Thompson, *The Making of the English Working Class* (Harmondsworth: Penguin, 1968); E. Genovese, *Roll, Jordan, Roll* (New York: Vintage Books, 1976), and G. Rudé, *The Crowd In History* (London: J. Wiley, 1964).

10. These Gramscian ideas were introduced into the English-speaking world by George Rudé (*Ideology and Popular Protest*) and Jorge Larrain (*Marxism and Ideology*). Basically, inherent ideas are those which are "a sort of 'mother's milk' ideology, based on direct experience, oral tradition or folk memory and not learned by listening to sermons or speeches or reading books," whereas "derived" ideas are those "borrowed from others, often taking the form of a more structured system of ideas, political or religious, such as the Rights of Man, Popular Sovereignty, Laissez Faire, and the Sacred Right of Property." See Rudé, *Ideology and Popular Protest*, 28 ff. It is easy to see that inherent ideas are more likely to be contained in oral sources than printed ones, particularly in the case of illiterate or semi-literate populations.

11. La Hausse points to the special need for oral history in such settings. See Paul la Hausse, "Oral History and South African Historians," *Radical History Review* 46—47 (Winter 1990). Southern African anthropologists such as Alverson and Comaroff have explored African consciousness through the use of methods of participant observation, the inferring of consciousness through the examinations of symbolic discourses, and interviewing. See H. Alverson, *Mind in the Heart of Darkness: Value and Self-Identity among the Tswana of Southern Africa* (New Haven: Yale University Press, 1970); Jean Comaroff, *Body of Power, Spirit of Resistance: The Culture and History of A South African People* (Chicago and London: University of Chicago Press, 1985).

12. Shula Marks, in her *Not Either an Experimental Doll: The Separate Worlds of Three South African Women* (Durban: University of Natal Press, 1987), makes imaginative use of a

series of letters between an African and a white woman to explore life history, experience and consciousness — but such sources are rare indeed.

13. Michael Frisch usefully has conceptualised what he calls the "more history" approach to oral history, in which it "functions as a source of historical information and insights, to be used, in traditional ways, in the formulation of historical generalisations and narratives." He distinguishes this from the more romantic and populist "no history" approach, in which, he suggests, oral history becomes "a way of bypassing historical interpretation itself, avoiding all the attendant elitist and contextual dangers. It seems to provide a way to communicate with the past more directly, to be presented with a somehow purer image of direct experience." M. Frisch, "Oral History and *Hard Times*: A Review Essay," *The Oral History Review* (1979), quoted in David E. Faris, "Narrative Form and Oral History: Some Problems and Possibilities," *International Journal of Oral History* 1, 3 (November 1980). It seems fair to say that in Southern African studies the former approach has been the prevalent one, although the "voices of the oppressed" approach has appeared in some popular literature in recent years. As will become clear, this study is not of the former type, but also attempts to avoid the pitfalls of the latter school, in which all interpretation is sacrificed.

14. The phrase is Luisa Passerini's, and derives from her path-breaking essay, "Italian Working Class Culture between the Wars: Consensus to Fascism and Work Ideology," *International Journal of Oral History* 1, 1 (February 1980), in which she asks Marxist questions, but refuses the positivist means of seeking answers.

15. Passerini, "Italian Working Class Culture," 4. In the same essay she writes

> it is no longer sufficient for oral history to claim the necessity of widening the horizons of historical research. The priority now is to question the validity of concepts borrowed by history from the social sciences and to proclaim our own ways of proceeding as practitioners of intellectual activities.... Oral sources refuse to answer certain kinds of questions; seemingly loquacious, they finally prove to be reticent or enigmatic, and like the Sphinx, they force us to reformulate problems and challenge current habits of thought

— precisely the point being made here.

16. I find Raymond Williams' formulation useful:

> We have to revalue "determination" towards the setting of limits and the exertion of pressure, and away from a predicted, prefigured and controlled content. We have to revalue "superstructure" towards a related range of cultural practices and away from a reflected, reproduced or specifically dependent content. And, crucially, we have to revalue "the base" away from the notion of a fixed economic or technological abstraction, and towards the specific activities of men in real social and economic relationships, containing fundamental contradictions and variations, and therefore always in a state of dynamic process.

"Base and Superstructure," 34. Larrain, *Marxism and Ideology*, discusses Gramsci's approach to this question.

17. As developed originally in phenomenological thinking by Alfred Schutz and Thomas Luckmann, in their *The Structures of the Lifeworld* (Evanston: Northwestern University Press, 1973), but more recently, argues Maurice Roche, implicit within the work of neo-Weberians such as Anthony Giddens, *The Constitution*. See Roche, "Social Theory and the Life World," *British Journal of Sociology* 38, no. 2 (1987), 283–87.

18. Paul Riesman, in his comprehensive and illuminating "The Person and the Life Cycle in African Social Life and Thought," *African Studies Review* 29, no. 2 (1986), shows that this idea has been used quite widely in Africanist research, mainly of an anthropological nature.

19. Similar to the idea of "life plan" used by R. A. LeVine, in his "Adulthood among the Gusii of Kenya," in N. Smelser and Erik H. Erikson, eds., *Themes of Work and Love in Adulthood* (Cambridge: Cambridge University Press, 1980), quoted in Riesman, "The

Person and the Life Cycle." The phenomenologist Alverson (*Mind in the Heart of Darkness*) suggests that the Tswana (male) informants he interviewed, in spite of their experience of colonisation and subordination, retain the power to translate their own lives as meaningful, partly through their holding on to a life-plan which consists of a series of "great works," which are attained through the process of living, rather than through the setting of goals to be "achieved" — a fascinating notion in the light of the material about Tswana women presented here.

20. Ernestina Mekgwe, interviewed by Mmantho Nkotsoe (MN) on 11–9–1981, p. 1, University of the Witwatersrand African Studies Institute Oral Documentation Project, Womens' Project [hereafter ODP WP].

21. As far as its theoretical background is concerned, in the early stages of the Oral Documentation Project, authors such as Paul Thompson, *The Voice of the Past: Oral History* (Oxford; Oxford University Press, 1978), and Theodore Rosengarten, *All God's Dangers* (New York: Avon Books, 1974) proved influential — more so, perhaps, than the existing Africanists who had worked with oral sources. The women's project in particular was influenced by the work of such Western scholars as Ann Oakley and Lillian Rubin, both of whom gave the voices of ordinary women a prominent place earlier than most. But a small and, as time went on, growing number of Southern African scholars came to use this method, and it now has a respectable pedigree, and is thoroughly reviewed in La Hausse, "Oral History."

22. Perhaps using the "more history" approach. See, for example, Helen Bradford, *A Taste of Freedom: the ICU in Rural South Africa, 1924–1930* (New Haven: Yale University Press, 1987).

23. See, for example, Tim Keegan, *Facing the Storm: Portraits of Black Lives in Rural South Africa* (Cape Town: David Philip, 1988); Malete Nkadimeng and Georgina Relly, "Kas Maine: The Story of a Black South African Agriculturist," in Bozzoli, ed., *Town and Countryside*; and T. Matsetela, "The Life Story of Nkgona Mma Pooe: Aspects of Share-cropping and Proletarianisation in the Northern Orange Free-State 1890–1930," in Marks and Rathbone, eds., *Industrialisation and Social Change*.

24. Charles van Onselen is writing a biography of Kas Maine, who was a sharecropper. A preliminary to the study is C. van Onselen, "Race and Class in the South African Countryside: Cultural Osmosis and Social Relations in the Sharecropping Economy of the South-Western Transvaal, 1900–1950," *American Historical Review* 95, no. 1 (1990).

25. Tapes of these early interviews are lodged in the ODP, but, with the exception of the Phokeng tapes, do not form part of this study.

26. Faris, "Narrative Form," 172.

27. I am grateful to Isabel Hofmeyr and Stephen Clingman for having drawn me into these analytical approaches, although they bear no responsibility for my failings in this respect.

28. Ronald Grele suggests that oral history interviews are in fact "conversational narratives" — a useful notion which approximates that used here, although perhaps it does not capture quite the range of ways in which the text of an oral history may be used. See R. Grele, "Movement Without Aim: Methodological and Theoretical Problems in Oral History," in R. Grele, ed., *Envelopes of Sound: Six Practitioners Discuss the Method, Theory and Practice of Oral History and Oral Testimony* (Chicago: Precedent Publishers, 1985).

29. There are a few studies of Phokeng and the surrounding area. See Graeme Simpson, "Peasants and Politics in the Western Transvaal, 1920–1940" (M.A. dissertation, University of the Witwatersrand, 1986); Naboth Mokgatle's *Autobiography of an Unknown South African* (London: University of California Press, 1971) includes important material on the oral traditions and early history of Phokeng. See also Georgina Relly, "Social and Economic Change amongst the Tswana in the Western Transvaal, 1900–1930" (M.A. thesis, University of London, 1978); and Graeme Simpson, "The Political and Legal

Contradictions in the Conservation and Dissolution of the PreCapitalist Mode of Production: The Fokeng Disturbances, 1921–6" (B.A. honours history dissertation, University of the Witwatersrand, 1981).

30. See Passerini, "Italian Working Class Culture," 8–10. Discussions of method are all too rare in Southern African studies.

31. I am not a symbolic interactionist, although this approach has proved useful — the ideas of Erving Goffman in particular have helped in the treatment of the "conversations."

32. However, in the physical sciences, too, we are told that great innovations and discovery often occur outside of what is formally defined as the "experimental situation."

33. This is one of many examples of the interviewees mentioning Mmantho's background, some of which appear in the body of the study. In another, Rosinah Setsome says to Mmantho, "You come from a local area" (ODP WP, MN interview with Rosinah Setsome, 12–9–1981, p. 17), while elsewhere mention is made of Mmantho's school, her surname, and the likelihood that she will know some of the people being discussed.

34. Mrs. Setshedi engages in a long discussion with her about the Setshedi clan, in which she assumes Mmantho has a knowledge of African history, and particularly of the Difaqane (early nineteenth-century wars between the Nguni and other ethnic groups in Southern Africa), and of its effects upon the Bafokeng. "They came here during the Wars. Isn't it that a person's surname is found all over the land; these people were scattered during the wars they had with the Matabele people." ODP WP, interview by MN with Naomi Setshedi, 31–1–83, pp. 31–33.

35. It should be stressed that at no stage was the impression given to the interviewees that these conversations were, or would remain, private. They knew full well their purpose. The tone of intimacy simply arises as a result of Mmantho's skill and acceptability to her subjects.

36. Jews, Germans, Boers, English, and policeman are the main ones.

37. See, for a comparative example, Philip Mayer's analysis of the attitudes of a sample of Sowetan blacks, in his "'Good' and 'Bad' Whites," paper presented to the Conference on South Africa in the Comparative Study of Class, Race, and Nationalism, New York, 1982. But while there are many studies of white South African attitudes towards blacks and other groups, there is extraordinarily little on the attitudes of blacks towards whites and others.

38. It was most frequently Western-derived feminist categories of analysis that proved difficult to transfer into this African setting — but more generally it was a case, as Passerini suggests, of existing social scientific concepts needing to be re-thought in the light of oral evidence.

39. ODP WP, MN interview with Ernestina Mekgwe, 11–9–1981, p. 2.

40. *Ibid.*, 11–9–1981, pp. 14–15.

41. *Ibid.*, 11–9–1981, p. 46.

42. It is important for positivistically inclined sociologists to recognise that questionnaire/survey methods of research were devised and evolved in Western settings, with high levels of literacy, good basic data from which to draw samples and construct questions, and the incorporation of even the poorer strata into a technocratic culture. People are used to filling in forms and ordering their perceptions. Even in those settings such methods have severe limitations. One of the reasons why sociological studies in South Africa have so often confined themselves to the white, middle class, literate, or dominant populations is that the discipline's own major heritage is faulty. These flawed instruments can barely be used amongst non-Western, peasant peoples, about whom basic raw data are almost entirely unknown, with low levels of literacy and a low level of absorption of technocratic values. African sociologists would do well to look to the discipline's non-positivistic heritage, and its social anthropological offshoot, for insight into performing research in such settings.

43. Luisa Passerini found it significant in the "spontaneous" part of her interviews with

Italian workers who had lived through Fascism, that they remained silent about the fact of Fascism itself—an important form of self-censorship which, she says, is "evidence of a scar, a violent annihilation of many years in human lives and memories, a profound would in daily experience" (Passerini, "Italian Working-Class Culture," 9). The women of Phokeng tend not to be silent about their own limited political experiences, and one or two express a clear wish to speak of these experiences. Many other examples of the patterns taken by the women's spontaneous responses are analysed in the body of the study.

44. This is in strong contrast with the experiences of interviewers in many Western settings, where the kinds of silences Passerini refers to appear to be common amongst poorer people who may have experienced harsh repression or taken part in strikes or other forms of protest without a sense of pride. See, for example, L. Shopes, "Oral History and Community Involvement: The Baltimore Neighbourhood Heritage Project," in S. P. Benson et al., eds., *Presenting the Past* (Philadelphia: Temple University Press, 1986), or Lillian Rubin, *Worlds of Pain* (New York: Basic Books, 1976), where the interviewees could not believe that their stories would be of interest to anybody. For an analysis of the sense amongst South African blacks of the living importance of their own pasts see B. Bozzoli, "Intellectuals, Audiences and Histories: South African Experiences, 1978–88," L. Callinicos, "Popular History in the Eighties," and L. Witz, "The Write Your Own History Project," all in *Radical History Review* 46–47 (Winter 1990).

45. I am grateful to Mike Kirkwood for first pointing out the rich storytelling capacities of particular interviewees, and for his creative editing of one of the woman's stories. See "The Story of Mrs. S," *Staffrider* 6, no. 1 (1984). For an analysis of this essay and other life stories run in *Staffrider* see A. Oliphant, "Staffrider Magazine and Popular History: The Opportunities and Challenges of Personal Testimony," *Radical History Review* 46–47 (Winter 1990). For further discussion of the role of the interviewee in structuring oral narratives see Samuel Schrager, "What is Social in Oral History," *International Journal of Oral History* 4 (June 1983); Passerini, "Italian Working-Class Culture"; Faris, "Narrative Form"; Jerome Bruner, "Life as Narrative," *Social Research* 4, no. 3 (1988); and I. Hofmeyr, "The Narrative Logic of Oral History," African Studies Institute seminar paper, University of the Witwatersrand, 1988.

46. This concept is linked to those of "inherent" and "derived" ideologies mentioned above; Gramsci's idea was that particularly knowledgeable and educated thinkers close to the working and poorer classes—the organic intellectuals—would be able to transform the incoherent "inherent" set of ideas into a more coherent and socially useful ideology. In putting this concept forward, Gramsci placed the emphasis on self-emancipation and subjectivity, and moved away from the Stalinist idea that all ideologies should stem from above and outside the people, from the "Party elite." He also argued that the ruling classes have intellectuals—often more efficient and successful ones who set the terms of hegemonic discourse—to organize their world views, an idea which I have explored in Bozzoli, *The Political Nature of a Ruling Class*.

47. See B. Bozzoli and P. Delius, "Radical History and South African Society," *Radical History Review* 46–47 (Winter 1990), for an overview of the revisionist thrust in Southern African studies over the past two decades, and for an elaboration of the arguments put forward so briefly here.

Prelude
Lives in Portrait

1. A few of the women's stories—those of Jacobeth Lekalake, Elizabeth Morobe, Lydia Phiri, Rebecca Phiri and Evelyn Rakola—have not been included because the information they yielded was relatively sparse; while biographies of those interviewed in the course of the research for the background for the study are not included here.

2. Chinese/African gambling in which runners take bets from various domestics, all of whom bet on symbols drawn from their dreams, to the central (originally Chinese) organiser, and then return with the name of the winning symbol, and the winnings themselves.

3. Sometimes the interviewees have given different information in the different interviews, and alternative dates or places given by them are placed in brackets behind the original.

Chapter 1
The Bafokeng: Myths and Realities of the Past

1. Sophie Serokane, who was not originally from Phokeng herself, praises Phokeng's high standards of education, saying that her grandchildren have benefited from the schools there: "I respect Phokeng schools. I think I came here late in my life. If I had come earlier, my children would have qualified as teachers and nurses." ODP WP, MN interview with Sophie Serokane, 27–5–1982, p. 23.

2. Well-known figures to have come from Phokeng include Naboth Mokgatle, whose *Autobiography* forms an important source for this study; and the Rangaka family of teachers, doctors, nurses, and other professionals.

3. See "A Tribe Hits the Big Money Jackpot," *Drum* (September 1969), in which it is said that revenue from the platinum mines was being used to improve housing and schooling in Phokeng.

4. *Ibid*.

5. Quotation marks are used here because it seems likely that there has been some form of "invention" of ethnicity going on side by side with the processes of economic growth and political change. I hope this book will not be used to assist this process.

6. See Michael Rowlands, "Repetition and Exteriorisation in Narratives of Historical Origins," *Critique of Anthropology* 8, 2 (1988).

7. See Margaret Kinsman, "'Beasts of Burden': The Subordination of Southern Tswana Women ca. 1800–1840," *Journal of Southern African Studies* 10, no. 1 (1983) for a definitive statement on the patriarchal character of Tswana social formations in general in the early nineteenth century.

8. P.-L. Breutz, *The Tribes of Rustenburg and Pilansberg Districts* (Pretoria: Department of Native Affairs, 1953), 11–12. A good deal of information is also contained on 56 ff.

9. D. F. Ellenberger, *History of the Basuto, Ancient and Modern* (London: Caxton Publishing Company, 1912).

10. James Walton, "Early Bafokeng Settlement in South Africa," *African Studies* 15, no. 1 (1956), 37.

11. Most references to such oral traditions are drawn from Naboth Mokgatle, *Autobiography*. Mokgatle, himself the grandson of one of the most famous chiefs of the Bafokeng, reproduces the oral traditions passed on to him by a sage uncle.

12. This paragraph and subsequent material is drawn from Breutz, *The Tribes of Rustenberg*; Mokgatle, *Autobiography*; R. Moffat, *Missionary Labours and Scenes in Southern Africa* (London: Snow, 1846); Karl Mauch, *Karl Mauch: African Explorer*, edited and translated by F. O. Bernhard (Cape Town: Struik, 1971); Ellenberger, *History of the Basuto*; I. Schapera, *The Tswana* (London: International African Institute, 1953); K. Shillington, *The Colonisation of the Southern Tswana* (Johannesburg: Ravan Press, 1985); and J. A. I. Agar-Hamilton, *The Native Policy of the Voortrekkers* (Cape Town: Maskew Miller, 1928).

13. Walton, "Early Bafokeng Settlement," 37.

14. Walton writes that "the Bafokeng also frequently married Bushman wives and lived with them in their cave dwellings.... The light skins and short stature of the present-day Bafokeng afford further evidence of the intermarriage which took place between their forefathers and the original Bush inhabitants. The Bafokeng themselves openly

state that they are the progeny of an early Bush-Bantu association." *Ibid.*, 37–38.

15. *Ibid.*, 37.
16. Mokgatle, *Autobiography.*
17. It is interesting, however, that Walton argues that pottery findings "indicate a migration route which is closely in accord with their tribal traditions." Walton, "Early Bafokeng Settlement," 38.
18. Breutz, *The Tribes of Rustenburg*, 16.
19. Ellenberger, *History of the Basuto*, 68.
20. *Ibid.*, 69.
21. Mokgatle, *Autobiography*, 16.
22. This is a typically Tswana agricultural pattern—farmland is at a distance from villages or towns; major agricultural work is undertaken in concentrated spells, which are spent away from home, camping or living in modest huts at the fields. The survival of this custom is attested to by the women.
23. It was from one of these branch villages that Mmantho came, reinforcing the ties between her and the residents of Phokeng itself.
24. Mokgatle, *Autobiography*, 20.
25. Sorghum.
26. Mokgatle, *Autobiography*, 30.
27. A point confirmed for the Tswana in general by Kinsman, "Beasts of Burden"; Alverson, *Mind in the Heart of Darkness*; and most other observers of Tswana society of the nineteenth century.
28. See, for discussions of the cultural attributes of the Bafokeng, C. A. MacDonald, "*The Material Culture of the Kwena Tribe of the Tswana*" (M. A. dissertation, University of the Witwatersrand, 1940).
29. Kinsman, "Beasts of Burden," 42.
30. *Ibid.* 53. It should be noted that Kinsman is referring to the Southern Tswana in general, and that many of her sources are not relevant to the Transvaal. But we can accept that the general picture she paints applies to the Bafokeng.
31. For a moving literary portrayal of the devastations of this period, seen from the Tswana point of view, see the novel *Mhudi*, by Sol T. Plaatje (Johannesburg: Quagga Press, [1930] 1975), and the Introduction to that edition by Tim Couzens.
32. Agar–Hamilton, *Native Policy*, 51.
33. Another ODP informant, Kas Maine (referred to in the Introduction above) was told by the Bafokeng that he could not obtain land in Phokeng because his ancestors had fled at the time of Mzilikazi. This scattering is also mentioned by Moffat, *Missionary Labours*, and R. B. Coertze, *Die Familie, Erf en Opvolgingsreg van die Bafokeng van Rustenburg* (Pretoria: Sabra, 1971), and appears in some of the women's testimonies.
34. This term is used in a variety of ways in this study. Historically, it is a word that has a legitimate status, and its use here simply refers to the Dutch-speaking settlers and farmers who came to the Transvaal during the Great Trek in the early and mid-nineteenth century. In the women's testimonies about their early history it may also have a legitimate historical status as a descriptive term. However, it has come to acquire a pejorative meaning amongst black South Africans and for this reason is placed in quotation marks where appropriate.
35. Quoted in Breutz, *The Tribes of Rustenburg*, 11; also interesting is Breutz's observation that "long before the first Europeans came, the locals were trading in beads," 9.
36. Agar–Hamilton, *Native Policy*, 50.
37. Coertze, *Die Familie*, 49–50.
38. Agar–Hamilton, *Native Policy*, 51.
39. Breutz, *The Tribes of Rustenburg*, 54. See also Kinsman's account of southern Tswana conquest, dispersal and regrouping; Kinsman, "Beasts of Burden."
40. Schapera, *The Tswana*, 16.
41. Mauch describes the early town. See Mauch, *Karl Mauch*, 157–58.

42. Mokgatle relates a fascinating anecdote which indicates the degree to which labour exactions were established by this time. See his *Autobiography*, 161–62.
43. See Schapera, *The Tswana*, 16; Shillington, *Colonisation of the Southern Tswana*, 136; Simpson, "Peasants and Politics," Ch. 2.
44. See Coertze, *Die Familie*, 50.
45. *Ibid.*, 50–51.
46. Breutz, *The Tribes of Rustenburg*, 65.
47. "A Tribe Hits the Big Money Jackpot." See also Breutz, *The Tribes of Rustenburg*, 65.
48. For a perceptive analysis of the *inboekseling* system, see Peter Delius and Stanley Trapido, "Inboekselings and Oorlams: The Creation and Transformation of a Servile Class." in Bozzoli, ed., *Town and Countryside*.
49. Mokgatle, *Autobiography*, 39.
50. *Ibid.*, 41.
51. See Breutz, *The Tribes of Rustenburg*, 42.
52. Mauch reports finding a Swiss mission station in the region during this 1869 visit. See Mauch, *Karl Mauch*, 155–56.
53. Mokgatle, *Autobiography*, 55.
54. *Ibid.*
55. *Ibid.*, 56. In fact this story is confirmed by one of the interviewees in this book, who remembers that members of her family went on the Durban journey; this is discussed in Chapter 3.
56. See Breutz, *The Tribes of Rustenburg*, 72.
57. This is confirmed by Breutz, *ibid.*, 64.
58. Mokgatle, *Autobiography*, 57.
59. *Ibid.*
60. Mokgatle, *Autobiography*, 60. This latter point is confirmed by Breutz, who suggests that only young people were Christianised at first.
61. Mokgatle uses the word *Sesotho* to describe the language of the Bafokeng in the broad generic sense—Setswana is indeed a part of the Southern Sotho family of languages.
62. Mokgatle, *Autobiography*, 62.
63. *Ibid.*, 65.
64. See Relly, "Social and Economic Change," 3.
65. See Breutz, *The Tribes of Rustenburg*, 63.
66. Relly, "Social and Economic Change," 30. Chiefs were said to have purchased land communally and then distributed it individually.
67. This must have been in the era of the chief who succeeded Mokgatle, August Mokgatle, also called August Molotlegi, who came to power in 1896, and of whom Chief Lepone was a direct descendant.
68. For these descriptions, see Relly, "Social and Economic Change," 8–9.
69. Today, indeed, the naming of districts in the Rustenburg area reflects this history, for every small partition in the area has a name such as Beerfontein, Diepkuil, Doornspruit, Elandsheuvel, and Goodgedacht. That white settlement is but a recent event in a long black history is evidenced by the fact that every farm also has a Tswana name, however, and that both names will be referred to in conversation.
70. Coertze, *Die Familie*, gives details of the various land agreements entered into by Mokgatle.
71. This argument is developed much more fully in Relly, "Social and Economic Change."

Chapter 2
Peasant Daughters, 1900–1915

1. The classic text on the South African peasantry is Colin Bundy, *The Rise and Fall of the South African Peasantry* (London: Heinemann, 1979). Little is known about the social effects of peasantisation upon the African societies transformed by it. See also W.

Beinart et al., eds., *Putting a Plough to the Ground* (Johannesburg: Ravan Press, 1986); and T. Keegan, *Rural Transformations in Industrialising South Africa* (Johannesburg: Ravan Press, 1986).

2. ODP WP, MN interview with Setswammung Mokgatle, 17–3–1983, pp. 5–6.
3. Although she identifies him as "Piet," this was almost certainly Paul Kruger, whose farm, ten miles from Phokeng, was called "Boekenhoutfontein."
4. For the background to this type of socially structured interaction see Van Onselen, "Race and Class."
5. ODP WP, MN interview with Setswammung Mokgatle, 17–3–1983, p. 2.
6. ODP WP, MN interview with Mmadiate Makgale, 16–3–1983, pp. 8–10.
7. *Ibid.*, p. 12.
8. ODP WP, MN interview with Setswammung Mokgatle, 17–3–1983, p. 3.
9. *Ibid.*
10. *Ibid.*; it is not certain why Mokgatle seems to have been allowed to keep three wives, if her memory is correct.
11. ODP WP, MN interview with Ernestina Mekgwe, 11–9–1981, p. 2. This is in direct contrast with Margaret Kinsman's suggestion for a much earlier period that women could not benefit from the cash economy. See Kinsman, "Beasts of Burden." But the question remains an open one—Ernestina's statement may well be exaggerated, or reflect a particular perception of family relations; on the other hand, Christianisation may have had some effect on women's ability to assert themselves.
12. ODP WP, Dennis Mashabela (DM) interview with Ernestina Mekgwe, 2–3–1983, p. 13.
13. *Ibid.*, p. 72.
14. ODP WP, MN interview with Nthana Mokale, 1–2–1983, p. 14.
15. *Ibid.*, p. 15.
16. *Ibid.*, p. 21.
17. ODP WP, MN interview with Mmadiate Makgale, 16–3–1983, p. 41.
18. ODP WP, MN interview with Nthana Mokale, 1–2–1983, p. 21.
19. ODP WP, MN interview with Mmadiphoko Mokgatle, 18–8–1982, p. 2.
20. *Ibid.*
21. ODP WP, MN interview with Mmadiate Makgale, 16–3–1983, p. 40.
22. *Ibid.*, pp. 36–37.
23. ODP WP, MN interview with Josephine Mokotedi, 25–11–1981, p. 4.
24. ODP WP, MN interview with Mmadiate Makgale, 16–3–1983, p. 2.
25. *Ibid.*, p. 45.
26. *Ibid.*, p. 46.
27. *Ibid.*, p. 38.
28. ODP WP, MN interview with Nthana Mokale, 8–10–1982, p. 4.
29. ODP WP, MN interview with Ernestina Mekgwe, 11–9–1981, p. 11.
30. For an outline of the main areas in which this sexual division of labour and of socialisation took place, see Kinsman, "Beasts of Burden." Initiation schools for girls and boys were different and Kinsman argues that they nurtured different cultures. However, both seem to have functioned to allow discipline over children to be ensured, and it is not clear whether discipline over girls was indeed stronger than that over boys, as she seems to imply. It rather seems to have been the other way around. See I. Schapera, *Bogwera: Kgatla Initiation* (Mochudi: Phuthadikobo Museum, 1978); and W. C. Willoughby, "Notes on the Initiation Ceremonies of the Becwana," *Journal of the Royal Anthropological Institute* 39 (1909). With the coming of Christianity, the discipline of the initiation schools was replaced by that of the church. This could have been one reason why chiefs were anxious to embrace Christianity—possibly they sought new legitimations for control and discipline over both male and female juniors.
31. ODP WP, MN interview with Nthana Mokale, 1–2–1983, p. 16.
32. ODP WP, MN interview with Ernestina Mekgwe, 11–9–1981, p. 2.

33. *Ibid.*, p. 3.
34. ODP WP, MN interview with Rosinah Setsome, 15–3–1983, pp. 31–32.
35. ODP WP, MN interview with Mmadiate Makgale, 16–3–1983, pp. 34–35.
36. ODP WP, MN interview with Nkwapa Ramorwesi, 25–5–1982, p. 7.
37. Mmadiate Makgale and her sister did all the cooking for the family, as well as helping care for younger children. See ODP WP, MN interview with Mmadiate Makgale, 16–3–83, p. 38.
38. ODP WP, MN interview with Ernestina Mekgwe, 2–2–1983, p. 15.
39. This is the finding of the comparative literature on the subject. See Esther Boserup, *Woman's Role in Economic Development* (New York: St. Martin's Press, 1970). However, Marcia Wright quite correctly warns us that Boserup's technicist determinism places far too much weight upon the productive processes as a cause of changes in gender relations, and suggests that a full examination of the entire economy and of gender relations in both the spheres of production and reproduction is necessary before generalisations can be made. See Marcia Wright, "Technology and Women's Control over Production: Three case Studies from East Central Africa and their Implications for Ester Boserup's Thesis about the Displacement of Women," paper presented to the Rockefeller Foundation Workshop on Women, Households, and Human Capital Development, 1982. Her warning is certainly appropriate to the case of the Bafokeng, where changes in gender relations, as this chapter demonstrates, are complexly related to the encroachments of mercantilism, colonialism, and peasant social relations, and not just to the introduction of new technology.
40. ODP WP, MN interview with Evelyn Rakola, 26–5–1982, pp. 9–11.
41. ODP WP, MN interview with Mahube Makgale, 27–11–1981, p. 2.
42. ODP WP, MN interview with Mokete Phalatse, 24–5–1982, pp. 3–4.
43. ODP WP, MN interview with Nthana Mokale, 20–8–1982, p. 2.
44. ODP WP, MN interview with Ernestina Mekgwe, 11–9–1981, p. 6.
45. ODP WP, MN interview with Nkwapa Ramorwesi 25–5–1982, p. 8.
46. ODP WP, MN interview with Setswammung Mokgatle, 17–3–1983, p. 16.
47. ODP WP, MN interview with Mmadiphoko Mokgatle, 18–8–1982, p. 5.
48. See ODP WP, MN interviews with Lydia Phiri, 12–9–1981, p. 6; and with Setswammung Mokgatle, 17–3–1983, p. 16. See also ODP WP, MN interview with Mmadiphoko Mokgatle, 18–8–1982, p. 11.
49. ODP WP, MN interview with Mmadiphoko Mokgatle, 18–8–1982 pp. 11–12.
50. *Ibid.*, p. 3.
51. This to some extent contradicts Margaret Kinsman's portrayal of Tswana society, for she seeks to argue that women's subordinate position and enmeshing in a variety of controlling networks prevented them from seizing the opportunities that were opened to them by the coming of cash relations. See her "Beasts of Burden."
52. ODP WP, MN interview with Nkwapa Ramorwesi, 25–5–1982, p. 1.
53. ODP WP, MN interview with Ernestina Mekgwe, 11–9–1981, p. 2.
54. ODP WP, MN interview with Nkwapa Ramorwesi, 25–5–1982, p. 21.
55. ODP WP, MN interview with Mmadiphoko Mokgatle, 18–8–1982, p. 3.
56. ODP WP, MN interview with Mmadiate Makgale, 25–11–1981, p. 1.
57. ODP WP, MN interview with Mokete Phalatse, 24–5–1982 p. 2.
58. ODP WP, MN interview with Mmadiphoko Mokgatle, 18–8–1982, p. 7.
59. ODP WP, MN interview with Ida Molefe, 19–8–1982, pp. 2–3.
60. ODP WP, DM interview with Ernestina Mekgwe, 2–3–1983, p. 5.
61. *Ibid.*, pp. 16–18.
62. ODP WP, MN interview with Josephine Mokotedi 25–11–1981, p. 2.
63. ODP WP, MN interview with Mmadiate Makgale, 25–11–1981, pp. 2–3.
64. *Ibid.*, p. 5.
65. ODP WP, DM interview with Ernestina Mekgwe, 2–3–1983, p. 18.

66. *Ibid.*, p. 19. It is not clear what she is actually trying to say here, other than to express some sort of desire to distance herself from boys.
67. ODP WP, MN interview with Setswammung Mokgatle, 17–3–1983, p. 18 ff.
68. ODP WP, MN interview with Mmadiate Makgale, 16–3–1983, p. 44.
69. ODP WP, DM interview with Ernestina Mekgwe, 2–3–1983, p. 20.
70. ODP WP, MN interview with Nthana Mokale, 1–2–1983, p. 30.
71. *Ibid.*, p. 21.
72. ODP WP, DM interview with Ernestina Mekgwe, 2–3–1983, p. 20.
73. ODP WP, MN interview with Setswammung Mokgatle, 17–3–1983, p. 16.
74. ODP WP, MN interview with Nthana Mokale, 1–2–1983, p. 17.
75. ODP WP, MN interview with Mmadiate Makgale, 16–3–1983, pp. 44–45.
76. ODP WP, DM interview with Ernestina Mekgwe, 2–3–1983, p. 16.
77. The name given to a characteristic blue–and–white, intricately patterned cotton cloth used by African women since it was first imported (by German traders or missionaries, perhaps) in the nineteenth century. Its other name is "German Print." Nthana Mokale says: "Our old-fashioned dresses were like those worn by the Xhosas, they traditionally belong to the Kgatlas and the material was called *motweisi*, a blue material sometimes called German material worn by African women. ODP WP, MN interview with Nthana Mokale, 1–2–1983, p. 17.
78. ODP WP, MN interview with Nthana Mokale, 1–2–1983, p. 17.
79. *Ibid.*, p. 16.
80. ODP WP, MN interview with Nkwapa Ramorwesi, 25–5–1982, pp. 3–4.
81. ODP WP, MN interview with Nthana Mokale, 1–2–1983, p. 20.
82. ODP WP, MN interview with Mmadiate Makgale, 16–3–1983, p. 36.
83. Maize or sorghum porridge.
84. ODP WP, MN interview with Mmadiate Makgale, 16–3–1983, pp. 39–40.
85. ODP WP, MN interview with Nthana Mokale, 1–2–1983, p. 16.
86. A Boer delicacy—sun-dried salted beef.
87. An Afrikaans word, indicating the degree to which Western Transvaal Tswana culture had become intertwined with that of Boers.
88. ODP WP, DM interview with Ernestina Mekgwe, 2–3–1983, pp. 16–17.
89. *Ibid.*, p. 13.
90. *Ibid.*, p. 5.
91. ODP WP, MN interview with Mokete Phalatse, 24–5–1982, p. 2.
92. ODP WP, MN interview with Mmadiate Makgale, 16–3–1983, pp. 38–42.
93. ODP WP, MN interview with Nkwapa Ramorwesi, 25–5–1982, p. 4.
94. *Ibid.*, pp. 8–9.

Chapter 3
Church, School, and Tribe, 1910–1925

1. Graeme Simpson quotes Petrus Mokgatle, giving evidence in 1924 in defence of the then chief at the time of the "Bafokeng Disturbances": "No one would have been disrespectful to him and call him a dog to his face, because he was a great chief." See Simpson, "Peasants and Politics," 240–41.
2. This is the argument made by Georgina Relly, in her "Social and Economic Change." Simpson ("Peasants and Politics") suggests that it then broke down in later times, as pressures for individualisation of land purchase undermined the redistributive impulses of the nineteenth-century chieftaincy.
3. Sociologists have perhaps tended to place too much weight on the indoctrinating capacities of missionaries. See, for example, Jacklyn Cock, *Maids and Madams* (Johannesburg: Ravan Press, 1980). The approaches of Bengt Sundkler (*Bantu Prophets in South Africa* [London: Oxford University Press, 1961]), and Deborah Gaitskell

("Female Mission Initiatives: Black and White Women in Three Witwaters and Churches, 1903–1939" [Ph.D. thesis, University of London, 1981]); or Jean Comaroff (Body of Power) while adopting varying theoretical assumptions, tend to regard Christianity as a set of ideas and symbols (a discourse in Comaroff's case), which may or may not perform the functions for which they were intended, and which may be seized by converts and used to other ends. This appears to be the way in which it worked for the Bafokeng.

4. This was Naboth Mokgatle's description, quoted above in Chapter 1.
5. This was a view which eminently suited the eventual rulers of the Transvaal in the late nineteenth century—the Boers. Kruger, it was said, consciously encouraged the Hermannsburg missionaries and actively discouraged the London Missionary Society, with its more active "Westernising" mission. The contribution of such missionary visions to the later evolution of Afrikaner ideologies of apartheid, separate development, and "Bantu education" has been explored by J. Hyslop, in his "The Concepts of Reproduction and Resistance in the Sociology of Education: The Case of the Transition from "Missionary" to "Bantu" Education, 1940–1955," *Perspectives in Education* 9, 2, (1987).
6. ODP WP, MN interview with Mmadiate Makgale, 16–3–1983, p. 11.
7. Mokgatle, *Autobiography*, 84.
8. ODP WP, MN interview with Mahubi Makgale, 27–11–1981, p. 3.
9. ODP WP, MN interview with Ernestina Mekgwe, 2–2–1983, p. 23.
10. ODP WP, MN interview with Nthana Mokale, 1–2–1983, p. 27.
11. ODP WP, DM interview with Ernestina Mekgwe, 2–3–1983, p. 26.
12. ODP WP, MN interview with Nthana Mokale, 1–2–1983, p. 29.
13. *Ibid.*, p. 32.
14. ODP WP, DM interview with Ernestina Mekgwe 2–3–1983, p. 28.
15. ODP WP, MN interview with Nthana Mokale, 1–2–1983, p. 32.
16. South African Archives Bureau (SAB), K/26 Evidence to the *Native Economic Commission* of 1930–32, State Archives, Pretoria (hereafter NEC 1930–32), by Ernest Penzhorn, p. 987. Penzhorn mentions the fact that "frequently" only the women in particular families were Christians, while men and even children were not.
17. ODP WP, MN interview with Nthana Mokale, 1–2–1983, p. 32.
18. ODP WP, MN interview with Mmadiate Makgale, 16–3–1983, pp. 29–30.
19. *Ibid.*, p. 13. This is an uncanny echo of the theme suggested by Deborah Gaitskell in her "'Wailing for Purity': Prayer Unions, African Mothers and Adolescent Daughters, 1912–1940," in Marks and Rathbone, eds., *Industrialisation and Social Change*.
20. Simpson, "Peasants and Politics," calls it the "state" church of the Bafokeng, implying that its alliance was mainly with the chieftaincy. Perhaps this ignores the complexities of the relationship between religious discourses and the broader commoner population.
21. ODP WP, MN interview with Nkwapa Ramorwesi, 25–5–1982, p. 12.
22. ODP WP, MN interview with Nthana Mokale, 1–2–1983, pp. 33–35.
23. ODP WP, MN interview with Mmadiate Makgale, 16–3–1983, pp. 59–60.
24. NEC 1930–32, Evidence of Ernest Penzhorn p. 977.
25. ODP WP, MN interview with Nkwapa Ramorwesi, 25–5–82, p. 2.
26. *Ibid.*, p. 9.
27. See Relly, "Social and Economic Change."
28. Although such succession disputes and splitting of communities are common in Tswana societies, Graeme Simpson suggests that this particular dispute presaged the later struggles within the Bafokeng community which were based on deep and modern differences. See Simpson, "Peasants and Politics."
29. Here I rely heavily upon Simpson's analysis.
30. This infamous act, passed by the first Union government, and at the time of writing being at last repealed, dispossessed thousands of African landholders, by declaring the majority of the country's land only available for ownership by whites, and designating

a much smaller percentage of land (the Reserves, some of them based upon older Reserves set up under former governments) for black ownership. It has been widely interpreted as the chief weapon of both mineowners and capitalist farmers, who sought to create a dispossessed labour force as well as destroy the black peasantry, at a stroke. The Bafokeng lands were already within reserved areas and have remained so.

31. ODP WP, MN interview with Ernestina Mekgwe, 11–9–1981, p. 7.
32. ODP WP, MN interview with Mmadiate Makgale, 16–3–1983, p. 46.
33. ODP WP, MN interview with Ernestina Mekgwe, 11–9–1981, p. 7.
34. See the story told by Setswammung Mokgatle above, p. 41.
35. ODP WP, MN interview with Mmamatlakala Moje, 1–10–1982, pp. 4–5.
36. This may not be true at the very highest levels of the society, where the stratum of better-educated Bafokeng included lawyers, doctors and teachers. But today women from the region are included among the African elite, as perhaps nurses and teachers themselves.
37. ODP WP, MN interview with Mmadiphoko Mokgatle, 18–8–1982, p. 7.
38. ODP WP, MN interview with Josephine Mokotedi, 25–11–1981, p. 3.
39. ODP WP, MN interview with Nthana Mokale, 20–8–1982, p. 3.
40. ODP WP, MN interview with Mmadiate Makgale, 25–11–1981, p. 6.
41. She says she started at ten, which must have been in 1913; and finished in 1920. Of course attendance may have been irregular.
42. ODP WP, MN interview with Nkwapa Ramorwesi, 25–5–1982, pp. 11–12.
43. She is referring to the system of education introduced by the National Party government in the 1950s, to replace the mission education of an earlier period. While Bantu education brought basic literacy to a far larger number of people than had been reached by the more elitist mission schools, the informant is quite correct to suggest that the quality of teaching was vastly inferior. See J. Hyslop, "State Education Policy and the Social Reproduction of the Urban African Working Class: The Case of the Southern Transvaal, 1955–1976," *Journal of Southern African Studies* 14 (April 1988).
44. It seems she was younger than some of the women, and benefited from Penzhorn's later move towards using the English language.
45. See Kinsman, "Beasts of Burden"; I. Schapera, *Bogwera*; and Willoughby, "Notes on the Initiation Ceremonies of the Becwana." But the emphasis in most studies is on boys' initiation.
46. Chiefs may also have supported this. In the evidence to the Native Economic Commission of 1930–32, one witness from the Western Transvaal, Stegmann, suggests that "the chiefs lately are trying to bring about something, some sort of ceremony, to be gone through for the coming-of-age of the children. Drilling and so on," when asked if circumcision schools were held. NEC, 1930–32, evidence of G. P. Stegmann, p. 1058.
47. Thomas Christopher Rangaka, "History of Rangaka Clan, Phokeng," mimeo, ODP, 18.
48. ODP WP, MN interview with Nkwapa Ramorwesi, 25–5–1982, p. 5.
49. ODP WP, MN interview with Ernestina Mekgwe, 11–9–1981, p. 10.
50. *Ibid.*
51. ODP WP, DM interview with Ernestina Mekgwe, 2–3–1983, p. 16.
52. ODP WP, MN interview with Setswammung Mokgatle, 17–3–1983, p. 17.
53. Rangaka, "History of Rangaka Clan," 18.
54. Kinsman, "Beasts of Burden," 49, quoting missionary sources.
55. ODP WP, MN interview with Mahube Makgale, 27–11–1981, p. 4.
56. Mokgatle, *Autobiography*, p. 66.
57. In fact one of the informants, Frances Nameng, claims that her father "brought" Morrison to Luka.
58. Mokgatle, *Autobiography*, p. 67.
59. ODP WP, MN interview with Frances Nameng, 26–11–1982, p. 6. Mrs. Nameng's father appears to have been educated at Tigerkloof and became a teacher, after which

he became an evangelist, presumably for the AME Church.

60. A great deal of the information in this section is taken from *"Sketches in the Life of K. E. M. Spooner, Missionary, South Africa,* collected and arranged by Mrs. K. E. M. Spooner, A. E. Robinson and Dr. P. F. Beacham, n.d.; Kenneth E. M. Spooner, *A Sketch of Native Life in South Africa,* undated pamphlet [hereafter *A Sketch*]; as well as Rangaka, "History of Rangaka Clan." Spooner, the *Life of Spooner* claims, "was remembered with respect" by his coreligionists as "one of the greatest missionaries" in Africa. His wife Geraldine, who outlived him by many years, comes across as having been crucial to his success.
61. Spooner, *A Sketch,* 31.
62. *Ibid.,* 12.
63. *Life of Spooner,* 73.
64. ODP WP, MN interview with Nkwapa Ramorwesi, 25–5–1982, p. 15.
65. Mokgatle, *Autobiography,* 84.
66. ODP WP, MN interview with Nkwapa Ramorwesi, 25–5–1982, p. 16.
67. Mokgatle, *Autobiography,* 82.
68. Spooner, A *Sketch,* 31.
69. *Life of Spooner,* 101–2.
70. ODP WP, MN interview with Ernestina Mekgwe, 11–9–1981, p. 9.
71. ODP WP, MN interview with Nthana Mokale, 1–2–1983, p. 28.
72. ODP WP, MN interview with Nkwapa Ramorwesi, 25–5–1982, p. 15.
73. ODP WP, MN interview with Naomi Setshedi, 1–3–1982, p. 22.
74. Rangaka, "History of Rangaka Clan," 20.
75. ODP WP, MN interview with Ernestina Mekgwe, 11–9–1981, p. 8.
76. ODP WP, MN interview with Nkwapa Ramorwesi, 25–5–1982, p. 15; a *rondawel* is a low, round thatched house.
77. ODP WP, DM interview with Ernestina Mekgwe, 2–3–1983, p. 25.
78. ODP WP, MN interview with Naomi Setshedi 1–3–1982, p. 22.
79. ODP WP, MN interview with Mokete Phalatse, 17–3–1983, p. 28.
80. ODP WP, MN interview with Naomi Setshedi, pp. 8–9.
81. Rangaka, "History of Rangaka Clan," 21.
82. ODP WP, MN interview with Naomi Setshedi, 1–3–1982, p. 22.
83. Rangaka, "History of Rangaka Clan," 20.
84. NEC, 1930–32, Evidence of Ernest Penzhorn, pp. 977–78.
85. ODP WP, MN interview with Nkwapa Ramorwesi, 25–5–1982, p. 16.
86. ODP WP, MN interview with Ernestina Mekgwe, 11–9–1981, p. 8.
87. ODP WP, MN interview with Nkwapa Ramorwesi, 25–5–1982, p. 15.
88. ODP WP, MN interview with Naomi Setshedi, 1–3–1982, pp. 21–22.
89. ODP WP, MN interview with Mokete Phalatse, 17–3–1983, p. 29.
90. ODP WP, MN interview with Nthana Mokale, 1–2–1983, p. 28.
91. ODP WP, MN interview with Nkwapa Ramorwesi, 25–5–1982, pp. 12–14.
92. ODP WP, MN interview with Ernestina Mekgwe, 11–9–1981, p. 10.
93. ODP WP, MN interview with Nkwapa Ramorwesi, 25–5–1982, p. 13.
94. ODP WP, MN interview with Naomi Setshedi, 11–3–1982, p. 21.
95. Spooner, *A Sketch,* 15.
96. *Ibid.*
97. This analysis is in contrast with that of Graeme Simpson, who gives far greater weight to Spooner, and sees his school and church as having given impetus to the rebels who attempted to depose the chief in the 1920s, discussed below. His analysis is suggestive, but perhaps reads too much into the documents, particularly Spooner's own account of his stay there. See Simpson, "Peasants and Politics."
98. ODP WP, MN interview with Mahube Makgale, 27–11–1981, p. 5.
99. Spooner, *A Sketch,* 62.

100. *Ibid.*
101. ODP WP, MN interview with Ernestina Mekgwe, 1–3–1982, p. 21.
102. ODP WP, MN interview with Nkwapa Ramorwesi, 25–5–1982, pp. 13–14.
103. Quoted in Simpson, "Peasants and Politics," 420.
104. ODP WP, MN interview with Mokete Phalatse, 24–5–1982, pp. 11–12.
105. ODP WP, MN interview with Nthana Mokale, 1–2–1983, pp. 26.
106. ODP WP, DM interview with Ernestina Mekgwe, 2–3–1983, p. 21–22.
107. This is Graeme Simpson's interpretation. See Simpson, *"Peasants and Politics,"* Ch. 4.
108. ODP WP, MN interview with Setswammung Mokgatle, 17–3–1983, p. 12.
109. ODP WP, MN interview with Naomi Setshedi, 31–1–1983, pp. 33–34.
110. ODP WP, MN interview with Mokete Phalatse, 24–5–1982, pp. 13–14.
111. Possibly the term *rebels* was influenced by its use to describe another popular revolt, the 1914 Boer *rebellie* against South African participation in the First World War, another example of influence of Afrikaans upon Setswana-speakers.
112. ODP WP, MN interview with Mokete Phalatse, 24–5–1982, p. 14.
113. An instrument that has been made from wood and a cow's hide and is blown to produce music.
114. ODP WP, MN interview with Mokete Phalatse, 24–5–1982, pp. 14–15.
115. ODP WP, MN interview with Setswammung Mokgatle, 17–3–1983, p. 13.
116. *Ibid.*
117. ODP WP, MN interview with Ernestina Mekgwe, 2–2–1983, p. 22.
118. ODP WP, MN interview with Naomi Setshedi, 31–1–1983, p. 34.
119. *Ibid.*, pp. 33–34.
120. *Ibid.*, p. 34.
121. ODP WP, MN interview with Setswammung Mokgatle, 17–3–1983, p. 13.

Chapter 4
Leaving Home, 1920–1935

1. Thus a neighbouring chief, in evidence to the NEC 1930–32, says one reason for male migration was that "the young boy" used to be in an age regiment that could be called upon as "tribal labour." See NEC, 1930–32, Evidence of Chief Shongoane, p. 1109.
2. At least according to Penzhorn in the 1930s. See NEC 1930–32, Evidence of Ernest Penzhorn, p. 990.
3. This view contrasts with that of Kinsman, who is at pains to demonstrate that young girls suffered particularly harsh constraints. See Kinsman, "Beasts of Burden."
4. See, for example, Bundy, *Rise and Fall*; W. Beinart, *The Political Economy of Pondoland* (Cambridge: Cambridge University Press, 1982); and P. Delius, *The Land Belongs to Us* (Berkeley: University of California Press, 1984).
5. See, for example, P. Harries, "Kinship, Ideology and the Nature of Pre-colonial Labour Migration," in Marks and Rathbone, eds., *Industrialisation and Social Change*; Delius, *The Land*; and P. Mayer, ed., *Black Villagers in an Industrial Society* (Cape Town: Oxford University Press, 1980).
6. See Keegan, *Rural Transformations*; and Bradford, *A Taste of Freedom.*
7. See B. Bozzoli, "Marxism, Feminism and South African Studies," *Journal of Southern African Studies* 9, no. 2 (1983), for a preliminary statement of the notion of "domestic struggles."
8. See NEC, 1930–32, Evidence of Ernest Penzhorn, p. 983.
9. NEC, 1930–32, Evidence of Major Anderson, p. 1026. Another witness, the Rev. G. P. Stegmann, said that the Bafokeng were more advanced than other local groups. See NEC, 1930–32, p. 1044.
10. NEC 1930–32, Evidence of E. Penzhorn, p. 972.
11. NEC, 1930–32, Evidence of Native Commissioner Thomas Emmett, p. 1061.

12. NEC 1930–32, Evidence of E. Penzhorn; see also evidence of T. Emmett, p. 1065. Some farmers grew tobacco, it was said, a crop requiring sophisticated techniques.
13. NEC 1930–32, Evidence of E. Penzhorn, p. 972.
14. It may be assumed he means *skottel* (disc) ploughs.
15. NEC 1930–32, Evidence of E. Penzhorn, pp. 964 ff.
16. *Ibid.*, p. 1011.
17. *Ibid.*, p. 1001.
18. *Ibid.*
19. *Ibid.*, p. 1012.
20. Gangsters.
21. NEC 1930–32, Evidence of E. Penzhorn, pp. 1009–1010.
22. This is certainly reinforced by the fact that not one informant had heard of the ICU, the largest African rural social movement of the 1920s. See Bradford, *A Taste of Freedom*.
23. NEC 1930–32, Evidence of E. Penzhorn, p. 1012.
24. Union Government (UG) 22/1914, Report of the Natives Land Commission, p. 335; Statement given by August Mokhatle (a different spelling of Mokgatle) and fourteen others to the commission; Statement dated 1st May 1914.
25. NEC 1930–32, Evidence of Mutle Mokgatle, p. 1095.
26. *Ibid.*, p. 1104.
27. NEC 1930–32, Evidence of E. Penzhorn p. 989.
28. *Ibid.*, p. 1000.
29. NEC 1930–32, Evidence of Chief H. Selon, of the neighbouring Matau group, p. 1117; see also Evidence of Mr. Stegmann, pp. 1033ff.
30. NEC 1930–32, Evidence of E. Penzhorn, p. 1010.
31. *Ibid.*, p. 973.
32. *Ibid.*, p. 974.
33. *Ibid.*, p. 1007.
34. *Ibid.*, p. 969.
35. *Ibid.*, p. 971.
36. *Ibid.*, p. 975.
37. *Ibid.*, p. 1016.
38. *Ibid.*, p. 1004.
39. ODP WP, MN interview with Naomi Setshedi, 24–11–1981, p. 4.
40. NEC 1930–32, Evidence of E. Penzhorn, p. 990.
41. ODP WP, MN interview with Nthana Mokale, 1–2–1983, p. 36.
42. ODP WP, MN interview with Ida Molefe, 19–8–1982, pp. 4–5.
43. ODP WP, MN interview with Mmadiate Makgale, 25–11–1981, p. 6.
44. ODP WP, MN interview with Josephine Mokotedi, 25–11–1981, p. 20.
45. ODP WP, MN interview with Mahubi Makgale, 27–11–1981, p. 33.
46. ODP WP, MN interview with Mokete Phalatse, 24–5–1982, p. 5.
47. ODP WP, MN interview with Naomi Setshedi, 24–11–1981, p. 4.
48. ODP WP, MN interview with Ernestina Mekgwe, 11–9–1981, p. 11.
49. *Ibid.*
50. ODP WP, MN interview with Naomi Setshedi, 11–3–1982, p. 4.
51. *Ibid.*, 31–1–1983, pp. 27ff.
52. ODP WP, MN interview with Nthana Mokale, 1–2–1983, p. 37.
53. ODP WP, MN interview with Sophie Serokane, 27–5–1982, p. 14.
54. *Ibid.*, pp. 14–15.
55. ODP WP, MN interview with Nthana Mokale, 1–2–1983, p. 37.
56. See, for example, P. L. Bonner, "'Desirable or Undesirable Sotho Women?' Liquor, Prostitution and the Migration of Sotho Women to the Rand, 1920–1945," African Studies Institute Seminar paper, 1988, in which the correlation between high bridewealth

payments and unstable marriages in the 1940s and 1950s is discussed. See also C. Murray, *Families Divided* (Cambridge: Cambridge University Press, 1981).

57. ODP WP, MN interview with Nthana Mokale, 1–2–1983, p. 23.
58. ODP WP, MN interview with Ernestina Mekgwe, 11–9–1981, pp. 11–12.
59. ODP WP, MN interview with Nthana Mokale, 20–8–1982, p. 5.
60. ODP WP, MN interview with Ernestina Mekgwe, 23–3–1983, p. 29; see also pp. 33, 39.
61. This was very likely Rainhill, the farm belonging to Mrs. Eleanor (called "Helen" by the women) McGregor, the local liberal with whom Spooner had associated in the Joint Councils movement.
62. ODP WP, MN interview with Mahube Makgale, 27–11–1981, pp. 6ff.
63. ODP WP, MN interview with Ernestina Mekgwe, 2–2–1983, p. 31.
64. *Ibid.*, 11–9–1981, p. 10.
65. *Ibid.*, 2–3–1982, p. 13.
66. Ernest Penzhorn, in his evidence to the NEC 1930–32, p. 1020, gives farm wages as about £1 per month for a youth, and up to £2 for older workers. It is doubtful whether women earned this much. Domestic wages were around £1–10s or more, which was thus reasonably good by these meagre standards; and the work was not as arduous.
67. ODP WP, MN interview with Ernestina Mekgwe, 2–2–1983, p. 33.
68. ODP WP, MN interview with Nthana Mokale, 1–2–1983, p. 38.
69. ODP WP, MN interview with Ernestina Mekgwe, 2–2–1983, p. 19.
70. *Ibid.*, p. 29.
71. *Ibid.*, 11–9–1981, p. 12.
72. ODP WP, MN interview with Naomi Setshedi, 31–1–1983, pp. 25.
73. ODP WP, MN interview with Nthana Mokale, 20–8–1982, pp. 5–6.
74. ODP WP, MN interview with Mmamatlakala Moje, 1–10–1982, pp. 8–9.
75. "We also can't hear."
76. ODP WP, MN interview with Josephine Mokotedi, 25–11–1981, p. 8.
77. *Ibid.*, p. 9.
78. ODP WP, MN interview with Ernestina Mekgwe, 2–2–1983, p. 33.
79. See, for an examination of the gender composition of the domestic labour force, C. van Onselen, "The Witches of Suburbia: Domestic Service on the Witwatersrand, 1890–1914," in his *Studies in the Social and Economic History of the Witwatersrand*, vol. 2 (London: Longman, 1982).
80. Maize porridge.
81. ODP WP, MN interview with Nthana Mokale, 1–2–1983, p. 43.
82. ODP WP, MN interview with Rosinah Setsome, 15–3–1983, pp. 45–46.
83. ODP WP, MN interview with Nthana Mokale, 1–2–1983, p. 43.
84. *Ibid.*, and ff.
85. For comparative material see Pam Taylor, "Daughters and Mothers—Maids and Mistresses: Domestic Service between the Wars," in J. Clarke, C. Critcher, and R. Johnson, eds., *Working Class Culture: Studies in History and Theory* (London: Hutchinson, 1979), amongst many others. The major existing study of domestic service, that by Jacklyn Cock, *Maids and Madams*, does not discuss suburban subcultures, although it may be that in the Eastern Cape, the case study she uses, such subcultures were weak or absent.
86. Basothos.
87. ODP WP, MN interview with Rosinah Setsome, 3–3–1984, p. 5.
88. *Ibid.*, pp. 8–10.
89. ODP WP, MN interview with Ernestina Mekgwe, 2–2–1983, pp. 35–36.
90. *Ibid.*, 2–3–1982, p. 3.
91. *Ibid.*, 2–2–1983, p. 37.
92. *Ibid.*, pp. 37–38.
93. ODP WP, MN interview with Nthana Mokale, 1–2–1983, pp. 47–48.

94. *Ibid.*, p. 46.
95. *Ibid.*, p. 42.
96. *Ibid.*, p. 50.
97. *Ibid.*
98. *Ibid.*, p. 45.
99. ODP WP, MN interview with Ernestina Mekgwe, 2–2–1983, p. 37ff.
100. *Ibid.*
101. Significantly, she was the daughter of a sharecropper who appears to have had considerable experience of the kind of rural paternalism exercised by white farmers.
102. ODP WP, MN interview with Sophie Serokane, 27–5–1982, p. 16.
103. ODP WP, MN interview with Mahube Makgale, 27–11–1981, p. 11.
104. ODP WP, MN interview with Mmamatlakala Moje, 1–10–1982, p. 9.
105. ODP WP, MN interview with Ida Molefe, 19–8–1982, p. 5.
106. ODP WP, MN interview with Ernestina Mekgwe, 2–2–83, p. 21.
107. ODP WP, MN interview with Mokete Phalatse, 24–5–1982, p. 6. In an even starker case of this type, one young girl's wages were paid directly to her father. See ODP WP, MN interview with Gosiameng Mokwene, 24–1–1982, p. 4. (Mrs. Mokwene was not part of the Phokeng project.)
108. ODP WP, MN interview with Mokete Phalatse, 24–5–1982, p. 9.
109. ODP WP, MN interview with Nthana Mokale, 1–2–1983, p. 46.
110. *Ibid.*, p. 50.
111. ODP WP, MN interview with Ernestina Mekgwe, 2–3–1982, p. 3.
112. The concept is derived from David Lockwood's "Sources of Variation in Working Class Images of Society," from A. Giddens and D. Held, eds., *Classes, Power and Conflict* (Basingstoke: Macmillan, 1982) — a concept convincingly shown to be inappropriate by Cock, *Maids and Madams*, for the South African case.
113. Cock, *Maids and Madams*, suggests that this is the case for the domestic workers she has studied, for whom deference is simply a "mask."
114. Whether all migrants see their situation in similar terms is a moot question — and one that has not been asked, because of the prevailing assumptions of the migrant-as-victim in recent historiography. These assumptions had their origins in the time when Marxists were, quite rightly, attempting to correct the liberal version of the origins of migrant labour, which saw it as lying in the operation of a "dual economy," and which emphasised its "voluntary" nature. But to acknowledge an element of choice and self-actualisation in the process of migrancy, at least for certain people in certain periods, is not to deny that larger determining social and economic forces were at work. It is simply to create a distance between these forces and human consciousness and subjectivity, a distance that economistic analyses are incapable of acknowledging, let alone analysing.

Chapter 5
Courtship and Marriage, 1925–1940

1. See P. Delius, "Sebatakgomo: Migrant Organisation, the ANC and the Sekhukhuniland Revolt," *Journal of Southern African Studies* 15, 4, (1989).
2. NEC 1930–32, Evidence of Chief Z. Shongoane, p. 1112.
3. NEC 1930–32, Evidence of Ernest Penzhorn, p. 976.
4. *Ibid.*, p. 987.
5. *Ibid.*, p. 977.
6. *Ibid.*, p. 987.
7. *Ibid.*, p. 990.
8. NEC 1930–32, Evidence of Chief Johannes Mamogale, p. 1103.

9. NEC 1930–32, Evidence of Mutle Mokgatle, p. 1104.
10. NEC 1930–32, Evidence of Pagiel Kgasoe, pp. 1114–15.
11. "Offender."
12. NEC 1930–32, Evidence of Ernest Penzhorn, pp. 990–91.
13. See, for academic confirmation that this was indeed the common purpose of bridewealth, E. J. Krige and J. L. Comaroff, eds., *Essays on African Marriage in Southern Africa* (Cape Town: Juta, 1981).
14. NEC 1930–32, Evidence of Ernest Penzhorn, p. 1004.
15. *Ibid.* This is in sharp contrast to the situation in Lesotho, where bridewealth prices were going up. See Murray, *Families Divided.* The difference is difficult to explain without a more detailed comparative study, but the peasantisation of Phokeng, and the concomitantly greater assertiveness of Bafokeng women, does appear to contrast strongly with the apparently increasingly weak position of Basotho women, in an economy that had become deeply dependent on migrancy. This difference was to affect the women of Phokeng, ultimately, as we shall see, because their move to the city was done from a greater position of strength than that of the Basotho women who followed them in the 1940s — and who formed a lower stratum in the townships of the Rand.
16. NEC 1930–32, Evidence of G. Stegmann, p. 1031.
17. An exceptional study that tries to locate bridewealth and marriage historically, and which does acknowledge the different perspectives on bridewealth taken by the various interests affected by it, including the women — but in a different part of Southern Africa — is Diana Jeater, "Marriage, Perversion and Power: The Construction of Moral Discourse in Southern Rhodesia 1890–1980" (Ph.D. thesis, Oxford University, 1990).
18. This, it may be suggested, is the implication of Jean Comaroff's argument, in her *Body of Power*, where she argues powerfully that Tswana culture as a whole contains discourses that are oppositional to the colonial/capitalist hegemonic order at large — but fails to see that particular groups within Tswana society itself (such as women, or junior men) may not accept its internal hegemonic discourses either.
19. ODP WP, MN interview with Naomi Setshedi, 31–1–1983, p. 14.
20. ODP WP, MN interview with Josephine Mokotedi, 23–3–1983, p. 30.
21. ODP WP, MN interview with Sophie Serokane, 27–5–1982, p. 15.
22. *Amalaita* — the name given to a particular gang active in the townships at the time, but also extended for use as a generic name for gangsters.
23. ODP WP, MN interview with Mahube Makgale, 27–11–1981, p. 10.
24. This probably suggests "playing the field" of girls.
25. *Doek*: a scarf, or headdress. Giving a *doek* to a boy could be symbolic of wanting to marry him.
26. ODP WP, MN interview with Mahube Makgale, 27–11–1981, p. 10.
27. ODP WP, DM interview with Ernestina Mekgwe, 2–3–1983, p. 32.
28. ODP WP, MN interview with Naomi Setshedi, 11–3–1983, p. 22.
29. ODP WP, MN interview with Ernestina Mekgwe, 2–2–1983, p. 33.
30. By Lutherans at Chaneng, near but not in Phokeng.
31. Referring to the overnight stays that friends had in each other's rooms.
32. ODP WP, MN interview with Josephine Mokotedi, 23–3–1983, pp. 29–30.
33. ODP WP, MN interview with Nthana Mokale, 1–2–1983, pp. 52–53.
34. ODP WP, MN interview with Nthana Mokale, 1–2–1983, p. 48.
35. Ida Molefe's first child was born before her marriage in 1939; all of Mokete Phalatse's were born before marriage; Josephine Mokotedi and Mmadiate Makgale each had one child before marriage.
36. ODP WP, MN interview with Mmamatlakala Moje, 1–10–1982, p. 13.
37. ODP WP, MN interview with Mokete Phalatse, 17–3–1983, p. 11.
38. See Jeater, "Marriage, Perversion, and Power."
39. ODP WP, MN interview with Nthana Mokale, 20–8–1982, p. 8.

40. ODP WP, MN interview with Nkwapa Ramorwesi, 25–5–1982, p. 22.
41. All taken from ODP WP, MN interview with Ernestina Mekgwe, 11–9–1981, pp. 12ff.
42. ODP, WP, MN interview with Nthana Mokale, 1–2–1983, p. 53.
43. ODP WP, MN interview with Mmamatlakala Moje, 1–2–1982, p. 12.
44. ODP WP, MN interview with Mmadiate Makgale, 25–11–1981, pp. 8–9.
45. ODP WP, MN interview with Naomi Setshedi, 31–1–1983, pp. 13ff.
46. *Ibid.*, pp. 14–15.
47. *Ibid.*, p. 15.
48. ODP WP, MN interview with Ernestina Mekgwe, 11–9–1981, p. 18.
49. ODP WP, MN interview with Nthana Mokale, 1–2–1983, p. 23.
50. ODP WP, MN interview with Josephine Mokotedi, 25–11–1981, pp. 7–8.
51. *Ibid.*, p. 9.
52. ODP WP, MN interview with Mahubi Makgale, 27–11–1981, p. 11.
53. *Ibid.*, p. 8.
54. ODP WP, MN interview with Nthana Mokale, 20–8–1982, p. 8.
55. ODP WP, MN interview with Mmamatlakala Moje, 1–10–1982, p. 10.
56. *Ibid.*, p. 9.

Chapter 6
Respectable Matrons, 1930–1945

1. ODP WP, MN interview with Mmadiphoko Mokgatle, 18–8–1982, pp. 10–11.
2. For a discussion of the formation of this segment of the urban population see David Goodhew, "Half a Loaf or No Bread: A Political Life of P. Q. Vundla," paper presented to the University of London, Institute of Commonwealth Studies, June 1990, and "No Easy Walk to Freedom: Political Organisation in the Western Areas of Johannesburg, 1918–1939," African Studies Institute seminar paper, University of the Witwatersrand, 1989; Julia Wells gives us a sense that such a class existed in Potchefstroom in her paper "'The Day the Town Stood Still': Women in Resistance in Potchefstroom, 1912–1930," in Bozzoli, ed., *Town and Countryside*. But the emphasis in recent studies, such as the work of Philip Bonner cited below, has been on later waves of immigrants to the city, and the "respectable" working class has, to some extent, been ignored.
3. See the work in progress of Kathy Eales (for example her draft paper, "Black Women and Influx Control on the Rand," p. 2) for a discussion of the pace of urbanisation of African women in the 1930s and 1940s; see also Bonner, "'Desirable or Undesirable Sotho Women?' Liquor, Prostitution and the Migration of Sotho Women to the Rand, 1920–1945," African Studies Institute seminar paper, University of the Witwatersrand, 1988; and J. Wells, "A History of Black Women's Struggle Against Pass Laws in South Africa, 1900–1960" (Ph.D. thesis, Columbia University, 1982).
4. See Bonner, "Desirable or Undesirable Sotho Women?"
5. Lebelo nevertheless makes a strong case for their existence. See M. S. Lebelo, "Sophiatown Removals, Relocation and Political Quiescence in the Rand Townships, 1950–1965" (B.A. honours dissertation, University of the Witwatersrand, 1988); see also, for a class-based analysis of township structures, P. Tourikis, "The Political Economy of Alexandra Township, 1905–1958" (B.A. honours dissertation, University of the Witwatersrand, 1981).
6. Wells, in "The Day the Town Stood Still," shows this for the Potchefstroom township population.
7. See Eales, "Black Women," for a discussion of this.
8. Goodhew, "No Easy Walk."
9. See, for discussions of the political expression of the "disreputables," P. Bonner, "The Politics of Black Squatter Movements on the Rand 1944–1952," *Radical History Review* 46–47 (Winter 1990); K. French, "James Mpanza and the Sofasonke Party" (M.A.

dissertation, University of the Witwatersrand, 1984); A. Stadler, "'Birds in the Cornfield': Squatter Movements in Johannesburg, 1944–1947," *Journal of Southern African Studies* 6, no. 1 (1979).

10. ODP WP, MN interview with Frances Nameng, 26–11–1982, pp. 14–15.
11. ODP WP, MN interview with Rosinah Setsome, 12–9–1981, p. 19.
12. ODP WP, MN interview with Naomi Setshedi, 1–3–1982, p. 12.
13. ODP WP, DM interview with Ernestina Mekgwe, 2–3–1983, p. 39.
14. ODP WP, MN interview with Rosinah Setsome, 3–3–1984, p. 4.
15. Alexandra was in those years run by a liberal "Health Committee," and not by local government officials, as were other townships. See Tourikis, "Political Economy" and D. Duncan, "Liberals and Local Administration: The Alexandra Health Committee, 1933–1943," *International Journal of African Historical Studies* 23, 4 (1990). But the use of the word "help" is surely significant—perhaps an acknowledgment of the relatively benign order the liberals attempted to create.
16. Getting a "pass" in this case refers to getting a residence permit.
17. Nostalgia about Sophiatown's supposed happiness and harmony is a common theme in literary and academic treatments of its history. See Trevor Huddleston's memoir, *Nought for your Comfort* (Johannesburg; Hardingham and Donaldson, 1956); Bloke Modisane's autobiographical *Blame Me on History* (London: Thames and Hudson, 1963); Don Mattera's autobiographical *Memory Is the Weapon* (Johannesburg: Ravan Press, 1987) and many others. While Lebelo "Sophiatown Removals," is quite rightly sceptical about the rosy hue such nostalgia has lent to the history of this freehold township (he points out that real class differences between its inhabitants, for example, are obscured by this nostalgic mode) it is interesting that some of the interviewees—who were of the working class, and who would hardly have been part of the literary intelligentsia seeking to "invent" a past—also have happy memories of their time there.
18. ODP WP, MN interview with Frances Nameng, 26–11–1982, p. 15.
19. *Ibid.*, p. 17.
20. Lebelo, "Sophiatown Removals".
21. ODP WP, MN interview with Frances Nameng, 26–11–1982, p. 17.
22. ODP WP, MN interview with Sophie Serokane, 18–3–1983, pp. 18–19.
23. ODP WP, MN interview with Ernestina Mekgwe, 2–2–1983, p. 17.
24. ODP WP, MN interview with Nthana Mokale, 1–2–1983, p. 19.
25. Porridge mixed with pumpkin-like vegetables; see ODP WP, MN interview with Nthana Mokale, 1–2–1983, p. 20.
26. ODP WP, DM interview with Ernestina Mekgwe, 2–3–1983, p. 15.
27. Naomi Setshedi recounts her mother's words to her on her death bed: "'My only daughter, the daughter to whom I gave birth to with the hope that later in life when I am ill, will look after me. Where is she now, here I am, suffering.' I tried to console her. Her last word was, 'Hold my hands together.' She then died." See ODP WP, MN interview with Naomi Setshedi, 31–1–1983, p. 5.
28. The naming of children also provides us with some interesting insights. Ida Molefe's second child, born during the Second World War, was given the second name of "Hitler": "They said he was raving mad, wanting to have the whole world to himself," admitted Ida. Mmantho asks, somewhat amazed, "Then you named your child after him?" "Yes." But then the unfortunately named "Hitler" was renamed "Pejana," "because he always liked to play with his genitals, and when he woke up in the morning he would scream right through the house "Pejana yo ka e kae" (where is my "old man"), and eventually he was called Pejana and the name Hitler died." Her third child was called Mmamotjhaena which means "China Girl," so named because "She was born just after I came back from running fah-fee." See ODP WP, MN interview with Ida Molefe, 19–8–1982, pp. 8ff.
29. ODP WP, MN interview with Mmadiate Makgale, 25–11–1981, p. 20.
30. ODP WP, MN interview with Ernestina Mekgwe, 2–2–1983, p. 41.

31. *Ibid.*, pp. 41–42.
32. *Ibid.*, p. 42.
33. ODP WP, MN interview with Mmadiate Makgale, 16–3–1983, pp. 32–33.
34. ODP WP, MN interview with Nthana Mokale, 20–8–1982, p. 12.
35. ODP WP, MN interview with Jacobeth Lekalake, 30–9–1982, p. 6.
36. *Ibid.*, p. 10.
37. According to David Goodhew ("No Easy Walk"), in fact, the townships of central Johannesburg did not house the classic proletariat—who in the early stages of South African capitalism lived in mine compounds, segregated from other Africans, or on the East Rand, which was where the major engineering firms were situated. Even today, Soweto, which inherited the population of the removed townships of the 1950s, has a disproportionately high number of residents in light industry or white-collar work. See Jeremy Seekings, "Why was Soweto Different? Urban Development, Township Politics and the Political Economy of Soweto, 1977–84," unpublished paper.
38. ODP WP, MN interview with Naomi Setshedi, 31–1–1983, pp. 16–17.
39. ODP WP, MN interview with Ida Molefe, 24–3–1983, p. 6.
40. ODP WP, DM interview with Ernestina Mekgwe, 2–3–1983, p. 11.
41. ODP WP, MN interview with Naomi Setshedi, 31–1–1983, p. 93.
42. *Ibid.*, p. 94.
43. ODP WP, MN interview with Ida Molefe, 19–8–1982, pp. 8–9.
44. ODP WP, DM interview with Ernestina Mekgwe, 2–3–1983, p. 11.
45. ODP WP, MN interview with Ida Molefe, 19–8–1982, p. 66.
46. *Ibid.*, p. 67.
47. ODP WP, MN interview with Naomi Setshedi, 24–11–1981, pp. 64–65.
48. *Ibid.*, p. 66.
49. ODP WP, DM interview with Ernestina Mekgwe, 2–3–1983, p. 15.
50. *Ibid.*, p. 9.
51. Her second and subsequent children, however, were born in Randfontein, the township to which she moved after her marriage in 1937.
52. ODP WP, MN interview with Nkwapa Ramorwesi, 25–5–1982, p. 22.
53. ODP WP, MN interview with Ida Molefe, 19–8–1982, p. 7.
54. ODP WP, MN interview with Nthana Mokale, 20–8–1982, p. 7.
55. ODP WP, MN interview with Ernestina Mekgwe, 11–9–1981, p. 19.
56. *Ibid.*, 2–2–1983, p. 40.
57. ODP WP, MN interview with Dikeledi Makgale, 28–5–1982, p. 8.
58. ODP WP, MN interview with Naomi Setshedi, 11–3–1982, p. 95.
59. This fact was perceived accurately by the women. See Josephine Mokotedi's testimony, where she says that in those days "there weren't firms to work in," ODP WP, MN interview with Josephine Mokotedi, 23–3–1983, p. 31.
60. ODP WP, MN interview with Nthana Mokale, 20–8–1982, pp. 14–15.
61. *Ibid.*, p. 19.
62. *Ibid.*, 1–2–1983, p. 72.
63. *Ibid.*, 20–8–1982, p. 19.
64. *Ibid.*, 1–2–1983, pp. 75–76.
65. *Ibid.*, pp. 56–57.
66. A substantial literature on these spheres of activity exists. See, for some examples, Ellen Hellman, *Rooiyard* (Cape Town: Oxford University Press, 1948), an exploration of conditions in a "slumyard," an inner-city area in which poorer, homeless people were crammed; see also, on these areas, E. Koch, "Without Visible Means of Subsistence: Slumyard Culture in Johannesburg 1918–1940," in Bozzoli, ed., *Town and Countryside*; Bafokeng do not seem to have lived in these types of areas. See also Bonner, "Desirable or Undesirable Sotho Women?"; Eales, "Black Women Oral Influx Controls"; C. Rogerson and D. Hart, "The Survival of the Informal Sector: The Black Shebeens of Johannesburg," *Geojournal* 12, no. 12 (1986).

67. ODP WP, MN interview with Ernestina Mekgwe, 2−3−1982, p. 12.

68. See B. Bozzoli, "Life Strategies, Household Resilience and the Meaning of Informal Work: Some Women's Stories," in E. Preston-Whxte and C. Rogerson, eds., *South Africa's Informal Economy: Past, Present and Future* (Cape Town: Oxford University Press, 1991), for a drawing together of all aspects of the "informal sector" activities that the women undertook.

69. ODP WP, MN interview with Naomi Setshedi, 31−1−1983, p. 12.

70. *Ibid.*, p. 9.

71. *Ibid.*, pp. 11−12.

72. ODP WP, MN interview with Mmadiate Makgale, 16−3−1983, p. 11.

73. *Ibid.*, p. 25.

74. ODP WP, MN interview with Mokete Phalatse, 17−3−1983, p. 32.

75. See Prelude, note 2, on p. 249.

76. ODP WP, MN interview with Mmamatlakala Moje, 1−10−1982, p. 20.

77. A deeply embedded urban savings-redistribution institution, which operates today much as Mrs. Setshedi describes it, although it takes different forms in each place and time. Members pool a designated portion of their income each month (sometimes virtually the whole amount will be given over), and *one* member will receive the full amount pooled for that month.

78. ODP WP, MN interview with Naomi Setshedi, 31−1−1983, p. 85.

79. See, for comparative material, Hellman, *Rooiyard*; Eales, "Black Women"; P. la Hausse, *Brewers, Beerhalls and Boycotts: A History of Liquor in South Africa* (Johannesburg: Ravan Press, 1988), and H. Bradford, "We are Now the Men: Women's Beer Protests in the Natal Countryside, 1929," in Bozzoli, ed., *Class, Community and Conflict*.

80. "Fietas" was the common name for the mixed inner-city poor suburb of Vrededorp. ODP WP, MN interview with Nthana Mokale, 1−2−1983, pp. 48−49.

81. ODP WP, MN interview with Ernestina Mekgwe, 2−2−1983, p. 37.

82. *Ibid.*

83. *Ibid.*, p. 38.

84. The rebellion of disaffected and impoverished Afrikaners against the decision of the government to support Britain in the First World War. See J. Bottomley, "The South African Rebellion of 1914: The Influence of Industrialisation, Poverty and 'Poor Whiteism,'" African Studies Institute seminar paper, University of the Witwatersrand, 1982. Quite a few of the testimonies suggest that the women were aware of the rebellion, and in this case, it appears to have actually affected Phokeng directly.

85. ODP WP, MN interview with Ernestina Mekgwe, 11−9−1981, p. 21. She continues to say that the Boers had sought refuge with "a German priest," but were found out and died a "horrible death." She also remembers that the departing English soldiers to whom they had given beer sang, "It's a long way to the prairie, It's a long way to go, It's a long way to the prairie, Sweetheart girl I know" — undoubtedly an improvement on the original.

86. ODP WP, MN interview with Rosinah Setsome, 15−3−1983, p. 34.

87. ODP WP, MN interview with Mmadiate Makgale, 25−11−1981, p. 11.

88. *Ibid.*, 16−3−1983, p. 41.

89. ODP WP, MN interview with Rosinah Setsome, 15−3−1983, p. 34.

90. ODP WP, MN interview with Mmadiate Makgale, 16−3−1983, pp. 73−76.

91. Name for a particular homemade beer.

92. ODP WP, MN interview with Mmadiate Makgale, 16−3−1983, pp. 12−13 and pp. 25−26.

93. ODP WP, MN interview with Sophie Serokane, 27−5−1982, p. 31.

94. ODP WP, MN interview with Frances Nameng, 26−11−1981, p. 16.

95. ODP WP, MN interview with Mmamatlakala Moje, 1−10−1982, p. 13.

96. She suggests it was a section of the northern suburbs of Johannesburg kept for blacks — but it is not clear what she meant.

97. ODP WP, MN interview with Mmamatlakala Moje, 1–10–1982, p. 15.
98. ODP WP, MN interview with Ida Molefe, 24–3–1983, p. 25.

Chapter 7
Subjectivity and Identity: Tales of Violence and Persecution

1. That their subjectivity has an historical base is a central tenet of the book, which distinguishes it from purely phenomenological studies such as those of Hoyt Alverson, as discussed in the Introduction.
2. This was a very early inner-city settlement, mainly inhabited by blacks, which was later demolished.
3. A corruption of "cab" — a common form of transport in the early days being horse-drawn cabs.
4. ODP WP, MN interview with Nthana Mokale, 20–8–82, p. 6. Nthana is emphatic that a *kepe* was not a rickshaw, but "a small carriage used to transport people during those days . . . a horse-drawn carriage with a roof, and they were owned by Indians."
5. ODP WP, MN interview with Mmadiate Makgale, 25–12–1981, p. 12.
6. ODP WP, MN interview with Ida Molefe, 24–3–1983, p. 13.
7. *Ibid.*, pp. 13–14, and 26.
8. ODP WP, MN interview with Ernestina Mekgwe, 2–2–1983, p. 40.
9. *Ibid.*, p. 39.
10. Thus the difference in the causes and experiences of migrancy between Bafokeng and Basotho women is instructive. See, for material that allows such a comparison, P. Bonner, "Desirable or Undesirable Sotho Women?", in which it is argued that "the mid-1930s marked the beginning of a sustained surge of black immigration to the towns which would carry on for another two decades," and that a high proportion of these new migrants were Sotho women, who had fled rural impoverishment and the ravages of migrant labour. In the towns they set themselves up as liquor brewers, engaged in prostitution, and did not settle into the stable marriages we have seen in the case of the Bafokeng.
11. ODP WP, MN interview with Ernestina Mekgwe, 2–2–1983, p. 5, and p. 16.
12. ODP WP, MN interview with Enestina Mekgwe, 11–9–1981, p. 18.
13. ODP WP, MN interview with Ernestina Mekgwe, 11–9–1981, p. 8; see also her interview on 2–2–1983, p. 23ff.
14. ODP WP, MN interview with Ernestina Mekgwe, 2–2–1983, p. 19.
15. ODP WP, MN interview with Nkwapa Ramorwesi, 25–5–1982, p. 18.
16. ODP WP, MN interview with Mmadiate Makgale, 16–3–1983, pp. 8–9.
17. It was the influx of thousands of Basotho women, defined by the authorities as "undesirable," which provoked a massive increase in attacks on liquor brewers. "From 1938–1940 the tempo of liquor raiding steadily mounted"; the new migrants were particularly threatening because it was during these years that municipalities sought to establish their own beerhalls, the revenue from which was to pay for housing. See Bonner, "Desirable or Undesirable Sotho Woman?" 2–3, for example.
18. ODP WP, MN interview with Sophie Serokane, 27–5–1982, p. 7.
19. ODP WP, MN interview with Ernestina Mekgwe, 2–2–1983, p. 36. "Dark City" was the name given to Alexandra by its inhabitants at the time, because of the lack of electric lighting (which is still the case in parts of Alexandra today).
20. ODP WP, MN interview with Frances Nameng, 26–11–1981, pp. 11ff.
21. ODP WP, MN interview with Naomi Setshedi, 1–3–1982, pp. 6–8, and p. 18.
22. *Ibid.*, p. 18.
23. *Ibid.*, p. 29.
24. *Ibid.*, pp. 30–31.
25. ODP WP, MN interview with Maria Mathuloe, 27–11–1981, pp. 9–11. For the background

to the activities of these gangs, see Paul Tourikis, "Political Economy," where the Msomi and Spoiler gangs are discussed (the latter obtained its name because it used to "spoil" parties by wrecking them); both operated protection rackets, and Shadrack Matthews was indeed the notorious leader of the Msomi gang. For comparative work on gangsterism on the Rand in this period, see J. Guy and M. Thabane, "The Ma-Rashea: A Participant's Perspective," in Bozzoli, ed., *Class, Community and Conflict*; T. Lodge, "The Destruction of Sophiatown," in Bozzoli, ed., *Town and Countryside*; and P. Bonner, "Family, Crime and Political Consciousness on the East Rand, 1939–1955," *Journal of Southern African Studies* 14, no. 3 (1988).

26. ODP WP, MN interview with Maria Mathuloe, 27–11–1981, p. 10.
27. ODP WP, MN interview with Mmamatlakala Moje, 1–2–1982, pp. 20ff.
28. ODP WP, MN interview with Sophie Serokane, 27–5–1982, pp. 20–21.
29. ODP WP, MN interview with Naomi Setshedi, 1–3–1982, pp. 140–41.
30. ODP WP, MN interview with Frances Nameng, 26–11–1981, p. 17.
31. ODP WP, MN interview with Mmamatlakala Moje, 1–10–1982, pp. 13ff.
32. ODP WP, MN interview with Rosinah Setsome, 15–3–1983, pp. 39–43.
33. Probably a corruption of the common Afrikaans name "Scheepers." That one policeman was well enough known to be considered a permanent persecutor is an interesting feature of this story—while the giving of Setswana nicknames to whites was and is a common way of indicating both distance and scepticism.
34. ODP WP, MN interview with Rosinah Setsome, 15–3–1983, pp. 39–43.
35. She and her husband had lived at Boons both before and after Alexandra. Her husband cared for a farm there. This anecdote probably refers to her later stay there.
36. ODP WP, MN interview with Rosinah Setsome, 15–3–1983, pp. 40–41.
37. ODP WP, MN interview with Mmadiate Makgale, 16–3–1983, pp. 70–73.
38. ODP WP, MN interview with Mmamatlakala Moje, 1–10–1982, p. 18.
39. ODP WP, MN interview with Mmadiate Makgale, 16–3–1983, pp. 70–73.
40. *Ibid.*, 25–11–1981, pp. 22–24.

Chapter 8
Resentment and Defiance, 1945–1960

1. Deborah Posel has correctly warned us against the assumption that the National Party was equipped with a "Grand Plan" on its assumption of power in 1948—and encourages us to see the implementation of Apartheid as the result of many political struggles "on the ground." See D. Posel, "Influx Control and the Construction of Apartheid. 1948–1961" (Ph.D. Thesis, Oxford University, 1987).
2. The classical sociological term "reference group"—allied to the notion of "relative deprivation"—has hardly found a place in the South African literature, which has been dominated by the idea of "absolute" deprivation—an economistic notion with no place for consciousness—as the basis for social protest, perhaps because of the extreme nature of the regime there. But it is an especially useful one when discussing the origins and bases of social movements, particularly those appealing to the stratum to which the women belonged, and has a great deal of application in the case of the protests discussed in this chapter. See G. Runciman, *Relative Deprivation and Social Justice* (London: Routledge and Kegan Paul, 1966).
3. The women's memories of World War Two appear to be mainly focussed on the deep resentment felt by "respectable" African men who had actually gone to war, at their treatment afterwards by white authorities, who thanked them by giving them bicycles, ploughs, and donkeys while white soldiers were given houses. See ODP WP, MN interviews with Naomi Setshedi, 1–3–1982, p. 13; Nthana Mokale, 20–8–1982, p. 11; and Jacobeth Lekalake, 30–9–1982, p. 8. This is a theme that clearly warrants further research.
4. See P. Bonner, "The Politics of Black Squatter Movements on the Rand, 1944–1952,"

Radical History Review, 46—47 (Winter 1990); K. French, "James Mpanza and the Sofasonke Party", M.A. dissertation, University of the Witwatersrand, 1984); and Stadler, "Birds in the Cornfield."

5. See Stadler, "Birds in the Cornfield," for a discussion of economic conditions after the war; and A. Stadler, "A Long Way to Walk: Bus Boycotts in Alexandra, 1940—45," in P. Bonner, ed., *Working Papers in Southern African Studies* (Johannesburg: Ravan Press, 1981), for a discussion of the resulting bus boycotts.

6. See, for example, D. Hindson, *Pass Laws and the South African Proletariat* (Johannesburg: Ravan Press 1988), who argues the latter, and D. Posel, "Influx Control," who tends to argue the former.

7. Townships such as Orlando, the earliest in Soweto, were not built under National Party rule, but later Soweto suburbs were. It would seem useful to interpret the National Party government as one that sought, not to deprive the urban working classes in an absolute sense, but to supply them with the housing and education that would fit them to the lowly, segregated, and exclusively proletarian jobs for which they were deemed suited. J. Hyslop's work on the educational policies of the National Party government, for example, shows that they did not simply involve the removal of educational opportunities from blacks, but their removal—by closing down mission schools—from mainly middle class or better-off blacks. For working-class blacks, in fact, the introduction of Bantu education involved an ironic and twisted expansion of opportunity to obtain basic literacy. Similarly, the building of the huge segregated townships was welcomed by the poorest squatters in the inner-city slums, as under the old system they had no housing at all. See J. Hyslop, "State Education Policy and the Social Reproduction of the Urban African Working Class: The Case of the Southern Transvaal, 1955—1976," *Journal of Southern African Studies* 14, 3 (1988). This makes it all the more essential to identify the existence of "relative" deprivation in urban people.

8. See Eales, "Black Women and Influx Control," for a discussion of earlier unsuccessful attempts at removals.

9. There had been numerous unsuccessful attempts to impose passes upon women before; see Wells, "The History of Black Women's Struggle"; and C. Walker, *Women and Resistance in South Africa* (London: Onyx Press, 1982).

10. See Tom Lodge, "The Destruction of Sophiatown," in Bozzoli, ed., *Town and Countryside*; A. Proctor, "Class Struggle, Segregation and the City: A History of Sophiatown, 1905—1940," in Bozzoli, ed., *Labour, Townships and Protest*; and Lebelo, "Sophiatown Removals." Alexandra was never removed and destroyed, as was Sophiatown, but many of its residents were moved out in the 1950s, and one or two of the informants link this to the swelling of political protest in this period. See Tourikis, "Political Economy."

11. ODP WP, MN interview with Maria Mathuloe, 27—11—1981, p. 8.

12. Tom Lodge, *Black Politics in South Africa Since 1945* (Johannesburg: Ravan Press, 1983), in particular, discusses how the ANC adopted a strategy based on mass action for the first time in 1949—with strikes, boycotts, and civil disobedience forming the core of its programme. While local township leaders had, in the preceding years, established a base and a following, it was only in the 1950s that a consciousness of the presence of the ANC reached the women, perhaps a sign of their relatively secure situation until then, as well as of the limited popular base of social movements in the 1940s.

13. None of the women, when asked, remembered the Industrial and Commercial Workers' Union—the biggest social movement of the 1920s, straddling both urban and rural repeal areas.

14. Julia Wells seems to support this suggestion. See Wells, "Black Women's Struggle," Ch. 8.

15. The studies by Wells and Walker cited in footnote 9 above give us an idea of the scale and nature of the women's movements of the 1950s. This chapter is not intended to be a replica of their analyses, but rather a rich filling-in, in personalised terms, of some of the forces they examine.

16. This concept, with its associated one of "inherent" ideology, is discussed in the Introduction.
17. The date 1948 has been given far too much weight in South Africa as the "turning point" at which true apartheid began. But in fact the National Party was only able to consolidate its power in the early 1950s, and thus the real bite of apartheid began to be felt then.
18. ODP WP, MN interview with Sophie Serokane, 27–5–1982, p. 22.
19. *Ibid.*, p. 21.
20. *Ibid.*, p. 22.
21. ODP WP, MN interview with Frances Nameng, 26–11–1982, p. 15
22. ODP WP, MN interview with Sophie Serokane, 25–3–1984, p. 10.
23. ODP WP, MN interview with Josephine Mokotedi, 25–11–1981, p. 21.
24. See Hindson, *Pass Laws.*
25. As did the newcomers to town, in the form of squatters' movements. See French, *James Mpanza*; Stadler, "Birds in the Cornfield"; Bonner, "Politics of Black Squatter Movements."
26. ODP WP, MN interview with Ida Molefe, 19–8–1982, p. 11.
27. ODP WP, MN interview with Naomi Setshedi, 1–3–1982, p. 14
28. Covered extensively in Wells, "Black Women's Struggle"; and Walker, *Women and Resistance.*
29. In one interview when the matter was raised, she said she wished to go to sleep.
30. ODP WP, MN interview with Sophie Serokane, 27–5–1982, p. 18; see also interview with Sophie Serokane, 18–3–1983, pp. 30–31.
31. ODP WP, MN interview with Sophie Serokane, 18–3–1983, pp. 30–31.
32. This word, from the ANC (and generalised) slogan "Mayibuye Afrika" — "Come Back Africa" — appears to have been used by the women to identify those who took part in the campaigns.
33. ODP WP, MN interview with Maria Mathuloe, 27–11–1981, p. 11.
34. ODP WP, MN interview with Nkwapa Ramorwesi, 25–5–1982, p. 28.
35. *Ibid.*, pp. 28–29.
36. ODP WP, MN interview with Ida Molefe, 19–8–1982, pp. 10–11.
37. ODP WP, MN interview with Ida Molefe, 19–8–1982, pp. 10–13. But later in a further interview, with a different interviewer, Ida is much more circumspect. When asked "Did you join the black organisations such as Women's League, Women's Federation or ANC?" she answered "I refused to join those organisations because of being afraid to be arrested. I only heard of people such as Mandela and Tambo." She mentions Fenny Gabashane, but does not tell how she knew of her, and denies knowledge of the famous march of protest against passes to Pretoria. See ODP WP, MN interview with Ida Molefe, 24–3–1983, pp. 14–15.
38. ODP WP, MN interview with Nthana Mokale, 20–8–1982, pp. 15–16.
39. See Wells, "Black Women's Struggle," for a discussion of the problems of transport for many women.
40. ODP WP, MN interview with Nthana Mokale, 20–8–1982, pp. 15–16.
41. Loosely translated as: "We will not be rehoused" — another example of the use of Afrikaans in black popular culture.
42. "Ons phola hier": We are staying here.
43. ODP WP, MN interview with Nthana Mokale, 1–2–1983, pp. 54ff.
44. This is an interesting reference to army headquarters — which also happened to be in one of the suburbs of Pretoria with which Phokeng women were familiar, because of the high number of Bafokeng domestics who worked there.
45. ODP WP, MN interview with Nthana Mokale, 1–2–1983, p. 54; see also interview of 20–8–1982, pp. 15–16.
46. ODP WP, MN interview with Nthana Mokale, 20–8–1982, p. 18.

47. *Ibid.*, pp. 17ff.
48. *Ibid.*, pp. 17–19.
49. *Ibid.*, pp. 15–16, although in discussing her involvement in the "Ons Phola Hier" campaign she says she did attend meetings in the evenings – but that was in Sophiatown where she says she did have more time.
50. ODP WP, MN interview with Nthana Mokale, 20–8–1982, p. 18.
51. *Ibid.*, 1–2–1983, pp. 59ff.
52. An ANC minimum wage campaign. See below.
53. Referring to domestic servants.
54. ANC colours.
55. A popular name for prison – one of the most notorious was No. 4 prison in Central Johannesburg.
56. Epithet for the characteristic "Black Maria" vans used to arrest blacks on pass and other offences; literally "get in, get in."
57. All the above is drawn from ODP WP, MN interviews with Ernestina Mekgwe, 2–3–1982, pp. 2ff; and 2–2–1983, pp. 43ff.
58. A relatively unsuccessful mass strike, held on the day of the all-white elections of 1958, for a minimum wage of £1 a day. For Mrs. Setshedi's admiring support see ODP WP, MN interview with Naomi Setshedi, 1–3–1982, p. 10. "We were one thing," she says (meaning, we were united).
59. ODP WP, MN interview with Naomi Setshedi, 1–3–1982, p. 9.
60. *Ibid.* Contrast this with the far less politicised Mrs. Moje, who was also in Alexandra during the potato boycott; "It was rumoured that people were being killed and their corpses were serving as manure on the potato farms.... people used to go about spreading that rumour.... We couldn't understand what was going on, therefore we used to eat potatoes occasionally. But some people never bothered themselves about the boycott." ODP WP, MN interview with Mmamatlakala Moje, 1–10–1982, p. 19.
61. See Tom Lodge, "We Are Being Punished Because We Are Poor: The Bus Boycotts of Evaton and Alexandra, 1955–1957", in Bonner, ed., *Working Papers.*
62. ODP WP, MN interview with Naomi Setshedi, 1–3–1982, p. 9.
63. *Ibid.*, pp. 14ff.
64. An open meeting-place in Alexandra.
65. ODP WP, MN interview with Naomi Setshedi, 1–3–1982, pp. 14ff.
66. *Ibid.*, pp. 15–16.
67. The above is from *ibid.*, pp. 14ff.
68. ODP WP, MN interview with Ida Molefe, 19–8–1982, pp. 10–12.
69. ODP WP, MN interview with Naomi Setshedi, 1–3–1982, p. 14.
70. A liberal women's organisation that was started in the early 1950s to protest against the Nationalist government's bypassing of the constitution, and which survived the subsequent four decades to fight against the many injustices of apartheid.
71. An interesting use of a Setswana word, to refer to Steve's role as a group or team representative.
72. ODP WP, MN interview with Naomi Setshedi, 31–1–1983, pp. 40ff.
73. ODP WP, MN interview with Nthana Mokale, 20–8–1982, p. 18.
74. ODP WP, MN interview with Naomi Setshedi, 31–1–1983, p. 39.
75. ODP WP, MN interview with Ida Molefe, 19–8–1982, p. 10.
76. ODP WP, MN interview with Naomi Setshedi, 1–3–1982, p. 15.
77. ODP WP, MN interview with Ida Molefe, 19–8–1982, pp. 10–12.
78. ODP WP, MN interview with Nthana Mokale, 1–2–1983, p. 62.
79. He was in fact assassinated some years later. She appears to connect this with the power of the women.
80. ODP WP, MN interview with Naomi Setshedi, 1–3–1982, p. 20.
81. This is a reference to the debate referred to earlier, the key point being that while these

protests all failed on one level, their weight and momentum did set limits to the government's willingness to impose full segregation, and forced it to come to terms with the urban working classes.

Chapter 9
Leaving the City, 1960–1980

1. But it should be stressed that this did not mean that all Bafokeng migrants left the cities — many stayed there permanently, but were of course not included in our sample, which was drawn from Phokeng itself.
2. ODP WP, MN interview with Mmamatlakala Moje, 1–10–1982, p. 23.
3. ODP WP, MN interview with Frances Nameng, 26–11–1982, p. 13.
4. ODP WP, MN interview with Ernestina Mekgwe, 2–2–1983, pp. 44ff.
5. *Ibid.*, pp. 4–5.
6. ODP WP, MN interview with Naomi Setshedi, 1–3–1982, p. 11.
7. *Ibid.*, p. 12.
8. *Ibid.*, p. 16.
9. *Ibid.*, p. 9.
10. *Ibid.*, 31–1–1983, pp. 30ff.
11. ODP WP, MN interview with Rebecca Phiri, 23–3–1983, pp. 12–13.
12. ODP WP, MN interview with Lydia Phiri, 12–9–1981, p. 17.
13. ODP WP, MN interview with Elizabeth Morobe, n.d., p. 4.
14. ODP WP, MN interview with Maria Mathuloe, 27–11–1981, p. 11.
15. ODP WP, MN interview with Sophie Serokane, 27–5–1982, p. 17.
16. *Ibid.*, p. 18.
17. *Ibid.*, 25–3–1984, p. 10.
18. *Ibid.*, 18–3–1983, p. 8.
19. ODP WP, MN interview with Mmadiate Makgale, 25–11–1981, pp. 11ff.
20. Evil spirit.
21. ODP WP, MN interview with Mmadiate Makgale, 25–11–1981, p. 18.
22. *Ibid.*, 16–3–1983, pp. 76ff.
23. ODP WP, MN interview with Mmadiphoko Mokgatle, 18–8–1982, pp. 36–37.
24. ODP WP, MN interview with Nthana Mokale, 20–8–1982, p. 20.
25. *Ibid.*, 1–2–1983, pp. 8ff.
26. *Ibid.*, pp. 10ff.
27. *Ibid.*, 20–8–1982, p. 20.
28. ODP WP, MN interview with Naomi Setshedi, 31–1–1983, p. 30.

Chapter 10
Grandmothers and Pensioners, 1980–1983

1. ODP WP, MN interview with Mmadiate Makgale, 25–11–1981, p. 10.
2. ODP WP, MN interview with Ida Molefe, 24–3–1983, p. 9.
3. ODP WP, MN interview with Evelyn Rakola, 26–5–1982, p. 3.
4. See ODP WP, MN interview with Mokete Phalatse, 17–3–1983, p. 25.
5. ODP WP, MN interview with Ernestina Mekgwe, 11–9–1981 p. 4.
6. ODP WP, MN interview with Naomi Setshedi, 12–3–1982, p. 3.
7. ODP WP, MN interview with Josephine Mokotedi, 23–3–1983, p. 21.
8. ODP WP, MN interview with Dikeledi Makgale, 28–5–1982, pp. 11–12.
9. ODP WP, MN interview with Nkwapa Ramorwesi, 25–5–1982, p. 27.
10. ODP WP, MN interview with Sophie Serokane, 18–3–1983, p. 24.
11. ODP WP, MN interview with Mokete Phalatse, 17–3–1983, pp. 25–26.
12. "He is too rich."
13. ODP WP, MN interview with Mokete Phalatse, 17–3–1983, pp. 21–22.

14. ODP WP, MN interview with Naomi Setshedi, 12–3–1982, p. 3.
15. ODP WP, MN interview with Mmamatlakala Moje, 1–10–1982, p. 23.
16. ODP WP, MN interview with Mokete Phalatse, 17–3–1983, pp. 19–20.
17. ODP WP, MN interview with Sophie Serokane, 25–3–1984, pp. 11–12.
18. ODP WP, MN interview with Ida Molefe, 24–3–1983, pp. 17–18.
19. ODP WP, MN interview with Mokete Phalatse, 17–3–1983, p. 20.
20. *Ibid.*, p. 21.
21. Indeed the Serokanes had known the chief's son when working in Johannesburg. "He is the person with whom we grew together, before he became a chief. We were just surprised when he was fetched to become a chief." He worked in a dairy in Johannesburg and knew Mr. Serokane. They used to play cards together.
22. ODP WP, MN interview with Sophie Serokane, 27–5–1982, p. 21.
23. *Ibid.*, pp. 14–15.
24. *Ibid.*, pp. 13–14.
25. ODP WP, MN interview with Evelyn Rakola, 26–5–1982, pp. 17–19.
26. ODP WP, MN interview with Mmamatlakala Moje, 1–10–1982, p. 24.
27. ODP WP, MN interview with Mokete Phalatse, 24–5–1982, pp. 16–17.
28. ODP WP, MN interview with Ernestina Mekgwe, 11–9–1981, p. 25.
29. ODP WP, MN interview with Mmadiate Makgale, 25–11–1981, pp. 3–4.
30. *Ibid.*, p. 6.
31. ODP WP, MN interview with Nthana Mokale, 1–2–1983, p. 65.
32. Water-induced enema.
33. ODP WP, MN interview with Nthana Mokale, 1–2–1983, pp. 33–35. As we saw in Chapter 3, Mrs. Mokale had some difficulty in resolving her inner conflict between traditionalism and Christianity, but eventually did so with the help of a sympathetic priest.
34. ODP WP, MN interview with Ernestina Mekgwe, 2–3–1982, p. 22.
35. *Ibid.*, p. 23.
36. ODP WP, MN interview with Sophie Serokane, 27–5–1982, pp. 22–23.
37. ODP WP, MN interview with Nkwapa Ramorwesi, 25–5–1982, pp. 33–35.
38. ODP WP, MN interview with Setswammung Mokgatle, 17–3–1983, p. 4.
39. ODP WP, MN interview with Ernestina Mekgwe, 2–3–1982, p. 11.
40. ODP WP, MN interview with Nkwapa Ramorwesi, 25–5–1982, pp. 24–26.
41. ODP WP, MN interview with Mmadiate Makgale, 25–11–1981, p. 21.
42. *Ibid.*
43. ODP WP, MN interview with Nkwapa Ramorwesi, 25–5–1982, pp. 8–9.
44. ODP WP, MN interview with Mokete Phalatse, 24–5–1982, pp. 17–18.
45. A second woman, Dikeledi Makgale, also suggests that paternalism had advantages which Bafokeng could use:

    How is life in Rustenburg compared with that on the farms?

    There is no difference at all. I can still go back and stay at the farms and still continue working if I feel strong. I know that the Boers will give *boermeel* [wheat flour]. . . .

    Money and taxes are amongst the burdens which were absent in those earlier days: "it was nice before, but these days there are so many things that irritate people, like sales tax." See ODP WP, MN interview with Dikeledi Makgale, 28–5–1982, p. 11.
46. Undoubtedly they continued to practise their Christianity, but possibly it took a somewhat more peripheral place than in their old age.
47. ODP WP, MN interview with Mokete Phalatse, 17–3–1983, pp. 8–9.
48. ODP WP, MN interview with Ernestina Mekgwe, 2–2–1983, p. 12.
49. ODP WP, MN interview with Setswammung Mokgatle, 17–3–1983, pp. 17–18.
50. ODP WP, MN interview with Mmadiphoko Mokgatle, 18–8–1982, p. 51.

51. ODP WP, MN interview with Mahube Makgale, 27−11−1981, p. 38.
52. ODP WP, MN interview with Josephine Mokotedi, 23−3−1983, pp. 26−27.
53. ODP WP, MN interview with Sophie Serokane, 18−3−1983, p. 26.
54. *Ibid.*, p. 27.
55. *Ibid.*
56. ODP WP, MN interview with Mokete Phalatse, 17−3−1983, pp. 29−30.
57. ODP WP, MN interview with Ernestina Mekgwe, 2−2−1983, p. 27.
58. *Ibid.*, p. 28.
59. ODP WP, MN interview with Nthana Mokale, 1−2−1983, pp. 32−33.
60. *Ibid.* Mrs. Mokale is, as we have seen, also a believer in ancestral worship.
61. Since this research was executed Peter Delius has suggested that burial societies played a crucial role in urban networking and even in politicisation. See his "Sebatakgomo." It is not clear whether this was the case here, as the women were asked very little about the role of the societies in the cities, and, as pointed out above, volunteered very little about the general role of religion in their middle years. Nkwapa Ramorwesi does hint at their importance:

> *Did you affiliate to any burial society during your stay in Cape Town? Or were there no such societies in Cape Town?*

> There were no organised societies like here in the Transvaal but whenever death occurred in our township we would contribute an amount of money so as to meet the bereaved family halfway concerning funeral expenses. I think the reason why we had no organised societies was because the township was composed of different ethnic groups, unlike in Johannesburg where one finds that the Tswanas or Sothos predominate in one particular township. In Cape Town we were a mixed society, therefore we had to organise a "society" only when death occurred. (ODP WP, MN interview with Nkwapa Ramorwesi, 25−5−1982, p. 27.)

But there is no indication that they played a part in political organisation, which is probably the case, since the Bafokeng women's politicisation was a phenomenon with roots in the townships rather than in the networks of migrancy.

62. ODP WP, MN interview with Nkwapa Ramorwesi, 25−5−1982, p. 26.
63. ODP WP, MN interview with Josephine Mokotedi, 23−3−1983, pp. 22−23.
64. ODP WP, MN interview with Dikeledi Makgale, 28−5−1982, p. 12.
65. ODP WP, MN interview with Frances Nameng, 26−11−1982, pp. 18−19.
66. *Ibid.*, p. 19.
67. ODP WP, MN interview with Mmamatlakala Moje, 1−10−1982, p. 24.
68. ODP WP, MN interview with Sophie Serokane, 18−3−1983, pp. 16−17.

Conclusion
Life Strategy and Social Identity

1. See Jerome Bruner, "Life as Narrative," *Social Research* 4, no. 3 (1988), 24.
2. Clifford Geertz, in *The Interpretation of Cultures*, (London: Hutchinson, 1975) evolved the idea of "thick description" to convey the overdetermined and complex meanings that particular cultural events possessed.
3. Non-African feminist studies, particularly within the discipline of sociology, tend to suffer from this lack of contextualisation, and detachment from any political economy. In some ways, feminist studies have been particularly affected by the "no history" romantic and populist approach, mentioned above, in which it is naively assumed that an untheorised "uncovering" of the words and experiences of women is possible.

SELECTED BIBLIOGRAPHY

Agar-Hamilton, J. A. I. *The Native Policy of the Voortrekkers*. Cape Town: Maskew Miller, 1928.

Alverson, H. *Mind in the Heart of Darkness: Value and Self-Identity among the Tswana of Southern Africa*. New Haven: Yale University Press, 1970.

Beinart, W. *The Political Economy of Pondoland*. Cambridge: Cambridge University Press, 1982.

Beinart, W., et al., eds. *Putting a Plough to the Ground*. Johannesburg: Ravan Press, 1986.

Benson, S. P., et al., eds. *Presenting the Past*. Philadelphia: Temple University Press, 1986.

Boggs, C. *Gramsci's Marxism*. London: Pluto Press, 1976.

Bonner, P. L. "'Desirable or Undesirable Sotho Women?' Liquor, Prostitution and the Migration of Sotho Women to the Rand, 1920–1945." African Studies Institute seminar paper, University of the Witwatersrand, Johannesburg, 1988.

———. "Family, Crime and Political Consciousness on the East Rand, 1939–1955." *Journal of Southern African Studies* 14, no. 3 (1988).

———. "The Politics of Black Squatter Movements on the Rand, 1944–1952." *Radical History Review* 46–47 (Winter 1990).

Bonner, P. L., et al., eds. *Holding Their Ground*. Johannesburg: University of the Witwatersrand Press, 1989.

Boserup, E. *Woman's Role in Economic Development*. New York: St. Martin's Press, 1970.

Bottomley, J. "The South African Rebellion of 1914: The Influence of Industrialisation, Poverty and 'Poor Whiteism.'" African Studies Institute seminar paper, University of the Witwatersrand, Johannesburg, 1982.

Bozzoli, B. "Intellectuals, Audiences and Histories: South African Perspectives 1978–88." *Radical History Review* 46–47 (Winter 1990).

———. "Life Strategies, Household Resilience and the Meaning of Informal Work: Some Women's Stories." In *South Africa's Informal Economy: Past, Present and Future*, ed. E. Preston-White and C. Rogerson. Cape Town: Oxford University Press, 1991.

———. "Marxism, Feminism and South African Studies." *Journal of Southern African Studies* 9, no. 2 (1983).

———. *The Political Nature of a Ruling Class: Capital and Ideology in South Africa, 1890–1940*. London: Routledge and Kegan Paul, 1981.

———, ed. *Class, Community and Conflict: South African Perspectives*. Johannesburg: Ravan Press, 1987.

———, ed. *Labour, Townships and Protest*. Johannesburg: Ravan Press, 1979.

———, ed. *Town and Countryside in the Transvaal: Capitalist Penetration and Popular Response*. Johannesburg: Ravan Press, 1983.

Bozzoli, B., and Delius, P. "Radical History and South African Society." *Radical History Review*, 46—47 (Winter 1990).

Bradford, H. *A Taste of Freedom: The ICU in Rural South Africa 1924—1930*. New Haven: Yale University Press, 1987.

———. "'We Are Now the Men': Women's Beer Protests in the Natal Countryside 1929." In *Class, Community and Conflict*, ed. B. Bozzoli.

Breutz, P.-L. *The Tribes of Rustenburg and Pilanesberg Districts*. Pretoria: Department of Native Affairs, 1953.

Bruner, J. "Life as Narrative." *Social Research* 4, no. 3 (1988).

Bundy, C. *The Rise and Fall of the South African Peasantry*. London: Heinemann, 1979.

———. "Street Sociology and Pavement Politics: Political Aspects of Youth and Student Resistance in Cape Town, 1985." *Journal of Southern African Studies* 13, no. 3 (1987).

Callinicos, L. "Popular History in the Eighties." *Radical History Review* 46—47 (Winter 1990).

Cobbett, W., and R. Cohen, eds. *Popular Struggles in Africa*. London: James Currey, 1988.

Coertze, R. B. *Die Familie, Erf en Opvolgingsreg van die Bafokeng van Rustenburg*. Pretoria: Sabra, 1971.

Cock, J. *Maids and Madams*. Johannesburg: Ravan Press, 1980.

Comaroff, J. *Body of Power, Spirit of Resistance: The Culture and History of a South African People*. Chicago: University of Chicago Press, 1985.

Delius, P. *The Land Belongs to Us*. Berkeley: University of California Press, 1984.

———. "'Sebatakgomo': Migrant Organisation, the ANC and the Sekhukhuniland Revolt." *Journal of Southern African Studies* 15, no. 4 (1989).

Delius, P., and S. Trapido. "Inboekselings and Oorlams: The Creation and Transformation of a Servile Class." In *Town and Countryside in the Transvaal*, ed. B. Bozzoli.

Duncan, D. "Liberals and Local Administration: The Alexandra Health Committee 1933—1943." *International Journal of African Historical Studies* 23, no. 4 (1990).

Ellenberger, D. F. *History of the Basuto*. London: Caxton Publishing Company, 1912.

Faris, D. E. "Narrative Form and Oral History: Some Problems and Possibilities." *International Journal of Oral History* 1, no. 3 (1980).

French, K. "James Mpanza and the Sofasonke Party." M.A. dissertation, University of the Witwatersrand, Johannesburg, 1984.

Frisch, M. "Oral History and *Hard Times*: A Review Essay." *The Oral History Review* (1979).

Gaitskell, D. "Female Mission Initiatives: Black and White Women in Three Witwatersrand Churches, 1903—1939." Ph.D. thesis, University of London, 1981.

———. "'Wailing for Purity': Prayer Unions; African Mothers and Adolescent Daughters, 1912—1940." In *Industrialisation and Social Change in South Africa: African Class, Culture and Consciousness, 1870—1930*, ed. S. Marks and R. Rathbone.

Geertz, C. *The Interpretation of Cultures*. London: Hutchinson, 1975.

Genovese, E. *Roll, Jordan, Roll*. New York: Vintage Books, 1976.

Giddens, A. *The Constitution of Society: The Outline of the Theory of Structuration*. Cambridge: Polity Press, 1984.

Glazer, C. "Students; Tsotsis and the Congress Youth League, 1944—55". History honours dissertation, University of the Witwatersrand, Johannesburg, 1986.

Goodhew, D. "'Half a Loaf or No Bread': A Political Life of P. Q. Vundla." Paper presented to the University of London Institute of Commonwealth Studies, June 1990.

———. "'No Easy Walk to Freedom': Political Organisation in the Western Areas of Johannesburg, 1918—1939." African Studies Institute seminar paper, University of the Witwatersrand, Johannesburg, 1989.

Greenberg, S. "Ideological Struggles within the South African State." In *The Politics of Race, Class and Nationalism in Twentieth Century South Africa*, ed. S. Marks and S. Trapido.

———. *Legitimating the Illegitimate*. New Haven: Yale University Press, 1987.

Grele, R., ed. *Envelopes of Sound: Six Practitioners Discuss the Method, Theory and Practice of Oral History and Oral Testimony*. Chicago: Precedent Publishers, 1985.

Guy, J., and M. Thabane. "The Marashea: A Participant's Perspective." In *Class, Community and Conflict*, ed. B. Bozzoli.

Harries, P. "Kinship Ideology and the Nature of Pre-Colonial Labour Migration." In *Industrialisation and Social Change in South Africa: African Class, Culture, and Consciousness, 1870–1930*, ed. S. Marks and R. Rathbone.

Hebdige, D. *Subculture: The Meaning of Style* London: Methuen, 1979.

Hellman, E. *Rooiyard*. Cape Town: Oxford University Press, 1934.

Hindson, D. *Pass Laws and the South African Proletariat*. Johannesburg: Ravan Press, 1988.

Hofmeyr, I. "The Narrative Logic of Oral History." African Studies Institute seminar paper, University of the Witwatersrand, Johannesburg, 1988.

Huddleston, T. *Nought for Your Comfort*. Johannesburg: Hardingham and Donaldson, 1956.

Hudson, W., G. F. Jacobs, and S. Biesheuvel. *Anatomy of South Africa*. Cape Town: Purnell, 1966.

Hyslop, J. "The Concepts of Reproduction and Resistance in the Sociology of Education: The Case of the Transition from 'Missionary' to 'Bantu' Education, 1940–1955." *Perspectives in Education* 9, no. 2 (1987).

———. "State Education Policy and the Social Reproduction of the Urban African Working Class: The Case of the Southern Transvaal." *Journal of Southern African Studies* 14, no. 3 (1988).

Jeater, D. "Marriage, Perversion and Power: The Construction of Moral Discourse in Southern Rhodesia, 1890–1980." Ph.D. thesis, Oxford University, 1990.

Jochelson, K. "People's Power and State Reform in Alexandra." *Work in Progress* (November–December 1988).

Keegan, T. *Facing the Storm: Portraits of Black Lives in Rural South Africa*. Cape Town: David Philip, 1988.

———. *Rural Transformations in Industrialising South Africa*. Johannesburg: Ravan Press, 1986.

Kinsman, M. "'Beasts of Burden': The Subordination of Southern Tswana Women ca, 1800–1840." *Journal of Southern African Studies* 10, no. 1 (1983).

Koch, E. "'Without Visible Means of Subsistence': Slumyard Culture in Johannesburg 1918–1940." In *Town and Countryside in the Transvaal*, ed. B. Bozzoli.

Krige, E. J., and J. L. Comaroff, eds. *Essays on African Marriage in Southern Africa*. Cape Town: Juta, 1981.

La Hausse, P. *Brewers, Beerhalls and Boycotts: A History of Liquor in South Africa*. Johannesburg: Ravan Press, 1988.

———. "Oral History and South African Historians." *Radical History Review* 44–47 (Winter 1990).

Larrain, G. *Marxism and Ideology*. London: Macmillan, 1983.

Lebelo, M. S. "Sophiatown Removals, Relocation and Political Quiescence in the Rand Townships, 1950–65." B.A. honours dissertation, University of the Witwatersrand, Johannesburg, 1988.

Levine, R. A. "Adulthood among the Gusii of Kenya." In *Themes of Work and Love in Adulthood*, ed. N. Smelser and E. Erikson. Cambridge: Cambridge University Press, 1980.

Lockwood, D. "Sources of Variation in Working Class Images of Society." In *Classes, Power and Conflict*, ed. A. Giddens and D. Held. Basingstoke: Macmillan, 1982.

Lodge, T. *Black Politics in South Africa since 1945*. Johannesburg: Ravan Press, 1983.

———. "The Destruction of Sophiatown." In *Town and Countryside in the Transvaal: Capitalist Penetration and Popular Response*, ed. B. Bozzoli.

———. "'We Are Being Punished Because We Are Poor': The Bus Boycotts of Evaton and Alexandra, 1955–1957." In *Working Papers in Southern African Studies*, ed. P. Bonner. Johannesburg: Ravan Press, 1981.

MacDonald, C. A. "The Material Culture of the Kwena Tribe of the Tswana." M.A. dissertation,

University of the Witwatersrand, Johannesburg, 1940.

Marks, S. *Not Either an Experimental Doll: The Separate Worlds of Three South African Women.* Durban: University of Natal Press, 1987.

Marks, S. and R. Rathbone, eds. *Industrialisation and Social Change in South Africa: African Class, Culture and Consciousness, 1870–1930.* London: Longman, 1982.

Marks, S., and S. Trapido, eds. *The Politics of Race, Class and Nationalism in Twentieth Century South Africa.* London: Longman, 1987.

Matsetela, T. "The Life Story of Nkgona Mma Pooe: Aspects of Sharecropping and Proletarianisation in the Northern Orange Free State 1890–1930." In *Industrialisation and Social Change in South Africa: African Class, Culture and Consciousness, 1870–1930,* ed. S. Marks and R. Rathbone.

Mauch, K. *Karl Mauch: African Explorer.* Ed. and trans. F. O. Bernhard. Cape Town: Struik, 1971.

Mattera, D. *Memory Is the Weapon.* Johannesburg: Ravan Press, 1987.

Mayer, P. "'Good' and 'Bad' Whites." Paper presented to the Conference on South Africa in the Comparative Study of Race, Class and Nationalism, New York, 1982.

———, ed. *Black Villagers in an Industrial Society.* Cape Town: Oxford University Press, 1980.

Modisane, B. *Blame Me On History.* London: Thames and Hudson, 1963.

Moffat, R. *Missionary Labours and Scenes in Southern Africa.* London: Snow, 1846.

Mokgatle, N. *Autobiography of an Unknown South African.* London: University of California Press, 1971.

Moodie, T. D. "The Moral Economy of the Black Miners' Strike of 1946." *Journal of Southern African Studies* 13, no. 1 (1986).

———. *The Rise of Afrikanerdom.* Berkeley: University of California Press, 1975.

Murray, C. *Families Divided.* Cambridge: Cambridge University Press, 1981.

Nkadimeng, M., and G. Relly. "Kas Maine: The Story of a Black South African Agriculturist." In *Town and Countryside in the Transvaal,* ed. B. Bozzoli.

Oliphant, A. "Staffrider Magazine and Popular History: The Opportunities and Challenges of Personal Testimony." *Radical History Review* 46–47 (Winter 1990).

Passerini, L. "Italian Working Class Culture between the Wars: Consensus to Fascism and Work Ideology." *International Journal of Oral History* 1, no. 1 (1980).

Plaatje, S. T. *Mhudi.* Johannesburg: Quagga Press, 1975.

Posel, D. "Influx Control and the Construction of Apartheid, 1948–1961." Ph.D. thesis, Oxford University, 1987.

———. "The Language of Domination, 1978–1983." In *The Politics of Race, Class and Nationalism in Twentieth Century South Africa,* ed. S. Marks and S. Trapido.

Proctor, A. "Class Struggle, Segregation and the City: A History of Sophiatown, 1905–1940." In *Labour, Townships and Protest,* ed. B. Bozzoli.

Relly, G. "Social and Economic Change amongst the Tswana in the Western Transvaal: 1900–1930." M.A. dissertation, University of London, 1978.

Riesman, P. "The Person and the Life Cycle in African Social Life and Thought." *African Studies Review* 29, no. 2 (1986).

Roche, M. "Social Theory and the Lifeworld." *British Journal of Sociology* 38, no. 2 (1987).

Rogerson, C., and D. Hart. "The Survival of the Informal Sector: The Black Shebeens of Johannesburg." *Geojournal* 12, no. 12 (1986).

Rosengarten, T. *All God's Dangers.* New York: Avon Books, 1974.

Rowlands, M. "Repetition and Exteriorisation in Narratives of Historical Origins." *Critique of Anthropology* 8, no. 2 (1988).

Rubin, L. *Worlds of Pain.* New York: Basic Books, 1976.

Rudé, G. *The Crowd in History.* London: John Wiley and Sons, 1964.

———. *Ideology and Popular Protest.* London: Lawrence and Wishart, 1980.

Runciman, G. *Relative Deprivation and Social Justice.* London: Routledge and Kegan Paul, 1966.

Schapera, I. *Bogwera: Kgatla Initiation.* Mochudi: Phuthadikobo Museum, 1978.
———. *The Tswana.* London: International African Institute, 1953.
Schrager, S. "What Is Social in Oral History." *International Journal of Oral History* 4, no. 2 (1983).
Schutz, A., and T. Luckmann. *The Structures of the Lifeworld.* Evanston: Northwestern University Press, 1973.
Shillington, K. *The Colonisation of the Southern Tswana.* Johannesburg: Ravan Press, 1985.
Scott, J. *Weapons of the Weak: Everyday Forms of Peasant Resistance.* New Haven: Yale University Press, 1985.
Seekings J. "The Origins of Political Mobilisation in PWV Townships 1980–1984." In *Popular Struggles in Africa,* ed. W. Cobbett and R. Cohen.
———. "Why Was Soweto Different? Urban Development, Township Politics and the Political Economy of Soweto, 1977–1984." Unpublished paper.
Simpson, G. "Peasants and Politics in the Western Transvaal, 1920–1940." M.A. dissertation, University of the Witwatersrand, Johannesburg, 1986.
———. "The Political and Legal Contradictions in the Conservation and Dissolution of the Pre-capitalist Mode of Production: The Fokeng Disturbances 1921–1926." B.A. honours history dissertation, University of the Witwatersrand, Johannesburg, 1981.
Sitas, A. "Moral Formations and Struggles Amongst Migrant Workers on the East Rand." *Labour, Capital and Society* 18, no. 2 (1985).
Spooner, K. E. M. *A Sketch of Native Life in South Africa.* Pamphlet, n.d.
Stadler, A. W. "'Birds in the Cornfield': Squatter Movements in Johannesburg 1944–1947." *Journal of Southern African Studies* 6, no. 1 (1979).
———. "'A Long Way to Walk': Bus Boycotts in Alexandra, 1940–45." In *Working Papers in Southern African Studies,* ed. P. Bonner. Johannesburg: Ravan Press, 1981.
Sundkler, B. *Bantu Prophets in South Africa.* London: Oxford University Press, 1961.
Taylor, P. "Daughters and Mothers–Maids and Mistresses: Domestic Service between the Wars." In *Working Class Culture: Studies in History and Theory,* ed. J. Clarke, C. Critcher, and R. Johnson. London: Hutchinson, 1979.
Thompson, E. P. *The Making of the English Working Class.* Harmondsworth: Penguin, 1968.
———. *The Voice of the Past: Oral History.* Oxford: Oxford University Press, 1978.
Tourikis, P. "The Political Economy of Alexandra Township, 1905–1958." B.A. honours dissertation, sociology, University of the Witwatersrand, Johannesburg, 1981.
Van Onselen, C. "Race and Class in the South African Countryside: Cultural Osmosis and Social Relations in the Sharecropping Economy of the South Western Transvaal, 1900–1950." *American Historical Review* 95, no. 1 (1990).
———. *Studies in the Social and Economic History of the Witwatersrand,* Vols. 1 and 2. London: Longman, 1982.
Walker, C. *Women and Resistance in South Africa.* London: Onyx Press, 1982.
Walton, J. "Early Bafokeng Settlement in South Africa." *African Studies* 15, no. 1 (1956).
Wells, J. "'The Day the Town Stood Still': Women in Resistance in Potchefstroom, 1912–1930." In *Town and Countryside in the Transvaal,* ed. B. Bozzoli.
———. "A History of Black Women's Struggle against the Pass Laws in South Africa, 1900–1960." Ph.D. dissertation, Columbia University, 1982.
Williams, R. *Problems in Materialism and Culture.* London: Verso Books, 1980.
Willoughby, W. C. "Notes on the Initiation Ceremonies of the Becwana." *Journal of the Royal Anthropological Institute* 39 (January–June 1909).
Witz, L. "The 'Write Your Own History' Project." *Radical History Review* 46–47 (Winter 1990).
Wright, M. "Technology and Women's Control over Production: Three Case Studies from East Central Africa and Their Implications for Ester Boserup's Thesis about the Displacement of Women." Paper presented to the Rockefeller Foundation's Workshop on Women, Households, and Human Capital Development, 1982.

INDEX